The Scholar and the Struggle

The Scholar and the Struggle
Lawrence Reddick's Crusade for
Black History and Black Power

....

DAVID A. VAREL

The University of North Carolina Press Chapel Hill

© 2020 David A. Varel
All rights reserved
Set in Charis by Westchester Publishing Services
Manufactured in the United States of America

The University of North Carolina Press has been a member
of the Green Press Initiative since 2003.

Library of Congress Cataloging-in-Publication Data
Names: Varel, David A., author.
Title: The scholar and the struggle : Lawrence Reddick's crusade
  for black history and black power / David A. Varel.
Other titles: Lawrence Reddick's crusade for black history and
  black power
Description: Chapel Hill : University of North Carolina Press, 2020. |
  Includes bibliographical references and index.
Identifiers: LCCN 2020016446 | ISBN 9781469660950 (cloth : alk. paper) |
  ISBN 9781469660967 (paperback : alk. paper) | ISBN 9781469660974
  (ebook)
Subjects: LCSH: Reddick, Lawrence Dunbar, 1910–1995. | African
  American scholars—United States—Biography. | Civil rights workers—
  United States—Biography.
Classification: LCC E185.97.R39 V37 2020 | DDC 973.07202 [B]—dc23
LC record available at https://lccn.loc.gov/2020016446

Cover illustrations: *Top,* detail from mid-1970s photo of Lawrence Reddick
(Photographs and Prints Division, Schomburg Center for Research in Black
Culture, New York Public Library, © Jack T. Franklin, courtesy of the African
American Museum in Philadelphia); *bottom,* detail from early 1940s photo of
Lawrence Reddick at the Schomburg Collection (Photographs and Prints
Division, Schomburg Center for Research in Black Culture, New York Public
Library).

To Michelle,
who made this book possible,
and to my fellow adjuncts,
in solidarity

Contents

Acknowledgments, xi

Introduction, 1

1 Coming of Age at Fisk University, 13

2 The Black History Movement during the Depression, 36

3 Librarianship for Democracy at Home and Abroad, 65

4 Cold War Civil Rights in Atlanta, 96

5 The Nonviolent Crusade from Montgomery to Madras, 122

6 The Search for Black Power in the Sixties, 154

7 Ebony Scholar in the Ivory Tower, 186

Conclusion, 222

Notes, 233

Index, 285

Illustrations

Reddick with his family in Jacksonville, circa 1920, 15

Reddick with his wife, Ruth Reddick, 1941, 45

Reddick at his Schomburg Library desk, early 1940s, 67

Reddick with City College of New York students, 1942, 71

Eleanor Roosevelt giving Atlantic Charter manuscript to the New York Public Library, circa 1942, 78

Reddick with Clarence Bacote at Atlanta University, circa 1950, 110

Reddick, Martin Luther King Jr., and Coretta Scott King with a group of Indians, 1959, 143

Reddick with Richard Wright and Martin Luther King Jr. in Paris, 1959, 145

Reddick with Leon Sullivan and Robert F. Kennedy at OIC meeting, 1966, 181

Reddick inducting Léopold Senghor into the Black Academy of Arts and Letters, 1971, 192

Reddick at Temple University, mid-1970s, 211

Acknowledgments

I'm happy to thank the people and institutions involved in making this book possible. The origin of the project lies in a postdoctoral fellowship in African American Studies from the Department of History at Case Western Reserve University. I benefited from the free time and $5,000 budget to conduct the early research for the project. I also received helpful feedback from Kenneth Janken, who was the scholar I invited to campus as part of the fellowship. He has continued to support my scholarly career since that time, and I'm happy to count him as a friend. Beyond the postdoc, I relied on a short-term fellowship from the New York Public Library to complete the archival phase of the research. At each archival repository I consulted—the Schomburg Collection of the New York Public Library, the Atlanta University Center Archives, the King Center, the Howard Gotlieb Archival Research Center at Boston University, the Beinecke Rare Book & Manuscript Library at Yale, the University Archives at Northwestern, the Fisk University Archives, the Special Collections and University Archives at the University of Massachusetts Amherst, and the Library of Congress—I encountered excellent librarians and archivists who aided me in my research. Michael Mery of the Schomburg Library was especially helpful. I'm thankful to them all.

My experience with shepherding the manuscript to publication was also a great one, thanks above all to the team at the University of North Carolina Press. Tim Mennel, my former editor at the University of Chicago Press, was one of the first people to look at the manuscript, and he gave me some good advice. My acquisitions editor at the UNC Press, Brandon Proia, expertly navigated the manuscript through peer review, and his immediate and consistent enthusiasm for the book meant a lot. His editorial suggestions also strengthened the book's prose. The two outside reviewers he arranged provided excellent feedback and affirmation. I'm grateful to both of them for performing the essential and thankless labor behind peer review. After the book was accepted for publication, I've been glad to work with the able folks at the UNC Press, including Dylan White, Cate Hodorowicz,

Dino Battista, Mary Caviness, and many others, all of whom had a hand in making the book what it is.

Yet this book, far more than most academic ones, relied principally on familial support. This is because since earning my PhD in 2015, I have had only a series of contingent faculty appointments that offered me very few resources to continue researching and writing. My parents and brother were therefore crucial, and they have supported me in all that I do. I still credit my brother, Steve Varel, with first interesting me in the liberal arts. As an ongoing exemplar of intellectual curiosity and moral commitment, he continues to be a daily source of inspiration both through his work as an appellate defender and beyond. My parents, Dennis and Sharon Varel, have made everything I do possible, and any virtues I have as a person stem from them. In the case of this particular book, though, it is my wife, Michelle Penn, who deserves the lion's share of the credit. She supported me financially during the full year in which I wrote the manuscript, as well as during the additional year in which I turned it into a book. She was the only person to read the manuscript as I was writing it, and her enthusiasm encouraged me to continue. I also relied on the library resources from her job to access the books and articles I needed. Hell, she even created the index!

It's impossible to convey all that Michelle ultimately contributed. She was my closest companion at a time of great dislocation and disconnection. Moreover, she never once questioned the value of dedicating myself to producing yet another scholarly book, even as I often did. The academic job market seemed hopeless no matter how much I produced, so spending over a year with no income on a book that would never recoup its expenses frequently struck me as insane. But I also loved the work and believed it would be of scholarly value, even if only for a profession that offered me no real place in it. My choices defied economists' logic at every turn, but maybe that was the point. My work on this book was in fact a quiet form of protest against an array of social forces: the defunding of higher education and the humanities, which threatens the very viability of humanistic research; the deepening elitism within the academy, which offers only the best-pedigreed scholars the chance for tenure-track positions (which offer the support needed to write academic books); the rise of social media and the attendant decline in social discourse, which distracts, degrades, and divides us at a time of great peril; and the narrowly utilitarian mindset that predominates in the capitalistic United States, which casts suspicion upon creative projects pursued for their own sake and thereby impoverishes our imaginations and limits our ability to live rich and meaningful lives. Michelle intuitively understood and valued my protest against these forces, and more than anyone else she made it possible. For that I am eternally grateful. I thus dedicate this book not only to my fellow contingent academic laborers, but especially to Michelle, with all my love.

The Scholar and the Struggle

Introduction

The Negro will have democracy or
there will be no democracy in America.

—Lawrence Reddick

In late September 1977, a Philadelphia public television station aired an explosive episode of *Black Perspective on the News* featuring Ku Klux Klan Wizard David Duke and American Nazi Party coordinator Frank Colin. As one journalist described it, Colin wore "a Hitlerian hair style, brown shirt with swastika on the left sleeve, riding breeches and boots," while Duke appeared "handsome, clean-cut, immaculately dressed . . . with no trace of the redneck in his carefully modulated speech." The two differently styled men nevertheless shared the same philosophy. "Hitler was right," Colin stated outright after both men's feverish rants on black people's biological and cultural inferiority and Jewish people's domination of business and the media.[1] They jointly called for a complete separation of the races in order to stave off "White second class citizenship," as Duke dubbed it.[2]

Two men sat across from the Klansman and the Nazi. One was Charles King, the black head of the Urban Crisis Center in Atlanta. The other was Lawrence Reddick, a black history professor at Harvard. As veterans of the civil rights movement, neither were at all surprised by the virulent racism of their interlocutors. King, who was often hired by companies and the government to run bootcamp-style seminars to confront racial prejudice, asked Duke and Colin to consider the hurt their words caused. Reddick, an activist-scholar committed to truth, objected repeatedly to their false statements. At one point, for instance, when Colin declared that Jews had controlled the slave trade, Reddick interjected and called the claim baseless. However, "his voice was lost in the melee" according to one commentator, giving a "relatively unobstructed path" for Duke and Colin's views.[3] Reddick and King were "too gentlemanly," complained another critic.[4] The show tested viewers' commitment to the First Amendment. It galvanized many to file lawsuits protesting its airing on public television and to condemn the program's journalistic integrity.[5] Underneath it all was a telling allegory of the black intellectual's struggle against white supremacy.

Duke and Colin epitomized racism at its most extreme and hysterical. Yet the maze of contradictions, rationalizations, anxiety, and denial they dramatized was in fact the default mode for the masses of white Americans who refused to acknowledge and confront their country's racist past and present. The task of challenging white supremacy thus fell largely to nonwhite people, whose lack of power demanded that they tread carefully, as Reddick and King had demonstrated with their "gentlemanly" demeanor.

But it was black people's very lack of power, coupled with their commitment to nevertheless survive and thrive, which endowed them with creativity, righteousness, and passionate resolve. Black thinkers understood white Americans' highest professed ideals, and they pressured whites to live up to them. They challenged falsehood and exposed hypocrisy, as Reddick did that September evening. They embodied dignity in the face of hatred and the threat of violence. They nurtured alternative cultures and traditions that enabled black people to endure the most severe forms of oppression. In doing these things, they lived lives of honor and meaning, and they advanced the universal cause of human freedom.

• • • • • • •

This book tells the story of Lawrence Dunbar Reddick, whose long and diverse career made him among the most notable African American intellectuals of his generation. When Reddick earned his PhD in history from the University of Chicago in 1939, he was among a select few African Americans to ever have earned that distinction. For the next fifty years he struggled for racial justice without ceasing. He served as a history professor at Dillard University during the 1930s before becoming the second curator of the Schomburg Library during World War II, the chief librarian at Atlanta University during the early Cold War, a history professor in Montgomery, Alabama, during the famous bus boycott there, a founding board member of the Southern Christian Leadership Conference alongside his mentee Martin Luther King Jr., the executive director of the Opportunities Industrialization Center Institute in the Black Power era, and a professor at Temple, Harvard, and various historically black colleges and universities in later years.

Behind these shifting job titles, Reddick's core identity was consistent. He remained an activist-intellectual committed to precipitating and extending some of the most earth-shattering developments of the twentieth century, including the defeat of Jim Crow, the decolonization of Africa and the Third World, and the building of African American history into a robust, indispensable field. Over the course of sixty years he came to see firsthand how great civil rights successes were only partial and subject to quick rollbacks. Indeed, the color line that had organized the modern world for the previous three hundred years would not simply melt away. Reddick's long career illuminates how black intellectuals dealt with the failures and the triumphs, the continuities and the changes, and continued pushing forward over the course of the century. His career also underscores how black thinkers recognized the political nature of scholarship and worked tirelessly to refashion it for black liberation. For them, scholarship and political struggle were two sides of the same coin.[6]

The field of history was the battleground where Reddick's struggle often played out. For much of Reddick's life, it was the preserve of white men who erased or caricatured nonwhite people while insisting on their own objectivity. Reddick's experiences on the wrong side of the color line made him wise to the game. He understood early on how white supremacy distorted American culture and thought, from professional history on down to popular films and children's books. Like other "race vindicationists" of his generation, Reddick spent endless energy contesting racist representations in textbooks, newspapers, movies, and comic strips.[7] One driving force was his righteous indignation over insulting caricatures, rooted in the love he felt for his own people. But Reddick and his contemporaries also knew that such representations were part of a sinister process to oppress an entire people. If you strip a group of their history, you rob them of their identity and render them unable to act collectively to demand equality and justice. At the same time, you stoke fear and resentment among others, making interracial alliances to create a fair and democratic society all but impossible. The solution was as simple as it was radical: to humanize black people in a society committed to dehumanizing them.

Along with a small contingent of professional black historians and many more lay historians, Reddick took every effort to combat racism while also doing the laborious work of building a field and popularizing its findings. It is hard to overstate the difficulty of the task set before them. When society's academic powerbrokers—including scholars, intellectuals, publishers, and foundation officers—denied the legitimacy of black history, there were few places to turn to support the timely and expensive work of not only challenging ideas but building archives, creating journals, organizing conferences, and funding research. Carter Woodson's Association for the Study of Negro Life and History (ASNLH) and its *Journal of Negro History* paved the institutional way for Reddick to take part in this effort, and indeed Reddick was among the handful of black historians in Woodson's inner circle.[8] Their labors eventually helped to transform the study of American history in the United States. The mainstream history profession consistently lagged decades behind the pioneering interpretations of slavery, the Civil War and Reconstruction, World War II, and the civil rights movement being published by ASNLH. Even more important, such work raised the self-consciousness of African Americans, who then channeled it to create one of the most transformative social movements in American history.

Reddick's turn to professional librarianship from 1939 to 1955 was a logical outgrowth of this mission to build up black history. A principal concern was to make available a range of sources that could be analyzed and turned into revisionist history books. Reddick therefore generally forewent publishing books of his own during these years and instead performed crucial functions such as having black historical newspapers microfilmed and made available at repositories across the country. Though this is not the type of work that grabs the headlines or makes a person famous, it is the *sine qua non* of history. Here he was accompanied by countless other unsung heroes, such as Sara Dunlap Jackson, a black woman archivist whose efforts at the National Archives in the middle decades of the twentieth century underpinned historians' efforts to remake African American history.[9] Reddick, Jackson, and many others were the quiet revolutionaries who built "liberation archives" that allowed—and continue to allow—scholars to write black people back into history.

Reddick's involvement with history and librarianship were central to his lifelong activism, but his engagement also transcended those fields. Through both calculated decisions and no small amount of serendipity, he became closely tied to some of century's greatest transformations. One month after he replaced Arturo Schomburg as the curator of the Schomburg Library in August 1939, World War II broke out and upended the global order. For a bird's eye view of the escalating crisis, there were few better perches than New York City. Reddick's tenure as curator thus involved doing much more than microfilming newspapers and writing notable articles. The Schomburg Library, located in Harlem, was one of world's richest repositories of records on African-descended peoples, but it was also a locus for political organizing and community outreach. In that milieu, Reddick quickly became an important figure in not only the African American community but also the global Pan-African one. Africans at that time regularly attended black colleges in the United States, and Reddick befriended many of the politically minded students, including Kwame Nkrumah, who became the first president of Ghana, and Nnamdi Azikiwe, who became the first president of Nigeria. Reddick helped to foster communication, collaboration, and solidarity among African-descended peoples of all stripes, and he leveraged foreign developments to put pressure on the color line at home.

Most notably, when World War II challenged European colonialism across the world, Reddick organized meetings in New York City to strategize over what he and others framed as a global black freedom struggle. Alongside W. E. B. Du Bois, Nkrumah, St. Clair Drake, Rayford Logan, and many others, Reddick helped to articulate demands for the colonial powers to relinquish control of Africa and to end white supremacy everywhere. In the decades that followed, Reddick repeatedly traveled abroad, invited Africans to the United States, and linked the American civil rights movement with its global counterparts. When Nkrumah and Azikiwe later invited Reddick to their presidential inaugurations as an all-expenses-paid guest, they testified to the success of Reddick's decades-long efforts to build ties among African-descended peoples.

Another twist of fate placed Reddick at the epicenter of the newly erupting southern phase of the civil rights movement in 1955. After losing his job at Atlanta University that same year, he just so happened to take a position as chair of the history department at Alabama State College in Montgomery, largely because of its proximity to Atlanta. When the Montgomery bus boycott began a few months later, Reddick was positioned to observe and document it firsthand while also participating in and writing about it for a national audience. What's more, during the boycott Reddick became a close confidant of the young Martin Luther King Jr., and he remained so for the rest of King's life. In consultation with King, Reddick wrote the first biography of the man, entitled *Crusader without Violence* (1959). It sated an international desire to understand the charismatic young leader who had come to embody the entire movement. Reddick also traveled to India with King and his wife, Coretta, that same year, and he helped to found King's activist organization, the Southern Christian Leadership Conference (SCLC), and served as the lone non-minister of its executive board for many years. As part of King's inner circle, Reddick shaped the contours of the civil rights struggle alongside Ralph Abernathy, Bayard Rustin, Ella Baker, and other better-known activists. He was thus a significant player in the classic phase of the civil rights struggle, and he effectively combined intellectual activism with grassroots struggle on the streets.

Cold War anti-Communism often had terrible consequences on the movement, and those consequences were visited on Reddick in 1960 when Alabama governor John Patterson fired him from Alabama State College for his civil rights activism. But this, too, was not all bad for Reddick. He found work in Baltimore and Philadelphia during the 1960s and 1970s, just as the Black Power era was dawning. He was therefore well positioned for a phase of the struggle grounded in the urban North and West. Against the backdrop of African Americans' more strident demands for self-determination, political power, and community control of resources, Reddick headed up the Opportunities Industrialization Center (OIC), a national job training program mainly for poor urban blacks. This was part of a practical effort to ensure that African Americans could access tangible economic resources, but it was also about cultural empowerment. Reddick made this clear when he made black history part of the OIC curriculum. Reddick also joined the faculty at Temple University to build up a Black Studies program there. In the process, he boldly confronted institutional racism while overseeing—along with Alex Haley of *Roots* fame—pioneering new research into the black family, as well as important investigations into the fate of black colleges in the post–*Brown v. Board of Education* world. Furthermore, he continued ASNLH's tradition of instituting black-controlled scholarly organizations by becoming a leader in the Black Academy of Arts and Letters.

· · · · · ·

By assuming all of these roles and placing himself in all of these spaces, Reddick offers a unique view into the radical, international, and intellectual dimensions of the twentieth century's long black freedom struggle. While the American public largely continues to equate the movement with only the southern struggle against Jim Crow from 1954 to 1965, scholars have expanded the narrative chronologically, geographically, and conceptually. Chronologically, historians have shown how the movement must be viewed over the longer term, from at least the 1930s through the 1970s—precisely the years of Reddick's principal activism. The long view contextualizes the southern struggle and underscores its more conservative nature, which owed in large part to the Red Scare at home. Geographically, historians have proven that the movement was both national and international in scope, stretching across the colonized world. Parallel struggles in the American North and West and in Africa and the Caribbean, for example, reveal how activists throughout the African diaspora understood their struggles as linked and labored together in tangible ways to advance it. They routinely framed their actions as part of the global battle against the world's color line. By conceptualizing the struggle in universal terms, by forging Pan-African relationships and solidarities, and by constantly moving across the country and the world in his decades-long freedom fight, Reddick testifies to the validity of these historiographical shifts while also making them more concrete.[10]

Chronological and geographical revisions have demanded conceptual and linguistic ones as well. Many historians now prefer the term "freedom struggle" to "civil rights movement" because the struggle involved much more than African Americans' fight for constitutional rights as citizens of the United States. Yet even if one does focus on that narrower aspect of the global movement, scholars have shown how its participants understood citizenship expansively, going well beyond the defeat of de jure segregation in the South. Theirs was always a far broader battle for the ever-elusive goal of full equality. For all the attention lavished on dramatic confrontations in the South during the 1950s and 1960s, less-heralded, parallel struggles for fair housing, fair employment, and the end of poverty and police brutality consumed the North and West. Underpinning these struggles was the cultural revolution of the Depression and the New Deal, which expanded the discourse of rights beyond negative rights (constitutional entitlements to free speech, due process, and equal treatment under the law, which the government cannot lawfully *deny*) to include positive rights (entitlements to protection from old age, illness, unemployment, and disability, which the government must *provide*). The broader conception of rights ensured that the movement would persist and evolve long after the legislative gains of the 1960s. The many unrealized objectives of full equality included the defeat of racialized poverty, the end of de facto segregation, and a fair share of institutional power throughout society. Reddick's involvement with the Opportunities Industrialization Center and his multipronged struggle against institutional racism highlight how the Black Power movement was a logical outgrowth of the failures of civil rights liberalism to transform the lives of most African Americans.[11]

In tracing this much longer freedom struggle, historians have often turned to biography. The study of participants has helped to challenge the flawed "great man" narrative of the movement, and it has made clear the central role that women and ordinary people have always played as organic leaders.[12] Reddick's own generation of largely black male historians largely overlooked this dimension of history. This oversight stemmed from both their patriarchal worldview and, especially for activists like Reddick, their belief that white Americans needed examples of respectable, charismatic male leaders in order to identify with the black struggle. Ironically, their approach sometimes led them to de-emphasize the importance of their own collective intellectual efforts as well. The rise of social history and especially black women's history has now helped to displace the sexist and elitist biases characterizing such earlier framings of the movement. Evaluating activists' lives over time has also helped to expand the chronological boundaries of the movement and reveal the ways that it evolved over many decades. After all, activists did not come out of nowhere or simply disappear after participating in a famous march. The ebbs and flows of an individual's life are thus informative, and they reveal how people are molded by society but also refashion it in their image. Furthermore, as our understanding of the struggle and its participants has grown exponentially, biography has likewise been useful in providing the ultimate "contingency narrative," as one biographer called it, enabling us to always assess and critique the larger generalizations being made about the movement.[13]

As part of King's inner circle, Reddick was an important part of the "classic" phase of the civil rights movement that looms large in the public mind and still deserves serious scholarly attention. Though King scholars have hardly acknowledged it, Reddick shaped the policy decisions of the movement's highest leadership. His role as SCLC historian and behind-the-scenes strategist and publicist is partly what has kept his contributions out of view. That makes it all the more important to foreground the process of activism in which he participated rather than the lives and personalities of only the most prominent figures in the movement. Crucially, too, the reason King and other younger activists turned to Reddick for guidance in the first place was precisely because of his role in the earlier, more radical civil rights movement.[14] Like with Bayard Rustin and Ella Baker, Reddick's battles for black history, for the decolonization of Africa, and for economic justice in the 1930s and 1940s gave him a broader view that younger activists eagerly sought out. Adding Reddick back into the narrative underlines how the movement was an intergenerational struggle and one in which secular leftists continued to play an important role even in more conservative times. The persecution and harassment of black radicals during the Cold War has continued to obscure their ongoing significance as both mentors and actors within the postwar movement. Reddick dramatizes these connections, for he experienced routine harassment for his leftist sympathies and associations but nevertheless rose to become a close mentor to King and the only secular figure on SCLC's executive board.

Attention to Reddick also complicates the simplistic distinctions that have framed the study of civil rights and black intellectual history. Reddick took part in what Robert Korstad first dubbed "civil rights unionism," which as Jacqueline Dowd Hall sums up, "combined a principled and tactical belief in interracial organizing with a strong emphasis on black culture and institutions."[15] Because that interwar tradition faded and was suppressed during the Red Scare, Reddick helps to resurrect it and trace its endurance beyond midcentury. Throughout his life he supported interracial movements for social change while continuing to promote racial solidarity, celebrate black culture, and build black-controlled organizations. The dichotomy between "integrationism" and "nationalism" within black intellectual history is therefore reductive and obscures more than it reveals. Reddick was always a black nationalist in the broader sense of the term, promoting black culture and pride while demanding black political and institutional power. But he also sought the full integration of African Americans into American life on pluralist, not assimilationist grounds. He insisted that desegregation be a two-way street in which black culture be maintained and black power be expanded, not diluted. Much of his righteous anger during the 1970s stemmed from his awareness that these demands were not being met.

The fluidity with which Reddick moved between integrationist and nationalist positions has special implications for another overblown dichotomy: that between civil rights and Black Power. A generation of "new Black Power studies" has overturned earlier narratives—first created by journalists—that portrayed Black Power as a sharp, violent, counterproductive break from the past spearheaded by male militants who usurped control and precipitated the end of what had been a virtuous, effective, and interracial civil rights movement. The facts no longer sustain that interpretation. Black Power activists, many of whom were women, built from a long tradition of black nationalism going back centuries, and they succeeded in proactively confronting problems not addressed by civil rights liberalism. They appealed to the masses by promoting black cultural pride and by discarding reformulated ideas about black criminality and dysfunction; they won elective office throughout the country and united peoples along multicultural lines; and they transformed—if only haltingly—the racial composition and character of American universities. These achievements were victories not for a narrow special interest group but for all Americans. Reddick embodied the continuities. When King was assassinated in 1968 and white America feared the rise of Black Power militants, Reddick continued fighting for black empowerment as he always had. Now, however, he seized upon Great Society largesse to increase black employment opportunities through the Opportunities Industrialization Center; he rode the wave of the black campus movement to build up a Black Studies program at Temple; and he confronted racism and demanded black institutional power in myriad other ways. Such activities underscore the many permutations of Black Power and their indelible connections to the civil rights movement.[16]

Above all, Reddick demonstrates the indispensable and multi-faceted role of intellectuals within the black freedom struggle. To be sure, countless ordinary people served as the foot soldiers of the movement and made it a movement in the first place. But their role is not diminished by an acknowledgment of the essential and interconnected labors of intellectuals. More than most, Reddick bridged the gaps between the intelligentsia and the broader public and engaged in an array of intellectual activities that bolstered, directed, and energized the movement. His example underscores the movement's reliance upon dense social networks and endless outreach to the masses. The black history movement of the 1930s and Reddick's work as curator of the Schomburg Library in the 1940s instilled in him an abiding public orientation that never waned. Understandably, many of his contemporaries' commitments evolved as life brought on new familial, financial, and professional concerns. Not so with Reddick. He refused to be pinned down in any one place or by any one job. Indeed, his wanderlust provoked complaints from several of his employers, but Reddick would have it no other way. He thus stands out as an exemplar of the myriad types of intellectual work that go into a movement: (1) scholarly: researching, publishing, and teaching about subjects central to the struggle, (2) archival: collecting, analyzing, and cataloguing the movement's primary sources, (3) library: managing "liberation archives," building collections, and reaching out to the community, (4) activist: strategic planning, mentoring and mobilizing people, and navigating public relations. From the black history movement of the 1930s to the "Save the Black College" campaigns of the 1980s, and through organizations ranging from ASNLH to OIC to SCLC to Phi Beta Sigma, Reddick performed this work with remarkable gusto. Thankless as it may have been, this unglamorous, day-to-day toil is what makes a social movement possible.

Uniting Reddick's disparate intellectual endeavors was a commitment to black empowerment. Ever a pragmatist, he took routes to black power that were as diverse and complex as the history of the twentieth century itself. Like almost every black intellectual, he moved strategically between what Manning Marable and Leith Mullings have dubbed the three poles within African American thought: integrationism, nationalism, and transformation (i.e., socializing the capitalist order).[17] Reddick came of age during the civil rights unionism of the Depression years. He was moved by the universalist principles underpinning World War II and decolonization. He was chastened by Cold War repression and in that context became an enthusiast for SCLC's model of change centered on charismatic male leadership (not necessarily as *the best* approach but as a useful one in which he was well-positioned to contribute). And he supported the nationalism of the Black Power era, personally adopting a more confrontational style while challenging institutional racism, even as he continued to promote pragmatic change through the government, the lecture hall, and the library. Despite the shifting styles, Reddick was nevertheless consistently a left-liberal of a secular stripe, as well as a nationalist committed to social justice as well as free thought.

Reddick's qualities led Herbert Hill, a contemporary of his and the one-time labor director of the NAACP, to describe him as part of the "independent black radical tradition."[18] Reddick consistently believed that the best path to black power began with solidarity among African-descended peoples, whom he saw as sharing a unique history and culture that furnished natural bonds of affection. Reddick therefore promoted Pan-Africanism, African decolonization, political self-determination, economic self-sufficiency, and black pride, even as he generally rooted his claims for black power in universalist principles. Reddick also promoted tactical interracial alliances, was critical of a simplistic racial "chauvinism," and found most schemes for racial separatism and emigration to Africa to be impracticable and counterproductive. Tracking Reddick's long career thus not only rediscovers an important figure within African American intellectual history, it also lays bare the contours of American life in the middle decades of the twentieth century and reveals how thinkers tried to both understand and remake a rapidly changing world.

In the end, it was Reddick's decision to often refuse more prestigious positions and commit to less-heralded activist work that makes him stand out among the more illustrious black scholars of his generation. No one better understood that than his close friend St. Clair Drake, a black anthropologist who had chosen to work at the predominantly white Roosevelt University in the late 1940s before later heading to Stanford. In contrast, Reddick "preferred to by-pass the prestige associated with being in the first cohort of 'integrated' Negro professors to stay where he was, Curator of the Schomburg . . . contributing mass education there through seminars, symposia, lectures, adult classes and the publicizing of work by Black writers and scholars." "And when he left there," Drake continued, "he went South—to Atlanta University. . . . He deliberately chose a different path from his distinguished contemporary, John Hope Franklin, who ended up as Chairman of the

Department of History at the University of Chicago."[19] Reddick's path may not have made him as renowned as contemporaries like Franklin, Drake, Rayford Logan, Ralph Bunche, and Benjamin Quarles, all of whom focused much more energy on producing first-rate monographs that would stand the test of time and ensure their legacy, but it did make Reddick exceedingly useful to the black freedom struggle. Like any social movement, that one, too, depended upon people giving generously—and sometimes sacrificially—of themselves in the hope of a better collective future.

Reddick's example should broaden our conception of intellectual work and abet a reorientation within civil rights historiography that gives intellectuals their due. The social turn succeeded in upending histories that prioritized the role of elites—especially charismatic male leaders such as Martin Luther King Jr.—in making history. Although Reddick himself wrote top-down histories, we need not revivify a great-man model of history to adequately appreciate the role that he and other intellectuals played, especially those (disproportionately women) who labored in quiet, underappreciated ways. In social history's haste to recognize the ordinary protester, it inadvertently slighted the role of the protest organizer. In narrating the dramatic street protests, it played down the efforts to inspire, coordinate, document, interpret, and teach about those same protests. The unglamorous nature of such labor may not easily lend itself to dramatic storytelling, but it does make for compelling history. It is part of the collective and unheralded work that binds people together and enables them to understand who they are, what they are willing to fight for, and how they may go about it.[20]

This book thus aims to resurrect Lawrence Reddick in American social and intellectual life, but not in the individualistic mode of popular biography which pits the exceptional lone man against the world. Rather, it does so in the spirit of mutuality, collaboration, and solidarity which animated his life. Reddick's lifelong crusade for black history—for a useable past—was the centerpiece of his larger struggle for black empowerment. He shared the movement's abiding wisdom that only equal power would make it possible for black people to lead full lives, to control their own destinies, and to speak for themselves. And because those demands for justice were in keeping with American founding principles as well as developing international norms on human rights, he also knew that the black freedom struggle was nothing short of a war for the soul of America and the world. His story helps us to connect the past with the present and to glimpse the outlines of the ceaseless struggle for racial justice.

1 Coming of Age at Fisk University

I was really educated, really put together at Fisk University.
For it was then that I felt that I was a part of whatever went on.
I was a part of the mainstream.
—Lawrence Reddick

Reddick was born and raised in Jacksonville, Florida, but it was at Fisk University where he truly came of age. Alongside Howard University, it was the best black college in the United States in the 1930s. In those years before *Brown v. Board of Education* disrupted black institutions, an education at Fisk rivaled one anywhere in the country. The nation's leading black academics—shut out from teaching at white universities—concentrated their talents there, joining some pioneering white scholars along the way. Reddick's five years at Fisk thus exposed him to the most cutting-edge intellectual trends in Depression-era America, and it built for him a professional network of scholars that would last throughout his life. "I feel that the education I received at Fisk was much better in many respects than that received at the University of Chicago," Reddick later avowed.[1]

Black colleges like Fisk provided a space to challenge the vicious racism of the wider society. Unlike at white schools, students were exposed to the history and culture of African-descended peoples, whether through classes or speakers or symposia. Furthermore, education occurred in an environment of solidarity with black peers who came from across not only the country but also the larger African diaspora. To feel "part of the mainstream," as Reddick later put it, was an invaluable gift that would nurture him as he waged his unending battle against the color line. After a childhood in Jacksonville, the emergence of Reddick the crusading intellectual began there.

Humble Beginnings in Jacksonville

Reddick got his start in Jacksonville, Florida. Lawrence Dunbar Reddick was born on March 3, 1910 to Amos Richard Reddick and Fannie Ethridge Reddick, who named him after the acclaimed black poet Paul Laurence Dunbar.

Lawrence had one older sister, Fannie M., born in 1901, and one younger brother, Harold N., born in 1914. The family was part of the black petty bourgeoisie, with Amos finding steady employment as a Pullman porter. This was a working-class job serving as an attendant on trains, but it was a coveted position that paid more than almost any other work African Americans could find in Jim Crow America. Indeed, it was sufficient enough to allow Lawrence's mother to stay at home with the children for at least part of their young lives. In a world in which most black women had to perform paid labor outside the home, often as nannies for white children while their own went unsupervised, this was no small thing.[2]

Looking back, Reddick felt that he was his mother's favorite child. He described the influence of his mother as "decisive." He recalled that they "got on very well together." "I liked her and she liked me," though it "was not an overly sentimentalized relation." Fannie was a forthright woman with a "strong sense of right and wrong." Yet she indulged young Lawrence and was sometimes reluctant to punish him for his "mischievousness."[3] This could be affirming, but it could also nurture a self-centeredness—a desire to "let me have my way," as he later confessed.[4] That quality stayed with Reddick, and it helps to explain why he would later have some explosive relationships throughout his life. Still, Fannie also instilled in Lawrence more than his share of redeeming qualities, including a seriousness of purpose and a love of learning, which went nicely with his levity and strong sense of loyalty. The love of learning came easily enough for such a precocious child.

Fannie died when Reddick was only twelve, so he looked elsewhere for nurturing during his adolescence. The local, segregated public schools he attended proved especially important. He recalled having some teachers who were "uncommonly good." Several decades later, he still remembered one second-grade teacher who would tell "wonderful stories . . . of China and Africa and of Europe and of this country—which started me off and I never lost this interest." In high school, he discovered poetry when one teacher's emotional response to a poem prompted him to take it more seriously. He wrote, "I said to myself if these lines mean so much to her they must be good and so I began to pay attention to poetry . . . after Cowper then Milton and Keats and the revolutionary Shelley and so many others."[5]

Although Reddick could not have fully appreciated it as a child, the strong education he received was the result of generations of struggle by the black community. For two hundred years, slaveholders had labored to keep black people ignorant and tractable, helping to pass laws making it illegal for

Lawrence Reddick, right, standing next to his mother, Fannie Ethridge Reddick; his sister, Fannie; his father, Amos Richard Reddick; and his brother, Harold, circa 1920. Courtesy of the Photographs and Prints Division, Schomburg Center for Research in Black Culture, New York Public Library.

slaves to be taught to read or even be caught with a book. After the Civil War, African Americans naturally threw many of their fledgling resources into education. During Reconstruction they allied with Northern liberals to make free public education a right for all citizens, which finally included them too after the adoption of the Fourteenth Amendment in 1868. In Jacksonville, as elsewhere, local African Americans organized and petitioned the Freedmen's Bureau and white philanthropists to help build schools for them. Thus the Edwin M. Stanton School—the precursor to Reddick's high school—was born. It was a modest institution named after President Lincoln's liberal-minded Secretary of War, General Edwin McMasters Stanton, but it would over time grow to become a first-rate school.[6]

Yet that growth was by no means inevitable. It was driven in no small part by the most famous African American from Jacksonville, James Weldon Johnson, who became one of Reddick's English professors and mentors at Fisk. Johnson was best known for his service as executive secretary of the National Association for the Advancement of Colored People (NAACP) in the 1920s, and for his contributions to the New Negro Renaissance and his service as a U.S. diplomat to Venezuela and Nicaragua. Before all that, Johnson served as the principal of Stanton. He had attended the school himself and knew how essential education was to black progress. So even after earning a bachelor's degree from Atlanta University and being admitted to the Florida state bar, he focused his early energies on strengthening Stanton. During his administration, the school expanded to include the ninth and tenth grades. By the time Reddick matriculated, the school had a proper high school with sufficient rigor to help him win admission to Fisk.[7]

Education was only one realm in which black Jacksonians homed their activist energies. Historian Paul Ortiz has documented how black Floridians slowly built up a statewide movement after Reconstruction in the face of a resurgent white supremacy that lynched, incarcerated, disenfranchised, and impoverished African Americans there to the same extent as throughout the rest of the Deep South. Florida in fact boasted the highest per capita rate of lynching in the country. Of course, the urbanization of port cities like Jacksonville provided black families such as the Reddicks greater opportunities than were available elsewhere in the region. The regular influx of immigrants from Central America and the Caribbean, furthermore, created a more cosmopolitan environment than elsewhere in the South, and this surely influenced Reddick's later engagement with Latin America. Yet it was the slow, grudging labors of countless black Floridians to resist oppression after Reconstruction that made it possible for them to organize what Ortiz has identified as "the first statewide civil rights movement in U.S. history" in 1920. The decades-long efforts to launch streetcar boycotts, use armed self-defense to prevent lynchings, and fight for higher wages and better working conditions—and to do so through a dense web of churches, lodges, and unions that promoted racial solidarity across class lines—all underpinned the movement's crystallization in 1920. The NAACP and leading national activists such as Mary McLeod Bethune and Walter White threw their weight behind the Florida voter registration drive and subsequently made Florida the "tip of the spear" of the NAACP's broader campaign against one-party rule in the South. Reddick was only ten years old during that registration drive, but his entire life and outlook were shaped by the opportunities, connections, and political consciousness that informed black Floridians' generations of activism.[8]

Nowhere were these opportunities more concrete than in the Jacksonville schools Reddick attended as a child. Reddick took advantage, graduating as valedictorian of the Stanton School in 1928. The broader environment of racial solidarity helped him understand that his successes were not simply the result of his own abilities or work ethic. This awareness was on display years later during a speech when he confessed that he "was not the best mind always or most of the time in my class." Many other students, he explained, were forced to stop their schooling early and work to support their families. Furthermore, at a time when only one in five hundred African Americans attended college (and only one in one hundred Americans), most of Reddick's peers had never even entertained the idea of an education beyond high school.[9]

Yet Reddick's mother pushed him to set high aspirations. She encouraged him to think about university life ever since he was a child, portraying it as "some form of place where young men and women had a nice time learning things and enjoying themselves." Thinking of his less-advantaged peers, Reddick wondered, "Would my mother have been as kind and tender and as interested in my going to college if she had had to work all day in somebody's kitchen and come home frayed, exhausted, and irritable and wornout?" Reddick's relative class advantages provided him a ladder to academic success unavailable to most of his peers, but he learned early on that it was his responsibility to "lift as he climbed" that ladder by continuing to help all black people fight for better lives.[10]

Even affluent African Americans in Jacksonville could not escape the growing malignancy of Jim Crow. The color line was being drawn ever more sharply during the first decades of the twentieth century, and it came to shape every social interaction. The situation caused Reddick and most southern blacks to fantasize about escaping to a utopian North. He later recalled, "the Mason-Dixon line had been so dramatized in my own mind that when the northbound train crossed it, I expected somehow a miraculous transformation. I expected general rejoicing and something akin to the ringing of bells." In that region, he dreamed, "certainly new friends would come forward with their right hands extended in fellowship and with their faces wreathed in smiles, saying, 'welcome, brother, to the jim-crow-less North.'"[11]

The North of Reddick's dreams did not exist, but in the South institutions as seemingly benign as libraries became battlegrounds and sites for the ritual subordination of black people.[12] During Reddick's youth, Jacksonian blacks still had access to the local, white-controlled library in town, so Reddick, ever the bookworm, made regular use of it. He had some great experiences there. Beyond being exposed to books that "gave me a vision of the world and the life that I have never known," he even had positive encounters with white librarians. One of them "paid me a compliment that I have never forgotten," which was that he selected books well—so well, in fact, that she would often read the same books when he returned them.[13]

Even so, Reddick learned from a young age that he was not the social equal of whites. He was pressured, often gently, to use a different set of stairs in the rear of the building in order to enact his difference and inferiority. Later on, when a lone black library branch opened up in Jacksonville, African Americans were denied access to the many white libraries, making it practically impossible for most of Jacksonville's 75,000 African Americans to make use of any library at all. Reddick was spared that fate, but he was forced to endure the Jim Crow rituals that humiliated all people of color.[14]

It was precisely that shared oppression coupled with the black organizing tradition in Florida that helped to bind black people together in solidarity and to nurture Reddick's budding political consciousness. The cruel and arbitrary unfairness of Jim Crow stoked in young Lawrence a righteous indignation that would never fade. His anger would help fuel a lifetime's worth of energy aimed at challenging a system that stole his opportunities, humiliated his family, denied his fellows the franchise, and murdered all too many black people with abandon. In order to make sense of such a cruel and bewildering world, Reddick did what so many African Americans of his generation did: he turned to the *Crisis*. As the official organ of the NAACP, the *Crisis* was unrivaled during the first third of the twentieth century in its coverage and analysis of black life. Reddick later wrote, "I remember, as a boy, in high school, how I used to wait each month for the mail man to bring the *Crisis* magazine that Du Bois was then editing. I waited excitedly for I knew that its facts would be accurate, its analyses acute and its editorials straight-forward." Even though he prided himself on being a freethinker, he confided, "Some times I could not make up my own mind on topics of the day until I had read the latest edition of the *Crisis*."[15] Because W. E. B. Du Bois regularly covered events in Africa, Reddick would have been exposed to the continent early on in life, planting the seeds of an interest that would blossom with time.

Yet it was another man and institution that would eventually attract even more of Reddick's attention: Carter Woodson and the Association for the Study of Negro Life and History (ASNLH). Reddick came to participate in that vanguard professional history association throughout his career, but his first exposure to it came during a memorable Woodson visit to his hometown. Woodson gave speeches before a local college and the Stanton School where Reddick was a student, and Reddick attended both. He was "immediately taken in by the force of his personality.... There were none of the flourishes and repetitions of the average speaker. He was a man who, quite obviously, had something to say. He came up to the point. Every sentence counted." With admiration, Reddick equated him to a "skilled boxer ... driving home blows deftly." At school, Woodson chastised a boy who was sleeping during his speech, decrying, "That is what we have been doing for decades; sleeping, sleeping away our rights!'" Reddick later traced his interest in Woodson and the black history movement to that moment. Subsequently, "During my high school and college days I read everything of his that I came across."[16]

By the time Reddick graduated as valedictorian from the Stanton School in 1928, he was ready to make the most of his college experience at Fisk. He no doubt wanted to honor his mother's legacy and to demonstrate to his father—another crucial role model during his teenage years—that he could be an independent man. He later described the moments with his father leading up to his departure to Fisk: "As we drove down to the railroad station I felt very friendly toward him and he said to me, 'You are going a long way from home and may be gone for sometime, are you alright?' and I said, 'Yes papa I am alright, I hope that you are alright', for he looked as if he was almost to shed a tear. So I put my arms around him and gave him a pat on the back as I took the train.... The truth is that I was glad to get away. I felt that I could manage my own affairs and I wanted to see what I could do on my own away from home."[17]

A Fisk Education

Nestled in Nashville, Tennessee, on an attractive forty-acre campus which had served as a Union army barracks, the coeducational Fisk University embodied the ideals of black uplift growing out of the Civil War. Indeed, its namesake was General Clinton B. Fisk, the assistant commissioner of the Freedman's Bureau, which was the lone arm of the federal government charged with the immense task of helping newly freed slaves get on their feet after the demise of slavery. Fisk was founded during the bureau's heyday in 1866, aided above all by the support of the American Missionary Association. White missionaries envisioned it as an elite institution that would train the best and the brightest African Americans who would then "civilize" the untutored masses. It grew out of the noble principles that black people deserved full political and civil rights, and that they were equally intelligent and capable of benefiting from a classical liberal arts education. The missionaries were silent on issues of social and economic equality, but their ideas were nevertheless radical for white people at the time. Most white southerners and white philanthropists—if they supported black education at all—backed only vocational training, which they believed would keep black people docile and at the bottom of the social, economic, and political hierarchy.[18]

After endless struggles to expand, secure funding, hire black personnel, and stave off white dominance over the years, Fisk had by the time of Reddick's matriculation emerged as a premier institution. The appellation "the Negro Harvard" was a testament to Fisk's elite status within the black community and to how a Fisk education offered graduates instant status and prestige. And not without reason. In 1928, Fisk was only one of four black colleges (along with Howard, Wilberforce, and Lincoln [Pennsylvania]) elected to membership in the Association of American Colleges. Even among those four, Fisk stood out. It was often considered to offer the best undergraduate education for students, and in 1930 it became the only black college to earn the highest ranking of Class A by the Southern Association of Colleges and Secondary Schools. In 1933, the Association of American Universities followed suit, ranking it among the top group of schools in the entire country. Only 16 percent of white public universities and 14 percent of white private ones shared that distinction. Such achievements were extraordinary for a college that enjoyed few economic resources and operated in a region in which black intelligence and refinement were seen as existential threats to the way of life.[19]

Fisk's success was due in no small part to the stellar faculty members—black and white—that it was able to recruit. In 1925, there were only two PhDs on campus, but by 1930 there were ten. Serving at one point or another during this period were famed sociologist Robert E. Park, Chicago School sociologist Bertram Doyle, reputed anthropologist Paul Radin, pioneering linguist Lorenzo Dow Turner, Rhodes scholar philosopher Alain Locke, Harvard PhD and historian Theodore Currier, future president of the American Sociological Association E. Franklin Frazier, historian and Carter Woodson protégé Alrutheus Ambush Taylor, prolific sociologist Charles S. Johnson, pathbreaking historian of education and college president Horace Mann Bond, and, of course, James Weldon Johnson. These figures, the majority of whom were black and thus shut out from teaching at white universities, raised the profile of Fisk and made it into a first-rate research institution, even as it maintained its mission as a small liberal arts college. The result was stunning, and the opportunities were many for students willing to take advantage of them. Reddick was one such student.[20]

Although Reddick began his freshman year with a nagging fear that he might flunk out, he quickly distinguished himself in the classroom. In fact, his academic record was unrivaled. He would go on to graduate as valedictorian of his class of 1932, which had over one hundred students, and as the only student to win magna cum laude honors. The following year, no student won that honor, and in 1934, only one did. Student friends such as Edmonia W. Grant, who later became Fisk's director of education, never forgot Reddick's "excellent academic record" as an undergraduate.[21]

Reddick's peers were not slackers either. John Hope Franklin, class of 1935, would go on to become the most influential historian of African American history in the twentieth century. Elsie Mae Lewis, class of 1932, would earn her PhD from the University of Chicago and become a historian at Howard. Lewis Wade Jones, class of 1931, became a sociology professor at Tuskegee Institute and pioneered studies of blacks in the rural South. Reddick continued to collaborate with each of these figures throughout his career, but at the time Jones was "the student who struck me most as a real intellectual."[22] However, Reddick later admitted that women like Lewis had it much harder in the male-dominated environment of Fisk, which in that way mirrored all of higher education at the time.[23]

In addition to academic rivalry, Reddick's peers offered him a sense of community and solidarity. Unlike in the larger white world, Reddick could be secure in his racial identity at Fisk. Like at the Stanton School and other black institutions, students could simply treat one another as fellow human beings with idiosyncratic personalities—distinctions which were erased within mainstream American culture. Reddick could learn the tragic and glorious history of black people and be encouraged to take up his responsibility to the freedom struggle, all in an environment generally free from the contempt and pity of white people. "At that time," Reddick later recalled, "the southern Black higher educational institutions, though segregated, looked upon themselves as happy community centers where, relaxed and intimate, everyone got to know everybody and could carry on a pattern of life with distinctive cultural features."[24] It is for these reasons that Reddick became a lifelong devotee of black colleges and other black-controlled institutions. It was empowering to be part of the mainstream, rather than a misunderstood and stereotyped minority.

To be sure, neither Fisk nor any other place could offer a complete refuge from Jim Crow horrors. This became painfully clear when a local black teenager named Cordie Cheek was lynched in the fall of 1933, shortly after Reddick had left Nashville. John Hope Franklin later narrated the shocking event that shook the campus to its core. He explained how Cheek "had been taken from his uncle's home at the edge of the Fisk campus and lynched. It was alleged that while chopping wood for a white family in Maury County, Tennessee, Cheek had taken a load of wood into the house and accidentally tore the dress of a white girl, whose brother then gave her a dollar to claim that Cheek had raped her. After his arrest, the grand jury refused to indict him on the basis of flimsy evidence, and he was set free. He left Maury County and went to live with relatives in Nashville." "The mob," he continued, "determined to bestow retributive violence on Cheek, followed him, seized him and returned him to Maury County. He was castrated and lynched, his body riddled with bullets as the barbaric participants passed a pistol from one to another."[25] The horrific lynching only underscored in stark terms what Jim Crow had already taught all black people: their lives were in constant peril.

The sense of empowerment and rootedness at Fisk nevertheless gave Reddick the courage to act boldly—even shockingly so—in the white world. As he later stated it, "I always felt that if I had two other Fiskites with me, we would meet any challenge, we would go anywhere." He recalled how "Once, when a waiter in a Cincinnati restaurant refused to serve the three of us, we threatened to break up the man's place. Even that wild lawless spirit was part of our feeling of identity. There was a certain sense of unity in black colleges, a certain sense of integrity that is very hard to acquire in other places."[26]

Serving on the debate team gave Reddick another forum to engage with the white world. While he was a member of the Fisk squad during his sophomore, junior, and senior years, the team challenged white schools from across the country. Most declined, but when Northwestern and New York University accepted, Reddick rose to the occasion. He surely had the same feelings about it as did John Hope Franklin, who wrote that "Debating . . . gave me my first opportunity to be in intellectual competition with white college students. That I could more than hold my own added immeasurably to my mounting confidence, an asset that would prove essential in graduate school and during the years that followed."[27] Reddick held his own too, and he became renowned for his speaking abilities, even winning oratorical contests on campus.[28] In one oration that earned him some press attention, Reddick issued a "manifesto" calling for "the dawning of a new era in which the intellectual can, if he will, assume control of our social system."[29]

Debating refined Reddick's skills of argumentation, forced him to take other perspectives seriously, and cemented bonds with scholars at Fisk. Reddick headed a small group of student debaters who regularly met with select faculty members to informally discuss political issues. The stakes were low among this group of "Wranglers," as they called themselves, and the participants were encouraged to try out ideas and spar with others. According to Reddick, it was "an intellectual joust for its own sake, having fun, not giving much of a damn about being [politically correct]."[30] All of this debating, both on the school team and with the Wranglers, made Reddick close with Lorenzo Dow Turner and Theodore Currier (both of whom coached the debate team), as well as Horace Mann Bond, Arturo Schomburg, and a range of professors who cycled in and out of the Wranglers group.[31]

The connection with Schomburg would be a consequential one. Schomburg was an Afro-Puerto-Rican bibliophile who collected materials from across the African diaspora, which he eventually donated to the New York Public Library before becoming curator of his own collection there. In 1939, Reddick would replace Schomburg as curator after he died, but the two of them first met during Reddick's Fisk days. Charles Johnson orchestrated the appointment of Schomburg as curator of the new Fisk library in November 1930. The two men had become good friends, and Schomburg helped Fisk build a library worthy of the university. The opening of the Erastus Milo Cravath Memorial Library on October 10, 1930, followed years of petitioning the foundations for funds.[32]

One of the first events at the library was a conference on the state of black libraries. Schomburg presented a paper entitled "Sketches for a Bibliography of the Earliest Negroes in America."[33] Through such talks and through regular attendance at Wrangler meetings, which he sometimes led, Schomburg exposed Reddick to the content of black history. But more fundamentally, he showed Reddick that black history as a field was inseparable from the source materials that gave it substance. Unfortunately, as Johnson, Schomburg, and the others at Fisk who pushed for the library understood, slavery and colonialism had erased many black archival records and muted the black voice, all in the service of white supremacy. To contest racial injustice, then, one needed not merely to write new nonracist histories but to first compile and organize the raw materials of the past that would make all other work possible.

During Schomburg's brief tenure at Fisk from November 1930 to December 1931, he put the library well on its way toward that goal. According to his biographer, the collections there came to reflect a "global character," including sources on "black domestics in Europe, along with extensive finds relating to blacks in Africa and the Caribbean."[34] The origins of Reddick's consuming interest in librarianship and the global nature of the black experience likely lie here. Indeed, Reddick decided to work as a student assistant in the library while he was an undergraduate.[35] Like others at Fisk, he was likely inspired by the huge Aaron Douglas murals adorning the library's reading room. Schomburg once noted, "I can look up to them for relief and pleasure and support when any of the so-called superior race comes to town to look at our wonder."[36]

Yet with history-minded professors like Horace Mann Bond and Theodore Currier, academic deans like Alrutheus Ambush Taylor, regular guest lecturers like Carter Woodson and W. E. B. Du Bois (a Fisk alumnus), and with Fisk's regular participation in ASNLH's Negro History Week, Reddick would have become intimately familiar with black history and black librarianship even if he had never met Schomburg.[37] Reddick recalled how Currier, a white Harvard PhD who taught most of his history classes at Fisk, "knew the 'literature' so well that his students were conversant with all major schools of thought."[38] Yet it was Woodson who ultimately became the greatest proselytizer for black history. Ever since Reddick's high school encounter with the man, he had become transfixed by the black history movement. He would not have missed Woodson's talks at Fisk, including his commencement address to the class of 1931 entitled "The Mis-Education of the Negro."³⁹ Two years later, Woodson published a book with the same title, and Reddick no doubt read every word.

Woodson, a mercurial fellow whose temperament at times made him difficult to get along with, did not intend *The Mis-Education of the Negro* to be a crowd-pleaser. But it was a widely read tour de force that laid out his ideas about black history, black education, and the role of ASNLH in fomenting social change—all of which would profoundly influence Reddick. The book was above all a sustained indictment of formal education in the United States. Woodson argued that modern education had been "worked out in conformity to the needs" of the oppressor, who uses it to justify "slavery, peonage, segregation, and lynching." The content of history courses was a case in point. History classes and textbooks chronicled the rise of Western civilization as a glorious triumph of democracy and freedom, all the while ignoring Africa "except so far as it had been a field of exploitation for the Caucasian." African Americans, meanwhile, "had no place in the curriculum" and were "pictured as a human being of the lower order, unable to subject passion to reason, and therefore useful only when made the hewer of wood and the drawer of water."⁴⁰

Woodson believed strongly that oppressed peoples needed a positive history to provide them with a sense of identity and empowerment. He therefore used his meticulous scholarship to poke holes in the colonialist version of history and share the proud history of black people, which he believed would inspire them to greatness. For instance, he celebrated that it was "Africans who first domesticated the sheep, goat, and cow, developed the idea of trial by jury, produced the first stringed instruments, and gave the world its greatest boon in the discovery of iron." His *Journal of Negro History* provided a scholarly forum to document and disseminate such research, but equally important was ASNLH's widespread public outreach through the annual conference, regular speaking tours, and especially the popular Negro History Week every February.⁴¹ When Reddick published an article in 1933 on the Ashanti people's encounter with British colonialists, he registered Woodson's influence.⁴²

While Woodson's positive message of black history found an enthusiastic reception within the black community, his indictment of black education ruffled some feathers. He argued that "the instruction so far given Negroes in colleges and universities has worked to the contrary" of liberation. The leaders of these institutions, he impugned, if they were black at all, were comprised of narrow-minded race leaders who "have turned away from" the masses and aped the educational model and curriculum of white schools. He could point to the fact that it was rare to find courses centered on black topics and experiences on most campuses. All too often black schools continued to emphasize vocational training and character-building in a paternalistic atmosphere that only eased black students' entry into the bottom rung of the social and economic ladder. Only through sustained student protests in the mid-1920s did Fisk begin to move more decisively against its own administrative paternalism and white control.[43]

Yet Woodson, who had long since given up working in higher education to concentrate on ASNLH, seemed to have lost sight of the many constraints facing those laboring within black colleges. They did not enjoy the same freedoms to speak and act as they saw fit—at least not without jeopardizing the economic viability of their institutions in the face of heavy dependence on white philanthropy. Even with philanthropic support, Fisk still depended upon its famed student choir, the Jubilee Singers, to tour Europe and the United States, often singing slave songs to white audiences to help raise funds.

At Fisk, Reddick had a mentor who helped him understand some of these dilemmas. Hired in 1928 to appease student demands for more black faculty members, Charles S. Johnson, like Woodson, had earned a graduate degree from the University of Chicago (a PhD in sociology, not history). He, too, had taken up a leadership role in editing a major black periodical—the National Urban League's *Opportunity* magazine, which became an important organ of the New Negro Renaissance. Also like Woodson, Johnson was a consummate scholar who dedicated nearly all of his energies to his professional work. Yet he chose a different path.

When Johnson arrived at Fisk, he rooted himself squarely in the black university, warts and all. He became a master at winning the support of foundations such as the Rosenwald Fund, the Rockefeller Foundation, and the Phelps-Stokes Fund. As a result, at Fisk he built the South's premier research center for the study of African Americans in the 1930s and 1940s. A number of the books he put out, including *Shadow of the Plantation* (1934), *The Collapse of Cotton Tenancy* (1935), and *Growing Up in the Black Belt* (1941), had a national impact.[44] However, that success was tied partly to his "gradualist" approach to race relations, which abstained from open indictments of Jim Crow and focused, rather, on describing objectively the nature of racial interactions and how they change over time.[45]

Reddick worked as a research assistant in Johnson's Division of Social Sciences, and he came to appreciate his mentor's efforts in building a black sociological tradition. Johnson was a genial man who let the rigor of his research do the talking for him. He was easy to get along with and difficult not to admire. Reddick later called him "the most far-seeing sociologist that I have ever known. His perception of what was likely to happen was so keen that we called him 'the man who could see around the world.'"[46] Reddick was especially interested in Johnson's work as part of the League of Nations commission appointed in 1929 to investigate the charge of slavery and forced labor in Liberia.[47] Generally, though, Reddick identified more with the fieriness of Woodson and others, and he ultimately found the crusade for black history more compelling than Johnson's gradualist sociology. Politically, too, Reddick found Johnson's more conservative approach to racial change less than inspiring. Johnson promoted change as a "sidelines activist," as his biographer called it, through his scholarship and his support of lukewarm liberal organizations like the Commission on Interracial Cooperation, which refused to condemn segregation but did organize to prevent racial violence.[48] Even during the Depression, Johnson never seemed to question the fundamentals of capitalism, though *The Collapse of Cotton Tenancy* did inform President Franklin Roosevelt's agricultural reforms during the New Deal. Reddick nevertheless learned from Johnson how to channel his anger into productive ends, and how to win support from the foundations. He would benefit from Johnson's connections.

Reddick's greatest mentor and soon close friend at Fisk was Horace Mann Bond. A deeply sarcastic, lighthearted but ambitious black southerner only five years older than Reddick, Bond appealed to Reddick immediately. "Horace Bond was the kind of professor who stayed up half the night and did his best writing after a snort of bourbon in the wee hours of quiet mornings," Reddick later came to know. "In the classroom, he was completely original and inspired."[49] Bond was just twenty-three years old when he started as an instructor at Fisk in 1928, but he had already earned a master's degree from the University of Chicago and published two important articles in *Crisis* and *Opportunity* on the racial biases of intelligence tests.[50] Like Johnson, he, too, would become a darling of the foundations, and he even worked full-time for the Rosenwald Fund from 1929 to 1930 while researching black schools in the South. He would complete his PhD in the history of education at Chicago in 1936. Reddick was on campus at that time, and he in fact helped file Bond's dissertation for him.[51] The prize-winning book that grew out of that research, *Negro Education in Alabama* (1939), was, according to Reddick, "one of the most penetrating inquiries into the economics of caste and class in public education in the South."[52] The two men corresponded and maintained close contact for decades, even as their impressive careers took them in different directions, with Bond rising to become the first black president of Lincoln University in Pennsylvania.[53]

Committed to an academic life in black colleges, Bond took issue with some of Woodson's broadsides about them. He articulated these most clearly in an influential book he published shortly after Woodson's entitled *The Education of the Negro in the American Social Order* (1934). Like Woodson, Bond analyzed education in relation to the larger social structure (a trademark of the Chicago School), and he agreed that it has been "the product and interpreter of the existing system." But he rejected Woodson's notion that changing the curriculum of a school—by, for instance, including black history courses and emphasizing black contributions to the world—would be revolutionary. "The school has never built a new social order," he maintained, and is only "a single institution" which can at best but "help transform the life of a people over a long period of time." Based upon that reasoning, Bond thought it more important that the whole of American education prioritize the same goals of "translating our common ideals into teachable forms." African Americans already live "in a psychical, often physical ghetto," so why, he questioned, should education further exacerbate social divisions by taking a fundamentally different approach based upon a person's skin color? He allowed that pupils' backgrounds could inform a teacher's selection of classroom materials, but he insisted that "The foundation stones need no reorientation for Negro children." This was necessary, he maintained, because "It is impossible to conceive of any future status of the Negro, or any social configuration of the American state, in which it will not be desirable to cultivate these qualities." In other words, African Americans would inevitably be minorities in this country, so they must be equipped to integrate fully into American society and not singled out for differential training. Bond's pragmatic argument sidestepped Woodson's most poignant critique: an education designed as a ladder to mainstream white society left black students unprepared to understand and appreciate their own culture (and therefore themselves), rendering them incapable of improving it. Reddick pored over Bond's words as he carved out his own positions on crucial issues of the day.[54]

Reddick would ultimately take issue with aspects of each of his mentors' stances. Like any independent thinker, Reddick stayed true to his own values, experiences, and goals. But he had a remarkable set of teachers to help guide him along the way. Whether it was in the classroom, on the debate stage, at a Wranglers meeting, or through the *Fisk Herald* (the student paper he edited and published in), his mentors encouraged him to try out ideas and approach issues from multiple perspectives. In their own professional work and personal interactions, they offered him an array of personality types, theoretical orientations, and political stances to consider.

But one thing was clear: Reddick wanted in. He endeavored to play a part in this black intellectual world where ideas mattered and knowledge was revered. Before he left Fisk, he had already begun carving out his own positions and making his voice heard.

A Southerner Takes His Stand

The thrill of graduating as valedictorian in June 1932 was sullied by the Great Depression, which led to "no jobs for magna cum laudes," Reddick bemoaned.[55] Indeed, the prolonged economic catastrophe colored Reddick's entire life and education during the 1930s. It radicalized him and created an experiential rift with those who had come of age during less calamitous times, even those only a few years his senior like Bond. At this historical moment, when many had come to believe that capitalism had finally proven itself a fundamentally bankrupt way to organize society, Reddick would adopt a more leftist perspective than his Fisk professors. For the rest of his career, both race and class would figure prominently in his thinking.

Hemmed in by the lack of job prospects but also pushed on by his commitment to further educate himself, Reddick upon graduation immediately reenrolled at Fisk in a one-year master's program in education. Besides potentially brightening his employment prospects, this provided a temporary shelter from the Depression's storm, which reached its nadir in 1933. Perhaps above all, the program enabled him to dedicate his energies to a single major research project that could make a real contribution. He already had an idea in mind.

Yet Reddick was never one to focus exclusively on any one thing. He also used the 1932–33 academic year to build a larger profile for himself by getting published in national periodicals. He wasn't always successful. Two years earlier, the twenty-year-old had already experienced the sting of rejection. He aimed to publish a short story in *Crisis*, but Du Bois rejected it, writing, "It has merit but somehow I do not think it quite gets the idea over."[56] Undeterred, Reddick kept trying, and he eventually met with success in *Opportunity*, maybe helped along by Charles Johnson's connections at the National Urban League. A number of the essays and reviews did not come out until shortly after Reddick had graduated and left Nashville, but they were nevertheless largely outgrowths of and commentaries upon his college years at Fisk.

Reddick's first national publication, a review of *Free Born: An Unpublishable Novel* (1932), made clear some of his burgeoning ideas. Reddick praised the book's ability to capture the burdens of blackness. The main character came to realize "the futility of his lot" in which "the usual avenues hold no opening for his black skin. Hard work?—you sank deeper into debt.... Education?—if the school house was better, the envious white folks burned it down. Even love had no protection against a white whim." As would be characteristic of all his reviews, Reddick used the forum to weigh in on larger debates. He criticized the book's author—and thus other black leaders at the time—for arguing that "the 'way out' for the black worker is to align himself according to class and to forget the matter of color."[57] This was precisely the position being advocated by a vocal group of young, radical black scholars at Howard, including E. Franklin Frazier, Abram Harris, and Ralph Bunche, who soon made their positions known at the NAACP's second Amenia Conference.[58] For Reddick, who was of a darker hue than many within the black intelligentsia, race was such a fundamental social division that notions of allying with white workers as equals seemed utopian. He reminded readers that "the entrance of Negroes into many industries has been in the role of a strikebreaker—a scab," and that "labor unions have not shown an excessive eagerness for his membership."[59] Although Reddick's specific policy positions and platforms would adapt to a changing world, a central tenet of his thought was always black nationalist: Black people's best hope for improving their lives began with racial solidarity and empowerment *as black people*.

Another review the following year underscores the point. Reddick praised George Bernard Shaw's *The Adventures of the Black Girl in Her Search for God* for what he viewed as its "fundamental indictment of Western Civilization," which for "all of the inventions, machines, and technological advance, '... the most wonderful thing that you have is your guns.'" Concluding with a passage from the book that rung especially true for him, he wrote: "'The next great civilization will be a black civilization, the white man is played out.'"[60]

Yet it was through a pair of opinion pieces in *Opportunity* that Reddick made his most important early contributions, wading into debates that his mentors were having over black education. Reddick assessed them from the grittier vantage point of the "younger Negro" in the Depression. College students like him used to subsist through grueling part-time and summer work as, for instance, "cuspidor cleaners and kitchen scullions," but as even those jobs disappeared, they were "stuck, no money, no jobs, and conditions worse down home."[61] If even the elite group of black college students was stuck, then it seemed that the whole system was rotten to its core. For Reddick, the crisis amounted to nothing less than "the collapse of the preachment of three generations" of black leaders who insisted on racial progress through education over agitation, assimilation over solidarity.[62] Agreeing with Woodson, Reddick laid the lion's share of the blame on black college administrators. In a controversial remark that was widely reprinted and debated in the black press, Reddick impugned, "There is not a single president of a Negro college who has an integrated philosophy of the definite function and place of his institution in the American social order."[63] In other words, the leaders of black colleges had no positive program for making their institutions relevant to black people during the Depression. Instead, all they did was "channelize the systems of control" by making ever-more-desperate students "knuckle-down," or kowtow to their superiors in the futile hopes of individual success.[64]

At a time when white America and much of black America was afraid of a burgeoning radicalism among African Americans (instigated above all by the Scottsboro Boys case and the inroads that the Communist Party USA [CPUSA] had made in the South), Reddick laid bare the prevailing conservatism of the younger generation. For him, this was an indictment. One might think, Reddick stated, that a proper education would make students "more sensitive . . . to the stifling meanness of American prejudice" and inequality, especially during the economic calamity they faced. Yet he observed no such thing: "Most of the students are a little sad, a little disappointed, but still the safe, obedient, and believing pupils of their teachers." His explanation was in part a class-based critique of the black bourgeoisie. "The Negro in college," he wrote, "is a middle-class American and . . . as a respectable bourgeoisie he is infected with the characteristic hope of becoming a petty capitalist. Most of the students at Howard, Fisk, and Atlanta University have parents who are either doctors, school teachers, or 'business men' and these same students aspire to be like their parents but with a finer car and a whiter collar." Hence, "Socialists? Communists? Practically none." Still, in observing that the CPUSA's support for the Scottsboro Boys had "made some dent," he continued to hope that black college students—and black Americans more generally—would adopt a more radical program equipped to address the scale of the crisis they faced.[65]

As Reddick kept his finger on the pulse of black America and weighed in on occasion, he focused most of his intellectual energies in the field of black history—the consuming interest of his career. He used his master's thesis as an opportunity to dig further into issues presented to him through years of engagement with the field, especially through the work of Woodson, Schomburg, and Du Bois, among others. The master's program encouraged him to consider black history from an educational standpoint. How was black history being portrayed to the public? How were black people being represented? The politics of representation, which center on the nature, origins, and implications of how a group is portrayed, comprised a chief area in which Reddick worked throughout his career. These were not arcane concerns. Reddick and other black scholars felt them viscerally and personally. The ways that black people were being portrayed were vicious and humiliating, and they amounted to an erasure of their humanity. By trying to understand these matters, black intellectuals could gain a semblance of control over them. By refuting stereotypes, they could translate their righteous indignation into a productive challenge to the culture.

In Nashville, Reddick experienced white scholarly racism up close. At neighboring Vanderbilt, a wealthy white private school endowed by railroad tycoon Cornelius Vanderbilt, a group of twelve white, male, southern intellectuals staked out an openly reactionary position to science, liberalism, and post–Civil War industrial society generally. Robert Penn Warren, John Crowe Ransom, and ten others dubbed themselves the Southern Agrarians and won national attention during the Depression. In 1930, they published their manifesto, *I'll Take My Stand: The South and the Agrarian Tradition*. In it, they portrayed the South as an idyllic refuge from the forces of progress and change dominating the rest of American society. They longed for the Old South, which was hierarchical and unequal, sure, but where relations were nevertheless "kindly and personal," and "people were for the most part in their right places." Slavery, wrote Ransom in the introduction, was "monstrous enough in theory, but, more often than not, humane in practice; and it is impossible to believe that its abolition alone could have effected any great revolution in society." Meanwhile, the Civil War was "disastrous" to the whole country, and Reconstruction was an era of "persecution" and "oppression" by the North and its "carpetbaggers."[66]

Years later, in the immediate post–*Brown v. Board of Education* era, Reddick criticized the Southern Agrarians in the *New Republic*. He made clear how Vanderbilt and Fisk, despite being highly regarded schools only a few miles apart, had "few contacts with each other." "There was no general fraternizing, no intellectual communion," so even though "I was head of the student council and the Wranglers Club, I did not know a single fellow undergraduate at Vanderbilt." For that reason, "it is understandable that we at Fisk never saw or talked with Professor Warren" and the others. Nevertheless, they certainly knew about these self-styled "fugitives," and they viewed *I'll Take My Stand* as "a plea for mythical ante-bellum days and a rejection of the modern world of urbanism and equalitarianism." Reddick found it infuriating that Warren, later comfortably ensconced at Yale, fashioned himself as an authority on southern race relations. He reminded readers how Warren's chapter on education in the manifesto was openly racist and elitist. Warren "argued politely that his aristocracy should study the liberal arts and that his Negroes—and perhaps poor whites—should be trained vocationally, mostly in agriculture. This was best, he concluded, for 'in the past the Southern Negro has always been a creature of the small town and farm. That is where he still chiefly belongs, by temperament and capacity.'"[67]

The Southern Agrarians only further energized Reddick to tackle and publish his research on racism in southern textbooks, which he did with remarkable speed. Within a year of graduating, Reddick revised his master's thesis into a notable forty-page article in the *Journal of Negro Education*.[68] Only two years earlier, in 1932, Charles H. Thompson had instituted the *Journal* at Howard University. It quickly emerged as one of the two most important forums for black scholarly research in the 1930s and beyond (the other being Woodson's *Journal of Negro History*). Shut out from mainstream organs, these few black-controlled journals created opportunities for professional advancement and dialogue otherwise unavailable to Reddick's generation of Jim Crow scholars.

Reddick's article, "Racial Attitudes in American History Textbooks of the South," highlighted the extent to which grade-school textbooks in all sixteen of the southern states were profoundly racist. Some of this was explicit in descriptions of black people as "docile" and "good natured" under slavery, or as "ignorant," "shiftless," and "vicious" during Reconstruction. But the more troubling racism was subtler. For instance, Reddick showed how all the textbooks ignored the contributions of black soldiers to American wars and said almost nothing about black activity and progress after Reconstruction. Black people were literally written out of that history. Even the explicit racism could be rendered invisible through the omniscient authorial voice and delicate phrasing of the textbooks. For example, slavery rose and fell naturally because of abstract economic forces rather than conscious political decisions; the experience of slavery was "not hard" and "the Negroes were good natured and sang songs during and after their work"; the Civil War was an unfortunate and unnecessary conflict that sprung only from misunderstanding; and Reconstruction was an ill-informed and counterproductive attempt to reunite the nation after a divisive war. In other words, the textbooks were merely presenting the same version of history that the Southern Agrarians were peddling.[69]

The full costs of such pervasive textbook racism were incalculable. Here they were, seventy years after the Civil War, and yet textbooks—the sole form of exposure to the nation's history for most Americans—continued to reflect a staunchly partisan, sectional interpretation of the past. Generations of students were being indoctrinated into a "Lost Cause" version of history that dehumanized African Americans and rendered them invisible and inconsequential, if not dangerous and threatening. Reporting on the article, the *Afro-American* noted how textbooks "stir up and ferment racial antipathy."[70] This was an appalling state of affairs, but it was hardly surprising to the initiated. Black intellectuals had observed firsthand how a defeated white South had embarked on a campaign to win in the history books what they had lost on the battlefield. The shocking thing was the extent to which they had triumphed in their struggle. Alongside lynching, disenfranchisement, and the rise of Jim Crow, the nation's account of its recent history—from professional history to popular culture—fell victim to vitriolic racism and distortion.[71]

The scope of the crisis, however, provided an opportunity for Reddick and other black scholars to embark on a campaign of their own to produce a truer account of the past. Reddick pushed to the forefront of that campaign. Remarkably, at the young age of twenty-four, he had already made a major contribution. He was among the first scholars to sound the alarm bells about the textbook crisis.[72] The NAACP contacted him shortly thereafter to expand his investigations into New York City schools.[73] Two black women scholars, Marie Carpenter and Edna Colson, soon followed Reddick's lead and authored major studies of their own.[74] Furthermore, these investigations only continued during the twentieth century, because even as professional history began to shift dramatically, textbook publishers proved remarkably resistant to change.[75] Later investigators, though, could at least look to Reddick's early contribution to the field as a role model, and many of them did.

Reddick's article and thesis provided a blueprint for his future professional work, and it foreshadowed how pioneering of a scholar he was destined to become. The research project amounted to a broad-based investigation of American historiography writ large. Reddick had studied not merely textbook accounts but also monographs by leading white historians who frequently coauthored many of the textbooks. What lay before him, he realized, was a full-on battle to defeat racist histories and build up the embryonic field of black history. His own vantage point made him attuned to the bogus politics of objectivity framing white historians' discussions of the discipline.[76] Reddick recognized that history, even among the foremost white scholars at the nation's leading universities, had all too often amounted to little more than "propaganda."[77] He sidestepped the hand-wringing over objectivity and committed to producing a more faithful account of the past, which he knew would only enhance the role of black people in the nation's history and empower them in the present. It is to those causes that he dedicated himself during his first heady years as a fledgling historian and professor during the Depression.

2 The Black History Movement during the Depression

> The work of [black historians] bears a relation to the reinterpretation of American history parallel to that furnished by the studies of Frederick Jackson Turner on the West.
> —Lawrence Reddick

In the six years that followed his graduation from Fisk, Reddick quickly distinguished himself as a historian. He placed himself at the vanguard of the black history movement, embracing a mission not just to catalogue the experiences of African Americans to promote race pride but also to inaugurate a fundamental "reinterpretation of American history and life," as he dubbed it. Because black people had played an indispensable role in every phase of American history, and because their treatment so regularly contravened American founding principles, Reddick argued, "the Negro has served as a test of the democratic idea" itself. Furthermore, "In those areas where the liberties of black men are least, freedom for all men is least." He thus pleaded that all Americans should join in the crusade to reassess the United States in light of the black experience.[1] Reddick's work in these years exposed the white bias masquerading as scholarly objectivity, and it exemplified how black intellectuals approached scholarship as but one part of the larger political struggle for black liberation.

From 1933 to 1939, Reddick shuffled between institutions, serving variously as a professor of history at Kentucky State Industrial College and Dillard University and as a doctoral student at the University of Chicago. After completing his PhD in the summer of 1939, he would embark on a tenure in librarianship at the New York Public Library. However, the character of his entire career was shaped by his experiences as a young professional during the Depression. He took important steps in building up the field of black history by compiling powerful new sources and laying out a prescient research agenda that would not be realized for decades. At the same time, he confronted boldly the racism that black scholars were encountering in books, classrooms, conferences, journals, and archives. His voice highlighted much that was rotten in American life, but it also pointed a way forward.

Out of the Mouths of Ex-Slaves

After earning his master's degree from Fisk, Reddick counted himself lucky in avoiding the bread lines. He landed a job at Kentucky State Industrial College, a small black college in Frankfort, the state's capital, located about fifty miles east of Louisville and two hundred miles northeast of Nashville. Reddick served as head of the Department of History and Government for the next two years, from the fall of 1933 through the spring of 1935. Despite the heavy load of teaching and administrative responsibilities, he worked hard to create the same collegiate opportunities for his students that had been available to him at Fisk. He headed up the debating team and established an undergraduate chapter of Phi Beta Sigma, a national black fraternity.[2]

The students at Kentucky State were less privileged and prepared for college than those at his alma mater, but they shared some of the same apathy. Struggling a bit with the transition from star student to professor, Reddick had his students in mind when he wrote that the average black college student—like the average white one—is "indifferent, tired, liquor-drinking, highly sex-conscious, and intellectually asleep." Not stopping there, he continued, "Many are immature, foolish, and there is that definite variety Collegius Moron Africanus."[3] Still, Reddick sympathized with his students and tried to enlist them in the invigorating historical work he was doing. That work helped to keep him motivated too, and it kept him in touch with broad networks of black scholars and professionals. In a small town like Frankfort, that was no small thing.

For community and solidarity, Reddick turned to Phi Beta Sigma. He had joined the two-decades-old fraternity while at Fisk. James Weldon Johnson was an active member, as were other major figures such as Alain Locke, Nnamdi Azikiwe, and Robert Russa Moton—who succeeded Booker T. Washington at Tuskegee Institute and shared his protégé's accommodationist approach to racial uplift. These figures represent the diverse array of men from all parts of the political spectrum who found a home in Sigma. Membership provided Reddick with an instant professional network and, not least, opportunities for social connection not easily found elsewhere. Indeed, Sigma had the distinction of being the only black fraternity that was constitutionally bound to a black sorority, Zeta Phi Beta, which made it especially valuable for meeting women.⁴ Sigma became a mainstay of Reddick's life, and decades later he even coauthored a history of the organization.⁵

Reddick took a more active role in Sigma after his move to Frankfort. He attended his first national conclave in Chicago in December 1933, at which point he competed for a leadership position in the organization. He was elected as editor of Sigma's periodical, the *Crescent*, a job he seemed to relish. The work set a precedent for the intellectual work he would perform in various other black organizations. The Depression had wreaked havoc on African Americans—Sigma men included—so a number of conclaves had to be canceled along with several editions of the *Crescent*. Reddick made do on a shoestring budget by organizing and publishing short newsletters.⁶

Reddick's editorial work at the *Crescent* underscores how his involvement with Sigma was about more than camaraderie. While many of his fraternity brothers seemed most concerned with the dances, the inside jokes, and the general frivolity, Reddick tried to steer the organization in more activist directions. This push and pull between "uplifting the race and creating social space for themselves," according to Jessica Harris and Vernon C. Mitchell Jr., was a perpetual tension within black Greek-letter organizations.⁷ At the time, most members of these organizations were part of the black elite, which tended to have a serious commitment to racial service but one which was articulated "in racial and middle-class specific, rather than in broader, egalitarian social terms," as historian Kevin Gaines explains it.⁸ But the Depression pushed Reddick and a younger generation of black fraternity members to begin promoting the latter form of racial leadership.⁹ Reddick used the *Crescent* to encourage political debate and activism, and he found that even generally conservative brothers were getting caught up in the political wave that swept Franklin Delano Roosevelt into the Oval Office in 1933. Although Americans "turned no further to the 'left' than the wealthy humanitarian . . . Roosevelt," as Reddick later wrote in his history of the fraternity, "the stirring 'one hundred days' of activity in the nation's capital were as bold and decisive as any the country had seen since the Civil War." Seizing upon that energy, brothers James Weldon Johnson and Emmett May encouraged Phi Beta Sigma to create a social action program, which the fraternity did at the December 1934 conclave. Yet there was disagreement over even that modest decision. As Reddick later recalled, "Its proponents ardently believed that it was the green light to the future; its opponents, with equal ardor, insisted that its color was not green but 'red.'"¹⁰

Reddick was squarely in the activist camp, and he organized the *Crescent* to highlight the work of the social action program. After expanding his role in Phi Beta Sigma by being elected the director of publicity and the overseer of the scholarship fund in 1934, Reddick put out a politically oriented newsletter in March 1935. He identified the program's four major goals: "(1) national and state anti-lynch legislation; (2) equality of wages and working conditions for Negroes; (3) elimination of race discrimination in federal state and municipal employment; (4) equality of educational opportunities." Reddick then included an article by a brother who called for Sigmas to "'buy black', that is, they should give first preference to Negro merchants and second preference to non-Negro merchants who employed Negroes." Such "Don't Buy Where You Can't Work" campaigns took off during the Depression and became a hallmark of civil rights activism for decades. Reddick heralded Phi Beta Sigma's politicization as a triumph. "At long last fraternities, at least one of them, had 'come of age,'" he penned.[11]

Involvement in Sigma allowed Reddick to sharpen his editorial skills and promote social change, but his most important work at the time centered on compiling the testimony of former slaves. The hunger for reform and the government's newfound willingness to confront the Depression offered many possibilities. Reddick was in fact the first person to use the New Deal to support the collection of slave testimonies. He became involved with interviewing former slaves when he was working under Charles S. Johnson at the Social Science Institute at Fisk. Johnson had begun a community study of the university and its environment in 1928, and in the process he and his assistant Ophelia Settle interviewed black residents throughout the community. Many of those residents turned out to be former slaves. Recognizing the immeasurable cultural value of these people's perspectives, Johnson enlisted students like Reddick to interview these community members.[12]

Johnson was certainly not alone in this venture. Carter Woodson had long since endeavored to record the testimonies of former slaves, but he lacked the time and resources to get very far.[13] A similar fate greeted the efforts of W. E. B. Du Bois, Walter White, Langston Hughes, and James Weldon Johnson. However, John B. Cade, a black instructor at Southern University in Louisiana, launched a more successful campaign in 1929. While teaching an extension course in U.S. history to teachers throughout the region, Cade had his students go out and interview as many former slaves as they could find. In all, Cade gathered eighty-two interviews from subjects who described various aspects of slavery from housing and working conditions to diet and their treatment from masters. Woodson celebrated the effort and had Cade present the material at an ASNLH conference and publish it in the *Journal of Negro History*.[14]

The stakes of these efforts were high, and their significance profound. Time was running out. It had been almost seventy years since the Civil War ended, and the number of former slaves still alive was dwindling fast. Black scholars either had to interview these people now or lose their firsthand experiences forever. Such urgency was only magnified by the polemical nature of the times. Race riots after World War I, the rise of the second Ku Klux Klan, and battles over eugenics and immigration restriction all registered a resurgence of white supremacy, and the white-dominated historical profession was not immune. The leading historians were portraying slavery in the same ways that only the most ardent pro-slavery voices in antebellum America had done. Ulrich Bonnell Phillips led the way. His book *American Negro Slavery* (1918) was held up as the masterwork on that subject for a generation. It performed all the usual tricks: downplaying the severity of slavery, emphasizing its positive, civilizing effects, and portraying slaves as generally happy and compliant. Relying almost exclusively on the records of wealthy Southern planters who naturally were committed to justifying the institution, Phillips wrote, "Severity was clearly the exception, and kindliness the rule."[15] Two other Columbia scholars, William Archibald Dunning and John W. Burgess, ensured that such racism would underpin multiple generations of scholarship on slavery, the Civil War, and Reconstruction.[16]

Black scholars believed that the testimony of former slaves had the potential to subvert the Dunning School. The power of white supremacy lay in its capacity not only to destroy black lives but to erase black voices. This was especially true under slavery when black literacy was criminalized. Yet here was one crucial way to document black perspectives on the institution. John Cade's pathbreaking article made this clear. For instance, he cited one former slave who said that she "would just as soon be in Hell" than in slavery, and another who reported, "I consider the days of slavery as the darkest days of the world," for "we were sold just as our masters would see fit, and many of us were driven and kicked about like dogs."[17] Cade's interviews also suggested the complexity of the experience of slavery, which could never be reduced to simple generalizations, and they highlighted the terrible difficulty of gathering reliable testimony from former slaves. While U. B. Phillips and others were quick to highlight the latter fact, black scholars knew that the testimonies were indispensable and no more flawed or biased than the records of slave owners.

Thus in 1934 Reddick seized upon the New Deal to attempt to subsidize a rapid expansion of the slave interviewing project. The Federal Emergency

Relief Administration (FERA) was the government body charged with providing relief to the desperate and unemployed, which it did through loans to states. Reddick recognized that he could kill two or three birds with one stone. With struggling college students at Fisk and Kentucky State in mind, he pitched the project principally as a jobs program for white-collar black workers. This endeavor ultimately became one of the only all-black relief programs of the New Deal. In addition to providing relief and jobs to black workers, the program would also provide sociological data regarding the immediate needs of former slaves as well as historical data on slavery and beyond.

It was a clever way to attract state funding, which he succeeded in doing from Kentucky in June 1934. The project, like the funding, was initially modest. Reddick began the Kentucky interviews with only a single student assistant, W. D. Bean. However, in September Reddick secured funding from the state of Indiana, which through FERA funds allowed for the employment of forty-five workers. Reddick's ambitious goal was to collect the testimonies of former slaves throughout the entire Ohio River Valley and then to swing "down into the Lower South ending in Texas."[18]

The project's successes never matched its ambitions, but they were nevertheless significant. This first attempt to interview former slaves under governmental auspices yielded 250 interviews—priceless voices that otherwise would have been lost forever. Reddick held on to these for many years, analyzing them before he presented the information to scholars and the larger public. For instance, at the November 1934 ASNLH conference in Houston, Reddick took part in the lively discussion over John B. Cade's interviewing project, and he later delivered an address of his own entitled "Why Interview the Ex-Slave?" An observer noted that Reddick "presented social, economic and literary aspects of which we have heard very little."[19] A few months later during Negro History Week in Frankfort, Reddick enlisted former slaves to speak for themselves about their experiences in antebellum America.[20] He did the same thing in New Orleans the following year, when "three ex-slaves from the Creole region" relayed "dramatic incidents from antebellum times."[21]

Just as Reddick had hoped, the slave-interviewing project soon took on a much larger scale, though it shifted out of his control in the process. The expanded project was launched under the Works Progress Administration (WPA), the hugely ambitious jobs program that replaced FERA in 1935, with white folklorist John Lomax at the head. From 1936 to 1938, the WPA launched a systematic effort to record as many life stories of former slaves as possible. As Reddick had conceptualized, interviewers panned out across seventeen states and, according to historian George P. Rawick, interviewed "approximately 2 percent of the total ex-slave population in the United States in 1937." The result was "over 10,000 pages of typescript containing over 2,000 interviews with ex-slaves."[22] That material was then edited, microfilmed, and made available in 1941 as the seventeen-volume *Slave Narratives: A Folk History of Slavery in the United States from Interviews with Former Slaves*. Today that work has been digitized, and it has abetted a transformation of the scholarship on slavery over the last several decades.[23]

Reddick's pilot project influenced the WPA's larger investigation in complicated ways. Certainly, it was only through the pleas and pioneering efforts of black scholars like Reddick that the WPA study ever came to fruition. Yet as historian Norman Yetman has argued, Reddick's project was not exactly a role model for the WPA, and its financial problems may even "have temporarily forestalled the adoption of a similar study under the Writers' Project."[24] From the beginning, insufficient resources had made administration difficult, and it resulted in unqualified and unprepared staff members carrying out the very difficult work of interviewing former slaves. The national director of the Writers' Project, Henry G. Alsberg, considered it "not well conducted and therefore discontinued."[25] Indeed, as the state director of the Louisiana WPA explained it to Reddick, his project would not receive further federal support because it "is technically inadequate and is of questionable value."[26] The "questionable value" comment is perplexing given that the WPA was in fact expanding the project at that time. Regardless, the WPA project was ultimately enfeebled when it turned more to white interviewers than black ones, because former slaves were far less willing to be frank with white interviewers.[27]

Though Reddick's efforts with the slave-interviewing project failed to earn him a leadership role in the WPA study, they nevertheless aided his rise within Carter Woodson's network. Woodson and Charles Johnson had both served as "continual advisors" throughout the FERA project.[28] Increasingly impressed with Reddick, Woodson granted him a greater role within ASNLH. He invited Reddick to present at the annual conferences, he supported Reddick in becoming a major speaker and organizer during Negro History Weeks, and he assigned Reddick books to review for the *Journal of Negro History*. In 1934, the *Journal* published two of those reviews, one of which won him the association's award for best review that year.[29]

The book reviews demonstrated Woodson's influence on Reddick. For instance, in his award-winning review of *Social Attitudes* (1931), which was an edited book featuring essays by Robert E. Park, Florian Znaniecki, Ellsworth Faris, and other leading sociologists, Reddick praised the volume's explanation of the complex social forces governing human life, including ones that biased intelligence tests against African Americans.[30] But Reddick took special issue with the essay by white sociologist Edward B. Reuter. Reuter had built a reputation for himself as an objective expert on the race question—a status automatically denied to any African American. In his selection, he argued that black people could make no distinctive contribution to American culture, for "The accomplishments of Negroes in America, as elsewhere, are achievements of individuals," not the group. At a time when white scholars were pointing to "backward" African heritage or bad genes to explain why black people were inferior, Reuter's position was in some ways progressive. But Reddick exposed the problem. Black people did have special contributions to make—not because of "remote origin in Africa" or "racial temperament," but because "the history of the Negro in America has been unique." "The alternating pressures upon the group and the reactions to these pressures," he maintained, "have generated a life and spirit which, if accurately interpreted, is not only revealed in definite arts, but in the determination and liberation of that spirit characterized as American." Woodson approved.[31]

A Season of Protest

The spring of 1935 was an auspicious time for Reddick. He gained admittance to the University of Chicago's doctoral program in history, won a fellowship from the General Education Board to subsidize summer study there, and accepted a job as the head of the history department at Dillard University in New Orleans. These were all significant achievements that boded well for the young historian's career. For the next four years, Reddick shuffled back and forth between Chicago and Dillard, managing somehow to complete all of his PhD requirements by the summer of 1939.[32]

The Dillard professorship marked a major step forward professionally. Dillard was a new university which opened that same year, and many administrators had ambitions for it to become a major research university on par with Fisk, Howard, and Atlanta University. Dillard never lived up to those ambitions, but it nevertheless emerged as a notable research center during the Depression.[33] Its greatest successes grew out of its recruitment of Horace Mann Bond as an academic dean, who then hired Reddick as a historian, Allison Davis as head of the Division of Social Sciences, Davis's wife, Elizabeth Stubbs Davis, as an instructor of English (she, too, was a talented anthropologist), and St. Clair Drake as an anthropologist.[34] The latter three were all involved in a monumental community study of Natchez, Mississippi, later published as *Deep South* (1941).[35] The book was the best study of the South in that generation, and it helped catapult Allison Davis to assuming the first full-time black professorship at a predominantly white university in 1942.[36] *Deep South* demonstrated how a class system overlay a racial caste one to circumscribe the lives of most Natchez residents.[37] Reddick was no big fan of the caste school of race relations, but he learned a great deal from his colleagues' anthropology. Together they created a lively intellectual environment at Dillard.

Reddick, again tasked with heading up a history department, now had to build it from scratch. This was not easy given that he had to teach five courses each semester and perform various administrative duties.[38] But the new position did allow him curricular freedoms. When he introduced courses in African American history, be became one of the earliest instructors to do so at an American college.[39] Reddick also developed a variety of timely courses. For instance, to help students make sense of the stunning rise of Adolf Hitler and Benito Mussolini, Reddick proposed a course on "Dictatorship in the Modern World." And given Dillard's proximity to the local Latin culture of New Orleans, he planned a course entitled "Historical Evolution of Latin America." As Reddick envisioned it, "Dillard might well avail itself of the opportunity to become distinguished as a depository of materials on the Negro in Latin America and the Negro in the Antebellum South."[40] The plan appealed to Allison Davis, who was developing a Caribbean Studies program and studying black peoples throughout the region.[41]

Dillard's longest-lasting impact on Reddick ended up being personal. In addition to deepening his connection with Horace Mann Bond, Reddick met his wife while in New Orleans. Ella Ruth Thomas was a schoolteacher and New Orleans native, and she married Reddick on Christmas Day in 1938.[42] She would remain his wife until he died fifty-seven years later in 1995. The daughter of a physician and a graduate of Boston University, Ruth was squarely part of the black bourgeoisie and shaped by the politics of respectability.[43] This was on display in 1938 when she spoke before the Tennessee State Federation of Colored Women's Clubs. A reporter noted that an address she gave "stressed health, education, spiritual development, security, love and affection, and a place in the home, observance of the Golden Rule and social adjustments."[44] Ruth confessed to Lawrence that she was not "the venturesome type," which sometimes made her peripatetic life with him

Lawrence Reddick, right, next to his wife, Ella Ruth Thomas Reddick, and musician Jimmie Lunceford at the Renaissance Casino in New York City, 1941. Courtesy of the Photographs and Prints Division, Schomburg Center for Research in Black Culture, New York Public Library.

stressful.[45] But she grounded her husband, kept the home while continuing to work as a teacher, performed the vital role of family socialite, and provided Lawrence the emotional support necessary to sustain his relentless work ethic. Ruth had her own ambitions too, later doing graduate work at New York University and publishing articles in the *Negro History Bulletin*, the popular periodical ASNLH began publishing in 1937.[46] It was nevertheless

Ruth's private relationship with Lawrence that made much of his activist life possible. This is a crucial point. Male scholars relied on a gendered division of labor that rendered women's work invisible while affording them more time to build their careers and burnish their stature as intellectuals. Ruth is remarkably absent from Lawrence's personal papers—and subsequently from much of this book—but that very absence speaks volumes. It should be a constant reminder that Reddick's contributions are not his alone.[47]

In addition to Ruth, Reddick befriended St. Clair Drake at Dillard. The two subsequently became close confidants who supported and shaped one another for their rest of their lives. The nature of their lifelong relationship is in fact far better documented than Lawrence and Ruth's, which is yet further evidence of the inherent sexism built into the archives. But Drake, one year younger than Reddick, matched his comrade's intellectual ability, political orientation, and activist sensibility. His father was from Barbados and became a significant figure in Marcus Garvey's Universal Negro Improvement Association, which laid the groundwork for Drake to become one of the great students of the African diaspora.[48] Allison Davis, Drake's professor at Hampton Institute, steered his pupil into social anthropology and then to Dillard.[49] Reddick liked Drake immediately. His geniality, brilliance, and fiery devotion to social justice was alluring. Drake was more of the absent-minded-professor type, while Reddick was always organized and disciplined. Their contrasting styles nevertheless proved complementary, and the two friends became roommates during graduate school at the University of Chicago. At Dillard, furthermore, the two bachelors both lived in university dormitories, where Bond would "drop in on them for impromptu chats" as they discussed the pressing issues of the day.[50]

Finding a political ally in Drake, Reddick was quick to involve him in his work. For instance, he encouraged Drake to join Phi Beta Sigma and then recruited him to write for the *Crescent*. In a series of newsletters from 1935 to 1936, Reddick organized an ongoing symposium entitled "Black America's Way Out—Which?"[51] He featured fraternity brothers' essays from across the political spectrum. On the conservative end, James Weldon Johnson wrote about the dangers that Communism posed for blacks, and others preached traditional messages of self-help. For a more progressive approach, Reddick solicited Drake, who "plugged for a cooperative society" and called for a broad-based social movement to confront both race and class inequalities.[52] Once again generational divisions were on display.

Reddick agreed with Drake, as did a growing number of others in the rapidly shifting political environment. When Reddick concluded his editorial for the December 1935 newsletter by writing, "Let us give a cheer, the sharecroppers of Arkansas are getting together and those in Alabama have *won* a strike," he was signaling his support for unions such as the Southern Tenant Farmers Union, which had seemed to rewrite the societal rulebook by eschewing Jim Crow norms and uniting across the color line.[53] And that union was only one part of a nationwide Popular Front of leftists and liberals uniting to confront capitalist domination along interracial lines. Their collective power pushed the federal government to move beyond the modest relief and recovery measures of the early New Deal and advance major structural reform, including the creation of Social Security and the welfare state. When President Roosevelt signed the National Labor Relations Act into law on July 5, 1935, guaranteeing the right of private-sector workers to organize into trade unions, he empowered workers to create a federation of industrial unions. The Congress of Industrial Organizations was instituted later that year. Reddick's conception of what social change was possible expanded exponentially in these years.

Seeking to play his part in the changes, Reddick pushed Phi Beta Sigma to get involved with the National Negro Congress (NNC). The NNC was, in historian Erik Gellman's words, "the black vanguard of the Popular Front," and it was slated to hold its inaugural meeting in Chicago in February 1936.[54] Therefore, when the director of the social action program recommended Sigma involvement during the December 1935 conclave, Reddick leapt in support. They convinced the fraternity to send representatives to the meeting despite "resistance to the 'radicalization' of the Fraternity" from some members. The spirit of reform was clearly afoot even among conservative brothers, who listened closely to Roy Wilkins's speech at that conclave. Wilkins outlined the NAACP's policy agenda, which included "entrance of black students to tax-supported schools of the South; non-discrimination in public transport; equalization of teachers' salaries; equal lengths of school terms; equal per capita school expenditures."[55] At that same meeting, Reddick was named the fraternity's director of education and reelected as the editor of the *Crescent*.

When the NNC met from February 14 to 16, over seven hundred delegates from twenty-eight states descended upon wintry Chicago, which was then being blanketed by a foot of snow.[56] Along with many Sigma brothers, Reddick bore witness to the unprecedented gathering and even ran a session on civil liberties. In his later history of the Sigma fraternity, Reddick recorded it as "the most representative and broadly based Negro convention of its kind in American history" where "intellectuals rubbed shoulders with labor leaders and high churchmen."⁵⁷ The goal was to coordinate the activities of all black activist organizations and to integrate them with the progressive labor movement. A. Philip Randolph was too ill to attend, but delegates listened to a speech he wrote that captured the spirit of the gathering. Randolph declared, "The problems of the Negro people are the problems of the workers, for practically 99 percent of Negro people win their bread by selling their labor power."⁵⁸ The speech was reprinted throughout the black press, and Randolph, a longtime socialist and organizer of the Brotherhood of Sleeping Car Porters (the first predominantly black labor union), was elected as president of the NNC.

The meeting was Reddick's first chance to interact seriously with leading black leftists and labor leaders. He recalled how John P. Davis, the "self-styled architect of the Congress," was clearly "the man in charge at Chicago." Reverend Adam Clayton Powell, a "young and dynamic modern preacher from Harlem," was also imposing. Max Yergan, another figure Reddick would become more familiar with in New York City, "inveighed against the 'imperialism' that had chased him out of Africa." Reddick was especially eager to see Angelo Herndon, the young man who in 1932 had been arrested and convicted for "insurrection" in Alabama—based upon a law dating back to slave times—for attempting to organize black and white workers together. He served almost three years in prison before his conviction was finally overturned in December 1935, shortly before the NNC meeting. Reddick recalled how Herndon, "frail and dreamy eyed, looked as though he had contracted 'T. B.' while in that Georgia dungeon."⁵⁹ Herndon's case became an international sensation, and Reddick made sure to continually remind his Sigma brothers about it. For example, in one *Crescent* newsletter he asked what Sigmas would "say and do about the *cause célèbre* right under their national conventions" in Atlanta. "O, where are our brave free college men?"⁶⁰

The convention did result in some concrete demands. Attendees called for a nationwide effort to organize industrial workers, and they criticized both company unions and the American Federation of Labor for their exclusionary and paternalistic practices.⁶¹ The Congress also, in Reddick's words, "fought fascism abroad and at home" and "called for the defense of Ethiopia against Mussolini; the abolition of jim crow in America and ending the exploitation of farmers and workers—especially sharecroppers."⁶² After the meeting, the NNC panned out and created local chapters all over the country, including the remarkably effective Southern Negro Youth Congress.

Reddick carried his enthusiasm southward as well. In New Orleans he took a visible role in a protest against a massive celebration of Italy's defeat of Ethiopia—the last independent African country on the continent besides Liberia. The blow was especially devastating to the black world given Ethiopia's long history of independence and high cultural achievements, and because it symbolized the rise of a white-supremacist, fascist imperialism that was on the march all over the world. As historian James H. Meriwether has shown, the invasion of Ethiopia "marked the start of black America's transformed engagement with contemporary Africa," away from a generalized indifference to a more intensive interest and identification with Africans.[63]

World War II and decolonization would only deepen that new relationship, but the protest in New Orleans already symbolized the shifting winds. The *Pittsburgh Courier* captured the striking scene: "Twenty-seven orders of the Italian union [featuring 2,000 marchers] . . . marched for three hours to the tunes of a double band, while over 10,000 spectators looked on. Exclamations of 'Vive L'Italians,' and the raising of the right hand in the fascist salute lent added color to the demonstration." Refusing to stand idly by, Reddick mobilized Phi Beta Sigma to coordinate with the NAACP, the League Against War and Fascism, and several other organizations to disrupt the proceedings. "Three university professors," the *Courier* reported, "L. D. Reddick, Byron Augustine, and St. Clair Drake, haunted the paraders throughout their march by trailing and sometimes cutting in front of them with an automobile bearing a placard, 'We Protest Against This Celebration of Aggressive War and Fascism.' . . . Police, after several futile attempts to frighten the professors away, finally surrounded the car and hurled threats while a group of angry Italians tore off the sign denouncing this celebration of war and fascism." It was a truly remarkable scene, and one rife with potential for violence. The professors luckily came away unscathed and seemed only emboldened to continue the protest. The paper reported, "Later in the evening, 3,000 Negroes gathered in the Freedmans' Auditorium to consider the imposition of economic sanctions against local Italian merchants as a sign of protest."[64]

Ebony Student in the Ivory Tower

As intoxicating as all the protest could be, Reddick believed he was best positioned to effect change through intellectual work. He thus brought his pugilistic spirit from the streets to the classroom, where he found white supremacy to be no less rampant. In the spring of 1936, Reddick got word that he had won a General Education Board fellowship to support nine months of full-time study at the University of Chicago, and he seized the opportunity to make a serious dent in his doctoral work. He later recalled how there had initially been "a tug among my profs as to whether I should go to Harvard or Chicago," but that his many Chicago-trained mentors ultimately convinced him that it was the better choice. The social sciences at Chicago, they averred, were more modern and scientific than Harvard's more traditional program.[65] Woodson, Bond, E. Franklin Frazier, Charles Johnson, and Lorenzo Dow Turner are only a few of his mentors who had preceded him at Chicago. Furthermore, Drake, Allison Davis, Elsie Lewis, Clarence Bacote, Luther Porter Jackson, and James Hugo Johnston are only a few of his peers who also studied at Chicago around the same time. That bastion of white power and privilege therefore had a few black paths forged through it.

Life in Chicago also had its perks. The Great Migration had created a vibrant black belt on the city's Southside, and this "Black Metropolis" surrounded the University of Chicago. With the formation of the NNC and the election of Oscar De Priest as the first African American to Congress in the twentieth century, Chicago was at the epicenter of political change. The same was true culturally. Chicago arguably displaced Harlem as the vanguard of black culture in the 1930s and 1940s, when its renaissance featured the likes of Louis Armstrong, William Edouard Scott, Gwendolyn Brooks, Margaret Walker, Richard Wright, Arna Bontemps, Lorraine Hansberry, Thomas Dorsey, and Earl Hines.[66] Ever an avid jazz fan, Reddick no doubt enjoyed the Savoy Ball Room and other draws of the famous nightlife, and he would not have missed the Reynolds Club, a student hangout playing everything from church choir music to the latest jazz. Reddick had already befriended Margaret Walker in New Orleans, and in Chicago he did the same with Bontemps and Wright.[67]

When Bontemps died in 1973, Reddick gave a eulogy that described his relationship to Bontemps and Wright within Chicago's dense network of artists and intellectuals. Reddick apparently encountered Bontemps as a neighbor, and the two of them "had many talks about writers and other artists—most black." Reddick recalled, "I learned a lot from Arna. He had read widely and knew so many writers personally; but he never seemed to put any of them down." Reddick had befriended black sociologist Horace Cayton through Drake, but it was Bontemps who acquainted Reddick with Wright. Bontemps "brought him around to my room one afternoon—and there Richard was, thin and shy. But once we got him talking, we could see that he was a natural and fascinating story-teller." In a fascinating bit of coincidence which revealed how much black art was rooted in concrete social experiences, Reddick recollected, "It so happened that I was rooming with Ulysses S. Keyes, the defense attorney in the local[ly] famous Nixon murder case. Wright and Keyes became friends and Wright's novel, *Native Son*, was largely based upon the Nixon trial."[68] Reddick and Wright remained casual friends for many years.

The thrills of the Black Metropolis could nevertheless be sullied by the pervasive racism that Reddick experienced not only in the city but also at the University of Chicago itself. Despite pockets of progressivism, the school mirrored the racist practices of the larger city and country. Historian Mary Ann Dzuback has documented the rampant racial discrimination on campus in the 1930s. As admissions officers labored to reduce the enrollment of both Jews and blacks, black students could not get haircuts at a campus barbershop, were denied equal access to medical treatment at the university hospital, and were refused apartments in university-owned buildings because the school honored restrictive covenants. Black fraternities, helpless before the discrimination, were forced to disband when they could not rent houses in the area. Furthermore, in stark contrast to black colleges like Fisk, Chicago lacked black professors who could truly empathize and support black students in their travails.[69] White students didn't make it any easier. Luther Porter Jackson, another black graduate student in the history program who had matriculated a few years before Reddick, observed that his white peers kept their distance from him even though they were "cordial and civil" enough in person.[70]

Despite the difficulties, Reddick plowed through five consecutive quarters of study at Chicago. His productivity during those fifteen months was astounding. He completed all the rest of his coursework, which involved passing no less than fourteen classes and a French language exam. The demands of such a schedule, coupled with the scholarly work he was doing outside of graduate school, contributed to Reddick's accumulation of two incompletes and a preponderance of Bs (he earned nine Bs and five As). Aside from one course in European history, the other sixteen of his seventeen courses (including three during the summer of 1935) were in U.S. history, especially southern history, the Civil War and Reconstruction, and Hispanic America. As was characteristic of the profession at that time, a heavy emphasis was given to political and diplomatic history—and hence to the white male dignitaries who were seen as the only ones to have "made" history.[71]

Reddick stood poised to challenge such biases, but he entered graduate school eager to soak up whatever he could from his professors. He reported to Bond, "The atmosphere is stimulating. . . . I have learned a lot—almost something every day."[72] Reddick then underscored how an elite education could be both invigorating and self-aggrandizing: "Think how ignorant all the other people must be who miss this daily advance."[73] His professors recognized the exceptional interest and enthusiasm characterizing their young black pupil. Bessie Peirce, a rare female professor whom Reddick liked, noted his "considerable zeal for research."[74] Fred Rippy, a Latin Americanist whom Reddick also liked, called him "a man of exceptional intellectual equipment and great industry" who ranked in "the upper five percent" in his classes.[75] Reddick especially liked U.S. colonial historian Marcus Jernegan, a Progressive School scholar who had written about how American Christians, acting out of narrow economic self-interest, had shamelessly adapted their faith in order to justify slavery.[76] Reddick beamed as he reported to Bond that Jernegan had "assigned two students to the class angles of the American Revolution" but then "dismissed the white boy's essay in two sentences and spent a class hour on mine."[77] Even that relationship, though, was sullied by racism. Jernegan's offhand remark about a "nigger in the woodpile" left a lasting impression.[78]

Reddick approached his white professors critically, and not with the deference and sheepishness characteristic of many graduate students. This was the case for even widely respected and politically powerful figures whom he admired, such as William E. Dodd. Dodd was a white southerner from humble origins who had mentored Woodson at Chicago decades earlier. Shortly after Reddick arrived, Dodd left the university to serve as the U.S. ambassador to Nazi Germany.[79] In that post, he famously resigned in protest of the Nazis' racist persecution of its own citizens. Reddick respected Dodd, but when called to write a review of his book *The Old South* (1938), he did not pull any punches. To be sure, he found much to praise about the book, and confirmed happily that "this is one of the few books of 'Southern History' written by a 'Southerner' which is not deformed by either regional patriotism or 'race' prejudice." Yet in a criticism that applied to every one of his white professors at Chicago, he complained that "very little space is devoted to the Negro," which he believed led to distortion because blacks were fundamental to every phase of American history. Furthermore, Reddick resented that white scholars like Dodd were positioned to get credit for ideas that black scholars had already been publicizing. Subsequently, when affirming Dodd's point that the first Africans brought to the British colonies were indentured servants and not slaves, Reddick made clear that "for some time a few of us have been submitting" that fact already. Reddick's informal education as part of Woodson's black history movement thus enabled him to critique his own renowned professors with remarkable cogency, even if those critiques were generally ignored within the white world.[80]

Considering Reddick's criticism of even the professors he liked, he was unsparing in confronting those he disliked. He got a chance to spar publicly with other leading white scholars in late December 1936 when twelve national scholarly societies descended upon Chicago for their annual meetings. Reddick was one of a dozen black scholars to attend these white-dominated organizations, which typically excluded black participants. Signs of change were further evident in Charles Johnson's election as vice president of the American Sociological Society.[81] While E. Franklin Frazier and Horace Cayton presented papers of their own, Reddick took on the role of audience critic.

Reddick made a full report to Bond that conveyed the revelry and bombast characteristic of a young man convinced of the validity and righteousness of his cause. After one scholar at the American Political Science meeting presented a paper arguing that religion created social harmony, Reddick relayed, "After I had hammered, for about three minutes, the stock in trade that economic and other social forces, are frequently stronger, all of the boys jumped upon this and destroyed the paper." He then recounted a similar incident the next day at the American Economic Association. He confessed, "Unlike the present mood, I felt quite seriously about the whole discussion. I had had a good night's rest and was composed and deliberate and I spoke into the mike in that gorgeous Stevens Hotel Grand Ballroom. Man, I felt like I used to feel in the old 'Wrangler days at Fisk . . . an intellectual joust for its own sake, having fun, not giving much of a damn about being politic."[82]

Reddick clearly enjoyed the rare opportunity to speak truth to white power, but he knew that the bigger issue involved was securing the right of blacks to participate in conferences at all. He began taking steps to challenge black exclusion, but not in the same way as his mentor Charles Johnson, who preferred a quiet, nonthreatening, gradual approach to integration. Reddick wanted to make people uncomfortable and to force the issue. He therefore worked with a group of scholars to force professional organizations like the Southern Historical Association to make difficult decisions about how and whether to exclude any black scholars who had joined the organization and wanted to participate in the annual meeting.[83] This group included sympathetic white scholars too, such as Howard K. Beale, another Progressive School historian who came to recognize the importance of black scholarship after reading Du Bois's *Black Reconstruction* (1935), which prompted him to rethink that whole era.[84] Reddick's frustration was that the meetings of professional associations were "arranged and executed without thought of the colored brother."[85] Or even worse, they were arranged with careful consideration about which type of black scholar would be welcomed and which would not. For instance, Reddick described how the American Historical Association (AHA) had welcomed politically conservative black scholars like Nathan Monroe Work to attend its conferences but excluded scholars from "a more aggressive tradition" like Carter Woodson and Charles Wesley.[86] Not wanting to highlight its discriminatory practices, the AHA simply reshuffled the membership of a committee when one member had recommended the participation of the more "aggressive" black scholars.

Reddick's protest of organizational discrimination did help him break an academic color barrier. In 1940, Reddick became the first black scholar to publish in the *Journal of Southern History*.[87] It was only a review of a book by another black scholar—Montague Cobb's *The First Negro Medical Society* (1939)—but it did mark a break from the past. Still, that journal did not publish another review by a black author (John Hope Franklin) for nine years, and it waited until 1955 to publish an article by one (Elsie Lewis).[88] Fisk alumni were thus at the forefront of this barrier-breaking, but there was little to celebrate. The institutional racism of scholarly organizations was overwhelming, and it ensured the marginalization of African Americans from conferences and journals for another generation.

Academic discrimination did not end there. No predominantly white universities hired even token black faculty members on a permanent basis until the 1940s, and the numbers remained very low for decades.[89] However, the problems for black scholars began much earlier, during the research process itself. Reddick was one of the first people to call attention to the issue in print. In 1937 in *Social Frontier*, an organ of the John Dewey Society, Reddick laid out the array of obstacles confronting black researchers.[90] While white researchers could access libraries and archives as they saw fit, black investigators had to navigate a veritable maze. Reddick confirmed that blacks were routinely denied access to tax-supported public libraries, private papers and collections, and archives with public records. Other times, they were allowed into the building but not the reading room, so they researched in hastily constructed, segregated quarters.[91] Yet such challenges could also be the seeds of ingenuity. "A stirring chapter could be written," Reddick wrote, "on the ingenious devices employed to gain access to the necessary books and documents. Ties of kinship are always useful. Often the old classmate in Harvard's 'History 400,' is helpful. The trick may be turned by a chain of letters to someone who knows someone who knows someone who knows the custodian."[92] More sinister than simply deferring to Jim Crow mores were the librarians who hid relevant material from scholars whose politics they opposed. Oftentimes, the mere interest in documents related to black history cast suspicion on a person. This constrained even white scholars like Herbert Aptheker, a Communist and pioneer in black history.[93] Reddick thus suggested, "A good practice is to denounce a pro-Northern history book on the Civil War." However, the prize for resourcefulness "should go to the passionate devotee who entered into conspiracy with the Negro janitor" to get research materials.[94]

Yet perhaps the greatest obstacle that Reddick faced on his own path to the PhD was his adviser: Avery O. Craven. An amicable enough man with North Carolinian roots, Craven was the resident faculty expert on the Civil War and the South. Given Reddick's interests, and with the departure of William Dodd and Marcus Jernegan, Reddick was all but forced to study under Craven. It did not end well. Reddick shared with Carter Woodson an anecdote from class that highlighted the divide:

> This joke may amuse you. Dr A O Craven, leading authority on all aspects of Southern History, was lecturing the other day on the "Crime of Reconstruction"—his very phrase. Well, after I had stood about thirty minutes of the wrongs done the "Southern People" by carpet baggers, scalawags and Negroes, I took advantage of a pause to ask: "Would it be scientific to consider the scalawags and Negroes as 'Southern People'?" It was a blow to the short-ribs. The man seemed to grasp his desk for support. He tried to stammer out some sort of an explanation. I did not push the point. I kept thinking of a bull in the bull fight reeling over the arena with the hilt buried in his head. The lecture was ruined. Apparently, his thesis had been predicated upon a certain notion that the planters et al. were "the Southern people." He seemed to be so happy when the end of the hour came that I felt a momentary eddy of sympathy for him. Altogether it is hopeful when such simple questions can bring down such high "authority."[95]

The story, besides illuminating Reddick's irreverent approach to Craven and the classroom, highlights the sectional biases framing Craven's entire corpus of scholarship. Unwittingly or not, he identified completely with the white planter class of the South, and his histories reflected their perspective. For instance, *The Coming of the Civil War* (1942) portrayed that great conflagration as an unfortunate and unnecessary war caused by abolitionists whom he dubbed "extremists" for first inventing and then inflaming sectional differences.[96] His interpretation rested on the idea that slavery was generally benign, and that blacks were uncivilized and unequipped for freedom. What is most striking about Craven is the overtness with which he expressed these ideas during his own classes—even those that included black students. For example, Reddick remembered Craven once musing, "You know, there is a remarkable parallel between the history of the Negro and the history of the mule."[97] In short, Craven was squarely part of the William Dunning and Ulrich Phillips Lost Cause school of historiography, which became Reddick's archnemesis.

Reddick's first idea for his dissertation involved tackling white scholarly racism head on. Rather than making a different argument about the war, he hoped to dissect the Dunning School historians themselves. The real story, he thought, was not about the war at all but about the generations of white historians who had reduced history to sectional propaganda. His proposed project, "The Racial Attitudes of American Historians," would be a social and intellectual history of American historians: who they were, where they came from, what racial ideas they held, how they disseminated those ideas, and the impact of their work on the public. He hoped to "show the historian as a functionary in a particular social, economic and political environment."[98] This would have been a radically innovative project. Besides being inspired by his own experiences with racist historians like Craven, it was also in keeping with the promising new field of intellectual history. For instance, Reddick cited Merle Curti's *The Social Ideas of American Educators* (1935) as a potential model.[99] No doubt Reddick was also influenced by the sociology of knowledge as articulated by Karl Mannheim and others, who came to wield a significant influence on that generation of social scientists.[100] However, for a variety of reasons including practicality, the forces of tradition in academia, and Craven's own discomfort, Reddick ultimately moved in another direction.

Reddick may have viewed Craven's lukewarm support for him as a badge of honor, but it did not make graduate school any easier. In a letter of recommendation for a Rosenwald fellowship in 1939, Craven included some negative comments about Reddick's personality which would have sunk most black scholars' chances for funding. He called Reddick's professional interest "rather unusual," and in a more damning fashion declared, "He has a rather aggressive personality and does not always cooperate as well as might be desired."[101] The white men who controlled the academy and foundations used such letters of recommendation to police the behavior of black scholars. Discussion of such negative personality traits signaled that Reddick could be a troublemaker and hence not worthy of a fellowship.

Black women scholars such as Elsie Lewis had it doubly bad. Lewis graduated from Fisk the same year as Reddick, and she also studied with him at Chicago, taking at least four classes alongside him. She would go on to become a true pioneer in earning her PhD and joining the history faculty at Howard. But the dual barriers of race and gender constrained her all the way. In letters of recommendation for her, white male Chicago professors felt compelled to speak about her feminine qualities. William T. Hutchinson wrote, "As a person she is most agreeable. She is careful of her attire, speaks well, and is courteous and cooperative." However, he continued, "She is race-conscious and perhaps for that reason sometimes over-strains to be a credit to her race." All of her recommenders measured her performance only in comparison with other black students, making any compliments inherently backhanded. For instance, Craven called her "the second-best Negro girl that I have had here at Chicago." J. Fred Rippy focused on her poor health and "frail" appearance but tried to offset those remarks by affirming that "in personality she is rather superior."[102]

In short, Lewis had to suffer both racial and gender proscriptions that made it impossible for her to be considered a true scholar. The very societal conception of scholar was gendered: men were the deliberative ones able to handle abstract thinking and scholarship; women were the emotional ones equipped to rear children and make men's lives aesthetically pleasing and morally upright. As men monopolized the universities, they conducted research that purported to prove that women were intellectually inferior.[103] Even worse, they constructed science as an inherently masculine pursuit to begin with, positing that only men were capable of the calm, rational thought necessary to be objective scientists. Even if Reddick was automatically dubbed a biased racial chauvinist, he could at least—and did—fall back upon masculine behavior (i.e., aggressiveness) and male claims of objectivity to establish himself as a reputable scholar.[104] Lewis had no such privilege. Her very existence as a scholar made her an oddity.[105]

Although Craven hampered Reddick and steered him away from his original research topic, Reddick nevertheless completed a dissertation that served as a stinging rejoinder to his adviser. While Craven portrayed abolitionists as extremists and propagandists, Reddick did the same for white southern journalists and newspapermen. Horace Mann Bond and others at Dillard made the project possible by copying local newspapers for him.[106] Reddick thus focused on the New Orleans press in the runup to the war from 1850 to 1860, a decade which "saw desperate efforts toward 'sectional nationalism' on the part of the South in resistance to the world sweep of the forces of urban industrialism and anti-slavery." Newspapermen, he contended, were the chief molders of public opinion and therefore played an outsized role in precipitating the war. Reddick analyzed four major New Orleans newspapers and sorted their subject matter into various categories while tracking their evolution over time. The key theme was the stunning rise of antiblack propaganda in these years. For example, Reddick identified "fifty-one terms derogatory to the Negro such as 'cuffee,' 'Sambo,' 'free buck,' and 'wooly heads,' while no such comparable terms of eulogy were discovered." The reasons for this assault, Reddick explained, stemmed from the newspapermen's role as "functionaries in a social system" that was built upon slavery. In other words, self-interest informed their commitment to slavery's preservation in the face of internal and external threats.[107]

Reddick's close scrutiny of New Orleans newspapers revealed a remarkably complex and conflicted society which exploded the romantic mythology of the Lost Cause at every turn. Instead of a peaceful, bucolic antebellum South, there was "great tension in ante-bellum Negro-white relations" all along. Instead of slaves being generally contented and compliant, "the Negro slave resisted his reduction, fought back and ran away." "Many of those who did not seek to break the system through insurrection and flight," he continued, "sought to maintain their personalities within the system through verbal and physical assaults and the destruction of property." Against the trope of white slaveowners and powerbrokers being a benevolent, genteel group, he offered up "the power and depth of the tremendous effort to eliminate the free Negro from the South, to drive him out of the land or into slavery," which was not unlike "the oppressions of ethnic minorities in modern Europe."[108] Reddick never published his dissertation as a book, so his landmark study was all but ignored. It nevertheless laid out a set of ideas about slavery that would not become common wisdom within the mainstream history profession for another half century. To be sure, the dissertation was also a product of its time and drew from the latest work in the social psychology of propaganda, the social anthropology of caste and class, and the sociology of stereotypes and racial attitudes. But the interpretations were remarkably prescient.[109]

Reddick waited until after he graduated to criticize Craven more directly. The immediate trigger was Craven's dismissive and insulting review of Charles Wesley's *The Collapse of the Confederacy* (1937) in the *American Journal of Sociology*.[110] In a barely two-hundred-word review, Craven impugned, "The conclusion is all too simple. The point of view is far too narrow. . . . Mr. Wesley has not proved his case."[111] But then, as Reddick told Bond, he "overplayed his hand" by concluding: "He has only demonstrated again how difficult it is for a Negro to write sanely of a period in which his race suffered such great injustice."[112] Craven was falling back on the racist politics of objectivity which presumed that all black people were biased and that only white men were capable of impartiality on the race issue.[113] However, the explicitness of Craven's admission provided Reddick an opening for attack. He corresponded with Bond to decide how to expose Craven's racism to the world.[114] The publication of Craven's lectures at Louisiana State University, *The Repressible Conflict, 1830–1861* (1939), proved auspicious.[115]

Under a pseudonym, and with Carter Woodson's courageous backing, Reddick leveled a lengthy four-page attack on Craven and his scholarship in the *Journal of Negro History*. It was unprecedented in its depth, tone, and frankness in rebuking a leading white scholar, which was not without risks for Reddick and the *Journal*. But it was exactly the kind of review that Reddick and other black scholars had always wanted to write. It first turned the politics of objectivity on its head, stating that Craven, "born in Randolph County, North Carolina, and married into a branch of the family of Tom Watson, Negro-baiting demagogue of the 'Nineties,'" could not be expected to produce an impartial account of the past. "He is an example of the effect provincial loyalties may have upon critical judgment," Reddick impugned, "and should be studied thoroughly as a document exhibit of the tenacity with which pedestrian attitudes maintain themselves in the face of professional training." The long review was punctuated by similar stark attacks upon Craven's professionalism. For example, Craven seemed "more interested in defending the Old South than describing it." And "Students of attitudes may be struck by the intrusion of pre–Civil War thought patterns into the paragraphs of a present day scholar." Craven's thesis about abolitionists causing the Civil War, furthermore, "requires little comment so disproportionate and inadequate is the analysis." Reddick concluded contemptuously, "Historians may be . . . hopeful that the standards of the craft may not be further debased by a sectional patriotism and race chauvinism of which the victim may not be altogether conscious."[116]

The review was not without its critics. James Hugo Johnston and Luther Porter Jackson, two of Craven's former black graduate students at Chicago, "rejoiced over the fact that someone has called Craven to task for his pro-Southern views," but they took issue with "the personal reference to him which would lead a reader to conclude that he is a fire-eater. He is not a person of that stamp."[117] Craven himself was furious, and he suspected it was Reddick. He wrote a letter to Jackson asking him to protest to Woodson, explaining that Reddick was "trying to damage me at every opportunity because I did not give him the grades he wanted in my courses."[118]

Those squabbles nevertheless distracted from the larger story of the day, which was that black scholars were subjected to gross double standards and profound institutional racism. Black academics were helpless when Craven dismissed Wesley's book and impugned his integrity in the pages of the most authoritative and widely read journal in all of American sociology. Issuing a rebuke of Craven in the marginalized *Journal of Negro History* was not at all comparable. Moreover, the outright biases and distortions characterizing Craven's books were the real problem. Reddick's review exposed them, if in the no-holds-barred manner that would come to define his style. Meanwhile, the reviews of Craven's *The Repressible Conflict* in the two leading American history journals simply praised the book in glowing terms.[119] Too, Craven was empowered by his long-term position on the faculty at Chicago, even rising to become president of the Organization of American Historians from 1963 to 1964, all of which gave him a powerful platform to share his deeply flawed and racist interpretations for decades. Today the OAH continues to honor Craven by offering an annual book award in his name, even as Reddick is ignored and forgotten.

A Rising Star in the Black History Movement

As cathartic as it was to "[tear] the hide off a pro-Southern professor of history at one of our greatest universities," as Reddick characterized it, he kept his eyes on the prize: advancing the black history movement.[120] In 1937 in the *Journal of Negro History*, he published a landmark state-of-the-field essay. Drawing from his array of experiences interviewing former slaves, living in New Orleans, studying at Chicago, writing for Phi Beta Sigma, and taking part in the National Negro Congress, Reddick issued a formidable critique of black historical writing to date, and he laid out a bold historiographical agenda that would not be fully realized for decades. While he supported the general "purpose-philosophy" of the black history movement—to discover the role of African-descended peoples in world history, to educate the majority populations about it, and to use that knowledge to create race pride among blacks—he questioned the larger political orientation and professionalism among black historians. "The whole group," he criticized, "has written under the influence of . . . liberalism," which gave undo weight to the individual in making history, and mistakenly folded all events into an arc of progress. Consequently, much of black historiography was "superficial" in relating factors together and in "determining the forces which have been influential" in shaping history. He attributed this failing partly to the amateurism of early black historians such as George Washington Williams, Booker T. Washington, and Benjamin Brawley, who lacked professional training in "scientific history." Hardening that divide, he claimed that "the history of Negro historiography falls into two divisions, *before* Woodson and *after* Woodson."[121]

If some of his critiques overplayed such distinctions and were less than generous to his predecessors, Reddick's recommendations for new directions in black history were prophetic.[122] He called for a new social history of ordinary black people instead of endless investigations into the "articulate professional classes." He suggested histories comparing the experiences of African Americans with other "racial, minority and laboring groups," and to others within the international arena. In particular, he called for examinations of black people in Africa and Latin America. Reddick also recommended new studies of slavery that explored slave resistance and viewed the institution "through the eyes of the bondsman himself." He got a little carried away in stating that "barring the discovery of new materials, the topic of slavery in the United States has been virtually exhausted. It is a further waste of time to continue to examine the few plantation records, the papers of the masters, or the usually superficial impressions of travelers." Later historians would read those same sources "against the grain" and garner fresh insights about the institution, but Reddick's emphasis on slave resistance and slave voices was farsighted. Finally, Reddick called for historians to investigate the economic basis of black history, which promised new ways to understand old events. For instance, the "whole matter of the North versus South," he contended, "seems to have been more the expression of the conflict between economic systems rather than a naturalistic geographic identification," as traditionally argued. This agenda reflected a larger one within the historical profession. Charles Beard and other historians of the Progressive School reinterpreted American history through an economic lens and eschewed the individualism and moralism of earlier accounts. Reddick cited Beard, but he emphasized instead books by black scholars such as Du Bois's *Black Reconstruction* (1935), which he called a "brilliant attempt to apply the Marxian dialectic to the Reconstruction tumult." Reddick's article was influential and continues to be discussed by scholars today.[123]

Reddick's state-of-the-field article also symbolized his entry into Carter Woodson's inner circle, which included at various points Alrutheus Taylor, Charles Wesley, Lorenzo Greene, Rayford Logan, Luther Porter Jackson, James Hugo Johnston, William Sherman Savage, William Brewer, Arnett Lindsay, and Louis Mehlinger.[124] Reddick owed his early career successes more to his involvement with this group than to any other source. They provided him with research leads, publication opportunities, conference forums, and social connections—not to mention a sense of purpose and inspiration. Far more than his doctoral work at Chicago, it was the black history movement that shaped Reddick and made him into the pioneering scholar that he was becoming. When Woodson finally bowed to pressure and created an editorial board for the *Journal of Negro History* in 1937, he included Reddick along with Jackson, Greene, Arthur Schomburg, Sterling Brown, and James B. Browning.[125] He also solicited Reddick to write a flurry of book reviews over the next few years.[126]

Yet few things came easy with Woodson. When Reddick joined the editorial board, Woodson had already had a falling out with Charles Wesley, and he had just precipitated the same with Rayford Logan, who had worked tirelessly alongside him for years.[127] The pretext was Logan's involvement with the Phelps-Stokes Fund's *Encyclopedia of the Negro* project led by Du Bois, which Woodson interpreted as undermining ASNLH's similar abortive project. He sent out a conspiratorial letter to the ASNLH executive board (which by then included Reddick) accusing Logan of treachery and announcing his prompt removal as an assistant editor of the *Journal*. Woodson called the *Encyclopedia of the Negro* nothing less than an attempt "to destroy the organization." The Phelps-Stokes Fund "has kept up an espionage system" in its "constantly waged war against the Association. . . . Are you with them or with us?"[128]

Given Woodson's belligerent position, there was little neutral ground for Reddick to hold. He told Woodson, "I deplore a division in the ranks of the 'Negro scholars,'" but he ultimately sided with the leader of ASNLH and assured him that he would never join a competitive project, professing, "I oppose and condemn any attempt to set up" one.[129] Reddick was gentler when corresponding with Logan, admitting that "my information is very incomplete on . . . essential points." He even wrote wistfully, "If you will pardon the sentimentality, I might add that all along I have admired the almost father-son relation of you and Greene to the 'Old Man'. It was quite beautiful."[130] Logan replied, "No one regrets more than I do the break between Dr. Woodson and me. . . . On the one hand, Dr. Woodson has been very kind to me. On the other, I took insults from him that I would not have taken from any other man." The underlying problem, according to Logan, was that Woodson "attempts to monopolize the field" of black studies, and "is prone to see a conspiracy against him whenever another group attempts to pursue a study of the Negro."[131] Despite the troubling signs, Reddick, like most within ASNLH, weathered Woodson's stormy personality to serve the larger movement.

Reddick had the capacity to alienate others in his own right. Admiring Woodson and perhaps wanting to prove his loyalty to him and the cause, Reddick at times adopted a cavalier approach to elder black historians. For example, his state-of-the-field essay followed Woodson in criticizing earlier black historians like Benjamin Brawley for being unscientific amateurs. Months earlier, Woodson had issued a press release that insulted Brawley's historical work and intelligence, chiding, "Brawley should have undergone sufficient mental development by this time to know that he is not an historian" at all.[132] When Brawley took offense at Reddick's article, the two men exchanged letters which only deepened the divide between them.[133] And Brawley was not the only one. Reddick's relationship with Logan soured in future years as well, no doubt influenced in part by Woodson's newfound contempt for him. It was one thing to alienate Avery Craven; it was another to sow divisions within the small community of black scholars.

It would nevertheless be a mistake to judge Woodson too harshly for any negative influence on Reddick, whose personal behavior ultimately reflected his own proclivities more than anyone else's. The fact was that Woodson, beyond dedicating his entire life to the black history movement and facing an endless stream of very real threats to ASNLH's viability, helped to make Reddick into a pioneering historian. He even influenced Reddick's decision to accept the curatorship at the Schomburg Collection in 1939. Woodson had all along insisted, "The need of the hour was not to write books from the scant materials available, but to collect and preserve sufficient data of all sorts on the Negro to enable scientifically trained men to produce treatises based upon the whole truth."[134] In other words, librarianship was at the center of black history movement, and without it little else could be accomplished. Reddick took the lesson to heart.

The Schomburg job offer was fortuitous, too, because Reddick lost his professorship at Dillard in the winter of 1938. The precise circumstances remain unclear, but in December 1938 Reddick and Horace Mann Bond were already discussing where else Reddick might find work.[135] The following summer, Edwin Embree, the director of the Julius Rosenwald Fund, corresponded with Charles Johnson and referenced a "Dillard debacle" that "might have permanently injured" Reddick's career prospects.[136] Embree rejoiced that he and Johnson had "kept this man from serious injury" and allowed him to reestablish himself and "continue a career which bids fair to be very useful."[137] It thus seems clear that Reddick was dismissed from his job. He and other allies, including Claude Barnett of the Associated Negro Press, worked behind the scenes to keep news of his departure out of the papers, and they seem to have succeeded.[138] The reasons for Reddick's dismissal may have had something to do with his involvement in local protests, which Dillard's president opposed. Indeed, the president dismissed St. Clair Drake a few years later for supporting a local NAACP protest against segregation.[139] Regardless, Reddick weathered the storm by working in Chicago in the spring of 1939 as he finished his PhD. He also managed to win a Rosenwald fellowship to study in Latin America before securing the Schomburg job that summer.[140]

In the end, Reddick's controversial departure from Dillard would only be the first of many throughout his life. Like most of those other instances, it also had the ironic result of rejuvenating his career. No other job in 1939 could have better positioned him to be at the center of the global black freedom struggle. Reddick's placement in New York City—the capital of the African diaspora and in many ways the West—proved auspicious indeed as World War II remade the world and shook the foundations of the global color line.

3 Librarianship for Democracy at Home and Abroad

> The task of democratizing the world . . . cannot be expected to go very far unless we embark, simultaneously, upon a drive for full democracy at home.
> —Lawrence Reddick

When Edwin Embree learned that Reddick had accepted the job at the Schomburg Collection, he stated its significance in no uncertain terms: "The curator of the collection automatically becomes dean of Negro history scholars." As he knew well, the curator was both "permitted and expected to give a good deal of his time to study and writing," all the while presiding over "the most important reference library on the Negro anywhere in the world."[1] And that was only the half of it. The collection, located at the 135th Street branch of the New York Public Library, served as the political, social, and cultural center of black Harlem, which was a locus for African-descended peoples from across the world. In ordinary times, such a post afforded nearly unlimited possibilities for engagement.

But these were no ordinary times. Reddick began the job on August 2, 1939, about one year after the former curator, Arturo Schomburg, had died. To honor his predecessor, Reddick renamed the Division of Negro History, Literature, and Prints as the Schomburg Collection of Negro History and Literature.[2] The name stuck. On Reddick's second day on the job, he wrote coolly to Horace Mann Bond, "The collection is swell. If I do not get at least a couple of books out in the next two or three years, it will be completely my own fault."[3] But fate intervened. Hitler invaded Poland less than a month letter and inaugurated a global cataclysm that threatened the very survival of Western democracy. The crisis cast a shadow over every activity during the next six years, and it upended Reddick's hopes of being able to sit back and write books.

Yet the war ended up being an immense galvanizing force for black activists like Reddick, much as the Great Depression had been. They knew well that the survival of the free world depended upon the support of colored peoples from across the globe. And they were committed more than ever to leveraging their wartime support for concrete social and economic gains. Their struggle strengthened connections among blacks across the diaspora, and it presented new opportunities to fight fascism both at home and abroad. If the West was engaged in a noble war for democracy and against Nazi racism, then suddenly the subjugation of nonwhite people worldwide posed new dilemmas. Reddick seized upon the universalistic language of the time to frame black civil rights as but one part of the broader human struggle for freedom and justice for all. As he put it, "A broadly gauged approach raises the limited and frequently obscure contest for minority rights to the level of the universals. On its American front it would battle for equal economic, political, social and cultural rights—irrespective of creed, color or class. On its world front, the objectives would include the Four Freedoms for all men—death to fascism and specifically the liberation of Africa, Palestine, India, China and the other subject millions."[4] As a prominent new public intellectual, Reddick was well positioned to fight the war on both fronts.

A Democratic Space

Reddick was always eager to make his voice be heard, and the curatorship gave him the perfect platform. Although he was only twenty-nine years old when he began the job, he quickly emerged as a major figure among the black intelligentsia. In addition to serving on the editorial board of the *Journal of Negro History*, he joined the Committee on Negro Studies of the American Council of Learned Societies in 1939. That same year he began serving as an editor of *Phylon*, a public-oriented black periodical headed out of Atlanta University.[5] Countless other leadership positions followed. For instance, along with Carter Woodson, Sterling Brown, John P. Davis, Dorothy Porter, and Henry P. Slaughter, he served on the advisory committee for a Library of Congress exhibition on black books and manuscripts in honor of the seventy-fifth anniversary of the Thirteenth Amendment.[6] He then attended a related White House reception organized by Eleanor Roosevelt.[7]

Reddick also joined the National Committee for the Participation of Negroes in the "American Common" at the World's Fair, which was held in New York City from 1939 to 1940. The American Common exemplified the growing cultural imperative to combat racism. Its guiding theory was that "all races, nationalities and cultural groups have contributed significant and specialized talents to make the United States the land of freedom and oppor-

Lawrence Reddick with an assistant at the Schomburg Collection in Negro Literature, early 1940s. Courtesy of the Photographs and Prints Division, Schomburg Center for Research in Black Culture, New York Public Library.

tunity it is today."[8] Reddick used the opportunity to give lectures and radio broadcasts on the "Negro's Contribution to American Culture."[9] On one such occasion sponsored by the Columbia Broadcasting System, Reddick adopted an increasingly common and resonant refrain among African Americans. He declared, "The only way we can prove to the world and to ourselves that we are not hypocritical champions of the democratic way of life is to see to it that the Negro enjoys full democracy. . . . We should counter-poise our ideology of freedom and equality over against the 'master race' creed of the Nazi."[10] This was the rhetoric underpinning African Americans' "Double Victory" campaign against fascism both at home and abroad.

Even as the curatorship placed Reddick in increasingly elite social circles, his work became ever more public-facing. This aligned with the nature and purpose of the Schomburg Library. As the Harlem branch of the New York Public Library, it was tasked with serving the local community. Harlem was predominantly Jewish when the branch opened in 1905, but it became heavily African American after the Great Migration of blacks northward during World War I. The *Pittsburgh Courier* captured the dramatic shift when it reported that patrons of the Harlem branch—once 95 percent white—had become 95 percent black by the mid-1920s.[11] A white woman named Ernestine Rose presided over the library during the transformation. She and Catherine Allen Latimer, the first and only black librarian within the entire New York Public Library system at the time, adapted to the changes.[12] In 1925, they helped form the Division of Negro History, Literature, and Prints "to preserve the records of the race; to arouse the race consciousness and race pride; to inspire art students [and] to give information to everyone about the Negro."[13] A year later, Arturo Schomburg bequeathed his breathtaking collection of materials on African and African-descended peoples to the library, transforming it into a major research repository. When Reddick took the helm as curator in 1939, he understood the institution's unique value and took its multipart mission seriously.[14]

Under Reddick's direction, the Schomburg Library functioned as a remarkably democratic institution laboring to serve the public good during a turbulent and exciting time. It focused on sharing ideas, bringing in speakers, and facilitating debates among black Harlemites and others. Reddick regularly convened nationally acclaimed authors for interviews and discussions. For instance, he had J. Saunders Redding "tell why and how he wrote *No Day of Triumph*," with Ralph Ellison serving as the critic.[15] He held similar events for friends such as Richard Wright, and also for St. Clair Drake and Horace Cayton upon publication of their landmark study of Chicago's black community, *Black Metropolis* (1945).[16] Some of the events could get quite lively. For example, the *Pittsburgh Courier* reported a "free-for-all discussion" with white author Lillian Smith in which "differences of opinion were sharp and serious" over how successfully her best-selling novel *Strange Fruit* (1944) had been turned into a Broadway play. The novel's depiction of interracial romance and sex was wildly controversial at the time, even provoking the book to be banned in several places across the country. Reddick ultimately welcomed the difference of opinion among the audience members, but according to the *Courier* he insisted that "The sincerity and high purpose of Lillian Smith were not debatable in that her consistent fight against racial segregation, her refusal to join with fake Southern liberal organizations, and her record as editor of the *South Today* had established her as a champion of human democracy."[17]

The Schomburg had a special ability to attract people from all walks of life, and to do so unexpectedly. The likes of no less than Du Bois, Kwame

Nkrumah, Richard Wright, Alain Locke, and Margaret Walker found occasion to drop in to make use of the Schomburg's holdings. Indeed, every student of the black experience could find unique, invaluable sources to consult there. And those collections only expanded during Reddick's tenure, as he built up holdings on Africa, Latin America, and the West Indies with the help of various foundation grants.[18] Margaret Walker, a key figure in the Chicago Renaissance, visited the Schomburg in 1942 after publishing her award-winning collection of poetry, *For My People* (1942). She recalled, "I found Lawrence Reddick serving as curator of that collection and we renewed a family friendship. . . . He proved an able teacher of southern history, and gave me excellent leads to Georgia's laws on Negroes. Our friendship and association continue to this day."[19] Reddick likewise helped Lorenzo Johnston Greene, a protégé of Carter Woodson, to revise his dissertation at Columbia and have it published as *The Negro in Colonial New England, 1620-1776* (1942).[20]

Yet more often it was ordinary people striving to improve themselves and learn about their history who inspired Reddick. He informally tutored one black boy from the Caribbean who visited his office every week seeking help in writing poetry. Sometime later, this young man named Ricardo Weeks published a book of poetry, and Reddick wrote the foreword. He penned, "These yearnings of Weeks may be multiplied by the spirit of hundreds of thousands of Negro youth. Their dreams and hopes are a vital part of America—a part which deserves to be encouraged and saved."[21]

During his first year at the Schomburg, Reddick also developed a new way to promote racial progress. To coincide with Negro History Week every February, Reddick published an "Honor Roll in Race Relations," which included a list of twelve African Americans and six white Americans who distinguished themselves in advancing race relations during the previous year. The list often included notable individual accomplishments such as Jane Bolin becoming "the first Negro woman judge in the history of America," or Benny Goodman "for his employment of distinguished musicians irrespective of color in his well-known orchestra." But they also included the work of organizations and groups of ordinary black people struggling for justice, such as those in Miami, Florida, who in 1939 led "a march to the ballot box to exercise their constitutional rights, despite threats of the Ku Klux Klan."[22] The honor rolls were thus popular ways to shine a spotlight on important efforts within race relations. The lists were widely reported and met with an enthusiastic reception each year. Coverage by CBS, the *New York Times*, and the hundreds of local outlets fed by the Associated Press and Associated Negro Press ensured a wide circulation of the results. Eleanor Roosevelt would often comment upon the honor rolls too, and in 1943 the Office of War Information included the list in its releases to soldiers stationed across the world. In this way, the honor rolls helped to shift American culture from an openly racist one to one in which "the American Way" could celebrate black achievement and improvement in race relations.[23]

Reddick nevertheless ensured that the honor roll was a black-controlled enterprise in keeping with his black nationalist predilections. The last thing he wanted was yet another forum in which white people were empowered to decide which black people were deemed deserving of recognition. So, each year he would send out a nationwide poll to a committee of one hundred diverse African Americans who were tasked with deciding the honor roll. As he saw it, this was "about the only regular arrangement whereby Negro leaders, after thoughtful deliberation, say who in their opinion is improving race relations in terms of the democratic ideal."[24]

In addition to his insistence on black control, Reddick was leery of attempts to celebrate accommodationist blacks. He kept that in mind while organizing the committee, and in his national calls for nominations he wrote (controversially) that "Obviously, all 'Uncle Toms' should be ruled out." This sparked some backlash. One disgruntled reader published a complaint in the *New York Age* which laid bare the political, educational, and generational divisions within the black community. The reader considered Reddick's honor roll "a protest against the Spingarn and Harmon Awards, which are for the same purpose" but run by less radical people at the NAACP and the Harmon Foundation. The barring of "Uncle Toms," he or she wrote, "is a form of discrimination, for we have known many so-called 'Uncle Toms' whose achievements were outstanding." More revealing, the author protested, "'Uncle Tom' . . . is applied by younger men to their elders. . . . One of the unfortunate results of university training in our present-day youth is to make those who receive this training belittle and sneer at the achievements of those who did not have the same educational advantages they enjoy. It was through the ambition and sacrifices of the so-called 'Uncle Toms' that many of these critics were able to secure the educational opportunities they now enjoy."[25] The complaints reiterated those of Benjamin Brawley years earlier, and they laid bare many of the same social divisions.[26]

Never one to be stymied by controversy, Reddick continued to push forward with other ways to engage the public. He found university teaching to be another fruitful avenue, and one that he missed from his years as a

Lawrence Reddick pointing to a map of Africa while four of his students from the City College of New York look on, 1942. Courtesy of the Photographs and Prints Division, Schomburg Center for Research in Black Culture, New York Public Library.

professor. He was quick to accept an offer from the College of the City of New York (CCNY) in 1941 when asked to serve as a lecturer in its history department. This made him only the second black professor to teach at CCNY and among the earliest to teach at a predominantly white university.[27] The fact that he was teaching a course in Negro History and Culture only made the milestone that much more significant, because such courses were all but nonexistent at white colleges at the time. Reddick covered material that was long excluded from traditional history courses: the ancient civilizations of Africa, the contacts between Africans and Europeans, and the history of blacks in North America to the present, all with an eye to ongoing problems and the "contributions of the Negro to American culture."[28] Reddick continued to teach at CCNY until he left New York in 1948.

Reddick's initial enthusiasm for the City College opportunity was, however, partly dimmed by the circumstances surrounding the dismissal of his predecessor, Max Yergan. Yergan became the first African American to teach at CCNY when he began teaching black history there in 1937. Like most racial milestones, it did not happen without a fight. It was the result of an intensive campaign led by the Douglass Society and the College Teachers Union at CCNY, both of whom "saw the need for presenting a true picture of the Negro people in the history and development of America."[29] Yergan had headed the International Committee of the YMCA in South Africa for fourteen years, and he later presided over the Council on African Affairs, winning both the Spingarn and Harmon Awards for his work. But he was also a Communist, and his association with the left-leaning National Negro Congress made him a target. When Communists took a greater role in the NNC in 1940, A. Philip Randolph stepped down as president and Yergan took over. That same year the New York State legislature established a committee that focused on "uncovering 'subversive elements' in the institutions of higher learning" within New York City.[30] The Rapp-Coudert committee regularly discussed Yergan's activities. In short, Yergan was likely pushed out of City College for political reasons, not because the history department simply wanted a professional historian for the post, which the department chair claimed.

The Yergan example highlighted for Reddick and others the limits on civil liberties, especially for African Americans. Reddick may have learned a lesson or two from the proceedings, but he was nevertheless an altogether different kind of leftist. Reddick was stridently independent in his left-leaning politics, and he was committed equally to social justice and free thought.[31] He thus had little patience for the ideological purity of the Communist Party. As the party came to dominate the NNC, Reddick continued to occasionally attend meetings, but only as a visitor. Although he found the party and the NNC to be imperfect allies, he was more than willing to work with those advancing the greater cause. Despite its many problems, the NNC laid out an action program in 1943 that was very much in keeping with Reddick's priorities, including "the abolition of a poll tax in this session of Congress, adequate utilization of all available man and womanpower, and democratization of the stage, screen and radio to secure an accurate interpretation of Negro life and culture."[32]

Reddick deftly navigated the racial politics of the white academy, and he took advantage of the newfound interest in black scholars that the war precipitated. One of his earliest addresses to his colleagues at City College was on "Why America Needs the Negro Scholar." He made the case that the black academic is "unblinded by the veil of 'race superiority' and is therefore able to see clearly the nature of the war and to point out the road to victory."[33] Such assertions took on new weight as the Japanese thrust their war machine into action, challenging notions of Western superiority. The sense of urgency and confusion created space for black scholars like Reddick to make their voices heard. Furthermore, as American culture shifted and Americans waged a war for democracy, a select few white universities joined City College and broke with tradition by hiring black professors. The recruitment amounted to only several dozen by the late 1940s, but it occurred "with a swiftness which has caught many of us unaware," reported the *Chicago Defender* in 1947."[34] New York City led the way, employing black scholars in eight out of its twelve universities, even though many of them were employed only part-time.[35] Kenneth Clark joined Reddick as a professor at CCNY, and Alain Locke joined Reddick as an instructor at the New School for Social Research, where Reddick began teaching around 1945.[36] Thus Reddick, both through his own example and his many talks on the importance of the black scholar, did his part to challenge segregation within American higher education.

A World View of the Negro Question

The title of the course that Reddick offered at the New School, "A World View of the Negro Question," symbolized how much the war had stoked an internationalist mindset among African American intellectuals. The Italian invasion of Ethiopia had ushered in a new era of black identification with and concern for Africa, and those solidarities only deepened during the war as the status of African colonies was newly thrown into question. To be sure, a Pan-Africanist movement embodied by W. E. B. Du Bois, Marcus Garvey, Amy Ashwood Garvey, Mittie Maude Lena Gordon, Celia Jane Allen, and others was active throughout the interwar period, but the world-historical events of the 1930s and 1940s greatly expanded the movement.[37] It was then that Reddick played a central role in building Pan-African ties and advancing the cause of decolonization. According to historian Kevin Gaines, Reddick "exemplified the vibrant wartime coalition of black American journalists and civil rights leaders who linked demands for freedom in the U.S. with anticolonial struggles in Africa."[38]

Serving as the curator of the Schomburg Collection naturally deepened Reddick's commitment to Pan-African solidarity. Now tasked with collecting, preserving, and presenting materials from across the African diaspora, Reddick made every effort to cultivate relationships with black people beyond the borders of the United States. He began in May 1941 by taking a monthlong goodwill tour of Haiti along with brief visits to the Dominican Republic, Puerto Rico, and Cuba.[39] The trip had been planned for a couple years, but the responsibilities of the curatorship delayed it. Now the timing was ideal because it could coincide with the inauguration of Haiti's new president, Elie Lescot. Hopes were high among Haitians after having ousted their American colonizers in 1934. Moreover, Haiti loomed large in the minds of African Americans ever since its African slaves had overthrown their French colonizers in 1804 and established the first black republic in the Western world. Reddick reveled in the visit, reporting to Melville Herskovits that he had "one of the most fruitful journeys of my life. I went all over the place, picked up books and manuscripts, took moving pictures of the Presidential inauguration, interviewed Lescot, Bellegarde, Price Mars, taxi drivers and peasants. Climbed the 4-1/2 miles to the Citadel."[40]

The main purpose of the trip was to deepen cultural ties between African Americans and Haitians. Toward that end, Reddick met with Lescot for forty-five minutes in the National Palace in Port-au-Prince.[41] Lescot enthusiastically supported the cultural exchange, and he called for African American teachers, doctors, dentists, and businessmen all to come work in Haiti.[42] Reddick encouraged the exchange of books, newspapers, government documents, and other materials. A few months later, Reddick shipped one thousand books to Haiti, and the Haitian Government promised to send copies of all its publications to the Schomburg.[43] Mercer Cook, later the U.S. ambassador to Gambia and Niger, was part of this new African American connection with Haiti. He worked as a professor at the University of Haiti from 1943 to 1945, and after reviewing recent Haitian literature, he wrote that it all "tell[s] the same story: that the American Negro is now being described as a brother."[44] Reddick's Pan-African labors in Latin America appeared fruitful.

Yet it was Africa itself that attracted the lion's share of Reddick's attention. He quickly involved himself with a group of young Africans who were living and studying in the United States. In 1940, forty of them organized the Association of African Students in the United States and Canada. John Karefa-Smart, the future foreign minister of Sierra Leone, and Akweke Abyssinia Nwafor Orizu, the future acting president of Nigeria, began the effort. They were both college students in Ohio in the late 1930s when they reached out to seventy other African students whom they could locate. The forty that responded joined an inaugural gathering of the group at Columbia University in the summer of 1940. Kwame Nkrumah, later president of Ghana, was one of them. He loved the idea of the association, and he whispered to Karefa-Smart and Orizu that he should become the president of the new organization. They had no objection, so in that casual fashion the organization was born and Nkrumah emerged as its titular head. The association continued to meet in New York City over the next several years, and they even put out a publication called the *African Interpreter*.[45] The students shared a broad Pan-African vision which they hoped would transcend regional rivalries among Africans, especially those between Nigeria and the Gold Coast. In 1963 Nkrumah founded the Organization of African Unity and emerged as the leading proponent of Pan-Africanism, but he was already developing that philosophy with his fellow African students in the United States. He recalled, "We believed that unless territorial freedom was ultimately linked up with the Pan-African movement for the liberation of the whole African continent, there would be no hope of freedom and equality for the African and for people of African descent in any part of the world."[46]

All of this activity thrilled Reddick. He later referred to these times as the "'good old days' when American Blacks and Africans, who came to Black colleges in [the] U.S.A. to study, were close friends and admirers." At Howard, Fisk, and Lincoln, he remembered a sense of solidarity among black students who shared a commitment to both liberating Africa from colonialism and defeating Jim Crow in America. That solidarity took tangible form in African American fraternities. Both Nkrumah and Nnamdi Azikiwe, who later became the first president of Nigeria, were members of Reddick's fraternity, Phi Beta Sigma. Reddick knew Nkrumah while he was a student at Lincoln University in Pennsylvania and the University of Pennsylvania, and they first met in New York City. Recalling their meetings, Reddick said, "We had fun and spent hours talking about freeing 'Black Folk.' Often we debated with others."[47] Reddick even published an article in the *African Interpreter*, which Nkrumah ran. Entitled "What the 'Brothers' Need to Know," the article laid out a program for promoting Pan-African communication and collaboration in familiar ways, including the exchange of newspapers, publications by activist organizations, and people themselves. "The splendid students who come over to attend American universities are exceedingly helpful," he wrote, "but we need to see some of the elder statesmen, scholars, and leaders.... If we cannot handle this *minor* task, how can we expect to perform the *major* task of freedom?"[48] Little did he know at the time that so many of these students would become the leading statesmen of an independent Africa.

Reddick's engagement with the African students took on a new urgency during the global crisis. No issue mobilized Pan-African activists more than the Atlantic Charter. On August 14, 1941, President Franklin Roosevelt and British Prime Minister Winston Churchill issued a joint declaration laying out their countries' war aims against the backdrop of a world rapidly succumbing to fascism. The Axis powers had subdued Europe, were bombarding the Middle East and North Africa, and in an about-face had declared war on the Soviet Union on June 22.[49] Meanwhile, the Japanese had taken over much of East and Southeast Asia. Roosevelt and Churchill thus felt compelled to enumerate the principles of the free world for which they fought. These included eight broad principles such as global disarmament and the freedom of the seas, but it was their third principle that galvanized the colonized peoples of the world. That one pledged that the United States and Britain would "respect the right of all peoples to choose the form of government under which they will live; and they wish to see sovereign rights and self-government restored to those who have been forcibly deprived of them."[50] Churchill had intended these words—which he broadcast all over the world in a radio address on August 16—to apply only to European peoples who had been conquered by the Nazis. However, colonized peoples read the words literally and highlighted the glaring contradictions. When Churchill attempted to walk back his statement and clarify his meaning before the House of Commons, he only stoked the anger.[51]

Reddick seized upon the Atlantic Charter to promote Pan-Africanism and decolonization. He was joined by a cohort of other African American intellectuals, including Walter White, George Schuyler, and Horace Cayton, all of whom followed the lead of Africans themselves.[52] Nnamdi Azikiwe was one of the most important. He used his influential Nigerian newspaper, the *West African Pilot*, to denounce Churchill's hypocrisy, complaining, "Are we fighting for the security of Europe to enjoy the Four Freedoms whilst West Africans continue to live under pre-war status?"[53] Reddick stood out among his peers for his ability to provide a forum for Africans in the United States to come together and make their own voices heard. For instance, on May 9, 1942, he organized a mass meeting at City College. The *Pittsburgh Courier* reported "an enthusiastic crowd packed and jammed" into the auditorium, where they heard several African leaders from all over the continent speak about the war. The *Courier* dubbed it "the first time that the Africans themselves have had an opportunity to make a full presentation of their case to the American public."⁵⁴

In the pages of *Opportunity*, Reddick gave an in-depth overview of the proceedings to the black reading public, hoping to counteract the "provincial nationalism of most Negro organizations in the United States."⁵⁵ He explained, for instance, how Joseph Schandorf of the Gold Coast "made it clear that the African people were anti-Axis" and "were definitely anti-imperialist," and how Kingsley Mbadiwe of Nigeria "denounced Churchill's misinterpretation of the 'Atlantic Charter.'" The gathering included non-black colonial peoples as well. M. A. Shamsee of India "emphasized the strong bonds . . . between the people of India and the people of Africa and urged joint action in the common struggle." Reddick made a point that had become a basic tenet of his entire thought: "The exploited and abused man can best speak for himself." The failure "to work or fight alongside of him on any terms short of equality," he continued, "is nothing less than a vicious paternalism." Reddick concluded the essay by specifying the concrete resolutions reached by the colonials at the meeting. These included:

1. That the Atlantic Charter and all other statements of the war aims and peace aims of the Allied powers should be specifically understood to apply to Africa.
2. That the freedom-loving people of Africa should be armed in order to overthrow the Nazi tyranny and establish freedom and self-determination for all peoples.
3. That African culture should be given its rightful presentation in the history of mankind.

These points, as he pitched them, were but one part of "the struggle for world liberation."⁵⁶ Here he captures the radical vision of these black anticolonial activists. They sought not to mimic the nation-building projects of the West but to construct a new, egalitarian global order free of racial and national domination.⁵⁷

Seeking to give further attention to these perspectives, Reddick—always a master of publicity—organized an exhibit at the Schomburg entitled "The War and the Whole People." As one hundred people looked on, he had Eleanor Roosevelt present a copy of the Atlantic Charter radio address for the exhibition. The *New York Times* covered the story and reported that the charter, along with nineteen other documents "from the pens of leaders of the United Nations," would be on view in a special room at the Schomburg

Eleanor Roosevelt handing Franklin Roosevelt's manuscript copy of the Atlantic Charter radio address to Francis R. St. John, Chief of the Circulation Department at the New York Public Library, while Lawrence Reddick looks on, circa 1942. Courtesy of the Photographs and Prints Division, Schomburg Center for Research in Black Culture, New York Public Library.

for the rest of the year.[58] Horace Mann Bond, keen to the public-relations coup, applauded Reddick for his "master stroke in obtaining the Manuscript of the Atlantic Charter."[59]

After organizing the exhibition and then facilitating another mass meeting among the Association of African Students in September, Reddick began publishing widely on Africa.[60] In *Opportunity* that same month, he commended *The Atlantic Charter and Africa from an American Standpoint* (1942) for injecting Africa into discussions of the war and underscoring that the Atlantic Charter should apply to Africans. But he also directed readers to books and articles by Africans themselves, such as Kingsley Mbadiwe's *British and Axis Aims in Africa* (1942).[61] A few months later in *Opportunity*,

Reddick demanded that the Allies "arm the African people and permit them full participation in the fight against fascism," and to "guarantee them . . . the Four Freedoms and a fifth freedom called self-determination."[62] In spring 1943, Reddick published an op-ed in the *New Masses* that criticized American policymakers' neglect of Africa. He also chastised newspapers for "conspir[ing] to reduce Africa to a *place*" for Western military heroics while ignoring that "Africa is also a *people*" with feelings, hopes, and demands for their place in the global order.[63]

Reddick emphasized these same points before various black activist organizations. In the summer of 1943, for example, he organized a panel for the national convention of the March on Washington Movement in Chicago. The movement, led by Bayard Rustin and A. Philip Randolph, had already won a landmark victory in 1941 when it mobilized the black masses to pressure President Roosevelt into issuing Executive Order 8802, which prohibited racial discrimination in the war industries. Now Randolph and Rustin continued trying to leverage black political power for further advances. Reddick had a strong opinion of what intellectuals could bring to such meetings. He wrote to Melville Herskovits, "I always try as best I can to assist the various organizations in giving some sort of intellectual content to their discussions at their national conventions. Heaven knows such is needed."[64] He presented as part of a panel entitled "The Negro in Peace and Post-War Planning: Africa, Caribbean and United States," which also included Herskovits, Eric Williams, Louis Wirth, and A. Philip Randolph.[65]

Reddick's presentation allowed him to test out ideas that he subsequently published in the *Crisis* as "Africa: Test of the Atlantic Charter."[66] This was his most thorough analysis of Africa and the war to date, even as it included many of the same points as before. However, because the Axis powers had by then been driven out of Africa and defeated at Stalingrad, there was fresh urgency about how the United Nations would deal with Africa after the war. Above all, Reddick demanded that Africans be represented within all international bodies charged with planning the peace, and within all local, regional, and continental governments. He used African wartime service and the Atlantic Charter to make forceful demands for African self-determination. Horace Cayton found Reddick's article compelling enough to give it special treatment in his regular column in the *Pittsburgh Courier*.[67] The editors of that same paper singled out Reddick and Du Bois as "two of America's most outstanding scholars" who deserve praise for outlining "concrete peace and post-war plans for the peoples of Africa."[68]

Yet even as Reddick fought boldly for African independence, he knew it was a grave mistake to view Africa only through the "traditional reference of European imperialism and colonial exploitation." In a groundbreaking exposé of South Africa, which had officially become independent in 1931, Reddick underscored how white supremacy could remain an omnipresent force even in postcolonial Africa. Reddick identified the purportedly free South Africa as "the worst place in the world for the Negro . . . where two million whites hold six and one-half million natives in slavery." The article provided a remarkably thorough overview of the historical, political, economic, and social conditions in the young nation. Reddick relayed how England's neocolonial economic domination continued to hamper the South African economy, but he argued that the gravest crisis was the systematic subjugation of the black natives. The level of poverty and illiteracy (80 percent) that he described was stunning, and it made the plight of African Americans look mild by comparison. Yet it was ultimately the similarities that most stood out. Black South Africans shared with African Americans similar predicaments of political disfranchisement, segregation, economic subjugation, social and cultural degradation, and police brutality. Any African American reading the article could not have helped but identify with the experience of black South Africans. Reddick concluded by calling for the United Nations to intervene, for "If fascism must be crushed in Europe and Asia, surely it should be wiped out in Africa, too."[69]

As the war neared its end in early 1945, Reddick began working closely with W. E. B. Du Bois and Rayford Logan to organize a colonial conference in Harlem.[70] Because the United Nations was set to convene in San Francisco in May to draw up the United Nations Charter, leaders of colonized peoples across the world needed a forum to meet and discuss their demands for the postwar order. Reddick offered to host the conference at the Schomburg on April 6, and Du Bois happily accepted.[71] Shortly before the conference, Reddick submitted to Du Bois a memo that included fourteen general points and six specific points that he thought should shape the conference proceedings. Many of these had a direct bearing on the resolutions that were ultimately adopted. The truly global character of Reddick's propositions is conspicuous. For instance, he even included a resolution that "the interest and welfare of the aboriginal people of Australia be brought within the purview of plans for world peace."[72] The whole conference suggested how much Reddick and other African American intellectuals were attempting to forge a broad coalition of all oppressed peoples, not just those within the African diaspora.

The resulting conference was a landmark event. In all, about fifty figures attended, and they represented peoples from such far-flung lands as India, Uganda, Barbados, and Indonesia.[73] The dignitaries voiced various concerns and platforms, which George Schuyler reported to the black public through the *Pittsburgh Courier*. Nkrumah was the boldest in calling for "complete independence at the end of the war." Maung Saw Tun of Burma demanded "a definite time limit for the granting of their independence." Julio Pinto Gandi, the secretary-general of the Nationalist Party of Puerto Rico, called for an end to the fifty years of "enslavement by the United States." Rayford Logan recommended an international trusteeship because "not all dependent areas are ready for immediate self-government." Reddick, along with Max Yergan and W. A. Hunton of the Council on African Affairs, submitted statements that supported Logan's more conservative proposal, which ultimately carried the day. Reddick then served on a committee of eleven that drew up conference resolutions.[74] The final statement declared boldly that colonialism must end, that an international Colonial Commission should be created to facilitate that end, that colonial peoples must have representation on that commission, and that the commission should focus on improving the social and economic conditions of all colonial peoples.[75] That such a disparate group of leaders could agree on these demands after only meeting for a single day has prompted historian Gerald Horne to call this conference "the most significant meeting of its type held in North America before or since."[76]

The Colonial Conference epitomized Reddick's lifelong engagement with the international movement. He continued to closely follow the meeting in San Francisco and the Pan-African Congress in Manchester later that year, not to mention the many more proceedings in coming years.[77] He continued to publicize the events and even tried to organize a couple of books about them. One called for Du Bois and other Pan-African leaders to analyze the movement.[78] Another, which fell apart after raucous Harlem meetings with Ralph Ellison, Richard Wright, C. L. R. James, St. Clair Drake, and Horace Cayton, aimed to set out black demands for the postwar world.[79] Reddick also tried to stay in touch with James, who was a central figure in the Pan-African struggle. He had more success with Du Bois, with whom he worked out an agreement whereby he was to "collect the documents on the demands of the colonial people" while Du Bois was to submit an essay for Reddick's prospective book project, "A World View of the Negro Question."[80] Although that project was never completed, it grew out of the successful courses of the same name which Reddick taught at the Schomburg and then the New School from 1944 to 1947. The classes featured an array of renowned guest lecturers at the forefront of the anticolonial struggle and black intellectual life. Krishnalal Shridharani of India, Ernest Kalibala of Uganda, Eric Williams of Trinidad, Lin Yu'ang of China, E. Franklin Frazier, and Charles Johnson were only a few of them.[81] Reddick thus kept his finger on the pulse of the global freedom struggle even as his work on behalf of the racial situation at home came to dominate his attention.

Fighting Fascism at Home

Reddick's increased emphasis on the universal rights of all oppressed peoples created space for new alliances at home as well as abroad. In reviewing Carey McWilliams's pioneering study of Japanese Internment, *Prejudice: Japanese-Americans, Symbol of Racial Intolerance* (1944), Reddick noted the expanded grounds for such solidarity: "The apparently separate problems of Americans of Negro descent, of Mexican descent, of Chinese and Japanese descent and so forth are all phases of the 'American race problem.'"[82] Racial and ethnic alliances should thus proceed accordingly.

Perhaps most consequentially, Reddick attempted to forge solidarity between Jews and African Americans, two stigmatized groups whom he believed had much in common. In the first volume of *Negro Quarterly*, a short-lived, New York–based periodical that Reddick had helped to found, Reddick organized a forum to confront the hostilities between Jews and blacks.[83] His article "Anti-Semitism among Negroes" explained the social origins of that animus, which he believed was relatively mild. Because any hostility at all was nevertheless counterproductive, he underlined "the need for the Jewish and the Negro peoples to identify their struggles as one."[84] In a widely circulated pamphlet, Reddick pared his article with a similar one by former *Jewish Survey* editor Louis Harap called "Anti-Negroism among Jews." Reddick happily reported, "The reader reaction has been tremendous. A flood of letters came in."[85] So, too, did an array of speaking invitations. The article also prompted editorials throughout the black press, many of which echoed an assertion by the *New York Amsterdam News* that blacks and Jews "could well afford to rid themselves of adopted prejudices and band together on a common front for the well-being of all."[86] Of course, there were also dissenters. The acerbic black commentator George Schuyler stated in an awful and not uncharacteristic remark, "There is nothing for the Negro to gain by association of his interests with the Jew because the latter is about to be eliminated."[87] Historian Clayborne Carson locates

Reddick's article as the beginning of a largely futile, stylistic response among African Americans to anti-Semitism in their midst, but in Reddick's case it did nevertheless mark a sincere effort to close ethnic ranks during the war.[88]

Although Reddick fought for the rights of other minority groups and exploited peoples of the world, his principal focus remained squarely on black people. At home and abroad, the war had created the greatest opportunity for racial change in Reddick's life to that point. Not least, its demand for labor thrust black people into military service and wartime jobs, and it fomented a cultural shift which made racism a problem like never before. Reddick took advantage by assuming a multitude of roles including librarian, sociologist, historian, public commentator, and community organizer. If the pace felt frenetic and occasionally stymied longer-term projects, the result was nothing if not invigorating. Reddick reveled in it.

It did not take Reddick long to score a public-relations victory. A truly remarkable event occurred before the United States had even officially entered the war—during the Japanese attack on Pearl Harbor on December 7, 1941. The first press releases covering the disaster noted that "an unnamed Negro messman" had rescued several navy men during the attack. Reddick, keenly aware of "the general disposition not to make heroes of Negroes," wrote repeated requests to the navy to identify the man. Only after several weeks of delays, and well after Reddick had listed the unnamed soldier in his Honor Roll of Race Relations for 1941, did the navy finally identify him as Doris "Dorie" Miller. The full story was more amazing than anyone could have imagined. As Reddick recounted it,

> At 6 o'clock on the morning of December 7, 1941, a messman, third class, on the good ship U.S.S. *Arizona*, was making his regular rounds, collecting soiled laundry. Japanese zeros dropped down out of the heavens, raining bombs on the United States Fleet, surprised and helpless in Pearl Harbor. The general alarm was sounded. This messman headed for his battle station, only to find that it had been wrecked by enemy torpedoes. He then went on deck, where he was ordered to help carry the wounded to places of greater safety. The ship's dying captain was one of those removed. Then, the messman, who had never before fired a machine-gun, manned one and began shooting at enemy planes. He kept at this for about fifteen minutes, until all hands were ordered from the sinking ship. He says that he shot down six planes; the Navy gives him credit for four.

Thus a black serviceman, kept in a lowly janitorial position and denied full military training, rose to the occasion and showcased a level of courage and marksmanship exceeding that of even the most seasoned experts. Like Crispus Attucks in the American Revolution, Miller became "the first American hero of World War II," Reddick happily reported.[89] Black communities celebrated by selling Dorie Miller buttons and singing folks songs about his exploits.[90] Indeed, African Americans have continued to share and find inspiration in the story.[91]

Yet Miller's story remained largely ignored by white America. The military and the press instead lionized Colin Kelly as the first real hero of the war. Kelly was an Irish-American captain who had sunk a Japanese battleship three days after Pearl Harbor. It was only through a sustained campaign by Reddick, the black press, and white allies such as politician Wendell Willkie that Miller was rightfully honored with a Navy Cross on May 27, 1942. The navy nevertheless refused to promote Miller, and much of the public remained oblivious—often willfully so—of his heroics. The insult was compounded by tragedy when Miller died unceremoniously the following year during a Japanese attack on his aircraft carrier. When the ship went down, Miller was still serving as a messman.[92]

The Miller case only underscored for Reddick what he already knew: America was wasting the talents of its black citizens, and it was essential for African Americans themselves to document black soldiers' wartime experiences. White America was indifferent, ignorant, or openly hostile to crediting African Americans with patriotic service. Historians, such as Christine Knauer, have now established how the War Department, for instance, "intentionally cut out African Americans from newsreel footage."[93] Black war correspondents tried to counteract the marginalization, but they faced heightened censorship and were regularly restricted from taking photographs of the conflict. Many thus did so surreptitiously.[94] Furthermore, when blacks were finally admitted into the military in equal numbers—which occurred only after the draft was instituted across all branches of the military—they were generally kept in subordinate, segregated roles that offered them far fewer opportunities to serve heroically in action against the enemy.[95] These same realities obscured the crucial role of African Americans in all previous American wars too.[96] Consequently, Reddick labored once again as an activist librarian to create an alternative archive that would ensure that black soldiers' experiences were adequately documented and appreciated.

Reddick's most important contribution came through his campaign to collect the war letters of black soldiers. Some he interviewed personally or solicited directly to share their experiences, but he knew that would only scratch the surface. Reddick therefore published calls for soldiers, their families, and anyone else to share black soldiers' wartime letters with the Schomburg Library. In the *Pittsburgh Courier*, Reddick declared, "These letters will tell us what the men have experienced in camps and on the fighting fronts, what they have seen, tasted and felt, how they have been treated and how they have treated others. Thousands of these letters are necessary so that a true history of the Negro in the war can be written."[97] As he had hoped, within a year several thousand letters had been compiled.[98]

The letters capture the rich diversity of the black soldiers' experience, which defies easy generalization. Many soldiers described the racial discrimination they faced both within the military and among civilians, while others emphasized the egalitarianism and even solidarity forged between black and white soldiers in the crucible of war. Among the letter writers were those who had won awards for their courage under fire, those who found tedium and mundanity to be the central features of the conflict, those who had endured humiliation and violence while stationed on military bases in the South, and those who were scarred by exposure to Nazi concentration camps. When Richard Wright consulted the developing archive in 1945, he recalled that "a sea of despair began to set in" as he read through letter after letter documenting the discrimination and injustices endured by black soldiers during the so-called war for democracy.[99] These letters are still housed in the Schomburg Library, and they have informed numerous scholarly investigations.[100]

Beneath the rich diversity of experience lay an almost universally held pride among black soldiers for their service, which for many of them translated into a determination to continue the freedom struggle at home. One soldier, Charles H. Dubra, stated this in no uncertain terms: "One phase of the fight against tyranny is over, but there remains yet, the second part."[101] He came to embody that spirit. After earning a master's degree from Boston University, he attempted, albeit unsuccessfully, to break the color line at the University of Mississippi in 1953 (James Meredith would follow his lead years later). Based on an assessment of numerous letters from black soldiers, a journalist for the *Pittsburgh Courier* likewise reported that black soldiers "will not go back to the old ways."[102] That journalist subsequently heeded Reddick's call and donated the letters to the Schomburg for safekeeping.

Building a robust archive of black soldiers' letters motivated Reddick to attempt his own history of African Americans in the armed forces during World War II. Charles Johnson encouraged him to take up the project, and together they worked with Edwin Embree to secure funding.[103] Embree helped Reddick convert a Rosenwald grant for a project endeavoring to microfilm Frederick Douglass's writings (much of which was completed anyway, in collaboration with Carter Woodson) to one focused on the black experience of the war.[104] The letters of black soldiers were an indispensable source for the project, but so were official military records and the testimony of white soldiers and officers. As Reddick told an official in the U.S. Army, he sought to investigate the "Who, What, When, and How" of the black soldier's experience, which could only be accurate if "it is based in large part upon the official records."[105] Unfortunately, Reddick encountered resistance from many within the armed services and was forced to curtail his wider ambitions. He nevertheless published two pioneering articles in the *Journal of Negro History* on the topic.

Reddick's articles, "The Negro in the United States Navy during World War II" and "The Negro Policy of the United States Army, 1775–1945," provided thematic introductions to the subjects and helped to lay the foundation for future investigations. Despite "effective 'diversions' and 'blocks'" from military officials, Reddick managed to consult thousands of documents and interview hundreds of officers and enlisted men.[106] The articles traced the remarkable wartime shift in military policy from black exclusion to segregation to integration. Furthermore, bolstered by the voices of black soldiers themselves, Reddick highlighted how the war forged interracial friendships and solidarities that boded well for the future. He also emphasized black soldiers' campaigns against racial discrimination *during* the war, which included boycotts, sit-ins, and strikes. Soldiers' "running fight against jim-crow" occasionally even rose to the level of armed confrontation with white soldiers who were harassing them, such as with U.S. Marines stationed in Guam in December 1944.[107] These insights continue to serve as fodder for contemporary historians writing about the war.[108]

Yet Reddick aimed to do more than lay the basis for future historical work; he sought to halt the advance of racism after the war. His research challenged a white power structure that was actively marginalizing the true black soldier's experience. In an address before the Society for Ethical Culture, Reddick exposed the "drive by racist myth-makers to build up anti-Negro sentiment" by portraying the black soldier as a coward who contributed little to the war effort. He then warned about how such lies could become truth, declaring, "If this campaign is not nipped in the bud, many more anti-Negro officers will write their memoirs, anti-Negro congressmen will quote the memoirs for the Congressional Record. Textbook writers will quote the Congressional Record and we will have a generation growing up believing that Negroes are inferior fighters and therefore deserve inferior citizenship rights."[109] That same process occurred across the centuries, and it made much of American history little more than race propaganda. Seeking to stem the tide, Reddick organized black veterans to meet at the Schomburg and voice their demands, and he even forced a concession from President Truman himself. After the veterans demanded that "the public mind be disabused of the belief that all Negroes were assigned to labor battalions," Truman voiced his approval. The *New York Times* then quoted him as saying that America "must include opportunities for the Negro veteran to contribute his skill on the basis of individual merit and capability without racial discrimination."[110]

Reddick's efforts to interpret and preserve the experiences of black soldiers had taken precedence during the war, but they remained only one aspect of his broader struggle to build an alternative archive at the Schomburg. One of Reddick's first tasks at the library was to gain a better understanding of the extant sources on the African diasporic experience. So much of it had not been well-documented. This was partly because many African civilizations had been oral ones, but also because Western colonization and the slave trade had killed off millions and denied basic literacy and political power to countless others. Reddick therefore went to work to provide a survey of library resources on black people, which he published in a preparatory volume of the *Encyclopedia of the Negro*. The result was the clearest portrait to date of what sources were available and where. Du Bois, growing closer to Reddick by the day, commended him for doing "a splendid job" on the article, which he noted was "especially strong . . . for use outside of the United States of which is so little known here."[111] Indeed, Reddick discussed many archives in Africa and especially Latin America, which at this point had been largely untouched by Western scholars. But he also noted how the cultural imperialism of the colonial era had an ironic result: "Art objects and written records were gathered and sent to European (and a few American) centers to such an extent that the finest collections of cultural objects produced in Africa by Africans are located outside of Africa itself."[112] Reddick thus devoted considerable space to describing archives in Europe and the United States.

While conducting the library survey, Reddick was also attempting to make key primary sources in African American history accessible to the public. One effort focused on the works of Frederick Douglass, arguably the most towering figure in all of African American history. In 1940, Reddick joined with Alain Locke, Max Yergan, Angelo Herndon, and Raymond Pace Alexander to head up the Frederick Douglass Historical and Cultural League. Condemning "the slight recognition accorded Frederick Douglass by white historians," the league sought to restore Douglass to his proper place in American history.[113] It successfully orchestrated the publication of a new edition of *Life and Times of Frederick Douglass*, Douglass's stunning chronicle of his escape from slavery. The book, originally published in 1845, exposed the horrors of slavery and galvanized the abolitionist movement. More than any other source, it forced white Americans to view the institution through the eyes of a slave. Yet as the Lost Cause version of the Civil War came to dominate American culture, interest in Douglass waned and white Americans showed little interest in a story that flatly contradicted that mythology.[114] Pushing back, Reddick and the League made Douglass's slave narrative available to the public for the first time in fifty years.[115] Equally important, Reddick had the Library of Congress microfilm many of Douglass's newspapers, including the *North Star* (1847–1851), *Frederick Douglass' Paper* (1851–1855), *Douglass' Monthly* (1859–1863), and *New National Era* (1870–1872). This paved the way for fresh interpretations of the towering figure.[116] To know Douglass, Reddick understood, was to know the true history of the nineteenth-century United States.

The success of the Douglass microfilming project encouraged Reddick to launch a broader effort to identify, assemble, and microfilm as many black newspapers as possible. At the time, there was little understanding about how many of these newspapers there had actually been because many were obscure, short-lived operations. Even so, Reddick recognized that no other source held a greater capacity to shed light on American history "*as seen through the eyes of Negroes themselves.*"[117] To support the expansive project, Reddick turned to the Committee on Negro Studies (CONS), a usually seven-member body of the American Council of Learned Societies (ACLS) on which Reddick served from its inception in 1940 to its demise in 1951.

CONS was a notable if ultimately disappointing body, and it symbolized both Reddick's prominence and marginalization within the scholarly world. The committee's mission was to offer a humanistic approach to the study of black people, especially along historical and cultural lines. The ACLS envisioned it as a counterweight to the Carnegie Corporation's more social-scientific orientation, which had come to dominate American investigations of domestic race relations when the landmark study it sponsored, led by Swedish economist Gunnar Myrdal and published as *An American Dilemma* (1944), monopolized the field. Yet CONS had little to show for its eleven years of operation. Its failures, as historians Jerry Gershenhorn and Robert L. Harris Jr. have shown, owe principally to its dominance by white anthropologist Melville Herskovits.[118] Herskovits was a student of the pioneering cultural anthropologist Franz Boas, and he was an innovative researcher who investigated the cultural influence that Africa exerted on blacks throughout the diaspora. But he was also an embodiment of the white scholars who controlled the academy and marginalized African Americans while using their research to burnish their own statures and reputations.

CONS is a case in point. Herskovits controlled it with an iron fist, and although he included black scholars on the committee, he scrupulously maintained a white majority and ensured his own final discretion over the direction of the body. Herskovits had a cordial relationship with Reddick and the other black scholars on the committee such as Sterling Brown, Lorenzo Dow Turner, and Eric Williams. But he seemed most concerned with furthering his own research agenda and shoring up his African Studies institute at Northwestern University. This translated into him undermining black-controlled African Studies programs, such as the one at Lincoln University in Pennsylvania, a black college, which was spearheaded by John Aubrey Davis and Horace Mann Bond (then president there).[119] It also translated into Herskovits's sidelining of Reddick's bold calls to confront racial discrimination and segregation in the scholarly world. CONS, Herskovits maintained, was to focus on "scholarly studies," not "programs of action."[120]

Despite CONS's failings, Reddick was able to leverage its resources to track down and microfilm many black historical newspapers. This in fact turned out to be the most significant accomplishment of the committee. To be sure, CONS also supported the research for Paul Lewinson's *A Guide to Documents in the National Archives: For Negro Studies* (1947), and it helped to fund the publication of Eric Williams's *Capitalism and Slavery* (1944)—a path-breaking book that placed slavery at the center of Western civilization.[121] The committee also created a bibliography for Latin American Negro Studies, identified a list of scholars studying black people, and solicited statements from historians who issued perceptive remarks regarding the state and future directions of black history.[122] Yet all of these paled in comparison to the committee's black newspapers project. Reddick first proposed the idea in 1944, and the committee embraced it. They tapped Armistead

Pride, the director of the School of Journalism at Lincoln University, to do the work. By 1947, the project had yielded a far more comprehensive list of black newspapers than had previously been known, and it microfilmed many of them and made them available at the Library of Congress and select black research institutions.[123] Historian August Meier claimed that this effort "revolutionized research into Afro-American history for just about every topic except slavery and opened important windows on the activities and thought of black Americans."[124]

Renaissance Man

During the turbulent times, Reddick's stature as the curator of the Schomburg also pushed him beyond his more familiar roles as historian, librarian, and even Pan-African organizer. This stemmed from the fact that the war had prompted a deep anxiety over the race problem at home. Waging a war against the Nazis, who took the theories of white supremacy to their logical, horrifying conclusion with the Holocaust, cast American race relations in a troubling new light. The closer one looked, the more one could see that everything from the Nazis' racial science to their political program of segregating minorities and stripping them of their rights had its counterpart in the United States. In fact, the United States was a model for racist states and colonial regimes across Western Europe.[125] Any burgeoning guilt among Americans combined with a fear of comeuppance as African Americans engaged in bolder forms of protest during the war and became more assertive than ever in demanding their rights.

The wartime race riots stoked the fears. The one in Reddick's own backyard of Harlem in August 1943 was only one of six uprisings across the country that year, ranging from Detroit to Los Angeles to Mobile, Alabama. The Harlem uprising, not uncharacteristically, broke out after a white policeman shot a black serviceman who was attempting to defend a black woman from assault. The shooting and the rumors surrounding it caused the community's simmering outrage over police brutality, poverty, and segregation to boil over. Black Harlemites concentrated their anger on the exploitative white businesses in the community, and they ultimately destroyed millions of dollars' worth of property. The police, gripped by fear and hate, overreacted and precipitated the deaths of six people and the arrest of six hundred others.[126]

Yet the depth of the racial crisis fomented a cultural sea change. Many white Americans began to see racism as a problem and even commit to combating prejudice. Toward those ends, New York City formed a Citizens Emergency Conference for Interracial Unity after the uprising. Reddick served as one of the twenty-five members of the executive committee, and at the conference he led a panel on "Organized Racial Antagonisms." As a report summarized, the group "unanimously agreed that winning the war and the establishment of a just peace depend upon national unity, which is gravely endangered by the activities of those persons, organizations and publications which organize racial activities to divide our people and confuse and disrupt our war effort."[127] This cultural imperative against prejudice and for national unity came to predominate during and after the war. Reddick, noticing that there was more discussion of the race problem "now than at any other time in our history since the days of the Reconstruction period," cited opinion polls which showed that between 34 percent and 50 percent of Americans believed that "extraordinary steps should be taken to 'improve' race relations."[128] What were those extraordinary steps? "'Revolution?' 'Oh, no!' 'New laws?' 'Maybe.' 'Education?' 'Yes, indeed!'" Reddick wrote wryly. Like most black intellectuals, Reddick believed that more fundamental reforms than education were needed to challenge racial oppression. However, he was willing to seize any available opportunity to extend progressive change. Reddick thus gave countless talks promoting tolerance and condemning prejudice, and he published a variety of articles that laid out effective programs of intercultural education and articulated the views and expectations of African Americans at the time.[129]

One of Reddick's most influential articles in this vein grew out of his long-standing concern with combating stereotypical representations of black people. He had already taken on history textbooks and professional histories through sustained scholarly investigations, but he was equally interested in racial stereotypes in popular culture. He routinely unmasked racist novels, films, radio broadcasts, and newspapers before anyone who would listen, and he expounded his ideas before the meetings of ASNLH, Phi Beta Sigma, social science associations, and at other public forums.[130] The article he published in the *Journal of Negro Education* in 1944 was only his most sustained indictment. In it he examined radio, newspapers, and libraries while dedicating the bulk of the article to motion pictures. He proceeded from the premise that mass communications had a "decisive influence . . . in determining public attitudes."[131] The statistics seemed to bear that out. At a time when only thirty million Americans were involved in formal education, he reported, ninety million Americans attended the movies at least once a week, forty-four million read daily newspapers, thirty million homes had radios, and ninety-six million citizens had checked out books from the library that year. Education, he logically concluded, thus needed to be defined much more broadly if it was to confront American prejudice.

When Reddick scrutinized a pop-culture education, he found much cause for concern. He reported that each form was saturated by antiblack messaging. The press, for instance, through its concentration on crime news, produced a distorted image of black people as dangerous and disproportionately prone to criminality. Yet Reddick was most struck by motion pictures, which through powerful visual, auditory, and narrative elements seemed to exert an undue influence on theater-goers. He gave special attention to *The Birth of a Nation* (1915) and *Gone with the Wind* (1939), two wildly popular and critically acclaimed films that were profoundly racist. In fact, they compelled Reddick to create a list of the nineteen most common black stereotypes in movies, such as "the savage African," "the devoted servant," "the petty thief," "the sexual superman," "the superior athlete," "the social delinquent," and "the mental inferior." Reddick complained, "Ideologically the South had won the Civil War. The defeat which it suffered on the field of battle was more than repaired by its victory over the minds of the American people through history books, novels, and now the motion pictures."[132]

Exposing the problem was one thing; changing it was another. Reddick called for "concrete plans to control these instruments of mass communication for the broad social purpose of bettering Negro-white relations."[133] In addition to various forms of agitation, he proposed the formation of censorship committees and other government bodies to regulate the racism within Hollywood films. He also recommended pooling together funds to support both educational productions and movies by black producers, who were positioned to offer a fuller portrait of black life. Although some interpreted his calls for censorship as heavy-handed, they stemmed not only from the pernicious racism that pervaded popular culture but also from a milieu in which many were using such propaganda to effectively sow division, hate, and war. Reddick continued to speak and write about racist representations for many years, and his list of stereotypes provided many Americans with a lexicon to discuss the problem.[134]

Finally, in addition to his role as media critic, Reddick took on the role of sociologist while at the Schomburg. The *Journal of Educational Sociology* broke with the long tradition of black exclusion from mainstream scholarly journals when it tapped Reddick to serve as a guest editor from 1944 to 1945. Reddick organized a special volume on African Americans in the North, which was a nod to the growing realization that "'the Negro question' in the United States is no longer a peculiarly 'southern' problem."[135] The *Pittsburgh Courier* relayed the findings to the wider public. Reddick's article surveyed the greater freedoms among blacks in the North while also highlighting the enduring realities of poverty, segregation, and discrimination.[136] He described how the new generation of northern blacks was bolder in demanding full citizenship rights, and he argued that any perceived criminality and deviance on their part stemmed from the denial of those rights. With keen insight he explained, "Resentment is not only expressed through the organized youth movements but also through the ready, profane language, 'talk,' 'zoot-suits,' knives and homemade guns of those who have been called 'hep-cat delinquents' and 'young hoodlums.'" These phenomena, he insisted, were in fact "social protests—protests against the neglect and maltreatment of individuals and groups within a society; protests which are not permitted to find expression within the legal framework of the social order." These were points that most sociologists—let alone ordinary Americans—failed to understand and appreciate. They illustrate Reddick's exposure to the Chicago School of Sociology generally but especially to the dynamic work of black scholars in that tradition, including Charles S. Johnson, E. Franklin Frazier, St. Clair Drake, and Horace Cayton, who interfaced it with the black experience.[137]

In 1945, Reddick also contributed to a special issue of the *Journal of Educational Sociology* that focused on race relations in the American West. He spent the summer of that notable year (which marked the end of World War II) traveling throughout the western states "interviewing hundreds of public officials, industrial, commercial and labor leaders and ordinary citizens" to examine black life in the region.[138] Today historians have documented how African Americans had a presence in the West going back hundreds of years, but at the time this was largely unknown.[139] The war did spark a key shift, however. The black population there tripled, increasing by over 250,000 as war industries and the military attracted over a million Americans to the region. As journalist Carey McWilliams discussed Japanese internment in another selection, Reddick highlighted the conditions of black life in this new frontier of race relations. What he found was in stark contrast to the romantic imagery pervading Americans' understandings of the West as an egalitarian frontier with democratic moorings. The West, rather, quickly reproduced the same hierarchies and discriminations characterizing black life elsewhere. Given the endemic oppression that Native Americans and Asian Americans experienced in the region, this finding was not altogether surprising, but it was dispiriting at this time of racial change. As usual, Reddick's work nevertheless laid the groundwork for future scholarly investigations into the important subject.[140]

・・・・・・

Reddick's multifarious efforts at the Schomburg were all the more impressive because of the consistent lack of funding available to support them. This would, unfortunately, be a persistent theme throughout Reddick's career, as the study of the black past and present remained marginal for most of his life. Consequently, by 1948, after nine years of relentless activity, meager pay, and constant headaches over financial concerns, Reddick was ready to move on from New York and the Schomburg Library. Furthermore, many of his hopes for creating a more just and peaceful world were dashed in the years following the war, as the United States and the Soviet Union careened into mutual suspicion, hostility, and Cold War. The forces of reaction at home seized upon the new environment to attempt to roll back the gains of racial minorities and women. Opportunistic politicians orchestrated a Red Scare that sought to settle old political scores and ensure a conservative agenda. Even New York City, "the hope of mankind" as Reddick once called it, lost some of its luster, as many of Reddick's leftist friends were caught in the crosshairs.[141] The coming days would see Reddick, too, harassed and spied upon for his various civil rights activities and associations. For now, though, that still lay in the future. Reddick and his wife, Ruth, welcomed the opportunity to start anew in Atlanta, where he accepted a position as the chief librarian at Atlanta University.

Yet Reddick was never one to go quietly into the night. He used his departure from the Schomburg as an opportunity to shine light on the city's neglect and underfunding of the library. Although the Schomburg had become one of the most important archival repositories in the world, Reddick reported to the press that it was "sorely in need of an increased staff, additional books, shelving space and facilities for preserving the valuable items" in the collection. He placed the blame squarely at the feet of "indifferent public officials who do find funds for other things while the Schomburg Collection starves."[142] Schooled in the black protest tradition and thus keenly aware that agitation was often the only way to galvanize change, Reddick directed friends and colleagues to weigh in and echo his complaints. Du Bois pleaded privately for Ralph Beals, the director of New York Public Library, to "come to the rescue" of the Schomburg.[143] In an op-ed in the *New York Times*, Horace Mann Bond declared, "I was astonished and grieved to learn that apparently this marvelous collection enjoyed so little appreciation on the part of those responsible for its administration."¹⁴⁴ George Schuyler added to the chorus as well, as did the *Times* editorial board. The board averred that "the Collection is badly handicapped," and it opined that "the loss of Dr. Reddick, after nine years of admirable service, is typical of what happens when we let our libraries starve."¹⁴⁵ Beals insisted that the Schomburg faced only the same problems as all other branches of the New York Public Library and that he was taking concrete steps to address them though he was limited by budgetary constraints.¹⁴⁶ What he seemed to miss was that the Schomburg had become much more than just another branch library in the city. It had developed into a repository of international significance which demanded additional support and maintenance. The raucous public debate sowed confusion among many New Yorkers, a group of whom picketed outside the library in the belief that it was being ordered closed.¹⁴⁷ In the end, the very public recriminations and protests alerted New Yorkers to the problem and seemed to succeed in building support for the Schomburg.

Reddick's controversial departure and the ensuing public spectacle, it turned out, proved tame indeed compared to the fate he would meet at Atlanta University seven years later.

4 Cold War Civil Rights in Atlanta

....

We cannot export our revolutionary traditions and nurture counter-revolution at home. If Jefferson and Tom Paine are good for Africa, they ought to be good for Alabama.
—Lawrence Reddick

Reddick's decision to return to the Deep South after a decade up north was not without misgivings. Like any good friend would, St. Clair Drake teased him about it. He asked Reddick how it was "down in Naziland" and wondered if he ever contemplated "a return to the civilized part of the United States."[1] Reddick admitted that the "shift was terrific at first."[2] He once again had to adjust himself to a land that continuously "relives" the Civil War, and "tends its memory with loving care."[3] Walking past the Eternal Light of the Confederacy in downtown Atlanta, for instance, never failed to unnerve. Even after almost a year in the city, Reddick reported in *Phylon* that he still was "not quite certain of the local race-relations etiquette." "Who is?" he wondered. "The damn thing is so contradictory and is always changing in some particular." His strategy was that "all avoidable humiliation ought to be avoided," so he generally stayed away from segregated theaters and public spaces.[4] But he did make an exception to attend a Dizzy Gillespie concert.

As the concert suggests, Atlanta also held its promise. The city rivaled Chicago and New York for its large and vibrant black community. Atlanta's black business district along Auburn Avenue supported an expansive middle class. The dense network of churches knit together black social and cultural life. And the black system of higher education within the Atlanta University Center (AUC)—a consortium of private colleges that included Morehouse College, Spelman College, Atlanta University, Clark College, Gammon Theological Seminary, and Morris Brown College—made it one of the most important sites for the education of black people anywhere in the world. It was thus no accident that Atlanta native Martin Luther King Jr. was a Morehouse man. King embodied the potential of the college students in the area, all of whom could find intellectual sustenance from the array of scholars within the consortium. Reddick was only one of them. He assumed the rank of full professor of history as well as head of the AUC's Trevor Arnett Library, and he worked alongside such notable figures as Hylan Lewis, a Chicago School sociologist with whom he shared a two-family house; historian Clarence Bacote, part of Carter Woodson's inner circle of black historians; and Benjamin Mays, the president of Morehouse and a renowned black theologian.[5] Reddick had already lectured at the AUC, edited its popular periodical *Phylon*, and admired its creation of the first black sociology program in the United States, which W. E. B. Du Bois inaugurated at the dawn of the twentieth century.[6]

The Trevor Arnett Library was also impressive. As the central library for the entire consortium, it was a major hub of intellectual and cultural activity. Furthermore, its collection of black archival materials, Reddick reckoned, was about "three-quarters as good as Schomburg" and capable of matching it because of Atlanta University's larger budget.[7] Relying upon the largesse of the black community and its commitment to black colleges and libraries was not without potential hazards, but it did offer Reddick an escape from the budgetary constraints imposed upon him by the whims of New Yorkers and the New York Public Library system. The only black college with greater collections was Howard University, but it, too, faced constraints because of its ties to the federal government. Reddick thus accepted his new position with pleasure and ambition. He set out to make Atlanta University "the Harvard of the South" with library materials capable of rivaling those in "Washington, New York, Boston or Chicago." Reddick's underlying goal was tailored to the politics of desegregation and their implications for black institutions across the country. "We intend," he declared, "to have it so strong that when the foolishness of racial segregation in education has passed away, students of all colors and creeds will clamor for admission to our classrooms."[8]

Reddick's grand goals, like so many of his activities, would be constrained by the Cold War environment. From 1948 to 1955, he would continue many of the same projects as before: cultivating Pan-Africanism, building a liberation archives, advancing racial desegregation, and achieving black political power. Now, however, the Red Scare hindered his work and drove the country's politics to the right, ensuring that Cold War civil rights would be a more limited campaign. Yet Reddick stands out for his refusal to follow many other black intellectuals and adapt more to the temper of the times. At great personal risk—and eventually cost—Reddick eschewed anti-Communism, condemned America's militant foreign policy, and continued to prioritize Pan-African solidarities, all the while envisioning a broader definition of black freedom than simply the end of Jim Crow.

Africa in America

Although Reddick never again reached the summit of Pan-African policy-making as he did at the 1945 Colonial Conference in Harlem, he continued to prioritize that struggle. As historian James Meriwether has documented, this made him rare among African American intellectuals in the early Cold War period. Meriwether tracks how black intellectuals generally reacted to the conservatism, militarism, and anti-Communism of the time by emphasizing their Americanness and conforming to President Truman's foreign policy goals, all in exchange for advancing an integrationist civil rights agenda at home. In this way, "international forces worked to fray African America linkages with Africa," he writes.[9] Reddick is important partly because he resisted these tendencies and believed that Pan-African solidarities continued to matter as much as ever.

To be sure, Reddick did not stand alone. Historian Sarah Azaransky identifies three strands of black internationalism that predominated throughout the interwar and early postwar periods: (1) Du Bois's leftist political project advanced through the Pan-African Congresses, (2) Garvey's black nationalist program institutionalized through the Universal Negro Improvement Association and its offshoots, and (3) a black Christian internationalism organized through churches and YMCAs.[10] Reddick is most closely connected with the Du Boisian strand, though he maintained contacts within each group. For instance, through St. Clair Drake he kept in touch with C. L. R. James and George Padmore, who provided Reddick with archival materials from across the diaspora.[11] He also conferred with James R. Lawson, a Garveyite who presided over the United African Nationalism Movement, which fought for African self-rule.[12] Furthermore, he was an associate of Benjamin Mays at Atlanta University, who along with Howard Thurman, Bayard Rustin, and others comprised a group of Christian internationalists who consulted other religious traditions and freedom struggles in order to strengthen the African American movement.[13] Mays in fact visited Gandhi to learn his tactics of nonviolent resistance a full generation before Reddick and Martin Luther King Jr. made their trip to India in 1959. Black internationalists were thus many, and as Reddick makes clear, many of them were closely connected with one another. Yet none of that takes away from Meriwether's broader point about the fraying of Pan-African sensibilities during the early Cold War. Because the roots of Reddick's internationalism were diverse, and because he advanced the Pan-African cause through an underappreciated institution—the black fraternity—he helps us better understand the myriad forms of black internationalism in this period.[14]

Although most Americans greeted the Cold War with a mix of fear and disillusionment, few emerged as outspokenly critical of it as did Reddick. Writing in 1953, he argued that "the past ten years or so deserve the label 'decade of war.'"[15] Certainly, Americans had little time to catch their breath between V-J Day on September 2, 1945, and the Truman Doctrine of March 12, 1947, which committed the United States to stopping the spread of Communism across the globe. American military mobilization continued apace, the nuclear arms race began in earnest, and declarations of an implacable Communist foe became commonplace. The subsequent calls for a peacetime universal military service only added to the martial atmosphere. Then, on June 25, 1950, the Cold War became hot when U.S.S.R.-aligned North Korea invaded U.S.-backed South Korea, propelling American combat troops back into action.

From the beginning, Reddick refused to view the Cold War through the bipolar lens being peddled by American and Soviet foreign policymakers. At the closing forum of Atlanta University's summer school in August 1948, Reddick declared that the root causes of the conflict were the "two giant economic systems represented by the United States and the Soviet Union," which were "competing for the mastery of the world." In the ensuing "struggle for raw materials and territories," the United States churned out endless propaganda "to influence the American people against the Russian people."[16] Reddick was not romanticizing the Soviet government, but it was impossible for him not to point out the difference between an "enemy whose theory and practice were based on racial equality" and an American society in which racial segregation remained the law of the land. If the Western democracies remained committed to white supremacy and colonial domination, as they had since their founding, then the nonaligned, Third World nations—and even America itself, Reddick provocatively argued—may become Communist. This is because "social change is their logical and natural ally," so "the unhappy minorities could not but join with revolutionary forces re-shuffling an unfriendly social order."[17]

It is hard to overstate the boldness of expressing these sentiments during the anti-Communist hysteria of the time. Reddick was aware of how "liberal and sentimental 'friends of the Negro' may deplore the very phrasing of it ('I wish you hadn't said that,' they moan)."[18] Conservatives and Red-baiters were another matter altogether. But Reddick stuck to his guns, and he ultimately demanded a new geopolitical order. Like Mohandas Gandhi, Albert Einstein, and other supporters of the World Federalist Movement, Reddick demanded a more powerful and democratic international body than the United Nations, which was dominated by its five permanent members: the United States, France, Great Britain, China, and the Soviet Union. He called for nation-states "to surrender sovereignty to a world government that will be strong enough" to stave off World War III.[19] "Modern war," he declared, because it was being waged by segregated armies in the service of a white-supremacist global order, "was a fraud and should be exposed."[20]

Given these predilections, Reddick's commitment to Pan-African solidarity and struggle remained as deep as ever. He did what he could within the spaces he operated. At Atlanta University, he taught courses on African history and culture, on "The Negro in America," and on "War as a Social Institution."[21] He organized African art shows, festivals, and meetings in the Trevor Arnett Library. He involved himself with the Atlanta branch of the African Students Association and hired African students to work in the library. Those efforts prompted the association to award Reddick a statuette replica of the "Torch Bearer," a symbol of truth and learning.[22] Furthermore, after the Committee on Negro Studies folded in 1951 (at the behest of Melville Herskovits and against the wishes of Reddick and the other black committee members), Reddick did what he could to support black-controlled African Studies programs. Above all, this involved working with ASNLH to help support Lincoln University's African Institute, which Horace Mann Bond and John Aubrey Davis presided over.[23] Lincoln (in Pennsylvania) had a remarkable track record in attracting top-flight African students—Kwame Nkrumah and Nnamdi Azikiwe among them. Bond continued this cross-fertilization in the postwar period, but as historian Jerry Gershenhorn has tracked, black-controlled African institutes like the one at Lincoln ultimately failed to attract the funding necessary to be viable over the long term.[24] The white-dominated foundations and universities ensured the ongoing marginalization of black scholars and black institutions during the Cold War.

In the hostile climate, Reddick turned to a familiar institution to promote Pan-Africanism: his black fraternity. Reddick had stayed involved with Phi Beta Sigma (PBS) throughout the years, but his participation had declined since the 1930s when he had held leadership roles in editing and publicity. He now renewed his commitment, recognizing the potential influence of the "usually worthless Greek-letter Frat," as he dubbed it in a letter to Bond, based upon its collective numbers, wealth, and assortment of notable members.[25] Nkrumah and Azikiwe were rapidly becoming the most significant Sigmas of all because of their rising stature in the African independence movement. Reddick played up that Sigma connection to Africa for all it was worth.

Reddick's greatest success was securing Azikiwe to speak before the Sigma conclave in December 1949. Azikiwe, a charismatic figure later called "the founder of Nigerian nationalism," had risen to a leadership position within the Nigerian legislature as that British colony pushed for independence. His Nigerian newspaper, the *West African Pilot*, which he had founded in 1937, continued to play an outsize role in building nationalist sentiment within this most populous of African nations. This prompted Bond to consider Azikiwe "one of the four or five most important people in the world today." Bond had only recently returned from a research trip to Nigeria, so he had seen firsthand the remarkable power and influence of the charismatic leader. Even a militant resistance group with no direct ties to Azikiwe labeled themselves "Zikists" in his honor. Bond was thus ecstatic about Sigma's success in attracting him to the conclave. In addition to his own attendance at the event, he began working to involve as many alumni of Lincoln University as possible. "I think such a display of allied Negro power would do the RACE a world of good," he noted, and it would certainly "help dramatize the colonial problem."[26]

Despite a series of hiccups that Reddick recounted at length for the fraternity, Azikiwe's speech was a notable success. As Reddick chronicled it, "the streets were jammed with cars" and "photographers and newspapermen were crowding us" outside of Benjamin Banneker High School in Washington, D.C. The audience at the event included "a sizeable white contingent" and some "high government officials," such as Liberian ambassador Charles King and Ambrose Carter of the U.S. Office of Education. Reddick, Bond, and Du Bois all shared the platform with Azikiwe and made their own brief comments. When Reddick introduced Azikiwe as "the Nehru of West Africa," he made explicit the global stature of Azikiwe. He hoped that Azikiwe would do for Nigeria what Jawaharlal Nehru, the freedom fighter who became India's first prime minister, had done for his country. Reddick also noted tellingly how colonial authorities prevented Azikiwe from making a stop in the Gold Coast during the 8,500-mile trek to the United States out of fear that "his very presence there might be the spark that would set off the powder keg of revolt."[27]

When Azikiwe began his speech, which radio broadcasts transmitted across the country, he gave voice to the fierce resolve among Nigerians for complete independence from Britain. As late at 1947, he said, Nigerians were still considering dominion status within the British empire, but when the British rejected that proposition, half measures would no longer suffice. Azikiwe chronicled the "riots and strikes" for independence and economic justice that had been occurring across Nigeria in recent years. He then made a special plea to Americans to support Nigerian independence. According to the *Atlanta Daily World*, he underscored that "the American people and government must deal directly with the African people" in these matters, and not broker agreements and compromises with the European powers, whom he said lacked legitimacy. Not surprisingly, the Truman administration ignored such demands; it was more concerned with shoring up European support while battling the Soviet Union. In doing so, however, the U.S. government only proved Reddick's point about why Third World nations often found the Communist-aligned world to be more appealing than the capitalist democracies of the West. Du Bois, a committed socialist by then, made a related point. He impressed upon the audience that independent Africans must not "'ape' the exploiting class-conscious capitalism of their masters." "There would be little gain for the masses of African people," he warned, "if the freedom movement only meant substitution of black masters for white masters."[28]

The entire event provided Americans, black and white, with a set of bold ideas and perspectives too often ignored within Cold War America. Reddick did all he could to publicize the event and parlay it into additional speaking engagements. After the visit, he began coordinating with Azikiwe to make another trip to the United States in the spring—this time for an entire month. It seemed that he had found through Phi Beta Sigma a clever way to leverage African American institutional power for Pan-African ends. However, as fate would have it, Azikiwe felt compelled to cancel that second trip at the last minute due to political crises enveloping Nigeria. The colonial government proposed a new constitution that would divide the large and diverse nation into a series of ethnic and religious groups. Nationalists like Azikiwe, Reddick said, believed that "Britain is paving the way for the kind of conflicts—Hindu versus Moslem—that have torn India apart." Furthermore, after a reported attempt by Zikists to assassinate the colonial governor, the government cracked down on the movement in mass arrests of its leaders. "For him to leave the country at this time," noted Reddick, "would look like running away."[29]

As the African independence movement reached a critical juncture, Reddick worked to shine a spotlight on it. He returned to editing the *Crescent* in 1949, and the following year he organized a special "Free Africa" issue of the fraternity's periodical. In it he published articles by Azikiwe, Ethiopian emperor Haile Selassie, Alain Locke, and Du Bois, as well as a "round up on developments in all parts of the erstwhile 'Dark Continent' by African Fraternity Brothers." The issue, Reddick recalled, also included a "striking cover design, showing the modern and the traditional of Africa."³⁰

In addition to editing the *Crescent* and organizing the special issue, Reddick shouldered the task of writing a history of Phi Beta Sigma, which was a long discussed but never attempted project among the fraternity brothers. He teamed up with fellow brother William Sherman Savage, a professor of black history at Lincoln University in Missouri. Savage had been part of Carter Woodson's inner circle and was a pioneer in studying blacks in the American West. Here he joined Reddick in devising the type of fraternity history that only trained historians could write. As Reddick explained it to the executive secretary of PBS, "Savage and I are very interested in putting the Sigma story in the proper framework of the nation and of the Negro people," which "not only makes the story more readable but it gives to it a significance which it could not have if it were to be restricted to the internal affairs of the organization."³¹ For Reddick, the international, Pan-African elements of Sigma were as important as any. Therefore, after Savage wrote the first draft of the manuscript, Reddick did his own research and went back and rewrote it to emphasize those ties. For one thing, this involved reprinting in entirety Reddick's narrative of Azikiwe's visit, which originally appeared in the Spring 1950 edition of the *Crescent*. Furthermore, Reddick tracked how Sigma "was making its influence felt outside of the United States," most notably by establishing a chapter in Liberia.³² Besides Azikiwe, the frat boasted Kwame Nkrumah as a member, who by the time of publication had already been elected prime minister of Ghana.

Reddick and Savage's book, *Our Cause Speeds On: An Informal History of the Phi Beta Sigma Fraternity* (1957), did more than exhibit Sigma's internationalism. It was intended for Sigmas themselves, so it never reached a wide audience. It was filled with its fair share of jokes and amusing incidents from annual conclaves, and it provided biographical portraits of many fraternity brothers over the years. The wider significance of the book, though, lies not merely in Reddick and Savage's placement of Sigma history in a larger historical context. It also rests in the nature of the project itself. The aim was to promote both black solidarity and historical consciousness—the twin goals of Reddick's entire career. Unlike many other black intellectuals at the time, Reddick did not spend the bulk of his energies trying to reach a national audience or establish a national scholarly reputation. The work that he found most invigorating and essential, rather, focused on empowering black people themselves.

Red Scare Civil Rights

The war against Communism at home was every bit as intense as the war against Communism abroad, and the reactionary spirit loomed ominously over the black freedom struggle. Historians such as Mary Dudziak have argued that the Cold War helped the civil rights movement because it created the context in which U.S. policymakers felt compelled to act against racial discrimination at home.[33] As the United States became the self-appointed leader of the democratic free world and acted to contain Communism across the globe, the argument goes, Jim Crow became an international embarrassment that undermined American foreign-policy goals and therefore pushed the government to grudgingly support civil rights. But as historian Glenda Gilmore has aptly put it, this argument "inflates the Cold War's contributions and discounts its costs."[34] The federal government actually did very little to support the movement either rhetorically or concretely until the mid-1960s. Meanwhile, the anti-Communism of the Cold War era ravaged the movement by hollowing out the left and placing questions of economic justice beyond the pale of acceptable discourse. The result was that the postwar struggle focused on the more modest goals of defeating de jure segregation and political disfranchisement. Reddick's struggles during this period testify to the hostile political environment, but they also make clear how radical black activists continued to push back against the era's conservatism.

A mere ten days after President Truman issued his Truman Doctrine laying out plans to defeat Communism abroad, he took breathtaking steps to attack it at home as well. With Executive Order 9835, he created a robust loyalty-security program for all federal employees, who were now to be screened for any Communist sympathies. As historian Ellen Schrecker has documented, the program was worthless because preexisting security measures had already eliminated such candidates. Furthermore, after the Hitler-Stalin Nonaggression Pact of 1939, there simply were not many American Communists to be found. Droves of leftists and Popular Front activists made the trek rightward in the 1940s, which meant that investigators were largely chasing a phantom. But that was never really the point. These were political battles, and politicians found in anti-Communism an uncontroversial issue in which they could win support and settle old political scores.[35] They thus jockeyed with one another to present themselves as the biggest and baddest Red-hunter of them all. That pressure is what pushed Truman to issue Executive Order 9835 in the first place. But the decision proved to be a fateful one. The loyalty-security program stoked Americans' fears and legitimated the anti-Communist crusade as only a president's actions could. Months later, the House Un-American Activities Committees opened investigations into Hollywood, and the charade only devolved from there, finally culminating in Wisconsin senator Joseph McCarthy's hounding of prominent state officials and military leaders in the 1950s. Schrecker aptly notes that these actions succeeded in "establishing anti-Communism as the nation's official ideology" during the Cold War.[36]

A couple of months after Truman issued his executive order, Reddick made perfectly clear where he stood on the issue. Horace Mann Bond had written him a letter complaining about how black Communists such as Paul Robeson and Max Yergan engaged in reckless forms of protest at home while romanticizing the Soviet Union as a land completely free of racism. He was particularly upset about the recent protests at Lincoln University in Pennsylvania, where he had become the institution's first black president. "Tell your Commie friends to quit trying to take advantage of the first Negro to be put in this spot," he told Reddick.[37] Reddick responded with a remarkably cogent statement summing up his philosophy.

> You are quite right about the nature and extent of race prejudice in Czarist and post–Czarist Russia. Unlike others, I was always wise enough or lucky enough to never get tied up intimately with the CP (though Marx et al. have helped me in my efforts to understand history and contemporary affairs); however, I don't go for the hysterical effort now to stomp them into the ground and I don't like to see Negroes . . . join in the mob. After all, *they* (the CPers) *are not the main enemy of the Negro people* and despite their bad points, it has been good to have them around. Though I am against their inclination to dominate or manipulate Negroes and the Negro question, I do believe that they are and have been, generally speaking, on the right side in the big fight and that they can be made by Negroes themselves to "straighten up and fly right."

Unfortunately, the space for such a nuanced position toward Communists was the first casualty of the Red Scare.[38]

The harassment of W. E. B. Du Bois made clear which direction the winds were shifting. After becoming the first African American to earn his PhD from Harvard in 1895, he established himself as the greatest African American intellectual of the twentieth century, editing the *Crisis* during its heyday from 1910 to 1934, organizing Pan-African Congresses, and completing pioneering historical, sociological, literary, and journalistic works. Yet his outspoken support for world peace, socialism, and Third World liberation made him a target during the Cold War. He railed against nuclear warfare and capitalism's dominance across the world, and he linked both with white supremacy in the West. These were all profoundly taboo positions. He took other stands, too, that white American politicians found shameful and dangerous. For instance, he was part of the postwar push by the NAACP and the Civil Rights Congress to have the U.S. government charged with genocide for its treatment of African Americans. Citing Genocide Convention law, the congress presented a case to the United Nations General Assembly charging that "the oppressed Negro citizens of the United States, segregated, discriminated against and long the target of violence, suffer from genocide as the result of the consistent, conscious, unified policies of every branch of government."[39] Unfortunately, the times—like most others—were not conducive to a judicious weighing of the facts of the three centuries of black enslavement, lynching, rape, segregation, and disenfranchisement, which in fact exceeded the UN's criteria for genocide. Rather, critical ideas themselves were viewed as threats, and Du Bois became one of many leftists harassed by the U.S. government. In 1949, the FBI opened its second investigation into Du Bois, and in 1951 he was put on trial after having circulated the Stockholm Peace Appeal, which demanded an absolute ban on atomic weapons.[40]

Many black leaders distanced themselves from Du Bois at the time, but Reddick was not one of them. Four days before the trial was set to begin on October 2, the National Council of the Arts, Sciences, and Professions convened a meeting in Washington to protest Du Bois's federal prosecution. The theme was "The Right to Advocate Peace," and the group had already compiled the signatures of over 250 figures who called for the withdrawal of the prosecution.[41] Reddick was one of a few individuals to speak at the event. The opening of Reddick's speech so struck Du Bois that he decided to reprint it in his own book on the trial, *In Battle for Peace: The Story of My 83rd Birthday* (1952).[42] Reddick began, "I have just come from a part of the country where the flag of the Confederacy is more popular than the flag of the United States of America; where Robert E. Lee is not only more of a hero than Ulysses S. Grant but also more than George Washington; and where the Governor threatens to close down the State's entire system of education if the courts should compel the public, tax-supported institutions that are presently maintained for whites only to admit a single Negro. . . . In such a land, the struggle for life and liberty is real and the issues raised by the case of Dr. W. E. B. Du Bois are clear." Reddick then paid homage to Du Bois's immense contributions, calling him an "*intellectual hero*—a champion of the spoken and written word; one who had the brains to know and the 'guts' to say what he knew to be true." After regaling the audience with anecdotes of Du Bois's own influence on him, making clear just how much Reddick admired him, Reddick concluded defiantly, "We may disagree with him but we do not repudiate him. He will not be disowned."[43] The speech struck a chord with Du Bois and with others. One woman wrote gratefully to Reddick, "It is courageous words such as the ones you spoke about Dr. DuBois which lead us on into the future."[44]

Not coincidentally, Reddick soon found himself caught up in the witch hunt. On February 5 and 11, 1954—during the height of McCarthyism—FBI agents interviewed Reddick at his home in Atlanta. He affirmed that he was not and had never been a member of the Communist Party, but the FBI had a report which contradicted that assertion. The report included two separate allegations, one by an unnamed woman and one by an unnamed man. The woman informant erroneously called Reddick "one of the most unpublicized members of the Communist Party" during his years in New York City.[45] Historian David Garrow later identified the male informant as Louis F. Budenz, a Communist-turned-informant who was one of many individuals to capitalize on the Red Scare by speaking out against former associates (as well as those he simply he didn't like) and then profiting from the exposure.[46] Budenz's allegations included blatantly false information, such as Reddick having worked as an instructor at the George Washington Carver School. They also linked him to interactions with Communists at the *Daily Worker*, the CPUSA's New York–based publication. During the McCarthy era, any connections to Reds—real or imagined—were enough to get a person put on trial, fired, blacklisted, socially shunned, or otherwise harassed. For Du Bois, the judge threw out the case before it even reached the jury, but the U.S. government nevertheless revoked his passport for the next eight years, which was a cruel punishment for the world traveler. As for Reddick, nothing yet came of the baseless claims against him. That would change as Reddick participated in the southern civil rights movement, and as white southerners grasped for anything at all to halt its advance.

Harassment of Reddick did not take long because Reddick, ever a joiner, quickly involved himself in local politics and established himself as a notable figure within black Atlanta. By 1952, he emerged as a leading voice challenging a racist plan by the all-white Metropolitan Planning Commission to weaken black economic and political power within the city. The plan, made public in April, proposed that businesses on Auburn Avenue—which were principally black-owned—be moved from downtown to the western part of the city. Under the guise of "slum clearance," it also detailed plans for the creation of six or seven "Negro-expansion areas" on the city's fringes that could house thousands of black residents. The plan naturally stoked outrage and provoked resistance from Atlanta's black community.[47]

The first complaints were aired at an April luncheon organized by Phi Beta Sigma. The Atlanta Business League and the Atlanta Negro Voters League selected Reddick as their spokesman. Reddick pulled no punches. After decrying the lack of black representation on the commission, he made clear how the plan would "cut the throat of Auburn Avenue business" and "go far toward destroying the *political* strength of the Atlanta Negro." Making matters worse, three of the expansion areas, or "ghettos," as Reddick rightly labeled them, were next to industrial sites that would expose blacks to pollution and other environmental hazards. One of the other sites, Reddick scoffed, "seems to strike the fancy of the Commission because it would be convenient for certain other people to have their domestic servants live there. This is what the report says on page 88!" He concluded by emphasizing how the plan would make Atlanta "more of a jimcrow city than it is today," creating "less chance of Atlantans of different backgrounds and colors to know each other as good neighbors."[48]

Reddick reiterated and expanded upon these remarks in May at the formal public hearings on the commission's plan, in which he was again designated as a spokesman. Here he thundered, "Do we want to build a city on the Nazi pattern, of one ghetto here for this group, another ghetto there for another group?" He also drew out the implications of these ghettos: "drawing lines between people tends to accent differences and antagonism" and thus precipitate race riots and other outbreaks of violence. Citing recent decisions by U.S. Supreme Court declaring racially restrictive covenants and zoning to be unconstitutional, he called for Atlanta to do better, and to build its future city "on the principle of *'One World,' of the United Nations, of the Declaration of Independence.*"[49]

Reddick was followed by nearly every black civic and business leader in Atlanta, including Benjamin Mays, veteran politician A. T. Walden, and the

Atlanta Daily World editor C. A. Scott. The combined force of black Atlanta ultimately succeeded in forcing the Metropolitan Planning Commission to squash the plan. Reddick, for his part, was widely quoted throughout the papers. The *Chicago Defender* even wrote that he "led the attack."[50] The *Atlanta Daily World* later credited him with helping to "work out the procedure and approach Negroes took in this fight."[51] When the commission presented a new plan three years later, it seemed to have been stripped of racism. Reddick labeled this "a victory for the democratic process," insisting that real democracy was "not merely a word" but "a way of life."[52]

Reddick's commitment to that philosophy, coupled with his desire to capitalize on the momentum, propelled him into action during that fall's election. Ever since he arrived in Atlanta, he had teamed up politically with his good friend Clarence Bacote, who in addition to being a Woodson protégé and an eventual history PhD from the University of Chicago, spent his forty-seven years at Atlanta University immersed in local politics. The 1952 election cycle struck both men as especially consequential. The presidential race pitted Republican candidate General Dwight D. Eisenhower against Democratic candidate Adlai Stevenson, the governor of Illinois. Stevenson represented the northern wing of the Democratic Party, which had become the party of labor and, increasingly, civil rights. However, Truman's adoption of a civil rights platform in 1948 and his steps to desegregate the military provoked an existential crisis for the southern wing of the party, which remained committed to white supremacy and Jim Crow. The controversy provoked some southern leaders such as South Carolina governor Strom Thurmond to temporarily flee the Democratic Party and form an alternative, pro-segregationist one—the Dixiecrats—in 1948. The Republican Party, on the other hand, had been founded as the party of antislavery and had fought for black civil rights during Reconstruction. Gradually, however, it became the party of big business and abandoned civil rights as the white South systematically disenfranchised African Americans.[53]

Reddick, Bacote, and other colleagues sought to harness black political power to further advance civil rights and marginalize the forces of reaction. After the Democratic National Convention in 1952, they repudiated local Democrats while endorsing the civil rights platform of the national party, declaring that it "give[s] great encouragement to our struggle for human dignity."[54] They issued a public statement encouraging all black voters to support Stevenson, and then sent it to all major black organizations in the South. The *New York Times* reported on their actions, interested as it was in gauging how influential an emerging black vote might become in national

Lawrence Reddick, right, with Clarence Bacote, left, and another colleague at Atlanta University, circa 1950. Courtesy of the Atlanta University Photograph Collection, Atlanta University Center Robert W. Woodruff Library.

elections.[55] Although most southern blacks remained disenfranchised, those in the North and West, and increasingly those in southern cities like Atlanta, were voting and therefore held the potential to swing elections one way or another. Of course, there was no consensus among African Americans over which party to support. Reddick and Bacote conducted a straw poll among students and faculty at Atlanta University and found that 75 percent of them supported Stevenson.[56] Yet other African Americans remained loyal to the "party of Lincoln" and were suspicious of Democrats, who in the South were synonymous with white supremacy and one-party rule. Critics raised these points and publicly contested Reddick's position in the press and in a series of debates staged throughout Atlanta, which were also aired on the radio.[57] The *Atlanta Daily World* quoted Reddick when he charged that Eisenhower "was trained as a soldier and knew little else than the art of war." Stevenson's training and experience, on the other hand, "have been in the arts of peace."⁵⁸ His endorsement by organized labor and the NAACP, Reddick underscored, testified to his progressiveness on social issues.

Reddick's politicking could not fend off an Eisenhower victory that year, but locally he found cause for optimism. The following May he published a celebratory article in the *Nation* entitled "Victory in Atlanta." "For the first time since Reconstruction days," he reported gleefully, "Negroes have been elected to public office in Atlanta." On May 13, Rufus Clement was elected to the board of education, and A. T. Walden and Miles G. Amos were elected to the city's executive council. This was an outgrowth of black Atlantans' enfranchisement and their commitment to voting. Reddick then catalogued Atlanta's thriving economy, its "unusually articulate and active" black community, and its generally liberal white population and newspapers, which "are quiet and polite about their pro-white views." He considered all this a "remarkable accomplishment . . . in a state where Herman Talmadge," a committed race-baiter, was governor. Reddick was rarely so sanguine, although he was not uniformly so. He also highlighted the rancorous battles necessary to achieve such progress. For instance, he described how the city's executive committee panicked when it appeared that Clement might be elected. Two days before the election, it convened a special meeting "to consider disqualifying Dr. Clement on the ground that he was a Communist or Communist-inspired." The measure was narrowly defeated in a five-to-four vote. Despite the struggles and the dirty politics, racial progress seemed to be the story of the day.⁵⁹

In that moment, Reddick could even look dismissively upon an attempt by Governor Talmadge to smear his own good name. In a dress rehearsal for Alabama, the governor accused Reddick of being a Communist and therefore a traitor to the United States. He produced a newspaper clipping that showed Reddick with Soviet ambassador Andrei Vyshinski during a "Get Together with Russia" rally held on December 2, 1946, at Madison Square Garden.⁶⁰ The accusation was part of Talmadge's project to harass civil rights leaders, in this case by demanding that private Georgia schools investigate the loyalty of their teachers. Talmadge's tactic would soon become the default one for white southerners looking to disrupt the civil rights movement after *Brown v. Board of Education*.⁶¹ For now, however, even the generally cautious *Atlanta Daily World* declared such "guilt by association" to be "an insult to American Democracy." Reddick, as usual, had a witty rejoinder: "I have been on the same platform with such notables as Mrs. Eleanor Roosevelt, the governor of Connecticut, Dr. Azikiwe of Nigeria and the mayors of New York City, Nashville, Tenn., and Atlanta. It has never occurred to me that in appearing on the same platform that all the views of all the speakers must be the same. I hope some day to appear on the same platform with Governor Talmadge. Will this mean that he will agree with my views against racial segregation?"[62]

Beyond the positive political developments in national and local politics, Reddick also found cause for optimism in the gradual—if also halting and hard-fought—advance toward desegregation. His most important scholarship of the period tracked the desegregation of the U.S. military since 1945. His earlier research had established the military's traditional policy toward African Americans, which governed all U.S. wars from the American Revolution through World War II. Although it was never codified, the policy, according to Reddick, involved four main principles: (1) exclude blacks from the military if possible, but if not, then (2) preclude them from positions of authority, (3) segregate them from other soldiers as well as "non-Negro civilians—especially women—at home and abroad," and (4) deny them awards for military service—if necessary, do so only for menial labor or for saving whites, not for "heroic performance, under fire, against the enemy."[63]

Despite centuries of such discrimination, the military policy was shifting decisively toward full integration. In 1953, as the Korean War grounded into a stalemate, Reddick reported that "During the past few years we have seen a social metamorphosis of wide import," making "the goal of an integrated Armed Force . . . a possibility of the immediate future."[64] The two articles he published on this topic, one in the *Journal of Negro History* and the other in the *Journal of Negro Education*, reflected extensive research.[65] They explained how the four branches of the military proceeded toward integration at different rates and along different lines, with the biggest branch of all—the army—being the slowest and most resistant. As usual, Reddick emphasized the centrality of black protest and agitation in forcing the changes while also highlighting the broader forces at work. The discussion challenged the simplistic and still prevalent notion that Truman's 1948 Executive Order 9981 spelled the end of military segregation. That "limited victory," Reddick explained, accomplished little in practice. Only ongoing agitation and the racial dynamics of the Korean War finally compelled the army to grudgingly abandon racial segregation.[66]

Besides the prospect of military desegregation, Reddick was buoyed by the decisive progress in school desegregation. The U.S. Supreme Court's landmark decision in *Brown v. Board of Education*, handed down on May 17, 1954, ruled racial segregation in schools unconstitutional. Shortly thereafter, Reddick published a perceptive essay on the nature, history, and early responses to the "Great Decision" in *Phylon*. He considered it "the most important ruling [the Supreme Court] ever has handed down on the question of human rights," as it bridged "the chasm between the general democratic dogma and our organic law." He also conveyed how shocking the ruling was, especially because of its unanimity. Believing that a unanimous decision would not have been possible if the Court had ruled simultaneously on how integration was to be implemented, Reddick praised the Court for separating the two issues and first deciding on only the constitutionality of segregation. This was something many activists would later come to regret, because in the intervening time the opposition mobilized and was able to greet the Court's weak, ambiguous directive on desegregation in *Brown II* (1955) with spirited resistance. At the time, however, the unanimity of *Brown I* warranted celebration because it "removed completely any constitutional grounds for mobilizing opposition on a legal basis," Reddick wrote. The Court's rulings the following week on public housing, theaters, and colleges only seemed to confirm that desegregation was to apply broadly throughout society, not merely within education. Indeed, Reddick reported that *Brown I* appeared to have stunned white southerners into stoic acceptance. Ardent race-baiters like Herman Talmadge, who pledged resistance early on, seemed to be in the minority.[67]

Aside from further white resistance, Reddick's article identified two other potential problem areas. The first related to the uneven dynamics within the different branches of government. In a stark reversal from the Civil War and Reconstruction days, the judiciary had now leapt far ahead of the legislative branch in the area of "human concern," as Reddick called it.[68] Congress refused to act on Truman's civil rights platform of 1948, while the Court now moved decisively against segregation. The potential hazards of that discrepancy were many. Beyond the inability to effectively address segregation, this also included a growing perception of the judiciary's politicization and hence its declining credibility. The other issue related to African Americans' response to *Brown I*. In an observation that resonated with employees at the *Chicago Defender* and prompted them to reprint his words, Reddick wrote, "Surprisingly, the reaction of Negroes to the decision has been rather timid. Where are the shouts of victory, the hilarious celebrations, the parades, the fireworks? A Joe Louis victory used to cause much more of a stir in Harlem or the Southside."[69] Reddick argued that this reaction stemmed not from apathy but rather from the inclination "to reassure the frightened whites" who had long been conditioned to equate civil rights with social equality and intermarriage, the ultimate taboo of the caste system. But there was "grave danger" in this response, Reddick warned. "The decision will never gain real and deep-seated acceptance unless it is embraced as a moral principle" and celebrated widely as a victory for all mankind.[70]

As Reddick emphasized these points, he joined with hundreds of other prominent black Atlantans to demand that local and gubernatorial candidates pledge to support the Constitution and honor the *Brown I* ruling. Even though the white South's "massive resistance" had not yet taken form, black Atlantans recognized the perils of that fall's midterm elections. Many of them therefore organized into a "Committee of One Hundred," which included Reddick, Bacote, Benjamin Mays, and Whitney Young. The group assailed politicians like Talmadge who "confuse and divide" the public to secure votes, and in the process leave "permanent scars after the current election races are over and forgotten."[71] In the coming days, these battles were to become even fiercer than these men had anticipated.

As the long battle against state-sanctioned racial segregation seemed to be nearing its end, Reddick shifted his attention to the potential problems and pitfalls for black institutions in an integrated society. This shift involved a remarkable change in his own rhetoric. Before the victory over de jure segregation was in sight, Reddick had little patience for those African Americans who publicly promoted the value of an education within all-black, segregated schools, believing that whites would seize upon such ideas to justify segregation and undermine the universal human right to an equal education. In 1947, for instance, in the pages of the *Journal of Negro Education*, he challenged the notion that black students get more inspiration or opportunities for social participation in black schools. He even argued that the color of a teacher's skin was largely irrelevant. The quality of the teacher, rather, was all that really mattered. Embracing the universalist ideas of the time, Reddick declared that "the mixed school is the logical, legitimate offspring of a democratic culture," and it was necessary to prepare all students and teachers "to live in One World with all kinds of persons from all kinds of culture."[72]

Yet as the realities of desegregation set in, Reddick adapted too. He would later reject the arguments he made in the 1940s, but for now he simply looked for a way to maintain the integrity of black institutions in the face of integration. In a letter to Horace Mann Bond only weeks before the *Brown I* ruling, he openly aired his fear that "whites will take over the whole shebang." "The blacks are so eager for integration," he lamented, "that they are willing to abandon all of their own institutions and go on over and join the whites. Aside from you and me, nobody seems to insist that the whites ought to integrate with us—at least now and then."[73] Reddick tried to accomplish that goal by making the Atlanta University Center and the Trevor Arnett Library truly first-rate institutions that would rival the Ivy League, or at least maintain their advantage when it came to library materials and professional expertise related to black people. In short, he feared exactly what he would later observe within historically black colleges and universities: a brain-drain to white institutions, an economic crisis as state governments and the black community withdrew their support, and the underlying existential crisis over the schools' nature and purpose in a post-*Brown* world.

One tangible way that Reddick attempted to make southern black colleges relevant was to place them at the forefront of the economic changes reshaping the region. Postwar America witnessed the rise of the South and the Southwest, or the "Sun Belt," as the emerging locus for manufacturing. By 1960, 80 percent of the nation's textile mills were already located in the South.[74] This came on the back of federal investments in infrastructure, such as the Federal Aid Highway Act of 1956, which facilitated commerce by stitching together the country through a web of interstate highways, and it stemmed from the flight of capital away from the heavily unionized Midwest and Northeast to the antilabor South. Struck by the tectonic changes and fearful that blacks were being left out of the gains, Reddick opened discussions with Julius A. Thomas, the industrial secretary of the National Urban League, and other black Atlantans. He was most concerned with how black colleges could adapt to the times and stay relevant.[75]

The fruit of these labors was a manifesto entitled *Our Colleges and the Industrialization of the South* (1953). Reddick edited and helped to write the booklet, and several Sigma brothers and AUC colleagues contributed essays. In the introduction, Reddick affirmed that whites routinely excluded African Americans from good jobs throughout the economy, but he underscored that black colleges, too, contributed to that state of affairs by overemphasizing "religious, humanistic and teacher-training education." The nature and tone of Reddick's critiques echoed his complaints about black colleges and administrators during the Great Depression. He again considered the colleges "derelict . . . with their eyes fixed on the medieval stars."[76] The new goal, which he reiterated throughout the black press, was for black colleges to become centers of scientific research and training which could win them national grants, bolster their reputations in an era of desegregation, and equip black workers to compete for good private-sector jobs in science, engineering, and management.⁷⁷ The *Atlanta Daily World* considered the ideas of these "enlightened professors" to be "most significant," and the *Chicago Defender* wholly backed the notion that black colleges should "re-examine their educational philosophy in the light of the changes that industry has brought to the South."⁷⁸

Given racial discrimination and black institutional inertia, Reddick's hopes proved overly ambitious. In 1955, after he had left Atlanta University, he sent a letter of lament to St. Clair Drake, who was then living in Ghana and encountering difficulties of his own in promoting black liberation. "As both Ruth and Elizabeth [Drake] might say, it serves us right, our disenchantment. No doubt we expect too much of these Negroes—African and Southern. This ideal of making AU the Harvard of the South, treating your staff like human beings and not like slaves," he bemoaned, "is foreign to the set-up. There is little real respect for manhood or intellectual interest. This I know in the worst way: my mission to the South to prove that when integration come[s] that the Negroes do not have to liquidate their institutions; only open the doors and let the whites in, etc., failed. The irony of it all is that my big fight was not with the Klan or Talmadge but with my Negro brothers!"⁷⁹

Dilemmas, Debacles, and Departures

Some of the very qualities that contributed to Reddick's intellectual accomplishments—his ambition, his loyalty, his morally uncompromising nature—could also at times fuel self-destructive behavior, especially when he did not get his way or feel that he was being heard. Reddick himself was fully cognizant of the complexities of human beings and their worlds. He once stated directly, "Everybody will know that it is not an honest book if it is a record only of achievements, wise decisions and victories, or if all of our men at every moment in history were prudent and forward-looking."⁸⁰ And so it is with Reddick, who in his years at Atlanta became involved in two controversies with other black leaders that were at least partly of his own making. The exact nature and context of those disputes can never be fully known, but taken together they suggest a tendency to occasionally succumb to conspiratorial thinking, reckless provocation, and an overblown sense of aggrievement. These warrant discussion so that we can appreciate Reddick as the complex, full-blooded human being that he was, but also so we can understand the trajectory of his career as well as the organizations and institutions that he shaped.

The first debacle grew out of the crisis facing the Association for the Study of Negro Life and History in the wake of Carter Woodson's sudden death on April 3, 1950. Woodson had maintained almost complete control of the association since its founding in 1915, so his passing left the organization unprepared to operate without him. Reddick, Luther Porter Jackson, Lorenzo Greene, John Hope Franklin, and others within Woodson's circle met at ASNLH's headquarters in Washington, D.C., shortly after Woodson's funeral. They discussed how the organization could continue even if they found someone else who could direct it while also editing the *Journal of Negro History* and the *Negro History Bulletin*. These were both full-time jobs which Woodson had insisted upon doing all by himself. The anxiety and despair only deepened two weeks later when Jackson, then only fifty-seven years old, died suddenly after emerging as the most likely successor to Woodson.[81] With ASNLH's leadership and finances in disarray, the association president Mary McLeod Bethune appointed Rayford Logan as the new director-editor. He was certainly qualified, but he was also controversial. Logan's role within ASNLH had diminished since his falling out with Woodson in 1936, which made Reddick and especially two of Woodson's closest disciples, William Brewer and Louis R. Mehlinger, perturbed by his appointment. Considerable tension arose not only over who the new leaders should be (Franklin, Greene, and Reddick were also viewed as potential successors to Woodson) but over how the organization itself should be changed to operate more efficiently and democratically in the post–Woodson era.[82]

Reddick had strong opinions. Logan had tasked Greene and Charles Wesley with recommending ideas for how the association and its constitution could be updated, so Reddick wrote to Greene, a friend of his, and conveyed his strong feelings that significant changes be made so that ASNLH "will operate in the manner of a 1st class learned society." This involved separating the editing jobs from those of business manager and promoter, specifying the duties and powers of the executive council and editorial board, and inserting some "new blood" on the council—more bluntly, "clear[ing] out the 'deadwood.'" He criticized Logan and other leaders of the council for wanting few if any changes in either personnel or the structure of the organization.[83] As historian Pero Dagbovie explains, Greene sympathized with both Reddick and Logan, and he tried to operate as a moderating force.[84] Greene nevertheless wrote a letter to Reddick stating that he agreed completely with his reform ideas. Greene intended to have everything "straightened out . . . in a lengthy business session at the Atlanta meeting" that fall.[85] Unfortunately, he fell ill and could not attend the conference at Atlanta University, for which Reddick and Bacote had done all of the planning. Thus the "plenty of fireworks" that Greene had anticipated at the business meeting became all too real, especially when the executive council, acting on a technicality, tabled the question of constitutional reforms until a later date.[86] Reddick exploded, furious that his and Greene's reform ideas were being arbitrarily dismissed. He ultimately resigned in protest from the council (to which he had been elected while he was out of the room), and severed all ties with ASNLH.[87]

Reddick's letter of resignation testified both to the depth of his convictions that serious reforms were necessary and to his penchant for overreaction. After laying out his reform ideas, he highlighted personal squabbles with Logan, whom he argued was not candid with him about a volume of essays commemorating Woodson which Reddick had been organizing, but which Logan, unbeknownst to him, had already been authorized by ASNLH to edit.[88] The overall frustration, long brewing, boiled over into utter distrust and dislike. Referring to Logan and Wesley, Reddick wrote, "I no longer have confidence in two key members of the present administration of this Association. I would suspect them. I would watch for their subtle moves. I would scrutinize the circle of friends within which honors and powers would be passed around." Believing that he "would grow to detest them" and "become an obstructionist" if he stayed around, he decided instead to sever all official ties with ASNLH.[89]

The association limped on for the next few years, plagued by continued infighting, financial problems, and leadership woes. Logan only lasted a year as the director-editor. He, too, then resigned in fury after being undermined at every turn by Brewer and Mehlinger.[90] Greene warned Reddick that his resignation was not the "best thing, either for yourself or for the Association." He also offered a poignant reminder of how "Wesley and I know what it means to be deeply injured, even by the founder, but we stayed in the Association because we deemed the cause greater than the individual."[91] Reddick was not yet ready to hear this. He continued to follow ASNLH politics from afar through Greene, Bacote, and Brewer, but the distance only seemed to deepen his conspiratorial thinking.[92] In a letter to Greene in 1951, he went so far as to allege corruption at ASNLH on par with Tammany Hall, with all of its "little tricks and stratagems."[93] Nevertheless, pleas from his friends eventually paved the way for Reddick to rejoin the association in 1953. After Wesley swallowed his pride and gently asked Reddick to return, Reddick did just that, and he quickly took up service on the editorial board.[94] In the context of a long career closely involved with the association, a three-year separation was not an especially long time. But for what it reveals about the internal politics of ASNLH as well as the personality of Reddick, the self-imposed exile speaks volumes.

The second major dispute during Reddick's Atlanta years proved more consequential, and it resulted in Reddick's dismissal from Atlanta University in 1955. The exact origins of the dispute are not clear, but the pattern in which it played out echoed Reddick's departure from Dillard, the Schomburg, and ASNLH. In April 1954, Atlanta University president Rufus Clement shocked Reddick by sending him an official notice of dissatisfaction with Reddick's performance as head librarian. He said that he would not be recommending Reddick for permanent status at Atlanta, charging, "You have not proved yourself to be one who is fully capable of recognizing the various needs of a library . . . [and] you have not taken your work seriously enough." He also noted that "you spend a great deal of time off the campus," and that "there had arisen in the minds of a number of persons the question of whether you were more interested in outside activities than you were in the University library."[95] Taken aback, Reddick quickly disputed all of the charges, noting, "In all my life I have never received a letter like yours of April 21. For a sensitive man with a house full of children to get a letter like that—so harsh and extreme—might be enough to cause him to commit suicide."[96] Reddick was not referring to himself, as he and Ruth never did have children (despite apparent attempts), but his jarring statement seemed to be a play for pity. To remedy the situation, Reddick proposed regular weekly meetings with Clement so he could better understand Reddick's work. He also recommended that outside experts examine the library to provide a neutral assessment of how well it was being run. Clement ignored Reddick's ideas and left things as they were until the following February.

In February 1955, Clement served Reddick with a notice of termination, making clear that the previous letter was merely part of the formal process of firing Reddick.[97] Reddick responded with shock and outrage. In a seven-page, single-spaced letter, he made the case that Clement's charges were largely groundless, and that the real issue was a personal dispute between Clement's wife, whom Reddick had reluctantly hired at the library in deference to Clement, and the rest of the library staff, with whom she did not get along. As Reddick described it, Clement's wife must have poisoned Clement's mind regarding the functioning of the library. Reddick did take an active role in outside professional organizations and local civic life, which could have potentially distracted him from work. And there were others who echoed Clement's criticisms. For instance, Glovina Virginia Perry Banks, an associate of Du Bois's who reported on southern conditions for him, said that Reddick "is not a trained librarian. He did neglect his work. He seemed to give too much time to boys. He was not a good public relations man . . . [and] was not able to set people to work and see that they did it."[98]

Separating fact from fiction, and rumor from truth, is not easy, but Reddick's case grew stronger when the Southern Association of Colleges and Secondary Schools launched an audit of Atlanta University that March. Its report that the library was "academically, professionally and personally of the highest order" made Clement's charges against Reddick appear baseless.[99] No matter, Clement was determined to fire Reddick, and Reddick's resistance only emboldened him. When Reddick wrote to Clement that "there will be more pain down the road if you force a course of action that I trust can be avoided," Clement considered it a "veiled threat," which only deepened his resolve.[100] Clement could barely conceal his rage when Reddick dared to mention his wife. He flatly refused any further discussion of the decision, calling Reddick's charges "absurd" and indicative of a "total lack of understanding of events."[101]

Reddick could see the writing on the wall. Privately, he began reaching out to friends for sympathy and help in finding new work. He remarked to Horace Mann Bond, "It seems that my happy days in the sunny South are rapidly drawing to a close."[102] He asked St. Clair Drake, "What about finding me a job in Africa? Perhaps the time has come for me to get out of the good old U.S.A. for a couple of years at least."[103] Du Bois also tried to help him, for he understood Reddick's plight all too well. Indeed, Clement had fired Du Bois from Atlanta University a decade earlier.[104] "Matters are shaping up at Atlanta as I have been afraid they would," Du Bois told Reddick, regretful that black college administrators had the power to fire faculty members at will.[105] Although Reddick's dismissal occurred at the same time that faculty members across the country were being censored and fired for harboring leftist views during the Red Scare, it seems that Clement's decision stemmed chiefly from personal animus and misunderstanding. Du Bois chalked it up to "the same old story: inner tricks, favoritism, narrow-minded envy and jealousy."[106]

Even as his departure from Atlanta University became unavoidable, Reddick continued to protest in a predictable pattern. He notified countless friends and colleagues about the proceedings, issued a complaint before the faculty senate, and after refusing to resign quietly and forcing Clement to fire him, he made a statement to the press explaining the circumstances.[107] In the statement he declared that Clement was "entrapped in a maze of contradictions, inaccuracies and hearsay," and that the only reason he did not speak out earlier was because Clement was "one of the few Negroes presently holding public office in the South"—an office which, ironically, Reddick had helped him secure. The statement further enraged Clement, who tried to humiliate Reddick two weeks later by convening the entire library staff and then personally handing Reddick his letter of dismissal. Clement even proceeded to read the letter aloud, which the *Cleveland Call and Post* reported on and called "unprecedented." That same newspaper then noted how Reddick handed the letter back to Clement and said to his staff that "the action . . . was obviously designed to humiliate him and that it reminded him of a Nazi General, who, when he was displeased with one of his junior officers, called that officer before his unit and stripped him of his commission, battle ribbons and medals."[108] Even if Reddick was not in the right regarding his leadership of the library—though evidence suggests he was—it is clear that his combativeness did not always serve him well in this instance.

Reddick persevered, and by May was already fielding numerous job offers. He decided to accept one as the chair of the history department at Alabama State College. This took him out of the library business and back into academic history, but its real significance ended up having little to do with the new job title. Because it placed him in Montgomery, Alabama, on the eve of the Montgomery bus boycott, the decision proved to be the most fateful one of his entire life.

5 The Nonviolent Crusade from Montgomery to Madras

....

> In the southern part of the United States it is like the days of the French Revolution.
> —Lawrence Reddick

When Reddick accepted a job in Montgomery, it was not out of any special interest in the place. For the longtime urbanite, it was a rather sleepy town whose chief attraction was its proximity to Atlanta, where he and Ruth continued to live. Lawrence made the 185-mile commute on weekends and stayed in Montgomery during the week, while Ruth remained in Atlanta, keeping her job as a schoolteacher there. Upon arrival, Lawrence was not quite sure what to make of Montgomery. He liked that African Americans made up about 40 percent of its 125,000 residents, but black social and cultural life there was dominated by religious institutions rather than the secular educational and entertainment ones that he preferred.

As it turned out, Montgomery churches were blessed with remarkable leaders with whom Reddick would soon strike up lasting friendships. Ralph Abernathy, who later became the second president of the Southern Christian Leadership Conference, headed up the largest black church in town, the First Baptist Church. Martin Luther King Jr., as a twenty-five-year-old about to earn his PhD in theology from Boston University, began his ministry at the Dexter Avenue Baptist Church in 1954, the year before Reddick arrived. Although Reddick's worldview was largely secular and materialist, he never lost sight of the church's essential role in black life. As a historian, he knew well that during slavery blacks had seized upon Christianity to proclaim their equality under God and to justify forming independent churches that nurtured black learning and leadership. Because Reddick soon became a key figure in Montgomery's black freedom struggle, he ultimately felt compelled to join Dexter.[1] The spiritual message may not have always resonated, but the church's practice and preachment of black solidarity never failed to inspire.

Black Montgomery was not all religion. Alabama State College, located only one mile from the state capitol building, loomed large within black cultural life. It had been educating black people since 1866 and had a proud legacy of teaching more than the rudiments of the arts and sciences. Abernathy was a student there in the 1940s, and he recalled "being taught all sorts of useful and subversive ideas by our faculty members, some of whom were openly urging us to make a difference in our people's struggle for freedom."[2] As head of the history department, Reddick quickly took up that mantle as well. That first fall semester of 1955 he gave a speech before the entire student body that beseeched them to cultivate their minds and take a stand "against materialism and conformity."[3] His own history courses provided them with the tools to do so. So, too, did Reddick's outside projects. For instance, Reddick quickly enlisted twenty-nine graduate students and two other professors in a wide-ranging study of racism in American encyclopedias. Unlike his analysis of American history textbooks two decades earlier, this American Teachers Association–sponsored investigation uncovered no derogatory references to black people in any of the encyclopedias. However, the research team found that each encyclopedia almost entirely excluded black people from entries not directly about them, such as those related to music and sports. "The segregated pattern of American life seems to be reflected also in the segregation of printed materials in standard American encyclopedias," Reddick reported to other educators.[4]

It did not take Reddick long to recognize the rich religious and educational environment within black Montgomery, but it was white supremacy that stood out most strikingly. All around him were signs that black life was as precarious in Montgomery as it was in Money, Mississippi, where on August 28, 1955, two white men mutilated and murdered Emmett Till, a fourteen-year-old black boy from Chicago, but were found not guilty by an all-white jury less than a month later. "A damn shame!" Reddick decried to Lorenzo Greene.[5] Montgomery had its own special tie to white supremacy: it was the original capital of the Confederacy, where the Confederate Congress first met and wrote its constitution ratifying the expansion of "Negro slavery" to the American West.[6] Such an ignominious honor was not one that white Montgomerians were ashamed of a century later; rather, they reveled in it. Driving in from Atlanta each week, Reddick was greeted by a sign that read: "City Limits, Montgomery, Cradle of the Confederacy." The Ku Klux Klan soon added a welcome sign of its own right beside it.

And that was only the half of it. As Reddick described, "Once inside the city, the visitor may be shown the statue of Jefferson Davis in front of the state capitol and nearby, an inscription marks the spot where he swore allegiance to the Confederate States of America. Across the street from the capitol building you would see what is known as the 'Little White House of the Confederacy.' Here old ladies—members of the Daughters of the Confederacy, of course—show the visitor the bed in which Jeff Davis slept, the chair in which he sat and the table at which he ate." The pageantry, as all blacks understood, was far from innocuous. After all, to celebrate the Confederacy was ultimately to celebrate what it stood for. Alex Stephens, the vice president of the Confederacy, had summed that up precisely: "Ours is the first government in the history of the world that was based upon the superiority of the white race and the inferiority of the black race."[7]

Yet when journalists from France, Germany, and Japan descended upon Montgomery only a few months after Reddick's arrival, it was not to report yet another Jim Crow outrage. Rather, they were covering an erupting black protest movement that seemed to catch everyone by surprise. As Montgomery emerged as the unlikely epicenter of the black revolution, it came to serve paradoxically as both the cradle of the Confederacy and the cradle of the modern civil rights movement. Reddick could hardly believe his good luck, noting to St. Clair Drake, "I could not have picked a better place than Montgomery for this year and may stick around a little longer."[8] He ended up sticking around for another four years. He only left then because Alabama governor John Patterson forced him out for his civil rights activities, attesting to Reddick's growing importance as a leader of the southern struggle.

Reddick's five years in Montgomery were arguably the most momentous of his life. Among other activities, he participated in the Montgomery bus boycott, helped form the Southern Christian Leadership Conference, completed joint book projects with King, made a trip to India with King and his wife, Coretta, and participated in the local student sit-ins. As always, Reddick tried to make sense of the revolutionary times while also clarifying them for others and attempting to steer them in productive directions.

Stay off the Buses!

The abuse black Montgomerians experienced on city buses was a microcosm of the entire Jim Crow order. The issue was not simply the physical separation of the races. To be sure, the demand that all black people ritually enact their social inferiority by sitting in the back half of buses was infuriating, but it was only one manifestation of a regime that systematically denied blacks political, economic, and social power. On a day-to-day basis, though, black citizens got most fed up with the utter absurdities and gratuitous cruelties confronting them in Jim Crow spaces like public buses. Even though black patrons comprised three-quarters of all bus riders—making the industry heavily reliant upon black patronage—drivers would routinely disparage them, pass them by at stops, refuse to make change or offer transfers for them, and demand that they re-enter the bus through the rear door after paying the fare at the front. Drivers would also force black riders to stand in the rear "Negro" section of the bus even if a seat was available in the front, just as they would force black passengers to give up their seats in the back if none were available for whites in the front. It was that latter humiliation which in 1955 alone provoked at least three black women to refuse to give up their seat, resulting in their arrest. The last of that triumvirate was Rosa Parks, who acted on December 1, 1955. Parks's arrest was nothing new. Nor was the fact that black Montgomerians protested it, either through issuing press releases or withdrawing patronage. Indeed, well before Parks, hundreds of black riders had refused to ride city buses because of discrimination.[9]

Parks's situation was novel only because of the scale of the protest it ultimately inspired. The previous two black women who had been arrested were only teenagers. One of them, Claudette Colvin, was fifteen and was rumored (falsely) to have been impregnated by a married man. For that reason, local leaders were hesitant to make her the face of a larger protest. Parks, on the other hand, seemed perfect, or at least could be made to appear so. She was middle-aged, middle-class, and a churchgoing woman whose protest many believed could arouse far more sympathy from white Americans. In fact, she was a veteran NAACP organizer at a time when white southerners were outlawing that group as a Communist front. Historian Danielle McGuire has documented how she was "a militant race woman, a sharp detective, and an antirape activist long before she became the patron saint of the bus boycott."[10]

Parks was well aware of the larger implications of her bus protest, and she worked in concert with a group of women activists associated with the local Women's Political Council to publicize her cause.[11] The council, after being founded in 1946 by Mary Fair Burks (the head of the English department at Alabama State College), quickly became the most important activist organization in Montgomery. The council's president, Jo Ann Robinson (who was also a professor in the English department at Alabama State), was responsible for circulating fifty thousand leaflets calling for a one-day boycott of all Montgomery buses on December 5. It succeeded beyond everyone's wildest expectations. The activists then capitalized on the momentum by continuing the boycott and instituting the Montgomery Improvement Association (MIA), a radically democratic organization committed to mass protest. Under the leadership of Robinson, King, Abernathy, and E. D. Nixon, the MIA extended the boycott from days to weeks, and then from weeks to months. Before long, nothing less than the complete desegregation of the buses would be acceptable to the boycotters.[12]

Reddick involved himself immediately. In April, he confessed to Du Bois that he felt overwhelmed because "this boycott movement has been so absorbing and the need for general and technical suggestions has been so great that I have scarcely answered any personal mail in six months."[13] As he told another friend, "If you had been here and seen these poor people struggling so manfully and with so little, you, too, would have taken time out to help out."[14] Indeed, the boycott was so impressive because of how difficult it was for black Montgomerians to function without the buses. Many of them would have to walk at least eight miles per day. Activists soon arranged for an intricate network of carpooling to help address the problem, but the police responded by harassing black motorists in creative ways. For instance, they resurrected arcane ordinances and rigorously enforced others that were long ignored, such as one specifying precisely where license tags on vehicles must be located.[15] Blacks turned to weekly MIA meetings both to lift their spirits and to stay informed about the rapidly evolving situation. "It had been almost like military headquarters in wartime," according to Reddick. "Conferences came daily—and nightly—for the moves of the enemy had to be checkmated and tactics had to be improvised as the movement expanded."[16]

Reddick helped MIA leaders devise strategy, but as a trained historian, he saw his principal role as documenting and analyzing the struggle. More than six months into the boycott, that role became official. The boycott still had no end in sight. The bus company was going bankrupt without black riders, but it preferred bankruptcy over submission to black demands. Accordingly, on May 24, 1956, King made a series of recommendations to the MIA executive board to "prepare ourselves for the long haul." The activists had already initiated a lawsuit against the bus company, and now they began putting out a bimonthly newsletter and created a history committee—so that "there may be a reliable and orderly record of the bus protest plus an accurate record of the origin, growth and future development of the Montgomery Improvement Association."[17] Reddick was appointed as chairman. He served alongside Jo Ann Robinson and Norman Walton, a junior member of Alabama State College's history department, who also published a five-part series on the boycott.[18] Together they testified to how much the black college served as ground zero for the movement.

Fourteen weeks into the boycott, Reddick published an article in *Dissent* that illustrates another type of intellectual work that he would perform for the larger movement: public relations. The article offered the American public a concise, objective overview of the basic nature and origins of the boycott. This was no small thing at a time when southern politicians were attempting to smear it as a Communist conspiracy to destroy the southland. Reddick, however, ever keen to the larger rhetorical battle, did attempt to frame the struggle in a way that would dramatize its moral righteousness and heighten its appeal for white America. This involved hewing closely to what historian Evelyn Brooks Higginbotham has dubbed the "politics of respectability."[19] That is, he emphasized those qualities and characteristics of black boycotters that he believed would most resonate with mainstream American values. He therefore excluded Rosa Parks's lifetime of militant protest and stated, rather, that she was "attractive and quiet, a churchgoer who looks like the symbol of Mother's Day." He portrayed her refusal to vacate her seat as an unprecedented, solitary act: "For some reason . . . Parks refused to 'move back.'" The protest that followed was likewise inexplicable, organic, and in no way the product of years of organizing on behalf of strong-willed black women activists: "Out of nowhere, it seems, written and mimeographed appeals appeared in the Negro community." Poor black women with any hint of controversy like Claudette Colvin were naturally omitted from the story.[20]

Reddick also offered up a portrait of King and Abernathy that aligned with America's individualistic, patriarchal, and self-consciously middle-class culture. He stressed their humility, writing that they were "not self-appointed 'leaders' but only 'spokesmen' of the movement" who were nevertheless the "real and obvious leaders of the mass upsurge." Black women leaders largely disappeared into that mass. King and Abernathy were also highly educated, masculine, and charismatic: "People have 'fallen in love' with King, a boyish-looking Ph.D. They look upon Abernathy, also young and an M.A., as a tower of strength." Lest white America fear strong and assertive black men, Reddick was sure to underline that both men were ministers committed to nonviolence who coveted only the universal human goals of freedom, justice, and democracy. Pitted against them, Reddick described, was an intransigent white resistance that contravened American principles to maintain their dominance. That part involved no embellishment. If anything, Reddick understated the depth of white hatred. He instead emphasized the desperate effort on behalf of white politicians, policemen, and the bus industry to break the boycott. Their efforts emboldened vigilantes, some of whom dynamited King's front porch and attacked other boycotters. In Reddick's hands, such hostility served as a useful foil for the rise of King the charismatic leader. King's courageous leadership and commitment to nonviolence, Reddick underscored, even in the face of direct threats to his and his family's lives, "saved the city from a race riot," shored up the nonviolent movement, and presented "a magnificent case study of the circumstances under which the philosophy of Thoreau and Gandhi can triumph."[21]

Reddick's framing stemmed partly from what historian Jacqueline Dowd Hall has aptly referred to as "the dance between activists and journalists."[22] Mainstream journalists largely ignored the plight of black Americans unless it made for a dramatic story that could sell papers. Civil rights activists, understanding the essential role that the media played in building public support for the movement, did their best to feed them those dramatic stories. They came to challenge white supremacy in ways that provoked a dramatic clash with segregationists, showcasing for the world how peaceful black protesters were hosed, beaten, and killed for pursuing basic citizenship rights. Reddick believed that any ceding of the moral high ground, any casting of blacks in an imperfect light, could and would become fodder for racists to undermine the movement. For that reason, he tried to control the narrative of the struggle so that it would appeal to the largest possible audience. Like any strategy, his was not perfect. In celebrating charismatic leaders, it devalued the power of ordinary people. In portraying leaders' larger-than-life qualities, it created an impossible standard to live up to. In hewing closely to the politics of respectability, it marginalized large segments of the black community. In emphasizing black people's courage and resolve, it left little room for their flaws and imperfections—in other words, their humanity. There were no easy solutions to these dilemmas, but each of them sparked arguments between Reddick and other black commentators in the days that followed.

After more than a year, the protesters finally emerged victorious and called off the boycott on December 20, 1956. It was not the economic pressure of the boycott that ultimately proved decisive; it was the lawsuit the boycotters had filed independently. To be sure, the boycott captured the world's attention, electrified African Americans, and created public pressure for change. Still, the bus company refused to relent. So just like in education, it was the U.S. Supreme Court that finally decided the issue. In *Browder v. Gayle* (1956), the Court declared bus segregation to be unconstitutional because it violates the equal protection clause of the Fourteenth Amendment.[23] A few days later, King issued a public statement stating that "our faith seems to be vindicated" because the ruling made "crystal clear that segregation in public transportation is both legally and sociologically invalid."[24]

The Montgomery bus boycott was a monumental victory in the struggle against Jim Crow, but as Reddick, King, and other local leaders understood, the fight was only just beginning. In the six months following the boycott, the Alabama Council on Human Relations recorded "seventeen bombings, four unsuccessful bombing attempts, several beatings, numerous telephone threats and scores of cross burnings and inflammatory Klan rallies in central and south Alabama."[25] Alabama Klan membership ballooned to around twenty thousand. The police continued harassing and assaulting the black community with abandon. Black children were beaten up and jailed.[26] Leaders like King, despite being international celebrities, were openly abused as well. In one incident recorded by the MIA, a policeman seized King, "pushed him into the street, twisting his arms mercilessly," while another "took him by the collar and choked him"—all in the light of day outside the courthouse.[27] White Montgomerians, too, became targets if they dared to break ranks and speak out against the treatment of blacks. One local librarian, Juliette Morgan, did so in the pages of the leading local newspaper, the *Montgomery Advertiser*. She was subsequently harassed and threatened day and night, at work and at home, rendering her unable to work, sleep, or eat—to the point that she actually died as a result. "Plain murder," a columnist at the *Pittsburgh Courier* called it, taken aback by the depth of white resistance and hate.[28]

White "massive resistance" to desegregation took its cues from the top. Reddick's initial optimism after *Brown v. Board of Education* quickly dissipated as southern congressmen voted overwhelmingly to support the "Southern Manifesto" on March 12, 1956, thus staking their political careers on fighting integration. In the statement, eighty-two members of the house and nineteen senators boldly declared *Brown* to be a "clear abuse of judicial power" with "no legal basis" that was "destroying the amicable relations between the white and Negro races" and "creating chaos and confusion" in the South.[29] Their intransigent position legitimated the ideas of white supremacists such as Tom P. Brady, a Mississippi judge who became the intellectual leader of the White Citizens' Council movement. His wildly popular treatise, *Black Monday* (1955), argued that the black race was biologically and culturally inferior, that black people had made no positive contribution to American history, and that *Brown* was a "socialistic doctrine" and part of a Communist plot to destroy America.[30] Inspired by these ideas, more affluent white southerners all across the region began forming Citizens' Councils as a more respectable alternative to the Ku Klux Klan, preferring boycotts, propaganda, and employment discrimination over violence to maintain Jim Crow. One handbill circulated at a Montgomery Citizens' Council meeting during the boycott read: "We hold these truths to be self evident that all whites are created equal with certain rights; among these are life, liberty and the pursuit of dead niggers."[31]

SCLC into the Breach

In the face of such opposition, it was imperative for the movement to develop new bases of power. The MIA would continue to fight for black Montgomerians for years to come, but the success of the boycott prompted Reddick, King, Abernathy, and others to ask, "Can this be done for the whole South?" In fact, there had already been boycotts in Baton Rouge, Louisiana; Columbia, South Carolina; and a dozen other southern cities. Moreover, during Montgomery's boycott, leaders from across the region had flocked to town to discuss strategy and exchange ideas. As Reddick recounted, "The common feeling grew: that we ought to do this regularly and systematically."[32] The feeling was especially urgent because white southerners had succeeded in outlawing the NAACP as a "foreign corporation" throughout much of the South, cleverly charging its lawyers with "barratry," or persistently inciting legislation. Recognizing the organizational vacuum, Ella Baker, Bayard Rustin, and Stanley Levison formed the New York–based group In Friendship to support the southern struggle.[33] They helped to organize the first meeting of southern leaders at Ebenezer Church in Atlanta on January 10–11, 1957. Sixty people from twenty-nine communities ultimately attended. Although the meeting was interrupted by news that vigilantes had firebombed Abernathy's church and home in Montgomery, the enthusiasm for instituting a new South-wide organization to coordinate nonviolent resistance could not be denied. The organization that would become known as the Southern Christian Leadership Conference (SCLC) was thus born.

Although SCLC was dominated by young black ministers from the South, including King, Abernathy, Joseph Lowery of Mobile, and Fred Shuttlesworth of Birmingham, the older generation of race leaders nevertheless had an important influence. For instance, Reddick recalled how Bayard Rustin, a committed leftist and pacifist, had taken charge of the initial January meeting and "prepared 'working papers' for the group, spelling out themes on a broad front."[34] Reddick himself was especially influential. He emerged as the lone non-minister on SCLC's nine-member board of directors, which included King as president. Reddick's official title was historian. The role underscores these men's understanding of the historic import of their new organization, but it also represents their deference to the "protest tradition" within black history. Sociologist Aldon Morris has demonstrated how SCLC activists drew heavily from that tradition for inspiration and guidance.[35] Through Reddick, that connection was direct and specific. As both a professional historian of the black experience and a well-connected activist during the 1930s and 1940s, Reddick offered a wellspring of knowledge that the ministers—especially King—were wise enough to tap. It was certainly convenient to have a historian in their ranks. Reddick not only provided a broad context for the black struggle, he also corrected the ministers' factual historical errors, as when he once told King, "I have meant to say to you some time ago that the Africans who were brought to Jamestown in 1619 were not slaves but indentured servants."[36]

Reddick played a key role in developing SCLC's constitution and bylaws. The organization's principal aim was "achieving full citizenship rights, equality, and the integration of the Negro in all aspects of American life." The preamble stated that the Declaration of Independence, the U.S. Constitution, federal civil rights laws, and recent U.S. Supreme Court rulings all "proclaim unequivocally that all American Citizens shall be accorded full citizenship rights and opportunities without discrimination." The means of achieving these goals were through education, voter registration and civic involvement, and "non-violent direct action."[37] Reddick made sure to add in a part on how industrialization and urbanization were transforming the South, creating new opportunities for a modern, prosperous society free from old racial divisions. Such divisions "will not disappear automatically," he wrote, so all citizens must work together to "cherish and defend our fundamental, democratic heritage." "To secure these ends," he concluded, "the [SCLC] is established, dedicating itself to justice, refusing to cooperate with evil, appealing to the conscience of man, working for social change but always in a spirit of good will and non-violence."[38] The SCLC would soon stand out for its role in supporting local mobilization campaigns across the South.

Ella Baker's early role in SCLC was as important as anyone's, but her experience was very different than Reddick's. SCLC leaders relied on her organizational skills even as they marginalized her in ways that bespoke the weaknesses of the fledgling organization. Baker proved indispensable in leading the conference in its early years, setting up a headquarters on Auburn Avenue in Atlanta with only a shoestring budget, taking charge of the 1958 Crusade for Citizenship voting rights campaign, stepping in as interim leader when King was stabbed, and generally promoting and publicizing SCLC through her dense network of grassroots activists. She was a veteran NAACP organizer who was second to none in building an activist group. Yet her efforts were not fully appreciated, and she was never seriously considered for the executive director position. As her biographer Barbara Ransby has documented, this stemmed in large part from the ministers' sexism. The ministers shared the patriarchal norms predominating American society in the 1950s, which envisioned women as primarily housewives and helpmates. For instance, Baker later recalled that the ministers were most comfortable talking to women about "how well they cooked and how beautiful they looked," and were put off by strong-willed women like her who spoke to them as equals and eschewed traditional trappings of femininity. Baker also struggled to respect men who committed adultery while preaching high moral principles from the pulpit.[39]

Reddick was enmeshed in the same patriarchal culture as were the other SCLC ministers. This was on display in a speech he gave upon returning from India in 1959. He had observed that Indian women "seem to have as their highest ideal, pleasing their husbands and sweethearts, fathers and brothers." "Wouldn't it be wonderful," he teased, "if we could import the spirit of the gentle women of India to America?"[40] Still, Reddick did admire Baker for her organizing abilities and strength of purpose. He seemed to have a greater capacity to treat her as an equal, perhaps because of their joint status as more elder activists. Like Baker, he believed that SCLC needed to be better organized, have a clearer agenda, and refrain from "long drawn-out 'country' meetings."[41] Furthermore, he, too, was not transfixed by King the way the other young ministers were. In his notes from one meeting, he recorded an anecdote that gently chided King and Abernathy for being late to meetings and that poked fun at their celebrity status. He wrote, "There was a good joke that when the chariot came to take Abernathy and King to town it would have to pick them up on a delayed schedule."[42] King was not amused.

Yet Reddick's entire life had been shaped by sharp gender divisions, and these came through in his social engagements and professional work. Phi Beta Sigma was an exclusively male organization, but others like the National Negro Congress and ASNLH could be almost as exclusive. Men also dominated American universities and publishing houses, thus reinforcing the notion that men were somehow better suited for serious intellectual work. Historical writing logically reflected this gendered view of the world, portraying men as the principal actors in history. Therefore, Reddick's marginal treatment of women in his article on the Montgomery bus boycott was not simply a strategic maneuver to appeal to a more conservative American public. It was also indicative of the patriarchal norms he shared with most of his generation.

Sexism would hamper SCLC and the larger civil rights struggle in important ways, but for tough-minded activists like Baker, the organization's fundamental problem had to do with leadership style. Scholars have identified two distinct traditions within civil rights leadership: community mobilizing and community organizing. The community-mobilizing tradition, according to historian Charles Payne, focuses on "large-scale, relatively short-term public events" that dramatize an issue, attract media attention, and leverage public pressure to support a specific cause.[43] The community-organizing tradition, on the other hand, prioritizes long-term grassroots organizing as a bulwark for sustained power. Whereas the former often relies upon charismatic leaders to attract attention, the latter depends upon ordinary people feeling empowered to be the forces of change in their communities. For Baker, sitting in awe of King's remarkable oratorical skills was not a productive way to empower individuals. She believed that hero worship actually disempowered people and created a weak, top-heavy movement that was overly reliant on the whims of one person. Baker stayed within SCLC until 1960. Then, amid the student sit-ins, she struck out and formed the Student Nonviolent Coordinating Committee, which practiced the community-organizing style of leadership she preferred.[44]

Reddick, on the other hand, was squarely part of the mobilizing tradition, and he committed himself above all to the public-relations arm of the struggle. This work took many forms, such as helping to craft official press releases and editing SCLC's periodical, the *Crusader*. It also involved sparring publicly with those who wrote about the movement in ways that he took issue with. For instance, in late 1957 Trezzvant Anderson, a journalist for the *Pittsburgh Courier*, published a seven-part series on the state of

Montgomery's black community one year after the boycott. Anderson was sharply critical of MIA leadership, sometimes gratuitously so. At one point he implied that MIA leaders may have firebombed their own homes to gain positive publicity—an allegation Reddick called "unforgivable."[45] "The theme grew to such a proportion," Anderson wrote, "that if one of the MIA leaders went down to the corner he had to do it to the accompaniment of a press conference. Publicity, all was publicity."[46] While Anderson argued that the circumstances of black residents had hardly improved, he portrayed King as reveling in the international fame and the potential riches from a book deal. After the second article in the series, Reddick shot back, complaining that Anderson's reporting "is based upon false assumptions and filled with insinuations and inaccuracies."[47] The *Courier* also published a retraction of a false claim made by Anderson.[48]

Anderson nevertheless made some legitimate criticisms that highlighted significant divisions over Reddick's public-relations strategy. Chief among these was his challenge to the ultimate significance of the boycott. Anderson's reporting revealed that most black Montgomerians were concerned with concrete issues in their lives and viewed the boycott as a success in defeating segregation and blatant abuses on local buses, though other goals such as the hiring of black drivers remained unmet. By many measures, the boycott simply did not transform black Montgomerians' lives. This was especially true on the economic front, where retributive job discrimination by white employers only compounded problems.

Meanwhile, Reddick's repeated emphasis on the symbolic and international dimensions of the struggle was beginning to grate. He once stated bluntly in the *Pittsburgh Courier* that "the test of the success of the Montgomery movement" is not "to be found in what it has done for the Negro community of this city. . . . On the contrary, the organization, strategy and sustained drive of the Montgomery Improvement Association have had a positive national and international effect, far more significant than any local effects."[49] Historian Troy Brown has suggested that Reddick's remarks "must have felt like a slap in the face to the foot soldiers of the movement."[50] That may be overstating it, but Reddick's views did magnify a lingering resentment over the media's obsession with King and his tribulations instead of those of ordinary boycotters. E. D. Nixon, a veteran local leader and president of the Montgomery's NAACP chapter, gave voice to this resentment when he told Anderson, "They bombed my house, too, but you never heard anything about it!"[51]

For Reddick, though, the emergence of King as the movement's charismatic leader offered an unprecedented opportunity to cast the whole struggle in a morally righteous, utterly respectable light. Reddick thus redoubled his efforts to cultivate King's public image and to mentor the young activist. For instance, he helped King frame the movement in global terms. This was not difficult given that King's fame put him in direct contact with anticolonial figures from across the world. In March 1957, for example, both King and Reddick attended Ghana's independence celebrations at Kwame Nkrumah's invitation. The festivities marked the beginning of the rapid decolonization of Africa, and they dramatized the links between all African-descended peoples in the fight against white supremacy.[52] In these years King also joined the American Committee on Africa, served as vice chair of the 1957 Declaration of Conscience (which opposed South African apartheid), spoke before a Human Rights Day celebration, and took up service on the American Negro Leadership Conference on Africa.[53]

Ever conscious of the broader struggle, SCLC leaders labored to establish their organization as the vanguard of the civil rights movement in the American South. It was slow going at first. SCLC first garnered national attention for its participation in the Prayer Pilgrimage for Freedom, which convened about thirty thousand people at the Lincoln Memorial to celebrate the third anniversary of *Brown v. Board of Education*.[54] SCLC's first major campaign, however, grew out of the Civil Rights Act of 1957. White southern congressmen watered down the bill, but it nevertheless created a Commission on Civil Rights and a Civil Rights Division within the Justice Department. Together these laid a groundwork for federal intervention over voter discrimination and disfranchisement, mainly by requiring all election officers to preserve voting records for federal review. Only days after President Eisenhower signed the Civil Rights Act into law on September 9, 1957, Arkansas governor Orval Faubus's flagrant disregard of federal power compelled Eisenhower to send federal troops to Central High School in Little Rock to integrate the school. All of these were tentative steps to intervene on behalf of civil rights, but they nevertheless broke an eighty-year precedent of federal government inaction and indifference over southern civil rights. Seeking to capitalize on the momentum, SCLC planned an audacious voting rights campaign in the South called Crusade for Citizenship. It began on February 12, 1958, when thirteen thousand people held rallies across twenty-two southern cities.[55] The Crusade put further pressure on the government to support black voting rights, and it began the long, arduous task of mobilizing African Americans to vote—and to feel empowered to fight Jim Crow generally—in a region where doing so meant jeopardizing one's life.[56]

Crusader without Violence

For all of Reddick's work planning and documenting SCLC activities, his greatest contribution stemmed from his joint book projects with King. Although Reddick had been working on a larger history of the boycott, he set that aside in the spring of 1957 to help King write his own personal account of it. Simultaneously, Reddick began working on a biography of King, first by interviewing him at length. The joint efforts would eventually yield King's *Stride toward Freedom* (1958) and Reddick's *Crusader without Violence* (1959), both of which were published by Harper & Brothers.[57] King's book became an international bestseller and an instant classic; Reddick's less so. Yet Reddick played an outsized role in both projects, and together they informed the world about the burgeoning southern struggle and its most charismatic leader.

Reddick's role in creating *Stride toward Freedom* was so important that Ella Baker once wondered if he wrote it alone.[58] In reality, as historian Clayborne Carson has documented, King's book was deeply collaborative and reliant upon input from many trusted advisers, including Reddick, Bayard Rustin, Stanley Levison, and Harris Wofford.[59] King's agent, Marie Rodell; his editor at Harper & Brothers, Eugene Exman; and a freelance editor hired by Harper, Hermine Popper, also played key roles in the book's production. Reddick nevertheless played as large a role as anyone, not least because he had participated in the boycott firsthand and had already analyzed and written about it as a professional historian. He helped King recount the general proceedings of the struggle, describe Montgomery in the second chapter, and frame the book's crucial final chapter, "Where Do We Go from Here?"[60] In short, *Stride toward Freedom* embodied the collaboration of movement activism generally, and in this case it testified to the direct role of more elder black leaders in mentoring the younger generation of activists.

Such intergenerational mentoring was not always smooth. King was only in his late twenties during these years, and he struggled not only to adapt to his celebrity but to find his own voice among a chorus of seasoned and headstrong mentors who were eager to weigh in. Consequently, before King decided he would write a memoir on the boycott, he resisted Reddick's plan to write his biography with the appellation, "As told to L. D. Reddick." "He thought that that phrase made it appear that he himself was incapable of writing," Reddick reported to St. Clair Drake.[61] Reddick's lack of sympathy sometimes translated into harsh assessments of King. He became particularly frustrated by King's concern over his portrayal of him. On one occasion, he even called King a "prima donna" who was "very sensitive."[62] On another, he told Drake, "As with your Nkrumah, my celebrity, too, was a bit greedy and suspicious. So, I pat myself on the back for an outstanding job of intellectual wet-nursing for the past twelve months."[63] For a man who was always deeply concerned about people being able to speak for themselves, Reddick might have been more understanding. In his Pulitzer Prize–winning book on King's early activist years, Taylor Branch notes accurately that Reddick was "devoted to King but prickly by nature and highly independent of mind."[64]

Private venting aside, *Crusader without Violence* testified to Reddick's high regard for King and his leadership of the burgeoning movement. The book provided an authoritative account of the young preacher who, despite being compulsively followed by the media, remained only superficially known if not outright "caricatured . . . by those who oppose the cause he serves." As King became the embodiment of the movement, casting him in an accurate light was critical. The book thus went to lengths to humanize King with great detail about his personality, relationships, experiences, ideology, and even physique. In twelve chapters, it tracked the rise of a bright, sensitive boy from Atlanta to his unlikely leadership of the southern struggle in 1958, when he was presiding over his own civil rights organization and had the ear of the U.S. president. Reddick argued that in a field crowded with other leaders, King emerged as "the spokesman, the philosopher and the symbol of the Montgomery bus boycott" because his philosophy of nonviolent resistance added a "fresh concept to social thinking" which electrified Montgomerians and helped them organize and give meaning to their struggle. In turn, as the boycott drew national and international attention, King's approach "drew a response from men everywhere who were followers of Jesus Christ or Gandhi," and from "all others who were weary of war and conflict."[65]

Explaining the nature and origins of King's philosophy of nonviolent resistance was paramount to the aptly titled *Crusader without Violence*. There was nothing inevitable about King's embrace of that philosophy. His parents did not share it nor did most within the black community. For King, it sprung from both his personal disposition and his own exploration of ideas.

From a young age, King had found violence anathema, prompting an early interest in Henry David Thoreau. Thoreau's pacifism—his "commitment to *non-co-operation with evil*"—set an early precedent for civil disobedience, which involved refusing to follow unjust civil laws in the service of higher moral ones. Jesus and Christianity also informed these commitments and schooled King in ethical principles that transcended the codes of man.[66]

Yet Reddick argued that Mohandas Gandhi influenced King more than any other because he had laid out an effective program of nonviolent resistance on a mass scale, contrary to Thoreau's individualistic approach. Around 1950, when King was a graduate student at Crozer Theological Seminary in Pennsylvania, he was introduced to Gandhi's approach during a talk from Mordecai Johnson, the first black president of Howard University and a leading minister who had visited India and came back preaching Gandhi's gospel of nonviolent resistance. After the talk, King became "fired up," according to Reddick, and he "began to read all the books on Gandhi that he could lay hands on." Gandhi seemed to have resolved for King "the paradox of the necessity of love and the necessity of force in bringing about social change." Specifically, Gandhi defeated British colonial rule of India through these tactics. He oversaw a movement in which the Indian masses would openly violate laws they deemed unjust, invite arrest, and stoically accept violence from police and others without retaliating. The point was to "activate his own followers to higher standards of conduct and living," to break the cycle of retaliatory violence, and to win over one's adversaries and the larger public to support the cause of human freedom and justice. Once he was thrust into the bus boycott in Montgomery, King successfully adapted that approach to circumstances on the ground and then began orchestrating a much larger black struggle based on those principles.[67]

While *Crusader without Violence* aimed to objectively portray King's life and thought, Reddick also framed the book to maximize its impact and to intervene in pressing debates at the time. Among other things, this involved minimizing King's socialist proclivities. McCarthyism had ebbed in most of the United States since 1954 but gained traction in the South after *Brown v. Board of Education*, when white southerners attempted to resist racial integration by associating civil rights with America's greatest enemy, Communism.[68] Civil rights activists had to tread carefully and minimize appeals for economic justice to retain moral standing with the American public. Those who refused, such as Du Bois and Paul Robeson, faced widespread demonization and harassment from the government. That was the last thing Reddick wanted for King, so he portrayed King as "a bourgeois leader of the masses" who "unequivocally rejects communism." Though no Communist, King opposed economic inequality and understood early on that there could be no racial justice without economic justice. Reddick played that down, writing, "Neither by experience nor reading is King a political radical. There is not a Marxist bone in his body. He accepts his society save where injustice and violence defile it." That latter exception, Reddick did not mention, left abundant room for critique. Furthermore, Reddick felt compelled to quote King directly regarding his position on Karl Marx's social theories: "I am not a materialist. I do not believe that all history is guided and shaped by economic determinism. . . . I cannot accept at all the theory of the necessity of violence." White segregationists bent on derailing King and his movement could not care less, but for those in the American public willing to consider King, such words mattered a great deal.[69]

Within the black community, *Crusader without Violence* weighed in on debates raging over the viability and righteousness of nonviolence. Nonviolent direct action had hardly been tested yet in the South, and there was much skepticism and confusion over what it even meant. The book clearly spelled out the method, but public debate revolved less around carefully reasoned books like Reddick's and more around dramatic public statements such as those made by Robert F. Williams in early 1959. Williams was president of a local chapter of the NAACP in Monroe, North Carolina, and after a jury acquitted a white man for the rape of a black woman, he issued a press conference and called for armed self-defense and "meeting violence with violence."[70] Williams was widely rebuked by black leaders, and the NAACP suspended him.[71] His feelings were nevertheless shared by many within the black community, and they foreshadowed the militant rhetoric of Black Power activists in the 1960s. Privately, even proponents of nonviolence routinely voiced very different sentiments. For instance, when Nat King Cole was attacked by an all-white audience who had paid to hear him sing in Birmingham, Reddick told Du Bois in no uncertain terms, "It is a pity that he was not fore-warned and fore-armed so that he could have shot his assailants dead on the spot."[72]

But public statements mattered, and Reddick had calculated that nonviolent direct action held the most potential for promoting positive social change at that time. He thus fought vigorously to promote the method and to quell misunderstandings. For one, Reddick explained that nonviolent resistance was a public protest strategy, not a directive for a private person to never defend himself or herself. Moreover, as he opined in the *Los Angeles Tribune,* "Non-violent resistance means vigorous resistance. . . . It is not do nothing-ism as so many people now seem to say witting or unwittingly. It is not cowardice. It is not merely negative 'not hitting back,' but it is the use of all forms of struggle except the deliberate leveling of violence upon the opponent."[73] In *Crusader without Violence*, Reddick clarified King's concept of love, a "much-used and abused word."[74] He quoted King describing three different types of love: *eros* (romantic), *philia* (brotherly), and *agape* (a generalized goodwill toward mankind). The call to "love one's enemies" referred to the latter type, he explained, which was about creating a transformative encounter, not simply loving as brothers those who hate you. Finally, the very title of Reddick's book may have been a rejoinder to the ideas and posture of Robert F. Williams, who in the months before had been printing his ideas in a periodical of his own entitled the *Crusader*.[75] The acrimony that accompanied debates about nonviolent resistance testified to how radical of an approach it was at the time.

Crusader without Violence ultimately did not make the splash that Reddick had hoped for among the white public. A few months after publication, Reddick wrote to Melvin Arnold of Harper & Brothers and noted that "the degree of enthusiasm . . .'twas not great this time." "People seem to assume that it carries the same story as *Stride*," Reddick grumbled. The fact that the press delayed publication of Reddick's book by six months to avoid competing with King's did not help matters. Reddick nevertheless did his best to promote it, notifying or sending copies to a wide array of figures, including Ralph Bunche, E. Franklin Frazier, John Hope Franklin, Howard K. Beale, Arthur Schlesinger, Earl Thorpe, Lerone Bennett, and even Vice President Richard Nixon. He questioned whether the press was doing its part: "I must be missing the promotion that Harper's is putting behind *Crusader without Violence*," he wrote Arnold.[76] All told, the book had sold about six thousand copies several months after publication.[77]

The reviews the book did get—many within black periodicals—were laudatory. Several reviews praised it for including little-known facts about a man covered so exhaustively by the media. For that accomplishment alone, Ernestine Cofield of the *Chicago Defender* hailed *Crusader* as "undoubtedly a book every American should read."[78] The reviewer in the *Negro History Bulletin* gushed, "Reddick cuts through . . . with facts" the "many fictions" surrounding King and the Montgomery story.[79] Many newspapers were happy to share some of the book's shocking findings, such as the *Los Angeles Tribune*'s discussion of how King had "tried to commit suicide" as a child, and how at Crozer "a white fellow student threatened to shoot him."[80] Much praise was rightly heaped on the book's portrayal of black America, which included leaders such as Roy Wilkins and A. Philip Randolph, institutions such as Morehouse College and Ebenezer Baptist Church, and business and cultural districts such as Auburn Avenue.[81] Another review in the *Chicago Defender* considered the book "the latest and most up-to-date account of what the Negro is struggling for."[82]

Black intellectuals generally approved.[83] James Baldwin used it to inform his investigative journalism into the movement, which he famously covered for *Harper's Weekly*.[84] J. Saunders Redding, keen to the book's literary qualities, noted in the *Afro-American* that Reddick "has filled the story with characters, pointed up its drama, indicated its complete meaning for today," all of which were "sharpened" by Reddick's "acute sense of history."[85] In the *Pittsburgh Courier*, Benjamin Mays called it a "moving book" which along with *Stride toward Freedom* was the most significant study of "the race question" in recent years.[86] In the *National Guardian*, Du Bois was also generally admiring of Reddick's efforts, but he had a less sanguine view of King himself. Reddick had become Du Bois's main source of information on King and the developing southern struggle, but King's approach seemed limited to him. Du Bois considered the portrait of King "a little disturbing. . . . His doctor's thesis is on a vague theological problem about the power of God as pictured by two of his theological teachers." Furthermore, King's nonviolent tactics seemed terribly inadequate to Du Bois, who had learned the hard way that "in order to stop lynching and mob violence, Negroes must fight back. . . . It is a very grave question as to whether or not the slavery and degradation of Negroes in America has not been unnecessarily prolonged by submission to evil."[87]

Crusader without Violence was the most important publication of Reddick's career, and the one for which he would become best known. Unlike most of his black scholarly friends, his contribution was no historical monograph pitched at an academic audience. Reddick's was fundamentally an activist book, written on an urgent subject and calculated to have an immediate public impact. Though informed by his broad historical training and insight, Reddick adapted those skills to advance the larger black freedom struggle. In doing so, he embodied the activist-intellectual type at its best.

Trip to the Land of Gandhi

Immediately after the publication of *Crusader without Violence*, Reddick seized another opportunity to promote King and SCLC. In the winter of 1959, he was the sole companion of Martin and Coretta during a monthlong sojourn to India. The trip had been years in the making, as various difficulties had delayed the Kings' acceptance of Indian prime minister Jawaharlal Nehru's official invitation. The Quakers greased the wheels by providing financial and logistical support, coordinating with the Gandhi Peace Foundation in India. Both organizations were committed to spreading nonviolence and thus found in King an important ally.[88] The trip was one that King had dreamed of making ever since he heard Mordecai Johnson's speech. Reddick, too, had long been interested in India's anticolonial struggle, and he frequently drew comparisons between those in Africa and South Asia. For instance, he never missed an opportunity to mention that Azikiwe had been dubbed the "Nehru of West Africa," or that "Zikism is comparable to Gandhism in India."[89]

Reddick later confessed to being honored but also a bit surprised by the Kings' invitation to join them. Nevertheless, it was a natural outgrowth of his relationship to Martin and the movement.[90] Besides being King's close mentor and friend, Reddick was an internationally minded historian who was well equipped to document and publicize the trip. He performed both tasks admirably. He helped prepare King's speeches, handled press conferences, adapted the travel itinerary as he saw fit, and took copious notes that formed the basis on an unpublished book manuscript entitled "With King through India: A Personal Memoir." King's inclusion of Reddick also underscored how the journey was intended chiefly to be a strategic one: to advance the black freedom struggle by attracting positive international attention to King and his campaign of nonviolent resistance.

The trip's clear political thrust, amplified by Reddick's heavy hand, ruffled some feathers. Reddick quickly butted heads with James Bristol, the Quaker representative in India, who had spent months organizing the trip and developing a detailed itinerary taking King across the country to give him face time with many prominent Indians. Reddick thought Bristol was overextending the Kings and not providing them with enough good publicity. He also resented that the Quakers seemed to consider Reddick an unnecessary addition to the travel party. Bristol, for his part, believed that Reddick was wrecking the itinerary and insulting Indians by focusing so extensively on media coverage. In a letter to a Quaker colleague at home, Bristol complained, "King leaned heavily on him for advice, with the result that Larry [Reddick] determined in probably 75% of the cases whom King would see or not see, which engagements would be kept or cancelled."[91] Furthermore, Bristol charged that "all three had an almost fanatical interest

Lawrence Reddick, second from right, sitting across from Coretta Scott King and Martin Luther King Jr. among a group of Indians, 1959. Courtesy of the Photographs and Prints Division, Schomburg Center for Research in Black Culture, New York Public Library. Reprinted by arrangement with the Heirs to the Estate of Martin Luther King Jr., c/o Writers House as agent for the proprietor New York, New York. © 1959 Dr. Martin Luther King Jr. © renewed 1987 Coretta Scott King.

in snapshots, pictures and newspaper publicity. Many Indians noticed this and even commented on it. Almost before greeting a person or group they were posing for [the] camera (they carried three wherever they went)." Clearly, Bristol had a very different conception of the trip's purpose. He came to resent that the Kings "seem almost totally disinterested in sightseeing, and shopping, and the remarkable art and craft work of India," and that their true aims were "to build up King as a world figure, and to have this build-up recorded in the US."[92] Reddick, occasionally prone to obstinate and curmudgeonly behavior, only deepened the divide by making his contempt of Quaker "interference" known.

As politically focused as Reddick and the Kings were, they could not help but be awed by the twelve-thousand-mile journey to and through India. In speeches afterward, Reddick shared some of his impressions. The first of these was the "crowded humanity" there, which created "big and staggering" problems over "poverty, housing, unemployment, malnutrition, etcetera." Yet though the country was "over crowded and half starved," Reddick marveled, "the Indian people do not quarrel and fight as much as we seem to." He was particularly impressed by India's leaders, many of whom he met as they traveled to the four corners of India, visiting major cities such as Bombay, Calcutta, New Delhi, and Madras. He observed admiringly, "The top men in government . . . are intellectuals," and "The dreamers and philosophers run India." The visit naturally included an education into Gandhi's life and legacy—Gandhi died in 1948—through visiting key historical sites and speaking with his contemporaries. Vinoba Bhave, "India's greatest living saint," most influenced Reddick and the Kings. He carried forward Gandhi's ideals by leading a land reform movement in which activists would walk "from village to village; from state to state, asking rich land owners to give up one-sixth of their holding to landless peasants."[93] Clearly inspired, Reddick told King that he could become the American Vinoba Bhave, but that doing so would require that he devote himself "full time to Crusading and thus give up his church and all other means of assured income." Reddick doubted that would ever happen. "He will continue to be a crusader in a gray flannel suit," he remarked.[94]

As Reddick's comment suggests, the political implications of the trip always took center stage. His chief public-relations strategy was to emphasize that the African American struggle was but one part of the global struggle for democracy and justice being waged by colonized peoples. This emphasis found a receptive audience. For instance, an activist author and political exile from South Africa, Pranshankar Someshwar Joshi, learned of King's visit to Rajkot, India, and wrote to King asking if they could meet to discuss "the problems of race discrimination in the U.S.A. and South Africa." He told King that Johannesburg "had an identical strike" to the one in Montgomery. "African workers walked 14 miles a day to and from Alexandria Township as a protest against the bus fare rise," he explained.[95] Furthermore, Indians generally seemed to identify with the African American plight, and leading Indian newspapers covered their struggle. African students at Delhi University likewise followed the events in Montgomery and eagerly sought out a meeting with King.[96]

Reddick cemented the international theme by shaping King's interactions and public statements. This began even before the traveling party had arrived in India. On a brief layover in Paris, he arranged for a private meeting between King and Richard Wright. He later recalled that "King was relaxed and philosophical while Wright was questioning and critical of the social order. Even so, each of them privately told me how great the other

Lawrence Reddick sitting between Richard Wright and Martin Luther King Jr., in Paris, France, 1959. Courtesy of the Photographs and Prints Division, Schomburg Center for Research in Black Culture, New York Public Library. Reprinted by arrangement with the Heirs to the Estate of Martin Luther King Jr., c/o Writers House as agent for the proprietor New York, New York. © 1959 Dr. Martin Luther King Jr. © renewed 1987 Coretta Scott King.

was. They embraced as we parted."[97] Eager to have this meeting of prominent African American intellectuals publicized, Reddick made sure King discussed it in subsequent public statements.[98] The meeting also renewed the friendship between Wright and Reddick, as they had lost touch since their shared years in Chicago and New York. Afterward, Reddick wrote to Wright, "I think of you as a sort of outpost for us, very strategically located where currents of attitudes from Europe, Africa, the Middle East and at times the Far East swirled together. To me it is valuable to have a man in such a spot and it is interesting that you've chosen to remain an American in Paris."[99]

When King sat down for the most important meeting of the trip—with Prime Minister Nehru on February 10—Reddick had already strategized with King about how to focus on nonviolence and the parallels between the

African American and Indian struggles.¹⁰⁰ He also encouraged King to ask about the possibility of Indian universities sponsoring African American students, which Reddick had long promoted as a practical means of supporting cultural exchange and international solidarity.¹⁰¹ In the trip's opening press conference the day before, King made sure to mention Nkrumah's commitment to nonviolence in Ghana and the successful bus boycott in Johannesburg.¹⁰² Furthermore, Reddick had a heavy hand in shaping King's comments upon his return to the United States, including in his press conference in New York City and his widely read article "My Trip to the Land of Gandhi," published in *Ebony* in July 1959.¹⁰³ Reddick seems to have written King's press conference remarks, in which King noted critically, "India appears to be integrating its untouchables faster than the United States is integrating its Negro minority."¹⁰⁴

Reddick had a smaller platform than King, but he emphasized the same themes in his own public comments. The Dexter Avenue Baptist Church in Montgomery and the First Congressional Church in Atlanta were two of his early venues. Trying to stoke solidarity across new national and ethnic lines, he told the black congregants about how Indians had embraced King as the American Gandhi. "We have found a land of 400 million new brothers," he declared triumphantly. Reddick was particularly effective at using the case of the "untouchables"—members of the lowest caste in Indian society who had been confined to lives of misery and ostracization—for both edification and critique. Despite the nearly unparalleled levels of stigma and oppression endured by the untouchables, Gandhi rather quickly transformed their status by adopting one into his family, by leading them by the hand into sacred temples from which they were excluded, and by threatening to fast himself to death if changes were not made. In a clever analogy, Reddick remarked, "Compare all this to what we have done in America on the Negro question. Do we see any of our top governmental officials in Washington taking Negro children by the hand leading them into Central High School in Little Rock? Do we see our leaders placing their moral force behind the decision of our Supreme Court?"¹⁰⁵

Reddick was particularly impressed by the Indian government's bold steps to attack caste inequalities. In addition to passing federal laws prohibiting caste discrimination, the government reserved a share of seats for untouchables in the Indian legislature and in the civil service, gave them preference in applications for college and public housing, supported a broad program of public education and propaganda to promote their cultural acceptance, and provided them monies for vocational training. These policies anticipated and, in fact, exceeded American Affirmative Action initiatives years later. Reddick helped to build the momentum, presenting a detailed overview of India's policies before the Institute on Non-Violence and Social Change in at Spelman College in July 1959.[106] Reddick would continue to reflect upon and write about his trip to India for years to come.

Sitting In and Casting Out

Though the bus boycott had compelled Reddick to stay in Montgomery, the student sit-ins ultimately precipitated his departure. For decades, African Americans had protested discriminatory treatment in restaurants and other public accommodations by refusing to leave until they were served or forced to leave.[107] In February 1960, however, those scattered protests exploded into a full-blown mass movement. These events, which began in Greensboro, North Carolina, when four black college students sat-in at a local Woolworth's lunch counter, signaled a new phase of the black freedom struggle in which young people rose to the fore. Within weeks, thousands of college students were engaging in sit-in demonstrations across the South. Those in Nashville were particularly successful, largely because they were spearheaded by a disciplined group of activists who had been training for months under James M. Lawson, an expert on the methods of nonviolent resistance who had helped King and countless others put them into practice.[108] Montgomery, too, emerged as an important theater for the sit-in movement, which once again placed Reddick in the right place at the right time. He again acted as a participant-observer of the dramatic events, but this time he would pay a price for his involvement.[109]

Segregationists in the border states greeted the student sit-ins with fierce resistance, but this paled in comparison to the wrath of Deep South states like Alabama. In the wake of *Brown v. Board of Education*, states in the Upper South generally resisted school integration by admitting only a token number of black students to white schools and then declaring themselves fully compliant with the law. Alabama chose a different path. In 1956, state legislators passed a law allowing school boards to close public schools rather than admit a single black student. The bus boycott in Montgomery had stoked a white rage that verged on hysteria. This became painfully clear when white Montgomerians elected to close fourteen parks, fill a city swimming pool with cement, and sell off the animals from a local zoo rather than capitulate to federal court orders to integrate.[110] Such a burn-it-all-down defense of Jim Crow is precisely what won John Patterson the state governorship in 1958. "If a school is ordered to be integrated, then it will be closed down," he promised voters.[111] Having staked his political career on preserving segregation, Patterson became an especially vicious opponent of the local civil rights movement. Alabama State College (ASC) had long ago emerged as one of his favorite targets, not only because it was home to many local civil rights leaders but also because it was partly supported by state funds and hence subject to government scrutiny. He oversaw a special state committee that sent evaluators to monitor the activities within the college's classrooms from 1958 to 1960. "The move was one of intimidation," Jo Ann Robinson understood well.[112] So when the sit-ins began among students at ASC, Patterson was quick to leverage all his powers to crush them.

The first sit-in began innocently enough. Levi Watkins, an administrator at ASC who became its president in 1962, recalled that the students were fired up by the larger movement and felt "restless to do *something* in Montgomery."[113] After careful deliberations among themselves and with Ralph Abernathy the night before, thirty-five students had a sit-down strike at the snack bar of the Montgomery County Courthouse on February 25, 1960. Employees there closed the restaurant after refusing to serve them, prompting the students to quietly return to campus, carefully obeying all traffic signals to avoid potential police harassment. They encountered no resistance. As Reddick recorded in his notes, the students felt "a deep sense of satisfaction that they had identified themselves with the sitdown movement."[114] They were proud of being the first ones to bring the sit-in movement to the Deep South.[115]

That first sit-in ended up being only the opening salvo of a months-long campaign that would transform the lives of ASC students. White men carrying bats were already roaming the streets and attacking black men and women when, on March 1, Governor Patterson ordered the expulsion of all the students who participated in the courthouse sit-in. Eighteen hundred students marched on the state capitol in response, uttering the Lord's Prayer and singing the national anthem. The following day, the state board of education ordered the expulsion of nine sit-in participants and placed the others on probation. On March 4, the Montgomery Improvement Association joined the protest and planned a march on the capitol for Sunday, March 6. As one thousand marchers gathered in Dexter Avenue Baptist Church that Sunday, six hundred law enforcement officers and upwards of ten thousand white people waited outside, many of whom were carrying knives and other weapons. The police made no effort to control the menacing whites as they hurled epithets at the protesters, but miraculously no serious violence broke out that day. Students protests over the student expulsions continued into the next week. During one protest on Tuesday, March 8, which featured students showcasing placards that read "1960 not 1860," "9 down, 2,000 to go," and "Democracy died March 4, 1960," the police arrested thirty-five students and one instructor on charges of disorderly conduct. This in turn sparked weeks of protests in which hundreds of students participated. Three hundred of these students were eventually thrown out of school on a technicality over class registration. And so it went. In the end, the governor, the police, and the state board of education joined forces to arrest, fine, expel, verbally abuse, and otherwise intimidate ASC students for daring to challenge Jim Crow.[116]

As with the bus boycott, Reddick attended the mass meetings and documented the fast-moving events as they unfolded. He also published another timely article in *Dissent* that captured the essence of the struggle. Entitled "The State vs. the Student," the article required no embellishment or literary flourishes to convey the drama. The most revealing incident that Reddick described, however, was a subtle one that grew out of his close involvement on the ground. It occurred as the police were breaking up the peaceful campus protest on March 8. One officer dared "the meanest nigger in the crowd" to step forward and challenge him, while another arrested "five of you nigger gals" and ordered them into his squad car. After this, an officer turned over a placard that read "It's a shame!" After a moment's pause, both the students and the police began laughing. Nothing could have better captured the absurdity of the moment, in which policeman were treating peaceful college students as dangerous criminals and existential threats. The "contestants" in this "racial war in Alabama," Reddick wrote, were a study in contrasts: "enlightenment vs. crudity, the book vs. the billet, a song vs. epithets, and black vs. white." Righteousness was squarely on the side of the students, and they knew it. "Jails, courts, police guns and badges have become symbols of a decayed social system now grown desperate and a bit absurd," Reddick explained. Segregationists' actions thus served to embolden rather than intimidate protesters, stoking a transformation that would infuse the rest of the decade with energy. "The young people have discovered sources of strength and courage within themselves. . . . Whatever happens," he concluded, "they have won, for all of the guards in Alabama cannot make men believe in a system that they know is evil and corrupt."[117]

Students were never Patterson's chief target, however. He was after the ringleaders of the local civil rights movement, many of whom he and the police believed to be professors at ASC and thus directly responsible for the students' rabble-rousing. Nothing came from the monitoring of classrooms during the last two years, so he took more drastic measures. On March 1, in addition to his calls for student expulsions, Patterson ordered the state board of education to investigate all faculty members for "disloyalty," which meant supporting civil rights. The state superintendent of education heeded the call and launched a full-scale investigation of the campus. Levi Watkins recalled, "State investigators and city detectives in plain clothes could be seen on and near the campus at any time."[118] When the state board of education convened on March 25, Patterson demanded that disloyal faculty members be fired, and he publicly rebuked ASC president H. Councill Trenholm for allowing "agitators" to run the school. Trenholm reluctantly bowed to Patterson's will.[119] Meanwhile, the *Montgomery Advertiser* piled on with its one-sided coverage.[120] One article quoted police commissioner L. B. Sullivan when he floated the idea of closing ASC altogether because of its faculty members' efforts to "incite racial violence" and churn out "graduates of hate and racial bitterness."[121]

Reddick feared a reprise of his firing from Atlanta University and saw the walls closing in, but he tried to defend himself. On April 12, he asked Trenholm for stronger contractual protection for his position as well as "assurance that I can continue to discharge a few of the ordinary rights and duties of citizenship." "I have always felt that you and I had an understanding about such matters," Reddick wrote, "but, here again, forces beyond us are presently intervening."[122] He also reached out to many others for support, making sure that a variety of national organizations such as the NAACP, SCLC, the American Civil Liberties Union, and the American Federation of Teachers were aware of the situation and were issuing public rebukes of Patterson and the school board.[123] King had moved to SCLC headquarters in Atlanta a few months earlier, but he remained deeply involved with and concerned for his friends in Montgomery. More than anyone, he and SCLC put pressure on Patterson, writing letters to all parties involved and issuing regular press releases.[124] For instance, on April 14, the SCLC wrote to Patterson decrying the "fantastic charges" against ASC teachers and pledging "our aid and support to any victim of the violation of academic freedom and the right of citizenship."[125]

To almost universal consternation, Trenholm refused to stand up to Patterson and defend his employees. His position was difficult if not impossible, but he seemed to believe that he could make reasonable compromises with an unreasonable man and thus refused to make assurances to his ASC colleagues. In conjunction with the campaign of harassment that the faculty and staff had endured, this prompted a wave of resignations at the end of the spring semester. Jo Ann Robinson and Mary Fair Burks, two key figures within the Women's Political Council and the Montgomery Improvement Association, were among them. So, too, was Reddick, who could hardly believe that he was being pushed out of yet another job. He resigned effective August 31, after the summer term.[126]

Yet Patterson was still not satisfied. He had built up a deep well of resentment toward local civil rights leaders, and after having made his crusade against them so public, he felt compelled to further humiliate and damage them. Because Reddick was a close associate of King's and an active participant in the sit-ins, he quickly became the chief target of the governor's vitriol. Patterson began gathering information on Reddick that could be used to discredit him. When the Alabama Public Safety Department handed him Reddick's FBI file, in which a few informants had accused him (falsely) of being a Communist, Patterson found his line of attack. By 1960, segregationists had firmly established in the public's mind the link between Communism and civil rights, so the tactic was not new. But it was effective. Patterson shared the report with the ten-member state board of education on June 14 as part of his push to have Reddick fired immediately. After reading the report, the board voted nine to one to do just that.[127] It allowed Reddick no hearing in which to defend himself (which was the reason for the one vote against the decision), and in eerily menacing language, it ordered him to leave town "before sunset."[128]

This stunning turn of events provoked a national backlash. Reddick was emboldened to fight back "tooth and nail," as he told Du Bois.[129] In remarks widely quoted throughout the press, he declared, "The real reason Governor Patterson fired me was because of the biography I wrote of Martin Luther King and because of the sit-ins that have taken place in Montgomery."[130] Elsewhere, he sounded the alarm that "Segregationists are out to punish any student or teacher who dares speak out with courage and dignity."[131] But more important than his own comments was how he and his allies galvanized various national organizations to condemn Patterson's behavior. Besides the NAACP, SCLC, and the MIA, the American Association of University Professors (AAUP), the American Civil Liberties Union (ACLU), the Interdenominational Ministerial Alliance, the University of Chicago's Department of History, and other organizations issued stern rebukes.[132] The ACLU stated, "We fear that you and the State Board of Education have fallen into the error of equating with Communism the indigenous Southern movement to attain racial equality by non-violent means."[133] Roy Wilkins of the NAACP reiterated that point. So, too, did SCLC, which avowed defiantly: "History will record who the true pro-communists are. They will not be the Negro citizens . . . but the Governor Pattersons, who through defiance of the law, undemocratic and unethical practices, and the tragic sabotage of justice, give Russia and all of her allies a strong propaganda tool to appeal to the uncommitted peoples of Asia and Africa."[134] Remarkably, even one white newspaper in Alabama, the *Lee County Bulletin*, criticized the governor for denying Reddick a hearing and "giving way to anger and hysteria."[135]

The national outcry notwithstanding, the school board refused to reverse its decision or to grant Reddick a hearing. And though the criticism caused irreparable damage to the reputation of Alabama's educational system, the greatest costs fell squarely upon Alabama State College. It lost many of its best professors, student enrollment plummeted, and the school lost its accreditation and faced censure from the AAUP for two decades for its violation of academic freedom and due process.[136] Moreover, even though Trenholm had kowtowed to Patterson, once stating publicly that the demonstrations were a product of "outside agitators" and that students would no longer be permitted to protest, he was pushed out as president of ASC.[137] At the same time, Patterson's actions only seemed to shore up support among his segregationist base and further cement the link between Communism and civil rights in the public mind. The *Montgomery Advertiser*'s shameless focus on Reddick's alleged Communist ties ensured that linkage in Alabama.[138] National papers played a role too. Leading papers like the *New York Times* chronicled the various Communist allegations against Reddick without contextualizing or critiquing them.[139] Meanwhile, former President Harry Truman was going around the country claiming that Communists were the ones orchestrating the student sit-ins.[140] "The present revival of McCarthyism is by no means confined to the South," declared the *Chicago Defender* in 1962.[141]

Reddick was by now accustomed to starting over after controversial departures. The national outcry upon his dismissal vindicated him, and like all ASC professors who had resigned that year, he consoled himself with job offers. He seriously entertained one from Lincoln University in Missouri, where Lorenzo Greene had invited him to replace William Sherman Savage upon his retirement that year.[142] To stay closer to the center of things, Reddick opted to take a professorship at Coppin State College, a black school in Baltimore named after Fannie Jackson Coppin, the first African American woman to earn a college degree in the United States.[143] He would continue to play a major role in SCLC and the southern movement, but as the physical and spiritual heart of the civil rights movement shifted to the urban North after 1965, Reddick once again found himself to be strategically located. A chapter he published in a notable anthology, *The Southerner as American* (1960), provided a fitting conclusion to his life in Montgomery. As usual, he went out with a flourish, calling upon all thinking people to "remind our nation, our section, our people, of the values, experiences, and dreams that we share. Therein we might discover at the least a common humanity and a universal destiny."[144]

6 The Search for Black Power in the Sixties

> The real struggle of the poor is not against illiteracy, hunger or disease, but against powerlessness. They want self-determination. This is the war they will join—the war to shape their own lives.
> —Lawrence Reddick

If Reddick ever allowed himself a moment of quiet contemplation in the late 1950s, he must have marveled at the dramatic changes both within his own life and the larger black freedom struggle. Africa was reaching its decisive period of independence, and two of his own friends, Kwame Nkrumah and Nnamdi Azikiwe, were spearheading it. Blacks in the American South were ushering in a new period of mass resistance, and he and his friend Martin Luther King Jr. had become important leaders of it. In early 1960, therefore, before being fired from Alabama State College, Reddick had surely been set on staying in the South and committing to the struggle there for the foreseeable future. But people rarely have the luxury of choosing the circumstances under which they must live. For Reddick, this felt especially true.

Yet the turbulence and drama of the 1950s ended up paling in comparison to that of the 1960s, and though Reddick could not have known it, his move to the urban North during that decade was serendipitous. The student sit-ins in the spring of 1960 inaugurated the activism of a new decade, ushering in a new phase of the movement that would shake the foundations of America's racial caste system. Reddick's involvement with SCLC placed him front and center. By the end of the decade, though, King lay dead, the interracial civil rights coalition was in shambles, a strident Black Power movement had risen to the fore, and a fierce white backlash was ascendant. As dramatic as the shifts were, the consistencies within Reddick's intellectual activism bespeak the broad continuities of the black freedom struggle, even as the mood of the country shifted dramatically. As Reddick exemplifies, the roots and routes of Black Power were many.

The Year of Africa

As he battled with Alabama governor John Patterson, Reddick looked to Africa to lift his spirits. His Pan-African agenda never felt more compelling or urgent than in the years surrounding 1960, when African nations began declaring independence at a rapid rate. Ghana in many ways inaugurated the procession in 1957. Reddick was thrilled to be able to attend the Ghanaian celebrations at Kwame Nkrumah's invitation that year. Upon his return, Reddick continued to follow African events closely. Although he could not afford to attend the notable All African People's Conference in Accra in December 1958, he did scrutinize the proceedings and publicize them at home, reporting happily to St. Clair Drake that "we received good coverage in this country."[1] Close friends like Du Bois, Drake, and Horace Mann Bond were all there, not to mention other notable African American intellectuals such as Mercer Cook, Claude Barnett, and John Aubrey Davis. The presence of so many prominent figures highlighted the transformations occurring within Africa at the time, which by almost any measure eclipsed what was happening in the American South. By 1960—the "year of Africa"— the wave of decolonization had become a flood, with seventeen nations winning independence in that year alone.

The All African People's Conference signaled the shifting winds. George Houser, an American Methodist minister and cofounder of the Congress of Racial Equality, documented the proceedings. He concluded, "The Conference announced clearly that African Freedom and independence are a necessity" and would be pursued with renewed vigor. Nkrumah set the tone by opening the conference with a declaration that "Africa is not an extension of Europe." Tom Mboya of Kenya, the conference chairman, followed suit. He played off the phrase "scramble for Africa"—used to refer to Europe's colonization of Africa in the late nineteenth century—to demand that Europe now "scram from Africa." However, serious issues rather than catchphrases dominated the Accra convention. Just as African Americans were debating the issue of violence versus nonviolence, so, too, were Africans. Most representatives agreed that Gandhian nonviolent resistance was the best method of struggle. The Algerian delegates took issue with that because their freedom fighters had determined that violent resistance was the only viable method for resisting their intractable French colonizers. The conference's final decision was thus to commend nonviolent tactics while allowing room for other methods when necessary. There were also regional tensions between Cairo and Accra, and strategic ones over allying with the United States or the Soviet Union, but overall Houser reported an overarching Pan-African sentiment that was broadening in nature. He paraphrased Drake as stating, "Whereas until recently Pan-Africanism has always been a racial concept ('Africa for the Africans'—meaning the black Africans), now a residential element has been added. Anyone living in Africa, white or black, could be a part of the Africa of the future so long as the basic principle of democracy ('One man one vote') is accepted." Clearly, tectonic shifts were underway.[2]

Reddick helped to broadcast the shifts by orchestrating the visits of African dignitaries to the United States. In May 1959, for instance, he helped bring Tom Mboya to Atlanta University. Mboya was a member of Kenya's Legislative Council and the president of the People's Convention Party, and he was a rising star within Africa. Reddick, Bond, Ella Baker, and William Gordon planned a successful Africa Freedom Dinner with Mboya, which aimed to promote Pan-Africanism and according to Reddick "introduce SCLC to the Atlanta intellectual community."[3] Mboya was effective at exposing how the colonizers' logic had warped discussions of Africa. When Western journalists asked whether Africans were ready for self-government, he rejected the premise, explaining how colonization was not about uplifting African people and training them for self-rule. Rather, "colonial systems . . . promote the human and material exploitation of the people and territories concerned," so independence was a necessary step for true progress.[4] During his speech at the dinner, Mboya defended the policy of nonalignment with the United States and the U.S.S.R., but he made clear that he felt solidarity with African Americans in their struggle. King had underlined those same solidarities in his stirring introduction of Mboya, although he framed them in universalist terms: "What we are trying to do in the South and in the United States is a part of this worldwide struggle for freedom and human dignity. . . . We are all caught in an inescapable network of mutuality. . . . Certainly injustice anywhere is a threat to justice everywhere."[5]

Africa's prominence in Reddick's mind was also evident in his persistent consideration of a visiting professorship on the continent. He had begun seriously entertaining the idea in 1955 after being fired from Atlanta University. Nnamdi Azikiwe, whom he had brought to the United States years before, offered him a position in Nigeria at that time. But after Reddick decided to take the position in Montgomery, the events there made it impossible to get away. By 1959, when things appeared to have calmed down at home, Reddick once again took up the proposition. He began working seriously with Drake to secure a position at the University College of Ghana, where Drake was temporarily heading up the Department of Sociology while on leave from Roosevelt University in Chicago. Drake urged Reddick, "I know that you would consider this the high point of your life if you came.... It would be a fitting climax to the many years of devoted work which you have given to the cause of Africa in the United States, and to the study of African history."[6] The two began working out details over salary and travel expenses, but the unreliable international mail service only compounded some of the practical difficulties of the arrangement.[7] Reddick's wife, Ruth, complicated matters through her reluctance to make the trying journey. Drake nevertheless kept encouraging him: "Do not miss coming out this year if you can possibly do so. The Queen visits Ghana in November, and this will be something worth seeing. Nigeria becomes independent in the fall of 1960, and you could see that show on the way home. This year will be a most important one in West Africa."[8] Reddick would continue to entertain the idea in the coming years, but each time the practical difficulties ultimately proved insurmountable.[9]

Yet Reddick was unwilling to miss out entirely on the Year of Africa. Even though he never secured a visiting professorship on the continent, he did arrange to attend the epic celebrations in both Ghana and Nigeria in 1960. His relationships with Nkrumah and Azikiwe allowed him to travel as an all-expenses-paid guest of both governments. Ghana celebrated its inauguration of Nkrumah as president that June, and Nigeria celebrated its independence and inauguration of Azikiwe as governor general that November. These were surreal occasions for Reddick, not least because of his longstanding friendships with both men.[10] They were also prime opportunities to further promote Pan-Africanism. After the ten-day trip to Nigeria, Reddick told the *Afro-American*, "The Nigerians want their American colored brothers to know they are concerned about U.S. race relations."[11]

The trip to Ghana was especially noteworthy. During his six weeks there, Reddick participated in a lecture tour in which he discussed African American mass movements and "the images that American Negroes have of Africans and vice versa."[12] The inaugural ceremonies lasted a full week, but the camaraderie and intellectual exchanges continued throughout. These were especially rich because, as historian Kevin Gaines has documented well, Ghana in these years was a mecca for African, West Indian, and especially expatriate African American leaders.[13] Reddick later recalled, "I talked with Nkrumah privately for a half hour, and with Dr. Du Bois, on another occasion, the three of us systematically reviewed histories and strategies. I enjoyed this tremendously. We talked a lot about the possibility of a 'United States of West Africa.'" The *Afro-American* reported how Nkrumah had called a meeting with Drake and Reddick only three days after his inauguration, symbolizing the significance of African Americans within that vanguard African nation. Nkrumah asked them "to bring him up-to-date on the latest phases of the civil rights struggle in the U.S.A." The men all compared the experiences of black people in both Africa and America, and they drew many parallels. The newspaper reported, "The President's dream of a United States of Africa, the Americans felt, is similar to the dream of a strong federal union for the U.S.A. during the dark days of confederation." Given the constitutional crisis at home, and thinking of his harassment in Alabama, Reddick noted sardonically, "Perhaps a United States of Africa may come first."[14] A few weeks after Reddick returned home from the memorable trip, the sublimity lingered. Drake wrote to him and recollected with his friend: "All of us were jubilant."[15] Yet as exciting as developments in Africa were, they soon took a backseat to those at home.

Servant to the King

In 1960, SCLC was a small, underfunded, and understaffed organization whose future remained in doubt. Five years later it had risen to become arguably the most influential civil rights organization in the country under the charismatic leadership of Martin Luther King Jr. Among other accomplishments, it played a pivotal role in the passage of the landmark Civil Rights Act of 1964 and Voting Rights Act of 1965. Reddick, as King's close friend, mentor, biographer, and fellow SCLC board member, played a significant role in these achievements. Along with other members of King's inner circle, including Ralph Abernathy, Stanley Levison, Clarence Jones, Bayard Rustin, Andrew Young, Wyatt Tee Walker, Cleveland Robinson, Harry Wachtel, Walter Fauntroy, and others, Reddick helped to steer SCLC policy, document its activities, craft King's public statements, fight the organization's public-relations battles, and generate funds. He also provided camaraderie and support for King, who bore the greatest burdens among these activists. Reddick's work on these fronts illustrates the deeply collaborative process of movement work. It also highlights the divisions and often raucous debates among leaders as they attempted to navigate a difficult and rapidly evolving set of historical circumstances. Furthermore, it suggests the important role of intellectuals—particularly those of an earlier generation—in helping to guide the young activists at the forefront of the movement. Years later Reddick opined, "What was missing so much during the black movement of the 1960s was the influence and leadership of intellectuals. We did not analyze enough. We did not write enough."[16] It is true that Reddick's activist work in these years kept him from writing and publishing as much as he would have liked, but in other ways his own example belied that critique. Reddick ultimately had a significant impact on SCLC, and therefore on America.

Progress was slow going at first. Now that Reddick was living and working in Baltimore while serving as a professor of history at Coppin State Teachers College, he lost the close daily interaction with King and others at SCLC. To keep up, he had to follow media coverage and carve out special time with King at SCLC board meetings, which he could not always attend.[17] At times the distance fostered miscommunication and frustration. For instance, in the preparation for the September 1961 SCLC convention in Nashville, Reddick offered to organize SCLC's newsletter until a permanent public-relations person could be hired.[18] This was familiar work for Reddick, and it complemented his ongoing effort to document SCLC's history as the group's official historian. But it was also time-consuming and difficult to manage while working full-time at Coppin State. Without pay, Reddick spent the next few months developing the newsletter. He tried to give timely and "mildly critical" coverage of the organization—"This, I'm told, is good for the soul and inspires confidence among our supporters that we are honest"—and its relation to the Freedom Ride movement of 1961. The Freedom Riders had transfixed the nation as segregationists firebombed buses of peaceful black and white riders who were testing the Supreme Court's *Morgan v. Virginia* (1946) ruling, which declared segregation on interstate transit unconstitutional.[19] Yet when the newsletter finally came out in February 1962, Reddick's contributions were not included. King apologized for the error and attributed it to "a lack of coordination" and "changing staff personnel."[20] But Reddick was not pleased. "I will, of course, forgive you, but this may be one way we sometimes rush ahead, losing friends and failing to favorably influence people," he warned.[21]

Despite the occasional miscommunication, King continued to seek Reddick's counsel throughout the remainder of his public life. Not all of King's advisers knew him so well or for so long—especially before he had become a celebrity. Reddick's strategic advice thus always carried weight with King, and Reddick was never shy about providing it. Littered throughout Reddick's letters to King are recommendations about what to say, when and how to say it, and to whom. For example, the election of a young, liberal, and intellectually minded northern Democrat named John F. Kennedy to the Oval Office in November 1960 boded well for progress on civil rights. But as Reddick and other black leaders knew well, Kennedy was going to have to be pushed and prodded to stand up for civil rights, especially because he did not want to alienate the staunchly segregationist southern wing of the party. This involved continuously notifying Kennedy of conditions on the ground and urging him to intervene.[22] It also entailed publicly praising the president when he took positive steps, such as when on March 6, 1961, he signed Executive Order 10925. The order prohibited racial discrimination among businesses contracting with the federal government and created the President's Committee on Equal Employment Opportunity to oversee it. Reddick told King, "John Kennedy should be commended for making a good start in restoring the faith of Negro Americans in the concern and fairness of the federal government." He also advised that Robert Kennedy, the president's brother and attorney general, "should be commended for his candor and political courage in coming to Athens, Georgia, and telling a white southern audience that civil rights laws and Supreme Court decisions will be enforced."[23]

Reddick also spoke out on these issues himself, and he was occasionally given a significant platform to do so. For instance, at the annual meeting of the Teachers Union of the City of New York in April 1961, which drew over two thousand people, Reddick was given the Union's Silver Jubilee Award for his "inspiring 'crusade without violence' for civil rights, intellectual freedom and human dignity."[24] After the *Nation* editor Carey McWilliams warned of the "new McCarthyism" spreading across the country—epitomized in Reddick's dismissal from Alabama State College—Reddick gave a poignant acceptance speech entitled "Africa, the Confederate Myth and the New Frontier." It called for President Kennedy to invigorate his New Frontier agenda in two ways: by supporting the decolonization and self-determination of African nations, and by advancing the black freedom struggle at home. Because 1961 marked the beginning of centennial celebrations of the Civil War, Reddick specifically demanded that Kennedy take a bold stance against the Lost Cause mythologies being touted with renewed vigor. Reddick argued that "all of these Confederate monuments, shrines, flags, holidays, pageants etcetera have done much to keep alive the memory and ideals of the 'Lost Cause,'" which in turn have created "a great emotional and sentimental wall . . . a barrier to the ideas and ideals of equality, of desegregation, of democracy and other aspects of modern life." He declared boldly,

"We ought to level to the ground every one of those Confederate monuments" and burn Confederate flags, just like Americans did in postwar Germany when "we would not permit the German people to make a hero of Hitler nor to make his war a sacred Lost Cause."[25] The *New York Times* and other national papers reprinted many of Reddick's remarks and put pressure on Kennedy to stand for civil rights.[26]

But Reddick was most concerned throughout the 1960s with making SCLC the best and most productive organization it could be. His most consistent counsel to King and other board members was to be better organized, more reflective and self-critical, and more attuned to practical considerations like financing. All of these proved to be herculean tasks for an organization that was constantly being stretched thin by calls for support from across the country, and for one that relied on donations rather than membership dues (so as not to compete with the NAACP and further divide the movement). Reddick began to sound like a broken record with his advice. Before the 1961 SCLC convention in Nashville, he told King and Wyatt Tee Walker to rein in those "long-drawn out 'country' meetings, in which every 'dignitary' present has to have his say." Rather, meetings should be "more modern and sophisticated," especially because "many thoughtful persons are wondering why it is taking us so long to build a mass movement in the South."[27] After the convention in Birmingham a year later, Reddick advised SCLC to "cut the oratory at bit" at future conventions and "have the Board members eat dinner together each day" to create space for strategic planning. "If the primary purpose of the convention is to think and decide, we subordinated that," he regretted.[28] In the run-up to the 1963 convention in Richmond, Reddick reiterated those points while also counseling King "go a little slow on staff expansion" and not "expand too rapidly" and thereby jeopardize SCLC's solvency. Furthermore, Reddick recommended convention sessions on "What Went Wrong at Albany" and "Lessons from Birmingham," underscoring that "We could learn a lot from reviewing critically our experience."[29]

Beyond such practical advice and strategizing, Reddick spent considerable time helping to craft King's public statements. Because the media had come to equate the movement with the man, King's words carried substantial weight and needed to be carefully constructed. King relied on Reddick and his other close advisers for this crucial public-relations work. The process involved beginning from what Clarence Jones has called an "ideological toolkit" of King's core values and principles and then adapting them into tailored messages for specific audiences. According to Jones, a black New

York–based attorney and one of King's closest advisers, this ideological toolkit included a "philosophical menu" of dozens of ideas, such as "the nonviolent approach to protesting, the idea that it is in the majority's own best interest that Negroes achieve equality, and the economic leverage of boycott."[30]

Although the approach to public relations was straightforward, finding agreement over the content of speeches among King's headstrong group of advisers proved daunting. The most famous speech of King's career—"I Have a Dream," delivered on Capitol Hill as the culminating event of the August 28, 1963, March on Washington—is a case in point. In 2011, Jones published an entire book, *Behind the Dream*, explaining the complicated backstory that went into crafting that speech. As usual, its earliest drafts were written by others: Stanley Levison and Jones. Then, on the night before the march, King met with his inner circle. Jones, Reddick, Bayard Rustin, Cleveland Robinson, Walter Fauntroy, Bernard Lee, and Ralph Abernathy all convened at the Willard Hotel in Washington to devise the final product. Also as usual, a raucous debate then ensued which both helped and flummoxed King as he sought to finalize the remarks. Jones recalled, "Cleve, Lawrence, and I . . . saw the occasion of Martin's address as a major opportunity to stake an ideological and political 'marker' in the national landscape of debate and discussion about civil rights." The ministers among the group thought the speech should draw from King's skills as a preacher and be more of a sermon. The more elder and secular of King's advisers, Reddick and Rustin, disagreed. "Amazingly, for a Christian-based movement, even the Bible wasn't safe territory," Jones remembered. "Bayard and Lawrence saw the use of biblical verse as sometimes obfuscating the 'real' concern, which in their opinion was the legal system. Criminalizing institutional racism would do far more to create a desegregated America than any quote someone could dig up from the New Testament, they argued." This was the type of nonspiritual, pragmatic advice that Reddick routinely offered King. In the end, though, King used the speech that Jones had originally written, but he then improvised the whole section on "the dream" after Mahalia Jackson encouraged him to do so. In short, King's final public statements were complicated, collective efforts, and ones for which Reddick played an important part.[31]

The months following the March on Washington marked a critical period for SCLC. The march had been wildly successful, drawing in a quarter million people and cementing King's status as America's moral authority and the foremost leader of the civil rights movement. Furthermore, coming as it did after the successful Birmingham campaign, which had pushed President Kennedy to send a comprehensive civil rights bill to Congress on June 19, 1963, King and SCLC were at the height of their power.[32] But such success only made the questions going forward that much more pressing. Prior to an October advisory meeting in New York, Reddick insisted that the group "go into some of the big, broad questions that are crying for attention," such as "Where do we go now, after the great March on Washington? Or, what do we do to help Congress pass a decent civil rights bill? What do we do if, in spite of all, Congress does not pass such legislation? And what's our plan, if Congress does?" Beyond such obvious questions, Reddick raised his own abiding concerns over labor and internationalism: "What about our weak labor base? . . . Internationally, should not we initiate private conversations with some of the UN people—especially from Africa and India—to explore the possibilities of legitimate support?" Finally, regarding unity among civil rights organizations, he queried: "Now that we have the big six (really five) civil rights organizations together, can we keep them so?" Reddick fretted over that last question, and he had long worked to resolve—or at least keep quiet—the simmering divisions between SCLC, NAACP, SNCC, CORE, and the National Urban League.[33] For instance, earlier that summer he wrote to both King and Roy Wilkins, the head of the NAACP, reminding them that "we will need every bit of unity we can muster." Any disputes should be resolved privately, he admonished, because "There is no issue between NAACP and SCLC . . . that will be settled in the pages of *Newsweek*."[34]

Such divisions also found their way into SCLC leadership, hobbling the organization as it struggled to navigate deep personal conflicts. The feud between Wyatt Tee Walker and James Bevel was deep and irreconcilable, but even Bayard Rustin, who had just brilliantly executed the March on Washington, became a frequent source of contention. King deeply valued Rustin's abilities, but Cleveland Robinson found him to be "a self-promoting manipulator unfit to be dogcatcher," according to Taylor Branch.[35] More serious were Rustin's documented Communist ties and his homosexuality. He had joined the Young Communist League in the 1930s, and in 1953 he was arrested for homosexual activity—then a crime. That controversial past is what led to Rustin's uneasy and unofficial relationship with SCLC all along. Reddick, choosing pragmatism over principle, contributed to Rustin's marginalization within SCLC. In an April 1959 administrative meeting, Reddick noted, "I pointed out the dangers of the 'enemy' using his record to smear SCLC and that if we used him it should be done unofficially."[36] Yet as with Du Bois, Reddick would never forswear Rustin and remained a friend and colleague. Therefore, after George Wallace (the governor of Alabama who had replaced Reddick's nemesis John Patterson in January 1963) went on the radio in October 1963 and smeared Rustin as "a sex pervert, a Communist, and a draft dodger" whose prominent role in the March on Washington made clear that it was a "communist movement," Reddick worked with Rustin and King to develop a response.[37] Rustin ultimately "demanded an apology from the station and equal time to respond to the attack," Reddick told King.[38]

A month later, after President Kennedy was assassinated in Dallas on November 22, 1963, SCLC had a much bigger public-relations issue to consider. Reddick wrote a detailed letter to King on November 27 suggesting how King should respond. Finding inspiration in Frederick Douglass's speech during the unveiling of an African American monument to Lincoln, Reddick recommended a "generous yet mildly critical" appraisal of Kennedy "from the point of view of our own people and our movement." He confided regretfully, "I do believe that if Kennedy had finished out his second term he would have ended up as completely on our side as was Lincoln at his second inauguration." Reddick counseled that the culmination of the speech should be a "re-dedication to non-violence," underscoring that "Nobody is safe in a violent social order." Kennedy's assassination was only the latest and most high-profile of a spate of murders which also included Medgar Evers and four black girls in a Birmingham church. "This is, you know better than I, inevitable in any society that resorts to violence in resolving differences," Reddick underscored.[39]

On January 21–22, 1964, King's advisers all convened in Black Mountain, North Carolina, for a two-day retreat to decide on SCLC strategy going forward. The same big questions Reddick had raised in September remained as pressing as ever, only now they were compounded by the 1964 election cycle and the entry of Lyndon Johnson into office. Along with Andrew Young, Wyatt Tee Walker, James M. Lawson, Clarence Jones, and Vincent Harding—a young black historian and soon-to-be PhD in history from the University of Chicago—Reddick was given a leadership role in the retreat. He was personally tasked with evaluating the "role of SCLC in this period of change."[40] Because there were no easy answers to strategy questions, serious infighting once again characterized the discussions. The breaks for ping-pong and softball failed to lighten the mood. One of the most urgent concerns was what to emphasize in the undrafted final chapter in King's second book, *Why We Can't Wait* (1964), which had been largely ghostwritten by Al Duckett and Nat Lamar.[41] The key question was how to approach poverty and race in the wake of President Johnson's call for a "War on Poverty" in his State of the Union address on January 8. Whitney Young, the head of the National Urban League, had publicly floated the idea of "preferential treatment" for black workers to confront the enduring legacy of racial discrimination in the workplace. But several of King's advisers, including Reddick, Jones, and Stanley Levison, urged extreme caution in tackling such a controversial issue.[42]

Reddick agreed with those who advised King to scrupulously avoid any platform that prioritized black workers over white ones. He believed that preferential treatment, or what would soon be called affirmative action, was a just policy but one that would backfire politically, alienating labor and undermining the fragile interracial coalition for civil rights. He had already observed white liberals' inability to seriously entertain such an idea when Norman Podhoretz had solicited responses from James Baldwin, Sidney Hook, Nathan Glazer, and Gunnar Myrdal in the pages of *Commentary* in 1963.[43] Instead, both at Black Mountain and in letters, Reddick implored King to focus on "maximum" training and educational opportunities for African Americans. Preferential treatment "is so contrary to the American spirit that our opponents would fasten upon it as our main objective and mobilize opposition against us."[44] As an intellectual who came of age during the Great Depression's Popular Front, Reddick was often concerned with building interracial class alliances. "What can we do to develop Negro-labor unity?" he asked at Black Mountain. "Are we not oozing blue-collar and white-collar whites because of their belief that we want 'preference' and not equality? Should we ask Phil Randolph to initiate a conference of labor and Negro laborers on this question?"[45] Reddick's advice had the intended effect: King gave greater emphasis to the effects of poverty on whites in his book, and in his policy agenda going forward.[46]

Another outgrowth of the Black Mountain retreat was the formation months later of a committee to counsel King and SCLC. This gave a formal structure to the intellectual work behind policy-making, and it is precisely what Reddick had long encouraged. The FBI, which by then was heavily surveilling and wiretapping King and his associates, recorded the development in its records: "On June 22, 1964, an advisory and research committee was formed, with King's approval, for the purpose of writing King's speeches and guiding his actions. Among the members of the group were Lawrence Reddick, Bayard Rustin, Clarence Jones and Harry Wachtel."[47] Cleveland Robinson and white trade unionist Ralph Helstein also joined the group. They aimed to meet once a month to brainstorm broad strategy at a time when King was perpetually busy and overburdened.[48]

Reddick got the advisory group off to a good start with a sophisticated analysis of George Wallace and national politics as they stood in June 1964. That summer was a momentous one. The Freedom Summer campaign recruited privileged white students to help register black voters in Mississippi, and in August the Mississippi Freedom Democratic Party challenged the exclusion of black participation in that state's Democratic Party. Meanwhile, King was bogged down in a campaign in St. Augustine, Florida, and the electoral year was in full swing. President Johnson had proven himself to be a deft politician who was generally sympathetic to civil rights. He had helped shepherd the Civil Rights Act through Congress, which officially became law on July 2, 1964. Yet such gains were already opening the door to a white backlash, and that captured Reddick's attention. George Wallace's campaign for the presidency exemplified the counterrevolution by making a strong showing in Democratic primaries outside the Deep South, including in Wisconsin, Indiana, and Maryland. Reddick observed with alarm that Wallace "actually got a majority (though silent) of Maryland's white vote." He underscored to the advisory group that "the wishes and fears of the average White American are worthy of our study and attention" because they could be "mobilized by the anti-Negro camp on an appeal that is reasonable and correlated with other long-time, deep-seated desires and irritations." With many Americans feeling "overwhelmed by gigantic forces," Wallace cleverly exploited people's fears while muffling his overt racism and emphasizing instead abstract principles like individualism and local control of government. It was on such grounds that Wallace justified his opposition to the Civil Rights Act while campaigning in the North. Moreover, Reddick observed how Wallace deftly reinforced white Americans' misgivings about racial integration by portraying the civil rights movement as aiming to take away the rights of white people. "He painted a picture that was somewhat frightening to the ordinary White citizen and his family—the specter of school bussing, integrated recreation, infiltrated or invaded neighborhoods, etc."[49]

In light of these disturbing developments, Reddick made the case for "new strategies and tactics" for SCLC. Always eyeing the fragile interracial coalition that was so crucial to political power, Reddick reminded his colleagues, "We cannot win without allies." Going forward, "our new strategy . . . must coincide with the democratic, equalitarian creed and must provide a good life and a promise of an even better life for the White as well as the Black American." He believed that many of the movement's successes had been rooted not in these principles but merely in opposition to the "rude and outrageous forms of Southern Jim Crow." As a result, progress would become exceedingly difficult as the struggle moved northward and encountered subtler forms of racism and inequality. To stave off the collapse of the interracial coalition augured by the Wallace campaign, Reddick again insisted that any reference to "preferential treatment" be abandoned. "We are not Negro patriots," he wrote, "rather we are against poverty, discrimination, segregation, etc., without regard for the color or the culture of the victims." Common cause had to be found with principled whites as well as poor whites, Native Americans, Asians Americans, Puerto Ricans, and Latinos. This program of action would become the operating logic of King and SCLC after 1965.[50]

In late 1964, after President Johnson had won a landslide victory over Barry Goldwater and temporarily allayed fears of a fracturing interracial coalition, Reddick's emphasis on the international dimensions of the civil rights movement scored a major victory when King was awarded the Nobel Peace Prize. Reddick again had the privilege of traveling abroad with the Kings as they made the trip to Oslo in December.[51] The award gave King a powerful new platform to link the African American struggle with those of other peoples across the globe. King's advisers spent a full month crafting the acceptance speech, and Reddick played a significant role. For instance, he was responsible for King's reference to Chief Albert Lutuli of South Africa, the Nobel laureate of 1960, which offered a tangible connection between African Americans and Africans. Reddick's other preliminary ideas drew from the "ideological toolkit" Clarence Jones identified. He mentioned how King should accept the award on behalf of the global nonviolent movement, stress that "domestic peace is but the other side of international peace between and among nations," and end with "a plea for all men to renew their faith in the courage, social intelligence and love for man—irrespective of race, creed or nationality."[52] King's final speech more or less did all of these things, stating boldly that "nonviolence is the answer to the crucial political and moral question of our time—the need for man to overcome oppression and violence without resorting to violence and oppression."[53]

Such speechwriting and subtle strategizing could at times feel trivial compared to the sacrifices being made by ordinary protesters. Not the least of these occurred at Selma, Alabama, where on March 7, 1965, five hundred marchers supporting a voting rights bill were viciously attacked by police on horseback wielding nightsticks and tear gas on Edmund Pettus Bridge. Other dramatic confrontations occurred closer to home for Reddick as the movement in Baltimore picked up steam. Reddick, though, was less involved in that struggle, choosing instead to devote his limited energies outside of work to his activism for SCLC—where his leadership role in the national organization naturally took precedence.

By the first half of 1965, as the Selma campaign pressured the federal government to pass the landmark Voting Rights Act of 1965, Reddick was playing the roles he was best positioned to play. Aside from his work in public relations and strategy-making, Reddick continued to serve as SCLC's historian and King's biographer. He had been closely documenting the organization and the man, and he had plans to write an updated biography of King.[54] Although that project never came to fruition, he did publish a booklet entitled "The SCLC Story," which provided a brief history of what had become one of the leading civil rights organizations in the country. It was a celebratory essay which called SCLC "a most decisive influence on the mass of Southern Negroes in the non-violent crusade for equality in America."[55] The jubilation was hard fought and well earned, for SCLC had played a critical role in the broad interracial coalition that had compelled the government to pass the Civil Rights Act of 1964 and the Voting Rights Act of 1965. These landmark bills spelled the end of Jim Crow and capped off the Second Reconstruction. The federal government had finally committed to enforcing the Fourteenth and Fifteenth Amendments to the Constitution, which—though ratified a century earlier—had been honored mainly in the breach. But there was little time for celebration as the national mood shifted rapidly.

The Search for Black Power

After 1965, the white backlash Reddick had been monitoring with apprehension metastasized. A perfect storm gathered to fracture the civil rights coalition and eclipse the authority of King and SCLC. Disturbances in urban ghettos had already broken out in 1964, but in the summer of 1965 they exploded with a new ferocity when the six-day uprising in the Watts neighborhood of Los Angeles produced a paroxysm of violence and destruction that left dozens dead and tens of millions of dollars' worth of property destroyed. President Johnson was particularly upset by the rebellions, seeing them as a personal betrayal of his efforts on behalf of civil rights. He also felt betrayed by King's decision to speak out against the Vietnam War, which

Johnson had fatefully chosen to escalate. The productive working relationship between the movement and the Oval Office was over.

Meanwhile, the alienation, despair, and hopelessness of many urban blacks across the North and West had only deepened after the civil rights movement had failed to meaningfully improve their lives. King's soaring rhetoric had raised hopes for change, so frustrations boiled over when the defeat of Jim Crow did nothing to combat the entrenched poverty, de facto segregation, discrimination, and joblessness characterizing their lives. Although King and SCLC would begin shifting their energies to the urban North, they found their style less resonant and their method less effective there. The vacuum of leadership was filled by a younger generation of Black Power activists whose defiant posture and militant demands frightened white Americans. Mainstream journalists, too, were shocked and alarmed by the Black Power movement. Their obsessive, uncontextualized coverage of the most extreme personalities, groups, and events sowed further alarm and confusion. As Reddick had predicted, crafty politicians like George Wallace and Richard Nixon exploited the fears to win electoral victories and halt the progress on civil rights.

Yet despite the tectonic shifts within American society, the black freedom struggle itself represented fundamental continuities. Earlier histories tended to follow the headlines and posit a decisive, overdetermined break between civil rights and Black Power, with the Voting Rights Act and the Watts rebellion serving as convenient signposts.[56] There is no question that "the mood of the nation has changed," as Reddick put it to King in 1966, but the sharp shifts in moods, media coverage, and rhetoric belie the consistencies of black activism throughout the 1960s and beyond.[57] Reddick testifies to the important continuities of the struggle which historians have only recently begun to emphasize.[58] His publications and scholarly activities, his continued work for SCLC, and his leadership role within the Opportunities Industrialization Center all make clear the deep roots and multiple routes of Black Power in these turbulent years.

Although the Watts rebellion, the meteoric rise of Stokely Carmichael and his "Black Power" slogan, and the advent of the Black Panthers all struck white Americans as alarming new developments, they in fact grew out of a long tradition of black nationalism reaching back many generations through figures ranging from Edward Blyden to Marcus Garvey and Malcolm X. Reddick's own writing helped to highlight that capacious tradition before it rose to public attention in sensationalized form during the 1960s. For example, in *Crusader without Violence* (1959) Reddick discussed black nationalism when explaining why it should not be a surprise that it was a *black* woman who stabbed King in a Harlem bookstore in 1958. The perpetrator seemed to be mentally ill, but she represented many within the black community who "totally disagree with [King] and reject his counsel." "They repose no confidence, as he does, in the good faith of white people," Reddick explained. "They feel that interracial co-operation is a snare, the campaign for racial integration a delusion." Alternatively, "Their immediate hope for a tolerable life in America rests in the doctrine of Negro cohesiveness—Negro businesses, Negro social organizations and Negro standards of culture and physical beauty. Their ultimate hope lies in actual or vicarious migration 'back to Africa,' where the black man will once again govern himself under his own flag and fig tree."[59]

Like most black intellectuals, Reddick moved tactically across the fluid spectrum from racial integration to black nationalism depending upon the circumstances.[60] Whether the best path to black empowerment came through solidarity among African Americans, all African-descended peoples, the working class, peace advocates, all colonized peoples, or some combination thereof was necessarily an open question. But the more militant of "these 'Negro Nationalists' or 'Black Zionists,'" with whom Reddick always disagreed, "feel that the Rev. Dr. King is 'soft' on the 'white enemy' and that he weakens and dilutes 'Negro integrity.'" In 1959, this whole segment of black America generally failed to register within the United States, which made its headline-grabbing appearance in the latter half of the 1960s especially shocking.[61]

As Reddick's own research and writing made clear, black nationalism was not only a legitimate and defensible political position; it was also an organic ideology that rose and fell depending on the perceived possibility for racial progress under the current order. The resurgence of black nationalism in the 1960s was therefore not what the media often portrayed it as: an unprecedented eruption of irrational, destructive behavior. Rather, it was a direct result of the failures of civil rights liberalism to meaningfully improve the lives of many black people.[62] Reddick committed tactically to SCLC's integrationist agenda during the 1960s, but even as he did so, he documented the limitations of desegregation and strategized over how to advance black power in a post–Jim Crow world. As Reddick and other black leaders recognized, desegregation often did not involve real integration, or it involved integration on white terms only, with a concomitant liquidation of black institutions, culture, and power. The Black Power movement was animated by a rejection of that very reality.

Reddick focused special attention on the fate of black colleges, which after *Brown v. Board of Education* came be called "historically black colleges and universities" (HBCUs) to account for the changing student demographics. In 1962, he published a timely literature review in the *Journal of Negro Education*, entitled "Critical Review: The Politics of Desegregation." After surveying the recent social science on HBCUs, he observed distinct problems for colleges in the Deep South versus the Upper South. In the Deep South, whites had defiantly resisted desegregation while continuing to starve HBCUs of state funding. To remedy this, Reddick recommended federal lawsuits and nonviolent mass action to compel integration, but he also emphasized how protest must be accompanied by a restructuring of black colleges to make them more modern and relevant, and hence more attractive to students of all races. Colleges in the Upper South faced very different problems. In Delaware, West Virginia, Missouri, Oklahoma, and Reddick's current home state of Maryland, integration was a reality. Indeed, at Lincoln University in Missouri, one-third of the students were white by 1962. Yet desegregation seemed to create more harm than good for the colleges. Seen by some as no longer necessary in a post–*Brown* world, many of them were closed or demoted to junior colleges in the face of declining enrollments and diminished funding. This precipitated the loss of good middle-class jobs for black faculty and staff. Colleges like Lincoln that were not shuttered faced other dilemmas. The special mission and purpose of these schools—black uplift—underwent a crisis when white students matriculated. So did the quality of campus life generally, because researchers found that many of the white enrollees were commuters who were less invested in campus life. Furthermore, among black students who now elected to attend white colleges, frustration and disillusionment were common reactions. Many of them had internalized the myth that "whatever white folks have or do is better," so the recognition that white colleges were sometimes worse than black ones, and that racism often accompanied an education there, was terribly disappointing.[63]

To address the many problems posed by college desegregation, Reddick encouraged African Americans to continue fighting back in ways they had already begun doing. For instance, Reddick highlighted Langston University, an HBCU in Oklahoma, which faced an imminent demotion to a junior college if not outright closure. The local black community came to reject that fate for its celebrated college, and it organized and petitioned to have the school continue as part of Oklahoma's higher-education system. They succeeded, making Langston University—like the four HBCUs in Maryland:

Coppin State, Bowie State, Maryland State, Morgan State—part of the state and thus able to survive while, crucially, maintaining black control. The victory would in some ways prove hollow given white domination of each state's educational system and budget, but the goal of black institutional control was prioritized given the dilemmas facing black communities in the post–*Brown* world.[64] Had white Americans read Reddick's article or otherwise engaged with the sober black discourse on the politics of desegregation, they might have understood this animating impulse behind the Black Power movement and not responded hysterically to it. But white understanding was yet another casualty of segregation. Whites were not reading the *Journal of Negro Education* and generally remained oblivious to black perspectives.[65]

The civil rights movement did, however, begin haltingly to effect change in the publishing industry. The movement was always a multipronged one with education and citizenship training as key parts. SCLC launched its Citizenship Education Program in 1960, and shortly thereafter brought in Septima Clark of the Highlander Folk School to teach adults—mainly disenfranchised blacks in the Deep South—how to read and participate in the political process. Her intent was clear when she used voter-registration materials as the course textbook.[66] Yet the fight for a real education and appropriate reading materials was a national one. In Chicago, Sterling Stuckey and a group of educators committed to black history formed the Amistad Society, and in 1963 they pressured the Chicago Board of Education to "radically revise its teaching of American history" by according African Americans proper treatment.[67] They testified publicly to the racism within history textbooks and staged the city's first demonstration at the Board of Education offices. Such demands, combined with white America's growing interest in black life because of the civil rights movement, made mainstream publishers take note.

Change nevertheless necessitated struggle even in those publishing houses eager to capitalize on the new market. Doubleday emerged as one of the first houses to commit to publishing a series of youth-oriented books on the history of racial and ethnic minorities in the United States. Reddick grabbed the opportunity to contribute to this Zenith Books series, for which John Hope Franklin served as a consultant and Rayford Logan and Hugh Smythe served on the advisory board. But none of that would have come about had it not been for a young black editor named Charles Harris, who had joined Doubleday in 1956 after serving in the army and graduating from Virginia State College, an HBCU. As a Virginia State man, Harris was aware of black history and such pioneering works in the field as Franklin's definitive overview, *From Slavery to Freedom* (1947). So when white colleagues at Doubleday laughed dismissively at his suggestion that African Americans had played a role in the Civil War, Harris sprang to action. From 1961 to 1965, he worked with countless educators, historians, textbook experts, and curriculum makers to lay the groundwork for the Zenith series, which began publication in 1965.[68]

Reddick had the opportunity to coauthor one of the first two books released in the series. His contribution, *Worth Fighting For* (1965), could hardly have better illustrated the ignorance of Harris's colleagues. The book was a narrative history of the black experience of the Civil War and Reconstruction. Reddick provided detailed outlines of the historical content and themes, while Agnes McCarthy, an editor in the Department of School Services at Wesleyan University, crafted the prose. This teaming up of a prominent scholar and an expert on children's literature was a hallmark of the Zenith series. *Worth Fighting For* ended up quickly becoming Reddick's best-selling book.[69] The Amistad Society celebrated its publication and compelled the Chicago Board of Education to add it to the city's basic textbook list for elementary and high school history courses.[70] Through its circulation within grade schools across the country, the book reached a wide audience. The *New York Times* helped matters along by praising its "superfluity of material" yet "brisk, readable fashion" as it recounted how "Negroes—unwanted by either side at first—ultimately took part in 200 battles, lost 36,000 men, and won 14 Congressional Medals of Honor."[71] In fact, *Worth Fighting For* contextualized the Civil War within the long span of African American history, and it effectively tied the past to the present, concluding: "Today, Negroes have taken up the battle again. They fight not with the sword and bayonet, but with the full force of the Federal Law behind them . . . to insure that every person can get the rights of full citizenship promised by the Constitution."[72]

The success of *Worth Fighting For* was satisfying for Reddick. He had long railed against racism in textbooks and called for black historians to fight back by writing textbooks of their own. As an avid reader since childhood, Reddick also knew the potential of books to transform young lives. At a lecture before a black sorority in the 1950s, Reddick remarked, "Some of our people who do not have a tradition of reading are easily persuaded to do so. Sometimes the simplest way is to start with books by and about Negroes' history and culture." African Americans can then "see themselves and . . . get an opportunity to grasp intellectually what they have known emotionally.

They get an opportunity to see their lives generalized and connected with thousands of other lives and they gain insight and strength from this nurture."[73] Of course, as Harris's colleagues made clear, the books were just as valuable for white Americans who remained largely ignorant of their country's diverse peoples and histories. The Zenith series thus offered an important precedent that was soon imitated by other publishers such as Educational Heritage Inc., which hired Wyatt Tee Walker to supervise its series on black history.[74] Even so, people of color continued to remain woefully underrepresented in children's books.[75]

Despite Reddick's positive experience with *Worth Fighting For*, he soon butted heads with Doubleday in a way that further highlighted the limits of racial integration. In 1966, the company tapped Reddick to coauthor another Zenith book on the slave trade. But by then, Charles Harris had taken a job elsewhere, leaving Doubleday lily-white and without an editor well-equipped to oversee the Zenith series. Reddick felt the impact immediately. He complained to John Sargent, the president of the company, that the new author he was working with was not following the outlines and themes he had provided. As he explained it, "I believe that some of the 'facts' that I included in the outline were so new that both the writer and the editor found them psychologically difficult to accept. African history and even the participation of the Negro in American history, most likely, were not a part of their education. Accordingly, the writer would go beyond my manuscript to traditional sources that I had rejected."[76] The writer thus produced a narrative that failed to "focus upon the enslaved people as the central 'character' of the drama" and "show their resistance."[77] The white-dominated American historical profession was still years away from following black historians like Reddick in adopting these themes and the very different sources and methodologies required to uncover the black experience of slavery, so commercial presses, not surprisingly, were much further behind.

The core issue was institutional racism. White-dominated universities and publishing houses offered only a token inclusion of black scholars, who continued to be marginalized and not credited as authorities in their fields.[78] To protest these circumstances and their impact on the slave trade book, Reddick ultimately abandoned the project. But he first made sure that Sargent heard him on the larger problem: "It is a pity that you do not have men of [Charles Harris's] type, scattered throughout your editorial corps. They could help in detecting some of the low-grade materials on the Negro and race relations that some ill-advised publishers are now printing. Moreover, they could be of real assistance in encouraging talented Negro authors (and others) to complete unfinished manuscripts that one hears about."[79] In the coming years, Reddick would focus even more attention on the racial politics of writing and publishing on black subjects, even though this was a long-standing concern of his. In 1959, for instance, he privately expressed concern to Du Bois about "the way white writers are moving in to exploit the expanding market for books on the Negro's theme." "Some of these writers are competent and serious," he conceded, but "most of them . . . are out for whatever cash or fame they can pick up, without too much regard for truth or understanding."[80]

Just as Reddick's scholarly activities revealed striking consistencies with the concerns of the Black Power movement, so, too, did the work of SCLC, which he continued to help lead. To be sure, the point is not to erase the significant differences between the civil rights movement and the Black Power one. SNCC, led by Stokely Carmichael in 1966, symbolized the divide when it pushed white members out of the organization and prioritized self-defense and black nationalism.[81] Furthermore, Carmichael and others rejected nonviolence as "an approach that black people cannot afford and a luxury white people do not deserve."[82] For SCLC leaders, this separatist, militant orientation was self-defeating in a country in which African Americans comprised only about 10 percent of the population. As before, they focused on creating an interracial coalition powerful enough to force further structural change through the political system. Toward that end, they remained committed to a nonviolent, universalist, equalitarian creed that could find common cause with all peoples but especially among other minorities and the poor. They believed that ceding the moral high ground would be a terrible mistake. Black Power leaders, however, found King's message to be out of touch with the lives of many African Americans, especially the urban poor for whom a more militant black nationalism had wider appeal. They envisioned themselves less as an American minority group and more as part of a global majority of nonwhite peoples. The opposing tactical paths—interracialism versus intraracialism—informed the strikingly different rhetoric employed by leaders of the two movements.

Yet such differences mask the shared objective of empowering black people, as well as the shared supposition that doing so after 1965 entailed a frontal assault on poverty and economic inequality. Reddick even thought that targeted violence was worth contemplating, for he recognized its place within various antislavery and anticolonial struggles of the past. "But, to *start* a riot and not be able to *stop* it, was indeed an indication of the bankruptcy of leadership and the height of irresponsibility," he declared in 1976.

"This was the great strategic blunder of the Black Power phase of the Black Revolution of the 1960s."[83]

Some figures within SCLC disagreed with King's increasingly Northern, urban, and economic focus, but Reddick was not one of them. SCLC had in fact been concerned with economic matters all along. In September 1962, it gave institutional form to economic matters when it launched Operation Breadbasket, which allied with businesses, labor unions, and clergy to pressure businesses to adopt fair hiring practices.[84] After Watts, however, King made black urban poverty his chief concern, launching his People-to-People tour of northern cities in 1965, his Chicago Campaign in 1966, and his Poor People's Campaign in 1968. Reddick supported the shifting focus. At Coppin State in 1963–64, he had personally helped inaugurate an on-the-job-training program to meet black economic needs.[85] At the April 1965 SCLC board meeting in Baltimore, he urged SCLC to support the launch of the federal Head Start program, which soon became the most effective arm of President Johnson's War on Poverty.[86] In November that same year, he represented SCLC at the White House Planning Conference on the Negro, where he served on the education committee and first encountered the Moynihan Report. That controversial memo drafted by Johnson's assistant secretary of labor, Daniel Patrick Moynihan, provided a bitterly stigmatizing assessment of the black family even as it advocated for structural reform.[87]

Yet when none of SCLC's post–Selma campaigns met with much success, Reddick shared his colleagues' frustration. Tempers boiled over for him at a New York board meeting in January 1967. The failures of the previous year's Chicago Campaign, in which city leaders signed agreements but failed to honor them, and in which Black Power activists heckled King while white Chicagoans formed the most "hate-filled mob" he had ever seen, weighed heavily on his mind.[88] So did the botched James Meredith March Against Fear. There Stokely Carmichael had stolen the show and caricatured King and his movement as passive and out of touch.[89] Those failures—in both policy and public relations—only compounded long-standing problems that bothered Reddick. One of those was financing, which had become especially grave now that donations were drying up. Reddick wrote a terse letter to King, Abernathy, and Andrew Young complaining that the board meeting was a waste of time. "Nothing appeared to be planned. All discussions were impromptu. No policy proposals were presented. No guidance was offered for the civil rights crises. Was the session worth calling together busy people from all parts of the country? Perhaps I expected too much." He then voiced the common feeling: "The civil rights movement is in disarray."[90]

Discord within SCLC grew even deeper over the question of Vietnam. King's advisers were almost unanimous in discouraging King from taking a public stand against the war. Even Bayard Rustin, a lifelong pacifist, questioned the wisdom of doing so. At a March 1967 board meeting, Rustin, Reddick, Cleveland Robinson, and Stanley Levison all discouraged King from participating in an April 15 antiwar march to the United Nations Plaza. According to Taylor Branch, Reddick pragmatically counseled that "the march would be sectarian and ineffective because the organizers welcomed all voices, including partisans of the Vietcong."[91] But King would not be deterred. On April 4, he gave the most thorough and passionate antiwar speech of his career at Riverside Church in New York City. It made clear the depths of his convictions, which as a Nobel Peace Prize recipient he felt it incumbent upon him to share. Indeed, the war was the ultimate contravention of his nonviolent method, and it approached genocide in its utter dehumanization and destruction of the Vietnamese. It also siphoned away precious funds for the War on Poverty and other social programs at home while relying disproportionately on poor, minority soldiers to do the fighting. Yet the reaction to King's principled stand was precisely what his advisers had feared. The press, including liberal papers supportive of the civil rights movement such as the *New York Times* and the *Washington Post*, roundly criticized King for stepping outside of his authority to make pronouncements on the war.[92] Even worse, the Johnson administration was irate and would never again partner with King in civil rights. When speaking personally with King, Reddick wrote gently, "I agree that the war is all wrong but I want to devote my limited energies to the urban rebellion."[93] Privately, he was blunter, calling King's move a "fatal blunder" and "a technical and decisive misjudgment."[94]

SCLC remained at an impasse in September 1967 when King's advisers gathered for a retreat at Airlie House in rural Virginia. Over five days of intense debate, the group considered various plans. Folksinger Joan Baez and James Bevel supported coordinating with the national antiwar movement. Hosea Williams recommended recommitting to voting rights in the southland where SCLC had proven itself more effective. Jesse Jackson, who had assumed leadership of Operation Breadbasket in Chicago, encouraged a mobilization in that city. But it was an idea by Marian Wright, a young black NAACP lawyer, that won over King. She suggested a national drive of poor people from across the country to descend upon Washington and camp out there, pressuring legislators to combat poverty. The operation would come to be called the Poor People's Campaign, and it would ultimately be carried out only after James Earl Ray had assassinated King on April 4, 1968, in Memphis, where King was supporting a sanitation workers' strike. Reddick was generally supportive of trying to rebuild SCLC's broad interracial coalition around economic concerns, but at Airlie he quickly grew tired of his colleagues' impractical proposals. Taylor Branch, relying upon the FBI's wiretapped transcripts from the retreat, recorded how Reddick at one point "stalked out with a prickly declaration that he would hear no more grandiose plans while SCLC remained functionally incompetent and nearly bankrupt."[95]

The Essence of OIC

While SCLC struggled to advance its economic goals, Reddick concentrated his energies on a vibrant new black self-help organization: Opportunities Industrialization Center (OIC). In 1966, he took leave from Coppin State to serve as the executive director of the OIC Institute in Philadelphia.[96] Two years later, he offered Coppin his official resignation, which was conspicuous as one of the only amicable departures of Reddick's entire career.[97] Reddick did continue teaching in these years, first as a visiting professor at Johns Hopkins for a year and then as an adjunct professor at Temple, but OIC demanded the lion's share of his attention.[98] From 1968 to 1970, he served as OIC's coordinator of policies and programs.[99] Reddick's four years as a leader of OIC represented a significant new phase of his intellectual activism, and they testify once again to the many routes activists took to black empowerment in the 1960s. Although OIC was a vocationally oriented self-help organization in the tradition of Booker T. Washington, it shared many ideas and approaches with other activist organizations at the time. Indeed, its commitment to community organizing and economic empowerment paralleled that of the Black Panthers and SCLC.[100]

The character of OIC followed that of its founder and leader, Leon Sullivan, who was a stridently independent Baptist preacher with humble roots in deeply segregated Charleston, South Carolina. A one-time colleague of Adam Clayton Powell and A. Philip Randolph, he was an optimistic and charismatic man who at six feet five had a powerful presence. After stints as a chief officer for the 1941 March on Washington movement and a preacher in South Orange, New Jersey, Sullivan moved to Philadelphia to assume the pastorate of the Zion Baptist Church. In the City of Brotherly Love, he focused special attention on the problem of juvenile delinquency—an abiding concern in 1950s America—and its roots in race and class oppression.

He and the 400 Ministers, a group of black clergy, launched a successful "selective patronage" campaign (boycotts were illegal in many places, hence the linguistic gymnastics) against white businesses that would not hire African Americans in anything but menial jobs.[101] After meeting with success, Sullivan turned to the intractable problem of black people's lack of job skills, which was especially acute in ghettos. In January 1964, he instituted OIC to prepare and then place poor blacks in jobs opened by selective patronage. The black community in North Philadelphia's ghetto greeted the program with enthusiasm despite its being headquartered in an abandoned jailhouse. People from across the nation soon flooded Sullivan's office with queries about setting up local OICs of their own, so in July 1966 Sullivan created the OIC Institute to focus exclusively on helping other communities create affiliates. Sullivan tapped Reddick, who already had experience working with the federal government on a job training program at Coppin State, to head up the important new arm of OIC.[102]

Of the many roles Reddick played within OIC, not least was the by now familiar ones of historian, documentarian, and popularizer of the organization. His most lasting contribution on this front came through the short book he published on the nature, function, and history of OIC, entitled *The Essence of OIC* (1971). St. Clair Drake and former Fisk classmate Lewis Wade Jones consulted with Reddick on the project, and they both helped revise the manuscript. The book focused on "the *ideas* of OIC," so even though it was targeted at people who were developing or supporting local OICs, it was a useful introduction for anyone interested in learning about the increasingly influential organization. Indeed, by 1970 ninety OIC affiliates had formed across the country from Boston to Los Angeles to Milwaukee to Jacksonville. Fifty thousand people had enrolled in OIC courses, and more than thirty thousand had found employment in training-related jobs, which netted an average income that was more than double that of trainees' pre-training jobs. In 1969, the organization had even formed an international branch, OIC International, which eventually developed programs in Ghana and Nigeria.[103]

The Essence of OIC does a fine job of explaining the evolution of OIC from a small Philadelphia jailhouse into a national powerhouse.[104] Reddick had originally intended to do a "socio-historical biography" of Sullivan similar to his book on King, but he ended up focusing instead on explaining the nature of OIC and confining a biographical sketch of the man to the appendix.[105] Reddick nevertheless subtly framed Sullivan's activities and OIC's growth within the larger national context. OIC had started as a black self-help operation funded largely by the black community, but it grew into one committed to helping all poor people through support from white reformers, employers, and the government. "It is obvious that the ghetto alone cannot support its economic and social rehabilitation," Reddick explained.[106] OIC cleverly parlayed Americans' cascading fears over the urban crisis, particularly after Watts, into jobs for those in the nation's predominantly black ghettos. In speeches across the country entitled "The Urban Rebellion and OIC," Reddick observed that "groups everywhere are falling apart and dropping out of society." He warned of their "turn away from non-violence and the turn toward nihilism, cultism and separatism."[107]

Such fears fed the tide of liberal reformism embodied in President Johnson's "Great Society." OIC took advantage, winning support totaling $45.9 million by 1969 from the Department of Health, Education, and Welfare, the Department of Labor, and the Office of Economic Opportunity—an arm of Johnson's War on Poverty.[108] Republicans like Richard Nixon likewise found Sullivan's "workfare not welfare" approach appealing, ensuring that the program would continue even after conservatives seized power and labored to roll back civil rights.[109] Thus Reddick, Sullivan, Johnson, and Nixon became strange bedfellows in supporting OIC.

OIC's operating structure nevertheless makes clear that the larger organizational objective was a more radical one centered on group empowerment. Despite the outside funding and inclusive framing, OIC was a black-controlled enterprise in which both employees and trainees were overwhelmingly African American. The whole program was bottom-up and demanded that local leaders take responsibility for setting up and operating all OICs. The OIC Institute would offer free guidance and support only when invited to do so. "Maximum feasible participation" of indigenous community members were the watchwords. Like Black Power activists, Reddick and other OIC leaders recognized that "The real struggle of the poor is not against illiteracy, hunger or disease, but against powerlessness." As a panelist at the Maryland State Conference on Social Welfare, Reddick explained, "They want self-determination. This is the war they will join—the war to shape their own lives."[110] *The Essence of OIC* thus goes to great lengths describing the best ways to identify and recruit local talent. Furthermore, the training itself was remarkably student-centered. As Reddick describes it, "Great emphasis is placed upon trainee initiative and participation, the use of audio-visual aids, programmed instruction and, above all, the nongraded class wherein the individual is never flunked out but makes progress at his own speed of learning." All of this was logical given OIC's aims, but

Lawrence Reddick, second from right, standing between Robert F. Kennedy and Leon Sullivan in an OIC classroom in Philadelphia, December 5, 1966. Courtesy of the Photographs and Prints Division, Schomburg Center for Research in Black Culture, New York Public Library. © Jack T. Franklin, courtesy of the African American Museum in Philadelphia.

it also highlighted how much Reddick and other black leaders had come to understand the limits of their authority over the masses in the wake of the urban rebellions.

The character of an OIC education further highlights the organization's radical objectives. Simply having a job, of course, could be radically empowering for those denied the social, economic, and psychological rewards of work. But one's ability to work at all often depended upon counteracting the cumulative psychological toll of living as a poor minority. In addition to counseling services, OIC therefore creatively offered courses in Minority History. These were in the "contributionist" vein of Carter Woodson and Negro History Week, laboring to improve the self-image of job seekers by showing them that "America was built by folks from many lands and that each ethnic group made valuable contributions to this upbuilding." Trainees learned of notable achievers among their group as a way to counteract the vicious stereotypes about minorities that saturated American culture. Black participants learned to link the past with the present by comprehending "the interrelatedness of current Civil Rights organizations and Afro-American and other minority heritage."[111]

Reddick personally developed this curriculum while leading OIC's management training program, which each year prepared a group of twenty recruits to head up local OICs. Reddick brought in business professors from Temple University and the University of Pennsylvania to ground trainees in modern business practices, but equally important to him was his use of the humanities and social sciences to promote group consciousness.[112] Reddick designed Minority History to broaden managers' sensibilities and enable them to appreciate "the possibilities in externally unattractive OIC recruits."[113] He seemed to have fun with this. The managers-in-training must have been taken aback when Reddick placed before them an ambitious exam which resembled one from a challenging college course:

I. Take 20 minutes and list important developments in African history that might be helpful for the world to study, in the following areas: (1) economic (2) political (3) social—especially family life (4) cultural.

II. Take 15 minutes and analyze the relation of the Atlantic (African) slave trade to (1) the development and exploitation of the resources of the New World and (2) its effect on Africa and its people.

III. Take 2 minutes on each of the following, identifying the personality or item: (1) Bishop Las Casas (2) Mohammed Askia (3) Zimbabwei (4) W. E. B. DuBois (5) *Capitalism and Slavery*.[114]

The future managers were also schooled in Urban Sociology in order to "further understand the community served."[115] Here Reddick relied on St. Clair Drake for "a run-down on who's doing what in this field of urban cultures with special reference to minority peoples."[116] Indeed, Reddick consulted with Drake about OIC throughout these years, and he even attempted to formalize those consultations into a research wing of the organization.[117] Implicit within all of this was the idea that the liberal arts were indispensable to the project of group empowerment.

To be sure, there were many limitations and conservative aspects of OICs as well. The organization, after all, accepted capitalism and focused on preparing recruits for the jobs that were available in an area. For residents of inner-city ghettos, there simply were not many decent jobs to be had given deindustrialization and capital flight to the suburbs and the Sun Belt. The structural problems of poverty and joblessness could not be addressed by OICs. Furthermore, in addition to the various financial and manpower limitations that constrained OIC job training, there were few ways to reach the most disenfranchised urban residents, including handicapped people, drug addicts, and alcoholics. More broadly, given the aim of job placement, OICs worked to acculturate workers into mainstream values and behaviors that would make them appealing to employers. This involved teaching punctuality, personal hygiene, and grooming; avoidance of slang or "jive" talk; and "easy, natural, graceful, 'lady-like' and 'gentlemanly' patterns of walking, sitting and moving about." The point was not to encourage unquestioned obedience to these norms but rather to make trainees aware of employers' expectations so that they could successfully find and maintain employment. Still, the instruction was striking when compared with the Black Power movement's unabashed celebration of blackness. OICs, as Reddick explained it, did not proscribe Afros, dashikis, and other symbols of black cultural pride, but they did suggest that workers would have to negotiate their appearance with employers.[118]

OICs were likewise conservative along gender lines. Like most activist organizations, they relied heavily on women to staff the local offices and lead the fundraising efforts. Yet the gendered division of labor relegated them to lower-level service roles throughout. When describing the responsibilities of counselors, Reddick lapsed into the "she" pronoun, later explaining, "It so happens that most of the counselors are female." But this was a symptom of systematic inequality, not happenstance. Women, as the male staffers understood it, were best suited for lower-level positions—especially those demanding "feminine" qualities like sympathy—while men were held to be above menial clerical work and best equipped for leadership roles that demanded "masculine" qualities like strength, reason, and charisma. Of course, these gender ideals were etched indelibly into the whole culture, and OICs administrators were concerned most with recruiting and preparing trainees by whatever means necessary. The messages OIC relied upon were thus often gendered, as when a popular radio disc jockey named Jockey Jock urged male residents to enter an OIC program by entreating, "Get up, get up out of that comfortable bed. Come on down to OIC and learn some skill so you can get a good job—and get your wife off relief. Be a man!" Since many men experienced that idleness as an affront to their manhood— to their ability to preside over a household as a breadwinner—OIC attempted to recruit them through the traditional tropes of masculinity that informed their identities.[119]

Although OIC had its limitations, it was never intended as a comprehensive solution to America's problems of race and class inequality but simply as one tool for empowering the most marginalized black people. Like many within the Black Power era, Sullivan observed the limitations of civil rights liberalism—in this case working with the government to pass and enforce antidiscrimination ordinances in the North. Time and time again, those ordinances had limited effect and left untouched the discrimination in the private labor market. So like Black Power activists, he turned away from interracial politicking and toward mass black protest. His selective patronage campaigns, which built from the 1930s-era "Don't Buy Where You Can't Work" campaigns, influenced not only SCLC but also nascent Black Power organizations such as Philadelphia's Revolutionary Action Movement. Upon meeting with some success, Sullivan developed OIC to tackle the next problem that cropped up: black people's lack of preparedness for jobs made available by selective patronage. In that arena, tactical alliances between white reformers, government, and industry proved essential to the organization's mission. But Sullivan's fundamental concern throughout was empowering black people in tangible ways. Historians Guian McKee and Matthew Countryman underscore this point in their interpretations of OIC.[120] Reddick shared those aims, so he was happy to contribute to an organization that was having a clear impact on the black community, especially when SCLC struggled to remain relevant.

In March 1970, Reddick concluded his services with OIC. Publicly, he explained his departure as a natural outgrowth of four productive years of inspiring but exhausting work. He reported to the papers that he felt comfortable leaving now that he had successfully initiated a "peaceful revolution" within OIC by decentralizing leadership and increasing job security for national officers.[121] He also professed to having grown tired of the relentless travel schedule which left little time for writing. Though he greatly admired Sullivan and considered him a genius, he would not miss the man "calling me up in the middle of the night, saying 'Hey, Doc, you know, I just got a new idea.'"[122] Internally, however, Reddick made clear to the OIC board that his departure was rooted in his great frustration with the organization, including the stalled "peaceful revolution" which he had publicly claimed as a victory. He underlined various "big mistakes of judgment" by OIC, including amateur fundraising operations and political errors that cost the organization hundreds of thousands of dollars. But the issue was more personal as well. He told that board that "during the past year I have felt increasingly that things were going wrong at OIC," the climax of which was a restructuring of Reddick's management training program that placed it under someone else's authority. "This was such a shock to me that I was prepared to go before the Board, the National Industrial Advisory Council and, if need be," he wrote, "before the public and expose this last as just one more example of the great blunders that had been made during the past year."[123] It was an empty threat but one that Reddick hoped would galvanize organizational changes that he viewed as essential. For Reddick, who tended to measure others' appreciation of him by the degree to which they shared his ideas, legitimate policy disagreements often felt like personal affronts.

・・・・・・

Throughout the 1960s, Reddick found many ways to advance the black freedom struggle, including cultivating Pan-African ties through trips abroad and speaking tours, guiding King and SCLC, helping to spearhead OIC, and continuing to research, write about, and document the mass movement. In the summer of 1970, he returned full-time to the academic world by accepting a full professorship at Temple, entering the final phase of his notable career. This role would once again place him at the vanguard of the freedom struggle. Now it coincided with the mass movement to confront institutional racism on college campuses, which was a fight that would forever change scholarly discourse and university life within the United States.

7 Ebony Scholar in the Ivory Tower

All along the line, we see the tendency—and determination—
to limit or exclude Blacks from the seats of decision making.
—Lawrence Reddick

In the late 1960s, American universities became sites of black struggle as never before. For decades, student activists had rebelled against paternalism and racism on black college campuses. Now, as part of the Black Power movement's commitment to confronting institutional racism, black students targeted historically white universities as well, which desegregation had finally opened to them in significant numbers. The extent of the rebellion was breathtaking: sometimes deadly protests rocked over a thousand campuses between 1965 and 1972. The results were no less striking: two hundred universities instituted Black Studies programs by 1972, and university culture became much more openly multicultural. Even as white domination and overrepresentation remained a fact of life at historically white universities, the institutionalization of Black Studies and allied fields including Ethnic Studies and Women's Studies ensured a persistent "formal space for oppositional consciousness," as Fabio Rojas has called it.[1] The extent of the victory has led two of the leading chroniclers of the movement to dub it a "revolution" that precipitated a "reconstitution of higher education."[2]

Activist-intellectuals like Reddick supported the student movement while working out new ways to interface with campus radicals and the Black Power movement. Taking the students' demands seriously, Reddick labored to place Black Studies on a permanent foundation, even as he also pursued a wide range of other intellectual activities. Figures like him benefited directly from how the black campus movement elevated the status of knowledge about black people and inaugurated Black Studies courses and programs. In 2001, historian Stephen Ward argued that the example of activist-intellectuals demand a "re-conceptualization of the Black Power Movement that recognizes the various ways in which black intellectuals, activists, and artists sought to mount a multifarious confrontation with and challenge to American institutional life."[3] Since Ward's essay, historians have only further broadened our conception of the nature and extent of a movement that included these and many other actors.⁴

Reddick's work during the final phase of his career must be understood within this context. As he assumed his first tenure-line appointment at a historically white university in 1970, he exemplified black scholars' varied attempts to upend the ivory tower and institutional racism more broadly. He challenged white dominance in academia, professional history, publishing, and local politics, and he participated in several independent black organizations, many of them brand new. His efforts testify to the changes afoot but also to the constraints that ultimately limited the scope of the transformation.

Intellectual Activism and the BAAL

As much as the academy became a site for concerted struggle, black intellectuals also spent creative energies forming new black-controlled institutions of their own. Reddick was part of this flurry of activity in the late 1960s and early 1970s, though he also continued to play a role in older organizations like SCLC. King's assassination in April 1968 had unfortunately only crystallized the group's decline. Ralph Abernathy took over as executive director, and he insisted on going through with King's Poor People's campaign in which three thousand Americans from across the country descended upon Capitol Hill in May 1968, camping out for two months to pressure Congress to act against poverty. The campaign was widely viewed as a failure because it generated negative publicity without moving legislators.⁵ When police officers destroyed the encampment in late June, *Newsweek* referred to it as "the end of the Dream," and it quoted Andrew Young as saying, "Whoever ran us out did us a great favor."⁶ Young's remark infuriated Reddick, who called for a "moratorium on statements to the press." But he nevertheless tried to assure Abernathy that the campaign was a success, and that the significant showing of white marchers during the culminating event on June 19 signaled the continued viability of an interracial movement for nonviolent social change. Still, he counseled patience, instructing Abernathy "that we ought to 'cool it' for a while, take stock, re-group and re-tool before we move on."⁷ The following year Reddick helped to coin the slogan "Billions for the Moon, Pennies for the Poor" to frame SCLC's July 1969 Cape Kennedy protest of the federal government's lavish spending on space travel while defunding antipoverty programs.⁸ Like so many of SCLC's efforts in these years, the righteous cause failed to gain traction, especially when the spacecraft that departed that July successfully landed a man on the moon and inspired awe throughout the country and the world.[9]

As SCLC's historian and King's former biographer and mentor, Reddick focused special attention on shoring up King's legacy. He continued to write and speak about King for the rest of his days, and he publicly took issue with representations he found to be inaccurate.[10] Furthermore, as he had done throughout his career, Reddick labored to build up an archival repository that would facilitate truthful renderings of the man and the movement for generations to come. Embodying the spirit of the time, he wanted King's papers to be reside in a black-controlled repository. He was critical of King's earlier decision to place many of his papers at his alma mater Boston University rather than the Schomburg Library or the Atlanta University Center. "Does not his special connections with the Negro people suggest some place that would symbolize this relationship?" he asked in 1966.[11] After King's death, Coretta King decided to build a permanent, independent repository in Atlanta called the King Center. Reddick took a position on the governing council of the center's Library Documentation Project (LDP), which was tasked with gathering and cataloguing the primary sources of the movement. Horace Mann Bond, John Hope Franklin, Ralph Abernathy, Harry Belafonte, Andrew Young, Marian Wright, C. Eric Lincoln, Julian Bond, Albert Manly, and others served alongside him on the advisory council that Vincent Harding presided over. By 1970, the project had already collected "over 450 audiotapes, 90 reels of micro-film, and 550 photographs" from all over the country, including the papers of SCLC, SNCC, CORE, James Forman, and Fred Shuttlesworth.[12]

Yet the LDP soon became mired in conflicts that revealed the enduring fault lines between the civil rights movement and Black Power. The King Center became increasingly frustrated by the activities of Vincent Harding, who in addition to leading the LDP presided over the Institute of the Black World (IBW), an Atlanta-based black think tank affiliated with the King Center. Harding and William Strickland formed the IBW to engage with the Black Studies movement, to foster "revolutionary scholarship" and exchange across the African diaspora, and to connect activist-intellectuals with the black masses in the freedom struggle. The IBW's unabashedly radical and nationalist orientation, however, alienated board members of the King Center, who were committed to shoring up the heroic life of Martin Luther King Jr. and his legacy of civil rights liberalism. The center thus took issue with the IBW's marginal treatment of King the man, its "deliberate avoidance" of nonviolence, its exclusion of white workers from the organization, and its willingness to include militant black nationalists like Stokely Carmichael in IBW events.[13] The center leveled similar complaints against the LDP in July 1970, which prompted the governing council to replace Harding with Julian Bond. Yet the council stood by its other practices, including the hiring of black staff members. Similar to Reddick's OIC, the LDP aimed to "deliberately and systematically provide every opportunity for gainful employment and the development of skills for Blacks."[14] In response, the King Center dissolved the LDP governing council, fired twenty-one of its thirty-three staff members, and severed the center's ties with the IBW altogether.

Such internal divisions were painful for Reddick, but he was among the black intellectuals attempting to stay relevant to the black community by interfacing directly with its resurgent black nationalism. This was not always easy for Reddick's generation given the stridency of black youths' demands. For instance, his good friend St. Clair Drake complained that Roosevelt University's Black Student Association "wasn't having much to do with me" around 1967 because he "talks black and sleeps white."[15] In other words, student radicals interpreted his marriage to a white woman as an affront to the Black Power ethos. Drake found this ironic because up until then it was white people who found his relationship objectionable—to the point that he did not consider it safe to live and work in the South.

There are signs that students had doubts about Reddick as well. At Coppin State, Reddick had supervised a program called Y-003 that prepared teachers for inner-city schools, mainly by training candidates who grew up in the inner city. The aim was to overcome the cultural divide between town and gown and to take seriously the indigenous knowledge of community members.[16] In a letter to Drake, after describing Y-003, Reddick remarked, "I think you could use it as a sort of propaganda item in persuading your students that I do identify with the brother and social change."[17] It seems that in this era of cultural nationalism and Black Power, everything from Reddick's clean-cut appearance to his ties to Martin Luther King Jr. and SCLC could arouse suspicion among militants about his true commitment to black liberation.

Reddick nevertheless responded sympathetically to such sentiments. He felt similarly to his friend C. Eric Lincoln, a black sociology professor at Union Theological Seminary, who acknowledged the "generation gap" but insisted that the black campus movement, despite its new confrontational tone and style, was ultimately a "friendly revolution" bent on making America a better, more just place.[18] At an April 1969 speech before Clark College in Atlanta, Reddick stated that "'student unrest' . . . is but an effort on the part of the objects of education to cease being objects and become activists, part and parcel of the collective will of their institutions." Recognizing the tensions on campus, he recommended that "instead of waging a war of attrition, why not simply and honestly make the students a part of the decision-making machinery of the college?"[19] He worked closely with Harding, Drake, and many other black scholars to support the institutionalization of Black Studies. The IBW, the Black Studies seminar at the Aspen Institute in July 1970, and other forums provided the space to formulate strategy along those lines.[20]

This was an era in which black intellectuals routinely broke with mainstream professional groups and formed new black-controlled ones of their own. The Black Academy of Arts and Letters (BAAL) grew out of this milieu, as did the Association of Black Psychologists (1968) and the Association of Black Sociologists (1970), which both emerged after dramatic fallings-out with their mainstream counterparts.[21] As Reddick would have been quick to inform any black militant, black scholars like himself had long been part of efforts to create alternative, independent institutions. In 1969, he was among the fifty black scholars who continued that tradition by instituting BAAL. Its focus on "defining and promoting cultural achievement by black people" reflected the cultural nationalism of the times.[22] The founders created the academy in the image of the first professional association of black intellectuals, the American Negro Academy (1897–1924). C. Eric Lincoln served as the president of BAAL, and he insisted that it was not a "separatist" organization. Rather, he and the twenty-seven other members of the steering committee including Reddick upheld a "non-racial standard of academic and creative excellence," but declared that "the ambiguities of American racism prevent unbiased judgments by that standard."[23] Accordingly, BAAL would serve as a counterweight to the ongoing marginalization of black people by providing a forum to celebrate and support black scholars and artists.

BAAL only lasted until 1973, but it included a who's who of African American elites and gave greater visibility to black America. Members included jazz musician and composer Duke Ellington, playwright Ossie Davis, artist and illustrator Romare Bearden, poet and novelist Arna Bontemps, actor Sidney Poitier, author and social historian Lerone Bennett, as well as a range of accomplished scholars such as John Hope Franklin, Benjamin Quarles, Oliver Cromwell Cox, St. Clair Drake, Benjamin Mays, John Henrik Clarke, Margaret Walker, Vincent Harding, Charles Wesley, and Martin Kilson.[24] Beginning in September 1970, BAAL began hosting annual banquets to promote black excellence in the arts and letters. One journalist set the scene for the inaugural convention: "In a mirthful mood, anchored to a spirit of self-determination and exuberant with self-assertion, some 600 persons" attended the culminating event which honored five people and inducted three more into BAAL's Hall of Fame.[25] Among the former were C. L. R. James and Paul Robeson, and among the latter were W. E. B. Du Bois and Carter Woodson. The selection of these figures was notable because all except Woodson had Communist ties and had fallen victim to America's Cold War repression. Celebrating the dawn of a new era, Benjamin Mays declared, "Whether we agree or do not agree with their philosophies, black people must not allow their names to be erased from the memory of black people. They fought for what every black man should be fighting for—the liberation of black people."[26]

Reddick played a prominent role throughout BAAL's brief existence. He rose to become its vice president in 1970, and his influence was evident in various organizational efforts, including the induction of Du Bois and Woodson—as well as Frederick Douglass and historian George Washington Williams the following year—into the organization's Hall of Fame. Even more, Reddick worked to expand BAAL membership beyond American borders while serving on the Credentials Committee on Membership. He succeeded in having the first African, and indeed the first non-American, join BAAL in June 1971 when Léopold Senghor, the president of Senegal, became a member. Senghor was an architect of Senegal's independence from France, and he was a cultural theorist who in the 1930s had conceptualized the idea of "Negritude," which posited an organic racial solidarity among Africans throughout the diaspora.[27] When Reddick introduced him at the BAAL induction ceremony, he beamingly declared, "Perhaps we have here a rare example of a 'philosopher-king.'"[28]

Reddick's lifetime efforts on behalf of Pan-Africanism prompted the U.S. State Department in 1975 to tap him for an educational tour of East and Central Africa to promote cultural relations between Africans and African Americans. This came after the devastating American defeat in Vietnam, and at a moment of profound transition and uncertainty for America's reputation abroad. After a disgraced President Richard Nixon resigned from office on August 9, 1974, Vice President Gerald Ford replaced him and moved toward détente with the Soviet Union, participating in the Helsinki Accords in July 1975. By then, the anti-Communist and anti-King hysteria, which had prompted the FBI to build a file on Reddick and closely monitor and harass SCLC, had ebbed. The young radicals associated with the Black Power

Lawrence Reddick inducting Senegal president Léopold Senghor into the Black Academy of Arts and Letters, June 1971. Courtesy of the Southern Education Foundation Records, Atlanta University Center Robert W. Woodruff Library.

movement now bore the brunt of the FBI's ire. It was in this context that the State Department now tapped Reddick to facilitate a cultural exchange intended to encourage African nations to become loyal allies of the United States. The turnabout was striking for Reddick, and he confessed to Drake, "I don't really know what's behind all this." But he was also not about to pass up the chance to make his fifth visit to the continent.[29] So over nineteen days, he visited Ethiopia, Kenya, Zambia, Tanzania, and Malawi and sat down with government officials, educators, artists, writers, and other notable figures.[30] In Kenya, he met with members of OIC Kenya and attempted to use those connections—and those with Drake—to meet Kenya's president, Jomo Kenyatta.[31] The trip proved to be yet another remarkable Pan-African event for Reddick. However, Africa already felt like a very different place than in previous years. The glorious days of African independence had all too quickly been replaced by a seemingly endless cycle of corruption, division, and regime change.[32] When the National Liberation Council deposed Kwame Nkrumah in 1966, the hopes for a united socialist Africa already felt like a distant dream.

Pilgrimage to the White University

Back home in Philadelphia, Reddick entered a battleground of his own when he joined Temple University's Department of History as a full professor in the summer of 1970. Although he had long taught at predominantly white universities, he had only done so on a temporary and usually part-time basis. He was therefore never responsible for administering departmental and university affairs alongside the mainly white men who dominated them. This arrangement would prove deeply contentious, and when Reddick narrated the trying saga later on, he referred it contemptuously as his "pilgrimage to the white university."[33]

Prospects appeared bright at first. Reddick had begun teaching part-time at Temple while working at OIC headquarters. He developed good working relationships with business professors there who had helped to lead training seminars for OIC managers.[34] Rather naturally he was invited to and began teaching courses at Temple in 1968, including an undergraduate Economics of the Ghetto course in the School of Business Administration, and later a graduate Afro-American Studies course in the history department. The chair of the history department, Donald L. Wiedner, told the *Philadelphia Tribune*, "We are delighted . . . for Dr. Reddick to move from part-time to full-time work in an area where, for 20 years, we have been trying to develop a fuller range of advanced instruction and study."[35] After four years of relentless OIC work, Reddick found the transition back to a calmer university life "altogether pleasant." "Everything and everybody at Temple was so friendly," he recalled. The dean even allowed him to bring his personal OIC secretary, Barbara Davis, with him to Temple. "And to my most delightful surprise," he remembered, "the President of the University revealed that he, too, welcomed me." At one of the receptions for new faculty members, the president "came up to me, shook hands and announced to the little group clustered about him, 'do you know that this is one of the outstanding Black historians of our country?'" Reddick always took a compliment well, but he was at least aware of it: "Perhaps I bathe in all of this sunshine and accommodation so naturally because I had been 'my mother's favorite child' and most of my life had been around people who, they said, 'let me have my way.'" "At any rate," he concluded, "my debut at Temple was rosy."[36]

Underneath the rosy exterior, however, roiled the same fierce divides and struggles that were rocking campuses across the country. Temple may have avoided the dramatic confrontations of San Francisco State University and the University of Illinois, but student activists there were nevertheless on the move. Indeed, the creation of Reddick's graduate course in Afro-American Studies only came about through student protest, and its realization was seen as only "a first step" toward creating an Afro-Asian Institute.[37] After three years of determined struggle by black students, Temple finally conceded in 1970 and created the institute. Such successes were nevertheless limited by other institutional realities, including the underrepresentation of people of color and the dearth of library materials relating to nonwhite peoples. Reddick set himself to attracting "talented black students" to Temple's graduate program, to stimulating "University-wide interest in black studies," and to staying relevant to the outside community.[38]

Pugnacious as Reddick was in speaking out against institutional racism, he also felt the weight of expectations placed on him as one of the lone black faculty members and worked to match the students' tenacity. In one instance, he drafted a report on university problems and presented it at an April 1971 faculty meeting. He stated bluntly, "The Library does not now possess the resources to sustain the classes in Afro-American Studies." He warned that "unless remedial action is taken soon, some sort of explosion may be expected." Dissatisfied with the faculty's lukewarm response and charging that it had "abdicated a major responsibility," Reddick took his complaints to the media.[39] Before *Philly Talk*, he asked incredulously, "Would you believe it? A university library that boasts of one million volumes does not have one-third of the books that are needed for Afro-American Studies?" He explained how this problem stoked student anger and made them believe that the university wanted the Afro-Asian Institute to fail. Intellectually, furthermore, beyond impoverishing coursework, it ensured that Temple students "get a very one-sided view of reality in the modern world." While information on black humanity and culture was hard to find, there was "shelf after shelf of material on the so-called mother countries of Europe." The implications were stark: endless volumes were filled with "innumerable apologies for slavery and the slave trade" alongside diatribes about what "'good hearted' whites did to free, happy, possum-chasing, watermelon-eating bondsmen of the South."[40] A library, Reddick knew well, was a politicized place. Temple's bookshelves bowed under the weight of a Western tradition that for centuries had ratified white supremacy and erased nonwhite perspectives.

Reddick remained creative as he confronted these circumstances. His students explained how he usually brought "a suitcase filled with books from his own library" to class, which they affectionately dubbed "Doc Reddick's travelling library."[41] The act was a pragmatic response to Temple's insufficient library materials, but it was also a bold declaration that black scholars had for decades been building up an impressive array of scholarship on black life. In his American Civil War class, he assigned his own *Worth Fighting For*, Charles Wesley's *The Collapse of the Confederacy*, Benjamin Quarles's *Lincoln and the Negro* and *The Negro in the Civil War*, as well as writings by John Hope Franklin and Carter Woodson, among other things.[42] In his Twentieth Century: Economic History course, he assigned such works as W. E. B. Du Bois's *The Souls of Black Folk*, Booker T. Washington's *Up from Slavery*, Abram Harris's *The Black Worker*, Horace Cayton's *Black Workers and the New Unions*, and again not shy about assigning his own work, Charles Sellers's edited volume *The Southerner as American*. The guiding questions for that course included: "(1) What happened to the Negro agricultural worker? (2) Historically and currently which unions are color-blind? (3) In what businesses have Negroes been most successful? (4) Are there Negro millionaires? (5) Does public assistance help or hinder?"[43] The implicit contention of Reddick's courses was that the black experience was fundamental to all of American history and life.

As with the Black Studies movement generally, Reddick maintained not only that the black experience was fundamental but that the black perspective was fundamentally oppositional. In 1969, a journalist for the *Philadelphia Tribune* interviewed him and posed the question, "What makes black history black history?" Reddick, allowing "a smile—half shy, half sly—to spread over his face," replied that "black history is not only concerned with putting in the missing pages from world and American history, but also with the distinctive institutions and points of view that have been developed in the black world." Furthermore, "as the sly part of his smile asserts itself, he says: 'What makes black history is that it examines the point of view of oppressed people in contrast to those of the nation.'"[44] The implication was profound: the view of black people was fundamentally different from that of the white majority. Indeed, the prevailing white view that the rise of the West was a story of progress—of the gradual unfolding of enlightenment, democracy, and civilization—was untenable from a black perspective. Any progress for certain white men had to be weighed against the extermination, enslavement, and disfranchisement of untold millions of nonwhite people. From the numbers alone, their subjugation was not a peripheral side note but the predominant reality, and one which made any of the alleged national "progress" possible.[45]

Both the novelty and the oppositional nature of Reddick's courses appealed to Temple students. Upon taking one of Reddick's black history courses, which covered African history through the civil rights movement, one white student reported, "I thought I knew something about it, but after getting into the course, I realize I knew nothing." He appreciated how Reddick had dispelled many of his misconceptions. A black student noted with awe, "For the first time in my life I'm learning about me, and I never realized there was so much about me to know."[46] Reddick's courses attracted a large share of both black and white students of more liberal political leanings, as well as both men and women. Many of them were teachers or teachers in training. But Reddick also shaped the careers of students who became notable scholars and public figures. For instance, F. Elaine DeLancey, later an associate professor at Drexel University and the founding editor of the internationally influential *Sonia Sanchez Literary Review*, studied with Reddick at Temple.[47]

Sharing the black campus movement's creed that Black Studies needed to serve the larger black community, Reddick's instruction also transcended classroom walls. For instance, in March 1972 Reddick attended the black political convention in Gary, Indiana, and he reported on the proceedings to his students and to various other groups on and off campus. The Gary convention exemplified the Black Power movement's shift toward electoral politics, which eventually netted the election of African Americans to a wide range of offices across the country.[48] The election of black mayors to major cities, such as Kenneth Gibson in Newark (1970) and Maynard Jackson in Atlanta (1973), proved to be some of the most lasting achievements of the movement. Reddick reported to various audiences that the convention was "perhaps the most important political gathering of American Blacks since 1864." He praised its inclusiveness ("All ideologies and shades of opinion were represented, from the Black Panthers and Black Muslims to the NAACP"), as well as its expansiveness ("It was truly representative, in that some 5,000 delegates and observers from 42 states were present"). Above all, he celebrated what he argued was a united front of black people at the convention. He summarized the prevailing sentiment as "We will go it alone as a political party, if necessary," but that black people will also make realistic demands on major political parties and seek out coalitions "with other dissatisfied groups such as Chicanos, Puerto Ricans, Indians, youth and women" where mutually beneficial.⁴⁹ His remarks were as much prescriptive as descriptive.

As his vocal complaints about inadequate library resources already attest, Reddick also believed that Black Studies scholars needed to extend the oppositional nature of their field to their personal interactions with white faculty members and administrators. His approach was one of disruption, and his years at Temple were filled with confrontations both large and small. For example, he routinely butted heads with history faculty members over his belief that people of color were inherently better interpreters—and also teachers—of their people's history.⁵⁰ This argument turned on its head the old racist dictum that black scholars were inherently biased on the race question, replacing it with the idea that one's blackness was an asset that enabled a black person to better, or at least more easily, understand the black experience. The point was not to essentialize blackness. "Negro thought is different from white thought," he once explained, "not because of race, but because of the general proposition that people who live differently think differently."⁵¹ The reasoning was sound, but white Temple professors such as the resident military historian resented the perceived affront to their historical abilities. For them, the notion that their racial privilege could be a handicap was simply too challenging to accept.

Another example of Reddick's confrontational approach is evident in his introductory remarks to a Vine Deloria Jr. talk on campus. Deloria was a leading Native American activist who coined the term "Red Power" and served as the second executive director of the National Congress of American Indians. He also authored *Custer Died for Your Sins: An Indian Manifesto* (1969), which established him as a major figure in the American Indian Movement. Deloria's speech no doubt posed a stark challenge to white America, but Reddick was intent on localizing that challenge at Temple. He declared, "At Temple as with almost every other American university, the voice of the non-white, the exploited and the pushed-back is seldom heard." Getting more personal, he queried, "Is it not true that the confidence of some of our European scholars is so great that when we demand that a few courses on the Blacks or the Indians be offered to our students, the European scholars themselves insist upon teaching such courses, contending that they with their Ph.D.'s know the story and that they even know what the Black or the Red man is thinking better than the Black and Red man himself?"⁵² The anger was righteous, but the breaking of decorum by calling out one's colleagues during introductory remarks unsettled some.

More challenging was a set of practical proposals Reddick recommended for administering African history at Temple. Insinuating that his white colleagues were inevitably biased, he proposed that the introductory course on African history be jointly taught by an African and a non-African. For similar reasons, he suggested that any papers "read by Euro-Americans" during a proposed conference on Africa "should be followed by critiques from African and Afro-American scholars." He also claimed that most African history courses taught by nonblacks were "mistaught" due to whites' "cultural imperialism." Further talking down to his white colleagues, he declared that "cultural imperialists may not be conscious of their basic European mythology."[53]

In being so indiscriminate in his belittling—if often accurate—accusations, Reddick won few allies. But Reddick's rhetoric and approach were now guided by the larger Black Power movement, not the civil rights liberalism of his earlier days. He thus openly advocated "community self-determination" and drew from the rhetoric of Harold Cruse, Kwame Ture, and Robert Allen in conceptualizing black Americans as an "internal colony" within the United States.[54] If nothing else, he succeeded in making his white colleagues uncomfortable and cautious about what they said. This was itself a partial victory, for it made them consider how the university was fundamentally a white space. Giving white colleagues a taste of the discomfort that black people experienced at Temple and elsewhere on a daily basis could also be satisfying. Nonetheless, the environment of fear and anxiety was hardly conducive to promoting intercultural understanding, and it alienated many. These circumstances would propel yet another dramatic falling out between Reddick and his employer later in the decade.

The White Takeover of Black History

Temple was only a microcosm of America's institutional racism, so Reddick channeled his disruptive efforts toward national struggles as well. No topic concerned him more than what he observed in the field of black history.

For generations, lay and professional black historians had slowly built up the field in the face of white hostility and neglect. Then, precipitated by the civil rights movement and the many dramatic racial changes in the country, whites suddenly grew terribly interested in black history. Newly encouraged by advisers at elite institutions, lavishly funded by grants from foundations, eagerly sought out by leading academic and commercial presses, and caught up in the righteous moral fervor of the times, white graduate students and scholars in the late 1960s and 1970s sought to overturn racist histories and ride the tide to professional success. In many ways, their newfound interest in black history and their commitment to evaluating it as a central part of American history were crowning achievements of the black history movement, which had long made the case for the field's significance along those lines. The changes also augured well for scholarship that was less flawed, less propagandistic, and better suited to foment a long overdue reckoning with America's racist past and present. But as Reddick and other black scholars observed, the manner in which this historiographic watershed had come about was problematic, to say the least. The very people who had built the field, safeguarded many of its key primary sources, and deserved to be empowered as its leading authorities often continued to be marginalized and forced into the background. "Racism today is more effective than ever," Reddick said of these trends, for it "is now well-mannered."[55] The stakes remained high, too, for history had taught Reddick that the field would never be on safe grounds if it were controlled by nonblacks.[56]

No year put the changes in the profession on display better than 1974. In that year alone, white scholars published several landmark books on slavery. These included such diverse works as Eugene Genovese's *Roll, Jordan, Roll*, Ira Berlin's *Slaves without Masters*, and Peter Wood's *Black Majority*.[57] These celebrated books testified to how far the profession had come over the course of Reddick's career. Truly, when Reddick completed his PhD in the 1930s, the Dunning School's "Lost Cause" interpretation of Southern history predominated. During the 1950s, liberal books such as Kenneth Stampp's *The Peculiar Institution* (1956) and Stanley Elkins's *Slavery* (1959) finally overturned that tradition by taking the opposite tract—painting slavery as utterly dehumanizing and oppressive, not unlike the concentration camps of Nazi Germany.[58] By the 1970s, white historians rebelled against such bitterly stigmatizing portrayals and finally began to take seriously the black experience. Genovese's Bancroft Award–winning *Roll, Jordan, Roll* focused on "the world the slaves made," or how they created culture, family, and traditions that enabled them to endure slavery.[59] Berlin's *Slaves without Masters* examined free blacks in the antebellum South—an always at-risk population whose very existence upended generalizations about blacks during slave times. Wood's *Black Majority*, meanwhile, was perhaps the most effective of all in taking black culture seriously and then tying it to the larger story of American history. Among other things, Wood showed how black people were coveted as laborers because of the advanced agricultural skills they had developed in Africa, and he explained how they turned to resistance and rebellion when conditions deteriorated in colonial South Carolina.

Accompanying the advancements, however, were ominous misfires. No book stirred up more controversy or justifiable alarm than William Fogel and Stanley Engerman's *Time on the Cross* (1974).[60] Focusing on "the economics of American Negro slavery" and drawing from the burgeoning field of "cliometrics," which used quantitative methods to lay bare social life, Fogel and Engerman rather unwittingly made the case that slavery was not so terrible. For instance, they claimed that "The nutritional content of the slave diet was quite high"; "The material . . . conditions of the lives of slaves compared favorably with those of free industrial workers"; and "The typical slave field hand received about 90 percent of the income he produced."[61] They conceded that they had no "meaningful index of the effect of slavery on the personality or psychology of blacks," but they insisted that their quantitative methods produced the most authoritative account of slavery ever written.[62] At the same time, they were generous—or as Reddick saw it, overly generous—to previous white historians. They stated that earlier scholars were "conscientious and diligent" and wrote generally without "personal bias or other idiosyncratic behavior."[63] Reddick, with memories of his Chicago advisor Avery Craven etched in his mind, was appalled.

For Reddick and many other alarmed black scholars, *Time on the Cross* was the last straw. Upon its publication, Reddick issued a stinging rebuke of the *New York Review of Books* for handing over its review to white scholar C. Vann Woodward, who had emerged as an outspoken critic of the cultural nationalism among black historians. For instance, in 1970, Woodward called it "preposterous" that only black writers could properly write black history, and he was quick to credit white scholars for conducting much of the seminal work in the field.[64] Reddick responded by dubbing Woodward an "ex-Southern liberal," assailing his review as the organ's "latest disaster." Reddick believed that the stakes were high for a book that he considered "the publishing industry's latest public relations package." Spotlighting the larger issue of institutional racism, Reddick asked, "Why does *The New York Review* so consistently turn over books on the Black experience to non-Black reviewers? . . . Is it another indication of 'liberal' racism that there are no recognizable names of Blacks on *The New York Review*'s editorial board?"[65]

In consultation with others, Reddick began organizing a conference of predominantly black scholars to discuss the latest history books and strategize over how to confront the institutional racism that he believed gave them rise. In April 1975, they convened at Queens College in New York, and their proceedings grabbed the attention of the *New York Times*. Much criticism was heaped upon *Time on the Cross*, which Reddick called "a shambles of inept methodology." Julian Ellison, an economist with the Black Economic Research Center, exposed the troubling history behind cliometrics. He claimed that it "developed out of the Federal Government's need some years ago for information to predict the behavior of Americans, especially blacks." Then criticism turned to other history books, including Genovese's *Roll, Jordan, Roll* and Berlin's *Slaves without Masters*. Fogel, Genovese, and Berlin were all apparently invited to the conference but declined to attend. With less merit, conference attendees condemned these very different books in broad strokes. Vincent Harding dismissed them as an attempt "to deny slavery, to deny the 'burden of slavery.'" Herbert Aptheker, a Communist historian who counted among the few white pioneers of black history, jumped on the bandwagon, calling the books a "travesty upon scholarship." However, the scholars' most justified indictment was of the "academic and publishing structures that produced" the recent history books.[66] Reddick told St. Clair Drake, unable to attend, what he missed: "The importance of the conference is that now we have another instrument that we can use to fight the battle against the reactionary white scholars who are taking over the Black Experience."[67]

Two months before the Queens College conference, the *New York Times* published an interview with Reddick that better articulated his criticisms for a public audience. Reddick, then busy crafting his conference paper entitled "Corporate Scholarship Takes Over Black History and Squeezes Out the Black Scholar," first gave a brief rundown of the historiography on slavery from U. B. Phillips to Kenneth Stampp.[68] Both types, he explained, lacked "the story of the slave himself," and relied upon white-created sources such as plantation records to understand the institution.[69] Meanwhile, black scholars had been writing alternative histories that placed the black experience at the center for over a hundred years. He referenced *The Underground Railroad* (1872) by William Still, a free black in Philadelphia who aided fugitive slaves and then wrote a book about it.[70] How, he challenged, could any legitimate study of slavery ignore sources created by African Americans themselves—from slave narratives to WPA interviews to Colored Conventions? His point was clear: black scholars knew better, and they were the true experts on these topics. Accordingly, they should be positioned institutionally to preside over the study of black people. But he did not see that happening. "Since slavery is becoming of interest to the reading public, you have corporate scholarship coming in to take over the field," he criticized. "You have the big universities that formerly weren't interested in it very much and you have scholars getting big grants to do these studies and these scholars tend to be white. And they tend to push out the black scholars."[71]

Reddick and the Queens College conference group by no means represented the majority opinion among black scholars. Although many people were sympathetic to their concerns, many found them unnecessarily alarmist, defensive, and divisive. For example, John Hope Franklin, who had risen to become the twentieth century's greatest historian of African American history, took a different view. He argued that "if [black history] is a valid area of intellectual inquiry, it cannot be segregated by sex, religion, or race. Historians must be judged by what they do, not by how they look." He maintained that Carter Woodson, too, would have been pleased with white scholars contributing to black history and appalled by the "bickering that enveloped the association in the 1960s over the question of whether white historians should be permitted to participate in the work of the association." He noted the important work done by white scholars in a variety of areas, not least in black intellectual history by August Meier. Furthermore, his autobiography devoted special attention to Theodore Currier, one of his and Reddick's white history professors at Fisk. Currier had a decisive influence upon Franklin, and in fact Franklin relied partly on financial support from Currier to subsidize his doctoral studies at Harvard. The important history of scholarly collaboration, mentorship, and friendship across the color line was easy to miss in the strident rhetoric of Reddick and his peers.[72]

Yet the very different trajectory of white scholars' careers attested to the ways in which Reddick's complaints were not mere petty griping or divisive identity politicking. Take, for example, the career of white historian David Brion Davis. Unlike William Fogel and Stanley Engerman, Davis's research on slavery was not controversial. He was one of the many emerging white scholars who *did* take black sources, black perspectives, and the black experience seriously, and his work was widely heralded for its rich portrayal of the institution and its central place within American life. His 1966 book, *The Problem of Slavery in Western Culture*, netted him the Pulitzer Prize.[73] However, Davis's experiences in the academy could not have been more different from Reddick's generation of black scholars. After serving in World War II, Davis earned a bachelor's degree from Dartmouth. In the mid-1950s, he met Kenneth Stampp and was first exposed to the new white historiography on slavery. He later confessed to being "totally ignorant of the work of . . . black historians" at the time.[74] He nevertheless took up the topic while a graduate student at Harvard, where he earned his PhD in 1956. Never once stepping down from his Ivy League perch, he subsequently served as a professor at Dartmouth and Cornell before settling in at Yale in 1970. In 1978, he was named the Sterling Professor of American History, which he held until his retirement in 2001. Over the course of his long career, he wrote or edited no fewer than sixteen books and advised two generations of scholars. Those scholars then took up prominent positions throughout academia and further bolstered Davis's stature.[75]

It is no slight on Davis's abilities to recognize the incalculable ways that his publications and influence were buttressed by his privilege as a white male Ivy League scholar. Reddick's generation of black scholars routinely taught five courses per semester in underfunded black colleges, had little support for their research, and were also expected to serve the larger black community. Davis, on the other hand, free of any responsibility to "lift as he climbed" and, backed by enormous resources, was able to throw his energies into research. His renown as a historian is thus inseparable from his race and class privilege. It was especially infuriating for Reddick when white scholars like Davis were credited with pioneering new fields of research that black scholars had long ago begun to build up. One need only consult Lorenzo Greene's *The Negro in Colonial New England, 1620–1776* (1942) or Eric Williams's *Capitalism and Slavery* (1944) to see the point.[76] The difference was that their work had to overcome many more obstacles and was often ignored within the profession.[77] In short, the marginalization of black scholars deprived them of the credit they deserved, inflated the contributions of white scholars, and ultimately impoverished scholarship more broadly.

Reddick's corrective helps us to see how the discussions surrounding academic production continue to be problematic and misleading. A more recent display of this dynamic emerged in the wake of Davis's death in 2019. His obituary in the *New York Times* praised him in effusive terms, citing many of his former students and colleagues. "No one," penned Columbia historian Eric Foner, "did more to inspire the revolution in historical understanding that places slavery at the center of American history."[78] The very stature of his former students was itself a case study in how the academy reproduces social hierarchies by granting the lion's share of research university professorships to those who attended a handful of elite schools. Yet this celebrity culture within academia persists with the backing of the racist, classist, and sexist academic division of labor, tainting even well-intended attempts to honor a notable figure like Davis. Reddick and his contemporaries would have surely greeted such inequities with righteous indignation.

Never short on righteous indignation, Reddick continued to expand his critiques and present them widely at conferences, universities, and other public forums.[79] In 1976, he published a revised version of his Queens College conference paper in *Social Policy*, a New York–based periodical that cosponsored that conference. The article, "Black History as a Corporate Colony," was a hard-hitting exposé of the systematic marginalization of black scholars. He linked present trends with the long history of cultural imperialism, in which white Westerners, knowing that political and economic domination was not enough to maintain power, labored to control culture and history as well. He also highlighted the striking contrast between the recent past and present. From the 1930s to the 1950s, he explained, black scholars controlled the study of the black experience, largely because white people were uninterested in it. By the 1960s and 1970s, however, there was a corporate "takeover of the Black experience."

Step by step, Reddick explained how the takeover operated in practice. Major research universities, still largely controlled by white men, handed out newly fashionable research topics on black history to predominantly white male graduate students. Foundations supported these efforts, giving grants to white scholars over black ones in hugely disproportionate numbers. For instance, Reddick described how over the course of a decade, two white Africanists received more grant money than all black Africanists combined. Publishing houses, beyond putting out the bumper crop of white-authored studies, cashed in by reprinting earlier books by black scholars whose copyrights had expired, therefore depriving them of royalties. "I do not claim that there is an ever-conscious and deliberate conspiracy to demand and destroy Black history and to silence and kill off Black scholars," Reddick declared. "But such an overall plot is hardly necessary, for there are cooperating forces within the normal operation of the social system which work toward the same effort." To resist them, Reddick recommended sounding the alarm, pressuring government agencies and foundations to spend public monies differently, and above all dramatically increasing the pool of black scholars.[80]

One way Reddick pursued these goals was through the Association for the Study of African American (formerly "Negro") Life and History (ASALH). In 1975, he chaired the program committee for the sixtieth annual conference in Atlanta. Along with old friends Clarence Bacote and Elsie

Lewis, the committee created a special session on "The Crisis of the Black Scholar," which prioritized the "ways and means of increasing the number and quality of training of black scholars."[81] The National Research Council's statistics certainly indicated a problem: in 1974, only 11 of the 456 PhDs in American history had been awarded to blacks. The committee's efforts had helped to foment significant change by the end of the decade: in 1979, blacks accounted for 27 of the 301 PhDs in the field.[82] At ASALH's annual meeting in Washington, D.C., in 1977, Reddick also participated in a session on "Research Dollars for the Black Scholar." There the director of the research division of the National Endowment of the Humanities (NEH) noted the organization's "dismal" record in awarding grants to black scholars, but he attributed it partly to the small number of black applicants. According to one observer, Reddick countered, "The experiences of blacks in securing grants and publications has been so disappointing that many are giving up."[83] Reddick then proposed that ASALH urge the new chairman of the NEH to allocate more funds to blacks and to request action from the National Advisory Committee on Black Higher Education. Both resolutions were adopted unanimously.

The corporate control of black history, as Reddick dubbed it, extended further into other areas of public life. Reddick entered the broader arena during a protracted struggle over Philadelphia's bicentennial celebrations. In the run-up to 1976, the city formed a bicentennial corporation that was tasked with planning the events and exhibitions. Black artists, administrators, and scholars like Reddick applied to work for the group in 1973, but many were turned away. Disgruntled, the local black community—which comprised almost one-third of the city's population—began sustained protest, recognizing that it could not entrust the white-dominated organization with including African Americans in the process or faithfully representing black history (and thus American history) in the exhibitions. On April 24, 1974, "the Bicentennial had received so much flack," Reddick explained, that it offered to build a black history museum in exchange for a cessation of protest. Reddick, as co-chair of the Afro-American Historical '76 Bicentennial Corporation of Philadelphia, was asked to preside over the meeting in which the corporation presented the offer to almost one hundred black Philadelphians. Looking out at the sea of committed black people around him, Reddick recalled, "It occurred to me and . . . to others that perhaps we ought not be satisfied" with that olive branch. Reddick thus headed up an investigation of the Philadelphia bicentennial to determine how to proceed.[84]

The investigation's findings were troubling, if not surprising. Reddick wrote the report and presented it to Philadelphia's black community in October. He described how no black people were heads of any significant departments, how black organizations only received 5 percent of the available funds (only $35,000 went to the restoration of the historic Mother Bethel Church while the Academy of Fine Arts received $5.9 million), and how the black community "would not even have control of the portrayal of the Black Experience."[85] In May, Reddick presented a "semi-final" report that focused especially on the latter issue. He spoke of the "audacity" of nonblack organizations in proposing that they should depict black history. One group apparently wanted to tell the story of slavery through the lens of only one white man's letters; another proposed telling two hundred years of black history. "What assurance would the Black community have that such a money-making oriented concern would not have a parade of cotton-picking scenes, Uncle Toms and Black-faced comedians?" Reddick questioned. "We should remember that even today the Black-faced minstrel tradition is still strong among some uninformed people. Anyone who catches a late T.V. show of some of the old Hollywood movies can testify to that."[86]

Reddick, ever the didact, also used the occasion to challenge the "false and superficial" interpretations of American history being proposed for the exhibitions. He was especially leery of attempts to romanticize, sanitize, and otherwise lionize the Founding Fathers. These men were "human beings and as such were liable to some mistakes. . . . We must give some attention not only to their wisdom and foresight but also to their blunders and blind spots." Those blind spots were achingly clear to nonwhites. Reddick pointed to the Declaration of Independence's reference to Native Americans as "merciless Indian savages, whose known rule of warfare is an undistinguished destruction of all ages, sexes, and conditions," as well as its failure to denounce slavery while grandly proclaiming that all men are created equal. "Was this failure because some of the men who wrote the Declaration or who signed it were themselves slave-owners and slave-traders?" Reddick asked sardonically. He also noted how the Constitution was drafted by a convention in which there were "no women, no Blacks, no indentured servants, no urban workers, only one small farmer but a great number of rich land owners, businessmen and lawyers." He again queried irreverently, "Is it not possible for us to understand that some of the shortcomings of the original Constitution are traceable to the fact that the Constitutional convention did not faithfully represent all of the American people?" Reddick concluded the report with a thinly veiled threat that should such flawed proposals appear in the exhibitions, "Philadelphia will be wracked with controversy, boycotts, the breakup of lectures, the destruction of exhibits and other forms of violence."[87]

The white higher-ups were not implacable, and the black community's complaints continued to win further concessions. Indeed, historian Andrea Burns argues that Reddick and other black leaders "successfully employed activist techniques to resist the city's exclusion (or token inclusion) of black organizations and projects during the Bicentennial."[88] But she also describes how Reddick's contentious approach, which at times misrepresented the facts, assumed the worst intentions of white Philadelphians, and called out collaborating blacks as Uncle Toms, deepened social divisions. The results were typically not satisfying for anyone. For example, the creation of the permanent Afro-American Historical and Cultural Museum was in many ways a significant victory for the black community, but fights over its location and ultimate control poisoned even that success. Reddick, for his part, had served on the museum's planning committee until 1975. Then he and Charles Blockson, a black bibliophile, resigned in protest because the committee refused to prioritize an archival repository and appoint a black curator to oversee it.[89] Blockson had hoped the museum could be a "Schomburg-like" institution for which his considerable holdings could have been the foundation.[90] Upon recognizing the lack of black control over the museum, he refused to donate his collection, and he and Reddick resigned in frustration.

To counter white efforts to narrate black history during the bicentennial, black scholars continued writing histories of their own. Reddick was one of six figures commissioned by the National Urban League to write a bicentennial essay "from a Black perspective." By this time, the notion of a monolithic black perspective had begun to ebb among black intellectuals. As historian Martha Biondi has shown, the rise of black feminism within Black Studies programs across the country had begun to fuel an exploration of the ways in which race, class, and gender intersected to create a multivalent black experience.[91] Yet the notion of a black perspective remained useful shorthand for critiquing the de facto "white perspective" within broader public discourse. Hence the six essays, according to the League's executive director, Vernon E. Jordan, "represent a major contribution toward providing a Black presence in the Bicentennial . . . on our own terms."[92] All were written for laymen. Reddick's essay, "Blacks and US Wars," addressed the American Revolution, the Civil War, and both World Wars. Along familiar lines, he explained how "at the beginning of every major war in the U.S.A.

blacks were not wanted for the fighting but before the war was over, blacks had to be called upon to help achieve victory." "Equally curious," Reddick argued, was the fact that "the nation's great moral justifications of each war coincided with the goals of black Americans for their own freedom and equality; but each time, the nation seemed reluctant to concede this."[93] Reddick followed the essay with discussion questions to help foster critical discussions of the material.

Departure from the White University

As contentious as Reddick's involvement in Philadelphia's bicentennial was, it ultimately paled in comparison to the bitter falling out he had with Temple University. Like so many of his battles in those years, the struggle ultimately revolved around institutional power, though mundane clashes over personality and departmental politics were also key precipitating factors. The problems began when Herbert Bass became chairman of the history department in the mid-1970s. Friendly with conservative-minded faculty members, including a military historian Reddick had long clashed with, Bass ran the department in a tight-fisted manner. Reddick bridled at this style, especially resenting the control Bass wielded over his teaching schedule and the department's course offerings in African American history. He felt that Bass unjustifiably limited those courses, posing a challenge to the entire "black revolution on campus."[94] As Reddick would increasingly come to articulate it, this reflected the "new racism" in which some black people were accepted on campus but then excluded from the seats of decision-making.[95] How neatly Reddick's circumstances at Temple actually mirrored those larger inequities, however, is not clear.

The issue came to a head at a departmental meeting on December 9, 1975, when Bass announced a plan to hire one or two new professors of black history in the wake of Reddick's scheduled retirement in June 1977. Because Temple had a mandatory retirement age of 67, Reddick was slated to retire at that time. However, Harvard had offered Reddick a visiting professorship, which he hoped he could take and then return to Temple to oversee the department's transition to new leadership of the black history program.[96] Reddick was in the midst of petitioning Temple's president, Marvin Wachman, to delay his retirement for a year or two on those grounds. In this context, Reddick greeted Bass's announcement of his scheduled retirement date and the plans to replace him as a power play and a personal affront.

He believed Bass was trying to humiliate him and did not appreciate Bass sharing his age with the faculty.[97]

Matters only deteriorated from there. The administration denied Reddick's request to work beyond 1977, and the department moved forward with plans to hire a new faculty member in black history. Reddick and two other black faculty members were on the hiring committee, but Bass chaired it, which Reddick again interpreted as a threat to him rather than a practice in keeping with departmental policy. Reddick thus began a fierce campaign against Bass, circulating statement after statement within the department and across the university. Before the January 28 departmental meeting, Reddick sent out a document that maligned Bass as a petty "tyrant" who was "aggressive, precise, clever and adept at manipulation and the accumulation of power."[98] When the faculty convened for the meeting, Reddick brought with him a group of sixty people to observe the proceedings. He orchestrated a faculty vote by secret ballot to decide whether Bass should maintain his chairmanship of the department. When the faculty voted overwhelmingly for Bass and his policies, Reddick was livid. His tactics had apparently alienated many who were previously supportive of him.[99]

The low point came on March 12, when Reddick circulated a bitter open letter announcing his surrender. "Whatever feelings of fraternity or identification that I may have had a few years ago are all gone now. . . . I reject the Department that has rejected me." Signaling once again how Reddick tended to equate friendship with complete loyalty and support for his positions, he sunk to describing the "ugliness of appearance" of one of his former supporters in the department: "I noticed for the first time that his feet are big, his knees knocked and his stringy, thinning hair can not hide a misshaped forehead that is speckled with freckles and blotches." As for Bass, he was "a covert enemy of the Black people" who had "surfaced on last December 9." In strikingly belligerent rhetoric, Reddick declared, "By the rules of war, I should seek his destruction." He concluded by suggesting his intention "to make public my disillusionment," referring to his friends at newspaper outlets and on television. "It is true that I am beginning to wonder if the Department of History is a good place for Black students or for Black professionals who are courageous," he warned ominously.[100]

True to his word, Reddick escalated the conflict from a departmental feud to a university-wide one. On April 27, he presided over a rally at the student center in which over three hundred students, university employees, and community members "declared war on racism at Temple University." They pressured the administration to combat institutional racism on campus by continuously calling, mailing, and otherwise confronting administrators. The campaign won ten of them an audience with President Wachman on May 20, when the Reddick-led group demanded, among other things, the hiring of a full-time black professor in big departments such as journalism, theater, psychology, biology, chemistry, and pharmacy, all of which had none. Their efforts met with some success when Wachman elevated Bernard Watson, a black scholar, to a vice presidency at the university. The group kept the pressure on, holding another rally on June 16. Reddick once again presided, now expanding his critique to the recent firing of 130 janitorial workers on campus, 80 percent of whom were black. "Our enemies may say that we want to hurt Temple or tear it down," Reddick proclaimed. "You know better than that. We want only to remove the infliction that is upon us. We want to build Temple up."[101]

Reddick went so far as to escalate the issue to the state level. He enlisted Bill Richardson, a Democratic representative from Philadelphia, and the nine other members of Pennsylvania's Black Caucus to hold hearings on racism at Temple. On June 21, Reddick and some twenty others traveled to Harrisburg and testified on the subject for six hours. Reddick presented information from a report he submitted to the legislators, which described a campaign of harassment that included unknown persons stealing his mail, monitoring his phone calls, and moving around his office materials. He also charged the administration with colluding with the two university publications—the *Temple Outlook* and the *Temple Times*—to discredit him and his allegations. He concluded with a new charge that "The children of the rich can find a place in our Medical school, if their parents and kinsmen have the proper political connection and or make a monetary contribution to Temple University."[102] Two days later, President Wachman testified in defense of the university and accused Reddick of pursuing "individualistic interests and concerns."[103] Then on June 30, representative Richardson moved to block state appropriations to Temple (a public university) until it took concrete steps to address its institutional racism. The moved failed when the legislature passed the appropriations bill by an overwhelming 182–9 margin, which included the defection of more than one member of the Black Caucus. Reddick's months-long crusade against Temple ground to a halt.[104]

The whole affair was a curious one. For Reddick, it was only the latest and perhaps greatest of his many controversial departures from institutions

Lawrence Reddick at Temple University, mid-1970s. Courtesy of the Photographs and Prints Division, Schomburg Center for Research in Black Culture, New York Public Library. © Jack T. Franklin, courtesy of the African American Museum in Philadelphia.

ranging from the Schomburg Library to Alabama State College. This one, however, sprang from the Black Power militancy of the times, and it targeted the subtler forms of racism that were ever-present throughout universities and the larger society. The episode also bore the imprint of Reddick's personality, warts and all. Regardless of its origins, Reddick's behavior certainly influenced the world around him, though not always in ways he would have liked. In this case, few people ultimately supported his tactics or his full message. A ten-member Affirmative Action Review

Committee at Temple issued a unanimous twenty-five-page report that rebuked Reddick for a "pattern of overreaction and provocation in his behavior toward members of the History Department in the last year."[105] Even the Black Faculty Caucus could not condone his behavior.[106]

Still, even if some of Reddick's charges were baseless or overblown, others were clearly justified. His campaign succeeded in giving significant public attention to problems of institutional racism that were otherwise being quietly ignored.[107] His broader work in institution-building also prepared the way for Molefi Asante and other Temple professors to develop the nation's first PhD program in African American Studies in 1988. When Reddick's efforts supported such concrete gains, they signaled the degree to which the black freedom struggle had begun to transform white spaces—from universities to state legislatures—into more multicultural ones. The problem, however, was that Reddick's zealousness also alienated many people and stoked divisions. More ominously, it sometimes clouded the actual racism at hand, helping reactionaries to paint the whole episode as but another example of a black person inventing racism where it did not exist. The age of colorblind racism had arrived.

A Black Perspective on the Black Family

Reddick excelled as an agitator, but his many efforts to disrupt institutional racism should not distract from the important constructive research and writing he completed in the 1970s. During his years at Temple and Harvard, Reddick was perpetually busy pursuing projects. At this point in his life, there was so much to do and so little time, and that challenge sometimes got the best of him. In the area of biography alone, he considered books on A. Philip Randolph, Leon Sullivan, and Ralph Abernathy, not to mention an update to his biography on Martin Luther King Jr.[108] None of those projects ever got off the ground. Others he began but did not finish, and some he largely completed but did not publish. His personal papers are thus filled with unpublished writings, abandoned projects, endless correspondence, and reams of documentary evidence from these years. Nevertheless, there were three topics on which Reddick did conduct significant research and find ways to disseminate it to the public: black family life, racism within higher education, and the history of HBCUs. By centering a black perspective, this research broke new ground and revealed how social science tended to disguise white perspectives as universal truths. In other words, Reddick fought to decolonize American social thought and to provide African Americans with a usable history to confront the era's new forms of racism.

The black family project grew out of collaboration with Alex Haley in the early 1970s. Haley had become famous for "authoring" *The Autobiography of Malcolm X* (1965), which became an international bestseller after Malcolm's assassination.[109] He used proceeds from the book to support a five-year, $70,000 intercontinental investigation into seven generations of his family's genealogy. As he was writing up his family's biography, tentatively titled *Roots*, he thought of creating a genealogical library devoted to the larger black experience. In the summer of 1972, he reached out to Reddick, whom he had first learned about through Martin Luther King Jr. The two of them began discussing a project that was breathtaking in scope and ambition. To create a black genealogical library, they would have to overcome the fact that centuries of slavery and the slave trade had severed the family ties of most African Americans. They would need to marshal every conceivable documentary source while also launching a massive oral history project that could tap into family lore on both sides of the Atlantic. "Even the mere contemplation of such an effort is staggering," Reddick conceded.[110]

Trying not to be overwhelmed, Reddick and Haley began taking steps to advance the project. Along with Leonard Jeffries, a professor of Black Studies at New York University, they met with officers of the Carnegie Corporation to gauge their interest in supporting such a study. Meanwhile, Reddick, George Sims, and others had begun making exploratory trips to the Library of Congress, the National Archives, and Harvard to work out a methodology for extracting valuable information from such repositories. By the end of the summer, the outlines of the project—dubbed the Kinte Library Project in honor of Haley's seventh-generation ancestor—were in place. Haley would serve as project coordinator, Reddick would lead the documentary phase, and others would head up the other two branches: Oral History USA and Oral History International. Haley later told the team, "There can't be quarrel that our strongest component is on the Archival side" because "our director there is Dr. Larry Reddick." The group succeeded in winning two full years of support from the Carnegie Corporation, which Haley said was "the largest funding ever entrusted to an independent all-Black project."[111]

Reddick cast the significance of the Kinte Library Project in broad terms. This was not an exercise in "filiopietistic pedigree hunting"; rather, it aimed to "reconstruct a history of Afro-America, based upon family continuities."

As he stated in the project proposal, it would "speak to the spirit of Pan-Africanism and provide handy documentation for scholars, writers and artists and should have salutary effect upon the self-esteem of Afro-Americans and respect and appreciation for them on the part of others."[112] In the final 550-page report, drafted by multiple authors and submitted to the Carnegie Corporation in the summer of 1976, Reddick underscored the larger issue: "The written history of the Red, Black and White experience in America has been almost exclusively fabricated according to the White perspective."[113] He regretted that situation, for he continued to believe that a "universal perspective" was possible if all peoples collaborated as equals to tell a truly inclusive story of multicultural America. Though that was not happening, Reddick believed that a black perspective held the potential to liberate social science from its white biases.

The challenge was herculean, however, because the European conquest of the New World extended to the archives. In his reports, Reddick asked rhetorically, "Has the Library of Congress over the years, with even-handed fairness, gathered the materials of the Black and Indian Experience . . . ? Would we as likely find there the memoirs of slave *captives* as we would of slave *traders*?"[114] He recounted frustrating visits to leading research libraries such as Harvard's, where he encountered librarians and archivists who were eager to help but largely unequipped to do so. "The staff there admitted that Harvard had not 'gone after' the papers of Black personalities." For the material that did exist, "there was no available guide or sufficient finding aids." All he and his team found was a thirty-six-page introductory guide to Afro-American Studies, which had been recently "thrown together in response to the demands of Black students that Harvard institute a program of Black Studies."[115]

Reddick approached the Kinte Library Project from the theoretical perspectives being advanced by Black Studies scholars at the time. They were discarding old assumptions and asking searching new questions. At a 1975 conference on the black family at Stanford, St. Clair Drake explained how previous generations of scholars—white and black, including W. E. B. Du Bois, E. Franklin Frazier, and Kenneth Clark—operated according to a "cultural assimilationist" viewpoint. He meant that they viewed certain black social patterns as pathological and in need of change to ensure equal opportunity in America. However, younger black scholars, molded by the Black Power movement, rejected the continued "derogation of 'Blackness'" evident in simply replacing theories of biological racism with ones of "cultural deprivation," which had been magnified publicly ever since the Moynihan Report. "'Black is beautiful,' they cried out, and asked, 'Why is white Anglo Saxon culture any better than ghetto subculture?'" Drake explained.[116] This framework was not quite as new as these scholars imagined, for marginalized black scholars such as Allison Davis had already developed a corpus of research from those same premises.[117]

A sea change was nevertheless evident, and scores of scholars looked anew at patterns of black life previously dismissed as embarrassing and problematic. Black sociologist Andrew Billingsley's *Black Families in White America* (1968) was an important landmark in the new tradition, as was an edited volume entitled *The Death of White Sociology* (1973).[118] In the latter, Billingsley contributed an essay that criticized "the white Anglo-conformity perspective which judges black people outside the context of their unique anchor in history." He emphasized "the strengths of the black community and the black family" that "have enabled black people to survive in a hostile environment for over 300 years."[119] Historians—black and white— likewise reacted against the stigmatizing images of black family life that pervaded America by writing histories of slave life that emphasized its strength and resilience over time. John Blassingame's *The Slave Community* (1972), George Rawick's *From Sundown to Sunup* (1972), and Herbert Gutman's *The Black Family in Slavery and Freedom, 1750–1925* (1976), were three landmarks in this vein.[120] Meanwhile, Vincent Harding, Sterling Stuckey, and other nationalist-minded black historians made similar claims while excavating the long tradition of black nationalism.[121]

As Reddick began to circulate his research findings at conferences and in articles, it was clear that he was operating at the cutting edge of the new black social science. In a 1974 conference paper he stated bluntly, "Social science today is largely a European development and is strongly European-American oriented . . . especially as to concepts, methodology and professional training." "So persuasive—perhaps insidious—is its influence," Reddick continued, "that many non-Europeans . . . once they have been put through the mill of an American or European graduate school, come out thinking and writing from a European perspective." His exhibit A was the scholarship on the black family. With works such as Daniel P. Moynihan's *The Negro Family in America* (1965), E. Franklin Frazier's *The Negro Family in the United States* (1939), and Kenneth Clark's *Dark Ghetto* (1958) in mind, he criticized the tendency to measure black families according to "the norms of the Euro-American family." He inquired, "Is the norm of the monogamous nuclear family appropriate to the Black experience? Instead, would not the necessity and the struggle for *survival* be a more fundamental and relevant life principle?" He pointed to black people's remarkable ability to not only endure slavery and increase in numbers, but to "survive psychologically" to the point that they became an indispensable part of the Union army during the Civil War. Reddick also excoriated the marginalization of nontraditional methodologies like oral history, which were essential to counteracting the racism of the archive and documenting the black experience. Furthermore, when white scholars did begin to take such methodologies seriously, Reddick decried how foundations heaped money upon predominantly white institutions such as Duke while ignoring black ones like Fisk—even though Fisk had originally pioneered oral history way back in the 1930s.[122]

Reddick conducted new historical research of his own, generating new insights. He shared some of these at ASALH's annual conference in Atlanta in 1975. Reddick's paper, "Myth versus Fact and the Black Family," was part of a panel that included Andrew Billingsley, Robert Hill, and his Kinte colleagues J. Herman Blake and Leonard Jeffries. Without elaborating, Reddick first cautioned that West Africans—who comprised most New World slaves—had a "very different family structure" than Europeans, and that this needed to be considered when assessing black family life in the Americas. He then cited marriage records from colonial New England to support his contention that "whenever the Africans were permitted to do so, they established and maintained family life." Slaves in the South, however, comprised a "special problem" for which "the methodology of the standard family historians usually fails." Because slave marriages were not sanctioned under the law, historians who relied upon legal records to evaluate marriage found little evidence of family life among slaves. "Our researchers," Reddick contrastingly underlined, "by looking at the family as a *functional* unit have been able to establish that there were strong slave families on the basis of mutual affection, commitment, [and] support in addition to sex and biological relationships." Indeed, "Some of these non-legal families proved to be more binding and lasting than the legal and formal marriages of the big house," Reddick explained, citing African Americans' persistent search for family members after the Civil War. Moreover, Reddick had spent considerable time studying black family life from 1850 to 1900. This included looking closely at records from the Freedmen's Bureau. Based on that research he argued that "the Black generation from 1865–1900 was perhaps the most achieving generation of the total Black Experience in America." This finding, he believed, was a direct refutation of E. Franklin Frazier, Ira Berlin, and other scholars who argued that black family life had been disorganized under slavery and had remained so long afterwards.[123]

As important as the Kinte Library Project was in challenging conceptions of the black family, it ultimately paled in comparison to the cultural revolution spawned by Alex Haley's *Roots* (1976).[124] Released during the bicentennial, *Roots* became a bestseller and netted Haley a Pulitzer Prize. Furthermore, it was adapted into a television series that aired on ABC over eight consecutive nights the following year. An astounding 85 percent of American households tuned in, making it the most watched television show in American history up to that time. It proceeded to earn thirty-seven Emmy nominations. As Henry Louis Gates Jr. recalls, "*Roots* wasn't just part of the pop culture conversation in 1977. It *was* the conversation." The book and television series forced white Americans to take slavery seriously, and it engendered pride and newfound genealogical interest on the part of black Americans. *Roots* also exemplified Reddick's and the Kinte Library Project's points about the resilience of the black family in the face of unimaginable adversity. It presented a compelling repudiation of entrenched ideas about the black family as pathological, and according to Gates it was nothing short of a "gateway to new worlds, genealogical, geographical, cultural, and psychological worlds."[125] Reddick argued with Haley and his publisher over the timing of *Roots*'s publication, concerned that it might diminish interest in subsequent publications stemming from the Kinte Library Project. As he came to see, however, there was no competing with the cultural revolution that was *Roots*. Upon observing it he wrote, "The whole nation has been reminded that slavery was no picnic," but "The even greater lesson of 'Roots' is the way the slaves survived their exploitation and degradation."[126]

The New Racism in American Higher Education

Despite the positive racial changes that *Roots* both symbolized and galvanized, the late 1970s was at heart an era of backlash and retrenchment. The Republican Party ascended as its politicians cleverly exploited the social divisions and resentments that boiled over during the 1960s. Most importantly, their "Southern Strategy," which played upon white Southerners' sense of racial grievance amid black gains in civil rights, succeeded in transforming the South from solidly Democratic to solidly Republican by the 1980s.[127] In a sad reprise of the Reconstruction era a century earlier, the severe economic recession beginning in 1973 only hastened the retreat from liberal policies aimed at tackling racial problems. Amid economic stagnation, Watergate, the failed Vietnam War, revelations of extensive government lying and spying, and perceived government overreach in social affairs, many Americans followed the Republicans' new motto and came to see government itself as the problem. Consequently, even as the successes of the civil rights movement supported the growth of the largest and most powerful black middle class in the country's history, structural poverty remained endemic, and a national backlash to racial change intensified.

Few examples better illustrate the shifting winds than the U.S. Supreme Court case *Regents of the University of California v. Bakke* (1978). The plaintiff, a thirty-seven-year-old white man named Allan Bakke, charged UC Davis with racial discrimination when it failed to admit him to its medical school while reserving sixteen of its one hundred spots for minority students. The Court ruled in Bakke's favor, declaring that such racial quotas were a violation of the Equal Protection Clause of the Fourteenth Amendment, and that race could only be one factor among many in determining students' admission to universities. The decision struck a blow to Affirmative Action programs, which were based on the simple premise that race-based inequities demanded race-based solutions. Race-neutral or colorblind policies, on the other hand, while purporting to be fair, merely maintained present racial disparities and thus upheld white supremacy. More sinisterly, the ruling legitimized the notion that race had become a liability for white people ("reverse racism")—and one which they needed to defend against.[128]

Against this backdrop, and after his own trying experience at Temple, Reddick pursued the last major research subject of his career: "the new racism of American higher education." The subject was really many subjects, and it evolved into overlapping projects on institutional racism at predominantly white universities, the existential crisis facing HBCUs, and the history of black colleges. The 1977–78 academic year inaugurated the new work. That year Reddick served as both a visiting assistant professor of Afro-American Studies at Harvard and as a research fellow in the Moton Center for Independent Studies in Philadelphia.

At Harvard, Reddick observed many of the same conflicts over institutional power as at Temple. He was on campus in April 1976 when students held protests over university policies that they argued threatened the existence of the fledgling Afro-American Studies Department. They railed against a proposed cutback in African and Third World culture courses and a tenure policy which did not adequately account for the community-activist work that Black Studies scholars routinely engaged in.[129] They found a cause célèbre when Ephraim Isaac, the first full-time professor of the department, was denied tenure. Students disparaged this as a "racist procedure," partly because he was evaluated by scholars with no expertise in his field. They also suspected that his ideology played a role: "Professor Isaac is being forced to leave Harvard because he refuses to become Harvardized. He insists on teaching African history, literature, languages, and culture from a proud Black perspective."[130] Reddick clearly identified with the struggle.

In his limited time at Harvard, Reddick developed wide contacts with both black and white liberal arts students.[131] He taught a reduced load of courses, but ones such as "What Happened to the Black Revolution?" and "The History of the Black Family in America" were timely and important.[132] He also encouraged students to approach the university's well-known white professors, especially Nathan Glazer, Daniel Patrick Moynihan, and Christopher Jencks, with skepticism. He would direct them to black scholars' critiques of these men and their ideas. "My point would be that a student at Harvard has to pick and choose carefully if he is to get a good education there and not become alienated from his personal experience," Reddick explained.[133]

Reddick also began a formal examination of the black experience at Harvard. His exploratory visit to Harvard's libraries for the Kinte project suggested the need for such a project. In his application for a National Endowment for the Humanities grant, he proposed to study Harvard's racial policies in concert with the personal experiences of black students from the nineteenth century to the present. He began sifting through class yearbooks, press reports, diaries, and private letters home, and he interviewed present and former students. His personal papers are filled with notes and manuscripts with such titles as "Hiding Blacks at Harvard." One of these discussed Harvard's marginalization of Richard T. Greener, the first black graduate of Harvard, and W. E. B. Du Bois, the institution's first black PhD. Like most of Reddick's projects in these years, he did not complete this one, but he did lay the groundwork for subsequent investigations.[134]

The Moton Center fellowship helped Reddick to prioritize other aspects of his research. In 1975, the center remade itself into a black think tank designed specifically to combat the "'brain drain' that has siphoned off some of the best black scholars from black colleges into other institutions."[135] Its support of a dozen or so postdoctoral fellows each year was an attempt to address the grossly disproportionate funding available to black and white scholars. For instance, the Center for Advanced Study in the Behavioral Sciences at Stanford had until then supported only five black scholars throughout its twenty-five-year existence. As a professor at Temple and then Harvard, Reddick was not the ideal candidate for a Moton fellowship, but the inclusion of distinguished black scholars raised the center's profile and facilitated productive discussions among fellows. He served alongside such eminent scholars as Helen G. Edmonds, a historian of Reddick's generation who shattered both race and gender barriers when she became the first black woman to earn a PhD from Ohio State University in 1946. When she began the fellowship, she had only just concluded her long professorial career at North Carolina Central University. Her Moton Center project, "Historical Research on the American Negro Woman," anticipated the rise of black women's history as a major new field—and one which Reddick's generation of predominantly male scholars had woefully neglected.[136] The launch of the Association of Black Women Historians in October 1979, spearheaded by Rosalyn Terborg-Penn, Eleanor Smith, and Eleanor Parker, gave institutional form to a field that would transform both African American history and American women's history in the coming years.[137]

Reddick's focus on racism in higher education also had special resonance for the Moton Center. At the spring 1978 seminar of fellows, Reddick announced that he had completed a 240-page manuscript on the subject and that he was negotiating with a publisher. Although it, too, was never published, Reddick's report clearly laid out his conclusions and critiques. "The new racism is institutional and structural, built into the 'normal' operation of education and employment," he observed. With Herbert Bass in mind, he wrote that this milieu had given rise to a "new social type," the *"competitive liberal* . . . who 'talks the talk' of liberalism" but "fiercely competes to limit and diminish the education and employment of non-Whites and their participation in decision-making."[138] This involved accepting blacks into predominantly white universities but then limiting their numbers, controlling what courses in Black Studies were to be offered, and deciding who was to teach them. It also entailed hiring black professors "who are 'assimilationists' or are 'compatible' or who have no obvious appreciation of their Afro-American cultural roots." Referencing the *Bakke* case, Reddick criticized white claims of "racism in reverse," which really meant the "discontinuance of any arrangement that would enable Black students, scholars or employees to 'catch up' from the previous decades of exclusion and tokenism." At the most basic level, Reddick concluded, "The New Racism seeks to dilute Black power, to isolate the Black struggle from the progressive forces in the society and the world."[139]

Reddick was clearly critical of the way black people were being integrated into predominantly white universities, but he was even more concerned about the flip side of the equation: the existential threat that desegregation posed to HBCUs. He reported that the most startling finding of his research was "the realization that maybe, on balance . . . Blacks have lost more through 'desegregation' than they have gained." He explained how the age of austerity had only increased the pressure from whites to shutter HBCUs so that state funds could be concentrated on white schools. At the same time, he found that while African Americans comprised less than 1 percent of faculty members at predominantly white universities in Georgia, that state's HBCUs experienced a "comparatively tremendous . . . influx of White instructors and administrators," who had come to hold about 14 percent of all appointments. Reddick's research was important in quantifying these trends.

The implications of Reddick's findings were profound. For one thing, the closing of HBCUs and the diminishing black control over them threatened good middle-class jobs for African Americans. Less quantifiable but even more disturbing, many storied black colleges "are now 'lost' as symbols of Black leadership, achievement, and unmatched inspiration of youth," Reddick lamented.[140] The scope of the crisis ultimately propelled him to do something personal about it: he elected to close out his remarkable if occasionally tumultuous career at an HBCU—one that he knew well. Although he had left Dillard University under a cloud of controversy in the late 1930s, he would return as a civil rights hero in the late 1970s.

Conclusion

· ·

Afro-Americans themselves should take heart, for if their ancestors could survive slavery, surely their descendants should survive and win today's war against racism.

—Lawrence Reddick

When Reddick decided to return to Dillard University in 1978, it was in many ways a homecoming for him. After almost a decade of crusading within white institutions, he was happy to conclude his long career in a familiar atmosphere of black solidarity. His wife, Ruth, had recently retired from teaching and was eager to move back to her native New Orleans, but Reddick's decision to return to an HBCU ultimately grew out of his commitment to shoring up black colleges at a time of crisis.[1] Other activist black scholars, too, had begun trading in their more prestigious, higher-paying jobs at white institutions for positions at HBCUs for similar reasons. Reddick's friend C. Eric Lincoln had set a precedent in 1973 when he left Union Theological Seminary for Fisk. He did so, he told the press, to address the "desperate need [for] black scholars with visibility at black colleges," who could offer "a new kind of hope and a new kind of pride."[2] Reddick's similar decision was made easier when Dillard's president, Samuel DuBois Cook, a former classmate of Martin Luther King Jr.'s at Morehouse, made him a "stunning offer" to serve as a Distinguished Visiting Professor of History.[3] The position entailed teaching only one course per semester, which left ample time to work on the two books he had under contract. Reddick happily accepted the offer in 1978, and he held the position until 1987.

As Reddick began his final years at Dillard, a national movement was under way to save black colleges. The roots of the campaign traced back to the early years after *Brown v. Board of Education* (1954), when various black communities began to observe the problems associated with desegregation. The black campus movement further elevated the issue.[4] By 1980, black columnist Tony Brown called it a "pandemic issue that is unifying Blacks in a manner that is unprecedented in recent history."[5] Indeed, on September 29, 1980, activists staged a Black College Day march and rally in the nation's capital alongside countless local demonstrations.[6] In New Orleans, a petition drive garnered several thousand signatures and galvanized the creation of the Louisiana Coalition to Save Black Colleges. Reddick was part of the coalition and spoke at its inaugural meeting. He moderated a workshop on the politics of desegregation held at Howard University on the eve of the march.

In the longer buildup to the national protests, Tony Brown interviewed Reddick at length and published the remarks in his nationally syndicated column. Reddick explained how "Under the cloak of desegregation . . . the situation in Louisiana is worse now than it was under segregation." Specifically, the predominantly white Louisiana State University now recruited the state's top black students and left HBCUs like Southern University and Grambling State University comparatively diminished. LSU was able to do this because its wealth and prestige—burnished by its receipt of ten times the level of state funding as those black colleges—made it a more reliable path to career success. Furthermore, integration continued to be one-sided. Ninety percent of the boards of trustees at state universities remained white, blacks held only 1 percent of faculty appointments at white colleges, and whites held over 25 percent of faculty appointments at HBCUs in the state. Reddick and others therefore called for a reallocation of state funds and an increased black presence throughout the system.[7]

On the other side of this divide were the many Americans, including many prominent African Americans, who viewed black colleges as little more than a racist remnant from a bygone era. Michael Meyers of the national NAACP declared, "There is no defense of either a 'white' or a 'Black' school except in the context of an undemocratic, racist society." Kenneth Clark said that black schools were "inferior institutions," and that "to spend money . . . on those Black schools in 1979 is simply an effort to keep them separate and unequal."[8] Interestingly, Meyers and Clark were reiterating arguments that predominated during the days of segregation. Reddick himself made such points during the 1940s, such as in a 1947 *Journal of Negro Education* article in which he took pains to refute those who believed that black schools could be better, more nurturing places for black students. The color of a teacher's skin does not matter, he declared, and students must learn to interact with whites and "live in One World."[9] But context was everything, and in those days activists were fighting to achieve desegregation as a universal human right. Toward that end, they called for blacks to close ranks and unite in their calls for integration. After that right was won, the struggle turned to maintaining and expanding black power—not surrendering it—during desegregation.

While Clark and Meyers seemed stuck in the past, Reddick doubled down on his defense of black colleges. In response to an article in the *New York Times* that treated black colleges dismissively, Reddick penned a stiff rejoinder.[10] He argued that the best black schools are as rigorous as the best white ones, and that his own experience was a testament to that. "I received a better education at Fisk University than at the University of Chicago," he declared, for Fisk boasted great scholars who were "equal to social scientists anywhere." Furthermore, those scholars "were like older brothers, who also gave valuable advice on making it in graduate school and in the competitive outside world." At Chicago, on the other hand, Reddick reported finding no such mentorship or even a single black professor to serve as a role model. "The great difference," he concluded, "seems to be social and psychological. . . . The black college provides a 'home' for teen-agers who need understanding and support, in a world indifferent or hostile to their desires and ambitions."[11]

As always, Reddick's scholarship followed his activist concerns. He set out to write an ambitious general history of black colleges. He enlisted St. Clair Drake and Benjamin Quarles in the effort, but both had to abandon the project early on after health problems and other priorities.[12] Reddick nevertheless persisted, and he gathered significant new research on the fate of black colleges in the age of desegregation. The most revealing information stemmed from a visit to Lincoln University in Missouri, the storied HBCU which had nearly lured Reddick as a faculty member in 1960. During the visit, he stayed with Lorenzo Greene, a longtime friend and retired professor of black history there, and his wife, Thomasina, a former Fisk classmate. Reddick was stunned by what he found: "I, myself, was amazed to learn, when I set foot on the campus, that White students outnumbered Black." In reviewing campus newspapers and documents, and in interviewing students, faculty members, and administrators, he observed that the spirit of black uplift—so palpable in earlier years—had all but disappeared after the "White invasion." Most of the white students, he found, were commuters who had little interest in the life of the university, much less in the special character of HBCUs. He came to understand a widely felt "bitter jest" within the black community at the time: "If this is integration, let's go back to Jim Crow!"[13]

Reddick never finished the larger history of black colleges, but the work he did complete was nonetheless significant. His personal papers remain a useful source for historians, and later scholars and documentarians would pick up his baton.[14] Stanley Nelson and Marco Williams's documentary *Tell Them We Are Rising: The Story of Black Colleges and Universities* (2017), both through its broad scope and its popular appeal, best mirrors Reddick's own ambitions with the project. For various reasons, many scholars in the late twentieth century came to prioritize narrower, more specialized investigations. Professional knowledge and expertise expanded exponentially, but so did the gulf between scholars and the American public. Reddick, for whom scholarship was always a form of activism, was never satisfied with that state of affairs. Indeed, Reddick's history of black colleges sought out "the American people in general—including educators and Congresspersons," on the premise that if they "really knew the actual history of the Black College, they would demand that its creative elements be preserved and enhanced for the benefit of the whole society."[15] His work and that of others ultimately helped HBCUs rebound and grow by 24.3 percent between 1984 and 1993, which in fact outpaced American higher education generally by 44 percent.[16]

Reddick also committed to Dillard itself, where his modest course load did not stop him from throwing his energies into teaching and the larger life of the university. He offered survey courses in African American history and advanced seminars on the civil rights movement. He participated in symposia and trained yet another generation of students. For example, in the spring of 1980, he and some of his students presented at a two-day symposium on campus called "The New Urban Syndrome." In his speech, Reddick set the tone for the conference by insisting that "New programs designed to bring about social changes as great as those that occurred during the 1960s are necessary." His influence on Dillard students was on display when the *New Pittsburgh Courier* printed conference remarks from several of his students. Five of them had made "intensive studies of civil rights leaders and their campaigns during the 1960s." One of them, Akwasi B. Assensoh, a Ghanaian who later became a history professor at Indiana University and the University of Oregon, echoed Reddick's view that Martin Luther King Jr. had erred when he "got tangled up in the Vietnam War." He also pointed out critically that "Dr. King did not control the press as did many of the African leaders."[17]

In other ways, though, Reddick showed his age as he struggled with a new generation of students who "seem not to enjoy reading" nor "look forward to becoming writers," as he told attendees at a 1981 Amistad Conference. In a complaint that cultural critic Neil Postman would soon make famous in *Amusing Ourselves to Death* (1985), Reddick noted how students "have become so habituated to television and the movies, that they seek to get not only the news by way of the picture tube but also much of history, literature, sociology, economics and even science."[18] Not giving in, Reddick continued pushing students to read and write. In 1988, he even self-published an eclectic mix of his students' creative writing. Themes of black self-determination, racial unity, and the power of history predominated.[19]

As usual, Reddick also involved himself in larger political struggles during his Dillard days. Nationally, he supported Jesse Jackson and his Rainbow Coalition during his two failed bids for the Democratic nomination in 1984 and 1988, seeing in Jackson the person best suited "to advance the unfinished Crusade of our beloved Martin Luther King."[20] However, the rise of Ronald Reagan to the Oval Office crystallized a new era of conservatism, and Reddick grew increasingly frustrated by "the reactionary policies that are now coming out of Washington."[21] As he often did, he turned to St. Clair Drake for edification and commiseration. "I realize that the whole nation and much of the world is not devoid of liberal and consistent change," he wrote to Drake in 1984. "But who's helping our folks in South Africa today? And who's contending for 'self-determination' in the Black Belt? . . . Has the third world idea and support vanished?"[22] Drake found some solace in the anti-apartheid campaign and the protests against Reagan's covert operations in Central America, but he also confessed to being in a "continuous state of psychological depression" over "how much of a mess I've made over my professional life." "I've frittered away energies that should have been put into the production of books that had been planned," he bemoaned.[23] Reddick tried to dispel Drake's misguided self-criticisms, but he also identified with his friend, remarking on another occasion about how "time bit by bit continues to take his toll."[24] It was bitter indeed for Reddick and Drake to see the resurgent conservatism undermining the civil rights gains they had spent their lives helping to win.

Yet the circumstances were not quite as dire as Reddick's and Drake's recriminations suggest. A landmark conference and the book that grew out of it, *The State of Afro-American History: Past, Present, and Future* (1985), highlighted one of the racial transformations that was not to be undone by the day's conservatism.[25] More than any other publication of the time, the edited volume testified to the remarkable maturation and growing sophistication of the field, and to its high place within American history generally. As John Hope Franklin explained in his influential historiographical essay in the volume, the newest generation of black scholars was by far the largest, most sophisticated, and most highly trained group ever.[26] To be sure, the relative number of black scholars in the American professoriate remained pitifully low, and the black institutional presence at predominantly white universities was diminished by the shuttering of nearly half of the approximately six hundred Black Studies programs across the country between 1973 and 1983.[27] Black scholars nevertheless exerted a sizable influence on the study of black history throughout the profession, and American history would never be the same. Race and the black experience could never again be ignored as constituent forces within American life.

Reddick's involvement with the conference and the book was characteristic of him. Ever suspicious of white control over black history, he clashed with the white editors and staff at Louisiana State University Press over the royalties and reproduction rights for authors of the prospective book.[28] The chief editor of the volume, Darlene Clark Hine, a black woman and an emerging force within black history, tried to assuage Reddick's concerns. But Reddick was not having it.[29] He ultimately refused to let the press publish his essay on President Lincoln and the freedmen, so the volume—in some ways a who's who of black historians at the time—would not bear his name, except in the footnotes.

Nonetheless, Reddick's engagement with Hine, Thomas C. Holt, James D. Anderson, Robert L. Harris Jr., and other emerging leaders in the field testified not only to how much black history was in good hands, but also to how much those scholars acknowledged and appreciated the work of their black scholarly forebears. Reddick was happy to help Harris in his notable article on the history of the Committee on Negro Studies.[30] And he was especially eager to engage with Anderson's conference paper on racism within high school history textbooks.[31] Anderson drew from Reddick's pioneering research into that topic, and Reddick in turn offered useful feedback on the conference paper.[32] For Reddick, who had made a name for himself in the 1930s by critically assessing the work of earlier historians, he had to respect the enthusiasm and vigor with which the new generation of black scholars approached the field. One would like to think that it gave Reddick some solace late in life. Perhaps the plight of the black scholar in the ivory tower was no longer quite so lonely as it had once been.

・・・・・・

Reddick passed away in New Orleans on August 2, 1995, survived by his wife, Ruth, and brother Harold. The *New York Times* published an obituary that captured the basics of his extraordinary career.[33] In the years since, Reddick has occasionally been honored, such as with a lecture series at Alabama State University and a scholarship award bearing his name from the Association of Third World Studies.[34] On the whole, however, Reddick remains very little known despite being one of the most notable African American intellectuals of the twentieth century.[35]

Several factors have combined to keep Reddick's life and contributions in the shadows. For one, a significant amount of Reddick's work and activism, especially in librarianship, was not the type to attract attention. The painstaking, collective work of building an archive or privately advising public figures gets marginalized in an individualistic culture that celebrates only the leaders who give the speeches and the writers who are credited as the authors. Second, although Reddick did publish a lot, he frequently did so in organs that did not reach a large national audience. For a long time, his generation of Jim Crow scholars had been shut out from mainstream publications, universities, and professional organizations. After that began to change, Reddick bypassed more prestigious posts to shore up black institutions and serve the black community, which the white world stigmatized as inferior and tended to disregard. His books on Phi Beta Sigma and the Opportunities Industrialization Center, for instance, were largely internal ones with narrow targeted audiences. At the same time, his activism got in the way of publishing his dissertation as a book or writing a monograph that would have lasting influence on the history profession. He elected instead to write an eclectic blend of timely articles and books, including *Crusader without Violence* and *Worth Fighting For*, which targeted a wide popular audience but had limited staying power. Third, Reddick was well known within the black intellectual world, but few people understood the full scope of his peripatetic career of over sixty years. As he habitually shifted professions between historian, librarian, and activist, he never stayed at any one institution or location for more than nine years—and often for only half that time. Reddick's variegated life has been lost in the process. Furthermore, unlike many of his contemporaries, Reddick never had children or a corps of doctoral students who might have been committed to retracing his path and carrying his legacy forward. Without such parties to take an interest, even prominent figures can be forgotten as the years go by. Finally, there was the practical obstacle that his papers were not processed or accessible at the Schomburg Library for many years.

Bringing Reddick out of the shadows and resurrecting him within American social and intellectual life are the first steps toward overcoming this historiographical neglect. By recovering his long, variegated career, we gain a clearer sense of the long black freedom struggle and its radical, global, and intellectual dimensions—topics the introduction spells out explicitly. This book has sought to cast Reddick not in the individualistic frame so typical within popular biography but rather in the spirit of mutuality, collaboration, and solidarity that animated his life. From this vantage point, we begin to see how one man's story has the power to reveal a great deal about the larger world in which he lived. More profoundly, it tells us about our own world, and about ourselves.

This point was driven home in April 2018, when the editorial board of the *Montgomery Advertiser* broke its silence about its complicity in white supremacy. The editorial, "Our Shame: The Sins of Our Past for All to See," followed the creation of the National Memorial for Peace and Justice—an Equal Justice Initiative memorial in Montgomery, Alabama, that documents the more than 4,400 lynchings of African Americans between 1877 and 1950. In the wake of white supremacists on the march in places like Charlottesville, Virginia, and with the U.S. president only emboldening them, the *Montgomery Advertiser* finally spoke out. "We were wrong," the board declared. "We propagated a worldview rooted in racism and the sickening myth of racial superiority." In particular, "*The Advertiser* was careless in how it covered mob violence and the terror foisted upon African-Americans from Reconstruction through the 1950s. We dehumanized human beings. Too often we characterized lynching victims as guilty before proven so and often assumed they committed the crime." The editorial then provided concrete examples of their racist coverage, which they confessed had played a role in "the history of these dastardly, murderous deeds." "We must never be as wrong as this again," the board concluded.[36]

Had Reddick been around to read this, he likely would have responded, "What took so long!?" After all, his 1939 dissertation had carefully analyzed southern newspapers in the run-up to the Civil War. Way back then he had detailed southern newspapers' participation in white supremacy, and he had explained how periodicals that were controlled by the white ruling class should only be expected to serve its interests. Reddick would have appreciated the novelty of a prominent southern newspaper like the *Advertiser* taking such a stand, but he also would have been frustrated by its carefully constricted admission of guilt. It did not wade past 1950 and confess to the paper's continued racism, such as its ridiculing of the civil rights movement and its leaders, or its reckless amplification of Governor John Patterson's Communist slanders against Reddick himself. Nor did it pause to admit its collusion with slavery, even though it had been regarded as "the leading paper of the Confederacy" during the nineteenth century.[37]

This tendency to only occasionally glance at history, and then to only selectively take responsibility for it, was precisely what Reddick and other black thinkers considered the great tragedy of the United States. They dedicated endless energies to counteracting Americans' historical ignorance, which they knew crippled the country from dealing productively with its problems and made life worse for everyone. "History . . . is not merely something to be read. And it does not refer merely, or even principally, to the past," James Baldwin expressed in a celebrated remark. "On the contrary, the great force of history comes from the fact that we carry it within us, are unconsciously controlled by it in many ways, and history is literally present in all that we do. It could scarcely be otherwise, since it is to history that we owe our frames of reference, our identities, and our aspirations."[38] Reddick understood history in the same capacious terms, and he worked tirelessly to provide not only African Americans but all Americans with a usable past—one true and messy and complex enough to allow Americans to link the past with the present and to glimpse paths through the morass. His story has much still to teach us.

Above all, Reddick underscores in bold terms how *black thought matters*. If Reddick's life should teach us anything, it is that scholarship at its best is organically connected with larger social struggles—that it both grows out of and informs contemporary concerns. The rise of Black Lives Matter, of the African American Intellectual History Society, and of other variants of the twenty-first century's freedom struggle testify to a growing hunger and still urgent need to take black thought seriously. For too long black voices, like those from other nonwhite and marginalized groups, have been muffled and disregarded within mainstream America. Reddick did as much as anyone to chronicle and protest that marginalization, but it still prevails from the halls of Congress to Hollywood studios to academic disciplines like U.S. intellectual history, which now incorporate some black voices while nevertheless refusing to centralize them. Yet it is precisely these voices—these perspectives—which the country so desperately needs right now. Black perspectives are not less important because they have been regularly excluded from the corridors of power. Rather, it's through observing their very marginalization that we can better understand and critique the powerful. In other words, it is on the peripheries of power where many of the most innovative ideas are generated. Reddick's decision to consistently situate himself within those peripheries—from black colleges to underfunded libraries to protest organizations—helps to explain why his perspectives continue to provide a wellspring of insight into American life.

Black thought also matters because it is frankly the most American, the most democratic thought of all. Reddick's bold calls for democracy, justice, equality, dignity, and self-determination for all peoples, which he voiced throughout his long life from the Great Depression to the Reagan Revolution, all testify to this fact. From their spaces of oppression, African Americans somehow found a way not merely to survive but to thrive. They did so by often adopting a higher moral code than white Americans, and especially by committing more fully to America's founding ideals, which white Americans routinely preached but rarely practiced. By marginalizing black perspectives like Reddick's, Americans are thus diminishing the best parts of their own tradition and culture, and they are losing sight of who truly embodies the principles they espouse. In his famous Letter from Birmingham Jail, Reddick's mentee Martin Luther King Jr. expressed this in a way that only he could: "One day the South will recognize its real heroes. They will be the James Merediths . . . facing jeering and hostile mobs and the agonizing loneliness of the life of a pioneer. They will be old oppressed, battered Negro women . . . who rose up with a sense of dignity and with [their] people decided not to ride segregated buses. . . . They will be the young high school and college students, the young ministers of the gospel and a host of their elders, courageously and nonviolently sitting-in at lunch counters and willingly going to jail for conscience sake. One day the South will know that when these disinherited children of God sat down at lunch counters they were in reality standing up for what is best in the American dream."[39] Yet over half a century later, that day has not yet arrived, and it does not seem near.

Black thought points the way forward. How better to overcome racial divisions than to commemorate black freedom fighters rather than white slaveowners or Confederate generals, as Reddick called Americans to do? How better to confront the "post-truth" era than by drawing on the black tradition of plainly speaking truth to power, which Reddick exemplified? How better to resist the rise of white supremacy or even global climate change than to remember the fundamental truth—so regularly spoken by black activists like Reddick—that human beings have more in common than not and that they are stronger together?

Perhaps as much as anything, Reddick's life and thought, like those of his comrades, should steady us in our own unsteady times. When we glimpse the profound, earth-shattering changes that occurred during Reddick's lifetime, including most dramatically the end of Jim Crow and global decolonization, we should be reminded that even the most stubborn and oppressive regimes are not beyond the forces of history. All regimes, all empires, and indeed all of human existence will come to an end with time.

But as Reddick's struggle reminds us, that larger truth should not tempt us into indifference or lethargy, for that history is yet to be written. People must actively refashion the world to make it a more just and habitable place. Reddick and his generation showed this time and again, and their example should be a call to action today.

Even as we confront our own inevitable limitations in changing the world, Reddick implores us to recognize that it's the struggle itself that's meaningful, regardless of the conclusion. W. E. B. Du Bois once wrote, "Life is not length of days nor plethora of pleasure, but satisfaction of work attempted."[40] Certainly by that measure, Reddick's life was one well lived. Few people ever pursued so variously or committed so fully to a life of purposeful struggle. If others should follow his example, then perhaps, as Reddick once dared to dream, we may "survive the days of anguish that are upon us." "Even in a mad world," he mused, "the spirit of man may yet prevail."[41]

Notes

Archival Abbreviations

Only collections cited frequently are abbreviated.

ARC-AU	Archives Research Center, Robert W. Woodruff Library, Atlanta University
DBP-UMAL	W. E. B. Du Bois Papers (MS 312), Special Collections and University Archives, University of Massachusetts Amherst Libraries
FUSC	Fisk University, John Hope and Aurelia E. Franklin Library, Special Collections
HMBP-UMAL	Horace Mann Bond Papers (MS 411), Special Collections and University Archives, University of Massachusetts Amherst Libraries
LDRP-SC	Lawrence D. Reddick Papers, Schomburg Center for Research in Black Culture, New York Public Library
LJGP-LC	Lorenzo Johnston Greene Papers, Library of Congress
MJHP-NU	Melville J. Herskovits Papers, Northwestern University
MLKP-AU	Morehouse College Martin Luther King, Jr. Collection, Robert W. Woodruff Library, Atlanta University Center
MLKP-BU	Martin Luther King, Jr. Papers, Howard Gotlieb Archival Research Center, Boston University
MLKP-KC	Martin Luther King, Jr. Papers, Martin Luther King, Jr., Center for Nonviolent Social Change, Inc.
SCDP-SC	St. Clair Drake Papers, Schomburg Center for Research in Black Culture, New York Public Library

Introduction

1. David Bittan, "'We've Got Each Other' a Good TV Effort," *Trenton Times* (Trenton, NJ), September 30, 1977.

2. "KKK on 'Black Perspective,'" *Racine Courier* (Racine, Wisconsin), October 1, 1977.

3. Walter Goodman, "How Should Public TV Handle the Inflammatory?," *New York Times*, December 11, 1977.

4. Bittan, "We've Got Each Other."

5. "Around the Nation: Station Allowed to Air Klansmen and Nazi," *New York Times*, October 1, 1977; John Carmody, "The TV Column," *Washington Post*, September 29,

1977; Jonathan Braun, "Liberals Feel Torn Apart over Nazi-Klan Show on Public TV," *New York Jewish Week*, September 11, 1977.

6. Manning Marable, *Dispatches from the Ebony Tower: Intellectuals Confront the African American Experience* (New York: Columbia University Press, 2000), xii–xiv.

7. For more on the "race vindicationist" tradition, see V. P. Franklin, *Living Our Stories, Telling Our Truths: Autobiography and the Making of the African-American Intellectual Tradition* (New York: Scribner, 1995), 15–16.

8. Little remains known about many of these important figures, with Reddick being only the most glaring. See Stephen G. Hall, *A Faithful Account of the Race: African American Historical Writing in Nineteenth-Century America* (Chapel Hill: University of North Carolina Press, 2009), 233. For the best work on black historians and historiography, see Pero Gaglo Dagbovie, *The Early Black History Movement, Carter G. Woodson, and Lorenzo Johnston Greene* (Urbana: University of Illinois Press, 2007); Pero Gaglo Dagbovie, *African American History Reconsidered* (Urbana: University of Illinois Press, 2010); August Meier and Elliot Rudwick, *Black History and the Historical Profession, 1915–1980* (Urbana: University of Illinois Press, 1986); and Earl E. Thorpe, *Black Historians: A Critique* (New York: Morrow, 1971).

9. Ira Berlin, "Dedication: In Memory of Sara Dunlap Jackson, May 28, 1919–April 19, 1991," *Federal Records and African American History* 27 (Summer 1997), National Archives, https://www.archives.gov/publications/prologue/1997/summer/sara-dunlap-jackson.html.

10. See Matthew J. Countryman, *Up South: Civil Rights and Black Power in Philadelphia* (Philadelphia: University of Pennsylvania Press, 2006); Kevin K. Gaines, *American Africans in Ghana: Black Expatriates and the Civil Rights Era* (Chapel Hill: University of North Carolina Press, 2006); Erik S. Gellman, *Death Blow to Jim Crow: The National Negro Congress and the Rise of Militant Civil Rights* (Chapel Hill: University of North Carolina Press, 2012); Glenda Gilmore, *Defying Dixie: The Radical Roots of Civil Rights, 1919–1950* (New York: Norton, 2008); Jacquelyn Dowd Hall, "The Long Civil Rights Movement and the Political Uses of the Past," *Journal of American History* 91 (March 2005): 1233–63; James H. Meriwether, *Proudly We Can Be Africans: Black Americans and Africa, 1935–1961* (Chapel Hill: University of North Carolina Press, 2002); John Munro, *The Anticolonial Front: The African American Freedom Struggle and Global Decolonisation, 1945–1960* (Cambridge: Cambridge University Press, 2017); Brian Purnell and Jeanne Theoharis, *The Strange Careers of the Jim Crow North: Segregation and Struggle Outside of the South* (New York: New York University Press, 2019); Robert O. Self, *American Babylon: Race and the Struggle for Postwar Oakland* (Princeton, NJ: Princeton University Press, 2003); Thomas J. Sugrue, *Sweet Land of Liberty: The Forgotten Struggle for Civil Rights in the North* (New York: Random House, 2008); Patricia Sullivan, *Days of Hope: Race and Democracy in the New Deal* (Chapel Hill: University of North Carolina Press, 1996); Jeanne Theoharis and Komozi Woodard, *Freedom North: Black Freedom Struggles outside the South, 1940–1980* (New York: Palgrave Macmillan, 2003); and Penny M. Von Eschen, *Race against Empire: Black Americans and Anticolonialism, 1937–1957* (Ithaca, NY: Cornell University Press, 1997).

11. Sugrue, *Sweet Land of Liberty*, xiii–xxviii.

12. See Katherine Mellen Charron, *Freedom's Teacher: The Life of Septima Clark* (Chapel Hill: University of North Carolina Press, 2009); Vicky L. Crawford et al., eds., *Women in the Civil Rights Movement: Trailblazers and Torchbearers, 1941–1965* (Bloomington: University of Indiana Press, 1993); Ashley Farmer, *Remaking Black Power: How Black Women Transformed an Era* (Chapel Hill: University of North Carolina Press, 2017); Joseph R. Fitzgerald, *The Struggle Is Eternal: Gloria Richardson and Black Liberation* (Lexington: University Press of Kentucky, 2018); V. P. Franklin and Bettye Collier-Thomas, *Sisters in Struggle: African American Women in the Civil Rights Struggle* (New York: New York University Press, 2001); Keith Gilyard, *Louise Thompson Patterson: A Life of Struggle for Justice* (Durham, NC: Duke University Press, 2017); Dayo F. Gore, Jeanne Theoharis, and Komozi Woodard, eds. *Want to Start a Revolution? Radical Women in the Black Freedom Struggle* (New York: New York University Press, 2009); Chana Kai Lee, *For Freedom's Sake: The Life of Fannie Lou Hamer* (Urbana: University of Illinois Press, 1999); Danielle L. McGuire, *At the Dark End of the Street: Black Women, Rape, and Resistance—a New History of the Civil Rights Movement from Rosa Parks to the Rise of Black Power* (New York: Vintage Books, 2010); Sherie M. Randolph, *Florynce "Flo" Kennedy, The Life of a Black Feminist Radical* (Chapel Hill: University of North Carolina Press, 2015); Barbara Ransby, *Ella Baker and the Black Freedom Movement: A Radical Democratic Vision* (Chapel Hill: University of North Carolina Press, 2004); Robyn C. Spencer, *The Revolution Has Come: Black Power, Gender, and the Black Panther Party in Oakland* (Durham, NC: Duke University Press, 2016); Jeanne Theoharis, *The Rebellious Life of Mrs. Rosa Parks* (New York: Random House, 2013).

13. Barbara Caine, *Biography and History* (New York: Palgrave Macmillan, 2010), 2. On the larger "biographic turn" within history, see Jeremy D. Popkin, *From Herodotus to H-Net: The Story of Historiography* (New York: Oxford University Press, 2016), 189–90; and "AHR Roundtable: Historians and Biography," *American Historical Review* 114 (June 2009): 573–661.

14. On the radical nature of the early civil rights movement, see Gilmore, *Defying Dixie*; Gellman, *Death Blow to Jim Crow*; and Sullivan, *Days of Hope*.

15. See Robert Korstad, *Civil Rights Unionism: Tobacco Workers and the Struggle for Democracy in the Mid-Twentieth-Century South* (Chapel Hill: University of North Carolina Press, 2003); Hall, "The Long Civil Rights Movement," 1254.

16. See Keisha N. Blain, *Set the World on Fire: Black Nationalist Women and the Global Struggle for Freedom* (Philadelphia: University of Pennsylvania Press, 2018); Farmer, *Remaking Black Power*; Peniel E. Joseph, "The Black Power Movement: A State of the Field," *Journal of American History* 96 (December 2009): 751–76; Peniel E. Joseph, *Waiting 'Til the Midnight Hour: A Narrative History of Black Power in America* (New York: Holt, 2007); "New Black Power Studies: National, International, and Transnational Perspectives," *Journal of African American History* 92 (Autumn 2007): 463–560; Nikhail Pal Singh, *Black Is a Country: Race and the Unfinished Struggle for Democracy* (Cambridge, MA: Harvard University Press, 2004); Spencer, *The Revolution Has Come*; Timothy Tyson, *Radio Free Dixie: Robert F. Williams and the Roots of Black Power* (Chapel Hill: University of North Carolina Press, 1999); Rhonda Y. Williams, *Concrete Demands: The Search for Black Power in the 20th Century*

(New York: Routledge, 2015); and Komozi Woodard, *A Nation within a Nation: Amiri Baraka (LeRoi Jones) and Black Power Politics* (Chapel Hill: University of North Carolina Press, 1999).

17. Manning Marable and Leith Mullings, eds., *Let Nobody Turn Us Around: Voices of Resistance, Reform, and Renewal* (New York: Rowman & Littlefield, 2000), xxi.

18. Herbert Hill quoted in Carol Polsgrove, *Divided Minds: Intellectuals and the Civil Rights Movement* (New York: Norton, 2001), 107.

19. St. Clair Drake, letter of support for Reddick's NEH grant application, 1978, box 8, folder 31, SCDP-SC.

20. For a look at how scholars have begun to broaden and revitalize African American intellectual history generally, see Keisha N. Blain, Christopher Cameron, and Ashley D. Farmer, eds., *New Perspectives on the Black Intellectual Tradition* (Evanston, IL: Northwestern University Press, 2018). See also Mia Bay, Farah Jasmine Griffin, Martha S. Jones, and Barbara Dianne Savage, eds., *Toward an Intellectual History of Black Women* (Chapel Hill: University of North Carolina Press, 2015).

Chapter One

1. Reddick quoted in Tony Brown, "Tony Brown's Journal," *Columbus Times* (Columbus, GA), September 23, 1980.

2. Fourteenth Census of the United States, 1920 (NARA microfilm publication T625, 2,076 rolls), Records of the Bureau of the Census, Record Group 29, National Archives, Washington, DC; "L. D. Reddick: Personal and Professional Information," circa 1955, box 8, LDRP-SC. Note: The Lawrence Reddick Papers are unprocessed. The folders are not numbered, and hence citations from the collection will only include box numbers. See Larry Tye, *Rising from the Rails: Pullman Porters and the Making of the Black Middle Class* (New York: Holt, 2004); and Elizabeth Clark-Lewis, *Living In, Living Out: African American Domestics in Washington, D.C., 1910–1940* (Washington: Smithsonian Institution Press, 1994).

3. L. D. Reddick, "Speech at Jacksonville, Fla Delta Affair," box 33, LDRP-SC.

4. L. D. Reddick, "T.U. Story: Pilgrimage to the White University," box 21, LDRP-SC.

5. Reddick, "Speech at Jacksonville, Fla Delta Affair."

6. Carter G. Woodson and Charles H. Wesley, *The Negro in Our History* (1922; repr., Washington, DC: Associated Publishers, 1962), 382–88; Stanton College Preparatory School, "Stanton's History," https://dcps.duvalschools.org/Page/10562 (accessed April 14, 2020).

7. James Weldon Johnson to Reddick, 1936, box 10, LDRP-SC; Malik Simba, "James Weldon Johnson (1871–1838)," The Black Past, http://www.blackpast.org/aah/johnson-james-weldon-1871-1938 (accessed April 14, 2020); Stanton School, "Stanton's History"; Joe M. Richardson, *A History of Fisk University, 1865–1946* (Tuscaloosa: University of Alabama Press, 1980), 136.

8. Paul Ortiz, *Emancipation Betrayed: The Hidden History of Black Organizing and White Violence in Florida from Reconstruction to the Bloody Election of 1920* (Berkeley: University of California Press, 2005), xv, xiv, xiv–xxii.

9. "L. D. Reddick Climaxes Brilliant Scholastic Career to Get Ph.D.," *Chicago Defender*, June 10, 1939; Reddick, "Speech at Jacksonville, Fla Delta Affair."

10. Reddick, "Speech at Jacksonville, Fla Delta Affair." For more on the contours and limitations of black middle-class culture at the turn of the twentieth century, see Kevin K. Gaines, *Uplifting the Race: Black Leadership, Politics, and Culture in the Twentieth Century* (Chapel Hill: University of North Carolina Press, 1996); and Evelyn Brooks Higginbotham, *Righteous Discontent: The Women's Movement in the Black Baptist Church, 1880–1920* (Cambridge, MA: Harvard University Press, 1994).

11. L. D. Reddick, "The Education of Negroes in States Where Separate Schools Are Not Legal," *Journal of Negro Education* 16 (Summer 1947): 290.

12. See Cheryl Knott, *Not Free, Not for All: Public Libraries in the Age of Jim Crow* (Amherst: University of Massachusetts Press, 2016); Wayne A. Wiegand and Shirley A. Wiegand, *The Desegregation of Public Libraries in the Jim Crow South: Civil Rights and Local Activism* (Baton Rouge: Louisiana State University Press, 2018).

13. Reddick, "Speech at Jacksonville, Fla Delta Affair."

14. Reddick; see also, Reddick to Marjorie Crump, July 28, 1959, box 41, LDRP-SC; Alpha Iota Sigma Chapter of Delta Sigma Theta Sorority presents Dr. L. D. Reddick, Founder's Day, A. L. Lewis Branch YMCA, Sunday, January 16, 1949, Reddick, L. D., Biographical Files, ARC-AU; and L. D. Reddick, "Where Can a Southern Negro Read a Book?," *New South* 9 (January 1954): 5–11.

15. "Text of the address of L. D. Reddick at the 'DuBois meeting' Town Hall, New York City," September 28, 1951, box 8, LDRP-SC.

16. L. D. Reddick, "As I Remember Woodson," *Negro History Bulletin* 17 (November 1953): 36.

17. Reddick, "Speech at Jacksonville, Fla Delta Affair."

18. Raymond Wolters, *The New Negro on Campus: Black College Rebellions of the 1920s* (Princeton, NJ: Princeton University Press, 1975), 28; James D. Anderson, *The Education of Blacks in the South, 1860–1935* (Chapel Hill: University of North Carolina Press, 1988), 239–41.

19. "Spelman and Morehouse Colleges Given Recognition," unspecified newspaper clipping dated January 19, 1930, A.A. Taylor Collection (original), box 114, folder 19, FUSC; Richardson, *A History of Fisk University*, 118.

20. Richardson, *A History of Fisk University*, 113–16, 138–44.

21. "L. D. Reddick Climaxes Brilliant Scholastic Career to Get Ph.D.," *Chicago Defender*, June 10, 1939; "Fisk University Will Hold 58th Annual Commencement," *Chicago Defender*, June 4, 1932; "HIGHEST," *Pittsburgh Courier*, June 18, 1932; see relevant "Annual Commencement Anniversary Programs," A. A. Taylor Collection (original), box 115, folder 11, FUSC; Edmonia W. to William C. Haywood, March 2, 1945, Fellowship Application, 1945, L. D. Reddick Fellowship File, Julius Rosenwald Fund Papers, FUSC.

22. Reddick quoted in George Breathett and Daniel T. Williams, "Lewis Wade Jones," *Journal of Negro History* 66 (Spring 1981): 85.

23. Reddick, "The Education of Negroes in States Where Separate Schools Are Not Legal," 298.

24. L. D. Reddick, "Black History as a Corporate Colony," *Social Policy* (May/June 1976): 1.

25. John Hope Franklin, *Mirror to America: The Autobiography of John Hope Franklin* (New York: Farrar, Straus and Giroux, 2005), 52.

26. Reddick, "Contrast: 1965 versus 1975," 8.

27. Franklin, *Mirror to America*, 45.

28. "Fisk Debaters to Meet New York U. Squad," *Chicago Defender*, March 7, 1931; "Hold Oratorical Contest at Fisk," *Chicago Defender*, June 13, 1931.

29. "Says Time Ripe for Young People to Take Control," *Norfolk Journal and Guide*, April 29, 1933.

30. Reddick to Horace Mann Bond, January 3, 1937, box 10, LDRP-SC.

31. "Pentagonal Debate, Fisk University vs. Talladega College," A.A. Taylor Collection (original), box 115, folder 52, FUSC.

32. Elinor Des Verney Sinnette, *Arthur Alfonso Schomburg: Black Bibliophile & Collector* (Detroit: Wayne State University Press, 1989), 154–56; "Who's Who," *Opportunity* 11 (January 1933): 1. For more on Schomburg, see Vanessa K. Valdés, *Diasporic Blackness: The Life and Times of Arturo Alfonso Schomburg* (Albany: SUNY Press, 2017).

33. Sinnette, *Arthur Alfonso Schomburg*, 154.

34. Sinnette, 154.

35. L. D. Reddick, "On the Road to Truth," review of *A Documentary History of the Negro People in the United States*, by Herbert Aptheker, *Phylon* 13 (1952): 168.

36. Sinnette, *Arthur Alfonso Schomburg*, 157.

37. "Negro History Week Being Observed," *Nashville Globe*, February 14, 1930; Stephen G. Hall, "Research as Opportunity: Alrutheus Ambush Taylor, Black Intellectualism, and the Remaking of Reconstruction Historiography, 1893–1954," *UCLA Historical Journal* 16 (1996): 51.

38. L. D. Reddick, "Is the White College Better—for Blacks?" circa 1980, box 25, LDRP-SC.

39. "107 Get Degrees from Fisk University," *Chicago Defender*, June 20, 1931.

40. Carter G. Woodson, *The Mis-Education of the Negro* (1933; repr., Hampton, VA: U.B. & U.S. Communications Systems, 1994), xii, 21.

41. Woodson, *Mis-Education of the Negro*, 21, 191–97. For more on Woodson and ASNLH, see Pero Gaglo Dagbovie, *The Early Black History Movement, Carter G. Woodson, and Lorenzo Johnston Greene* (Urbana: University of Illinois Press, 2007); Jacqueline Goggin, *Carter G. Woodson: A Life in Black History* (Baton Rouge: Louisiana State University Press, 1993); and Darlene Clark Hine, "Carter G. Woodson: White Philanthropy and Negro Historiography," in *Hine Sight: Black Women and the Re-Construction of American History* (Bloomington: Indiana University Press, 1994), 203–22.

42. L. D. Reddick, "Prempeh: Last King of the Ashanti," *Norfolk Journal and Guide*, March 18, 1933.

43. Woodson, *Mis-Education of the Negro*, 29, 53; W. E. B. Du Bois, ed., "The Unrest Among Negro Students," *Crisis* 34 (August 1927): 187–90, 208; Lester C. Lamon, "The Black Community in Nashville and the Fisk University Strike of 1924–1925," *Journal of Southern History* 60 (May 1974): 225–44.

44. Charles S. Johnson, *Shadow of the Plantation* (Chicago: University of Chicago Press, 1934); Charles S. Johnson, Edwin R. Embree, and W. W. Alexander, *The Collapse of Cotton Tenancy. Summary of Field Studies & Statistical Surveys, 1933–35* (Chapel Hill: University of North Carolina Press, 1935); Charles S. Johnson, *Growing Up in the Black Belt: Negro Youth in the Rural South* (Washington, DC: American Council on Education, 1941).

45. Richard Robbins, *Sidelines Activist: Charles S. Johnson and the Struggle for Civil Rights* (Jackson: University Press of Mississippi, 1996), 64–76.

46. Reddick, "Is the White College Better—for Blacks?"

47. "Negro Accomplishments," *Tennessean*, January 27, 1931; P. Olisanwuche Esedebe, *Pan-Africanism: The Idea and Movement, 1776–1963*, 2nd ed. (Washington, DC: Howard University Press, 1994), 95.

48. Robbins, *Sidelines Activist*, 76.

49. Reddick, "Is the White College Better—for Blacks?"

50. Horace M. Bond, "Intelligence Tests and Propaganda," *Crisis* 28 (June 1924): 61–64; Horace M. Bond, "What the Army 'Intelligence' Tests Measured," *Opportunity* 2 (July 1924): 197–202.

51. Reddick to Horace Mann Bond, November 23, 1936, box 10, LDRP-SC.

52. Reddick, "Is the White College Better—for Blacks?"; Horace Mann Bond, *Negro Education in Alabama: A Study in Cotton and Steel* (Washington, DC: Associated Publishers, 1939).

53. "Fellowship and Scholarship Application," January 15, 1930, Horace Mann Bond fellowship file, box 394, folder 10, Julius Rosenwald Fund Papers, FUSC; Wayne J. Urban, *Black Scholar: Horace Mann Bond, 1904–1972* (Athens: University of Georgia Press, 1992), 40–44.

54. Horace Mann Bond, *The Education of the Negro in the American Social Order* (New York: Prentice Hall, 1934), 13, 9, 8.

55. L. D. Reddick, "What Does the Younger Negro Think?," *Opportunity* 11 (October 1933): 312.

56. W. E. B. Du Bois to Reddick, September 15, 1930, DBP-UMAL; Reddick to the *Crisis*, April 30, 1930, DBP-UMAL.

57. L. D. Reddick, review of *Free Born: An Unpublishable Novel*, by Scott Nearing, *Opportunity* 11 (January 1933): 25.

58. Jonathan Scott Holloway, *Confronting the Veil: Abram Harris Jr., E. Franklin Frazier, and Ralph Bunche, 1919–1941* (Chapel Hill: University of North Carolina Press, 2002), 4–19.

59. Reddick, review of *Free Born*, 25.

60. L. D. Reddick, review of *The Adventures of the Black Girl in Her Search for God*, by George Bernard Shaw, *Opportunity* 11 (October 1933): 314.

61. Reddick, "What Does the Younger Negro Think?," 312.

62. L. D. Reddick, "The Younger Negro Looks at His College," *Opportunity* 12 (July 1934): 211.

63. Reddick, 211; "Claims Presidents of Race Colleges Are Incompetent," *Pittsburgh Courier*, July 14, 1934; William H. Ferris, "College Aims to Train Men for Restricted Status," *Afro-American*, July 28, 1934; George B. Nesbitt, "Urban League

and N.A.A.C.P. Called Two Schools of Thought in Battle for Racial Equality," *Chicago Defender*, August 4, 1934.

64. Reddick, "What Does the Younger Negro Think?," 312.

65. Reddick, 312.

66. John Crowe Ransom, "Reconstructed but Unregenerate," in *I'll Take My Stand: The South and the Agrarian Tradition*, by Twelve Southerners (1930; repr., Gloucester, MA: Peter Smith, 1976), 14, 15, 17.

67. L. D. Reddick, "Whose Ordeal?," *New Republic* (September 24, 1956): 9.

68. L. D. Reddick, "Racial Attitudes in American History Textbooks of the South," *Journal of Negro History* 19 (July 1934): 225–65.

69. Reddick, "Racial Attitudes in American History Textbooks," 237, 257.

70. "History Texts Blamed for Development of Prejudice, *Afro-American*, July 28, 1934.

71. David W. Blight, *Race and Reunion: The Civil War in American Memory* (Cambridge, MA: Harvard University Press, 2001), 258–72.

72. James D. Anderson, "Secondary School History Textbooks and the Treatment of Black History," in *The State of Afro-American History: Past, Present, and Future*, ed. Darlene Clark Hine (Baton Rouge: Louisiana State University, 1986), 254; Pero Gaglo Dagbovie, *African American History Reconsidered* (Urbana: University of Illinois Press, 2010), 71.

73. Mary W. Ovington to Reddick, December 21, 1936, box 10, LDRP-SC.

74. Marie E. Carpenter, "The Treatment of the Negro in American History School Textbooks: A Comparison of Changing Textbook Content, 1826 to 1939, with Developing Scholarship in the History of the Negro in the United States" (PhD diss., Columbia University, 1941); Edna M. Colson, "An Analysis of the Specific Reference to Negroes in Selected Curricula for the Education of Teachers" (PhD diss., Columbia University, 1940).

75. Council on Interracial Books for Children, *Stereotypes, Distortions, and Omissions in U.S. History Textbooks* (New York, 1977); Michael B. Kane, *Minorities in Textbooks: A Study of Their Treatment in Social Studies Texts* (Chicago: Quadrangle Books, 1970); James W. Loewen, *Lies My Teacher Told Me: Everything Your American History Textbook Got Wrong* (New York: Simon & Schuster, 2007).

76. See Peter Novick, *That Noble Dream: The 'Objectivity Question' and the American Historical Profession* (Cambridge: Cambridge University Press, 1988).

77. Reddick, "Racial Attitudes in American History Textbooks," 265.

Chapter Two

1. L. D. Reddick, "The Folklore of White Historians," *Equality* 2 (February 1940): 20, 33.

2. Lorenzo Greene to Reddick, January 11, 1934, box 33, folder 5, Lorenzo Johnston Greene Papers, Library of Congress.

3. L. D. Reddick, "The Younger Negro Looks at His College," *Opportunity* 12 (July 1934): 211.

4. Matthew W. Hughey, "Constitutionally Bound: The Founders of Phi Beta Sigma Fraternity and Zeta Phi Beta Sorority," in *Black Greek-Letter Organizations in the Twenty-First Century*, ed. Gregory S. Parks (Lexington: University Press of Kentucky, 2008), 95.

5. See W. Sherman Savage and L. D. Reddick, *Our Cause Speeds On: An Informal History of the Phi Beta Sigma Fraternity* (Atlanta: Fuller, 1957).

6. Savage and Reddick, *Our Cause Speeds On*, 82–84.

7. Jessica Harris and Vernon C. Mitchell Jr., "A Narrative Critique of Black Greek-Letter Organizations," in *Black Greek-Letter Organizations*, 145. For a broader history, see Lawrence C. Ross Jr., *The Divine Nine: The History of African American Sororities and Fraternities* (New York: Kensington, 2000).

8. Kevin G. Gaines, *Uplifting the Race: Black Leadership, Politics, and Culture in the Twentieth Century* (Chapel Hill: University of North Carolina Press, 1996), 20.

9. Gregory S. Parks and Matthew W. Hughey, *A Pledge with Purpose: Black Sororities and Fraternities and the Fight for Equality* (New York: New York University Press, 2020), 70–122.

10. Savage and Reddick, *Our Cause Speeds On*, 82, 91.

11. Savage and Reddick, 91–93; L. D. Reddick, ed., "The Crescent News-Letter," December 1934, box 27, LDRP-SC; "Phi Beta Sigma Business Forum," n.d., box 27, LDRP-SC; John Aubrey Davis, "We Win the Right to Fight for Jobs," *Opportunity* 16 (August 1938): 230–37.

12. Norman R. Yetman, "The Background of the Slave Narrative Collection," *American Quarterly* 19 (Autumn 1967): 540–41.

13. See Brenda E. Stevenson, "'Out of the Mouths of Ex-Slaves': Carter G. Woodson's *Journal of Negro History* 'Invents' the Study of Slavery," *Journal of African American History* 100 (Fall 2015): 698–720.

14. John B. Cade, "Out of the Mouths of Ex-Slaves," *Journal of Negro History* 20 (July 1935): 294–337.

15. Ulrich Bonnell Phillips, *American Negro Slavery: A Survey of the Supply, Employment and Control of Negro Labor as Determined by the Plantation Regime* (1918; repr., Baton Rouge: Louisiana State University Press, 1966), 307.

16. Reddick, "The Folklore of White Historians," 20; Norman R. Yetman, *Voices from Slavery: 100 Authentic Slave Narratives* (Mineola, NY: Dover, 2000), 340–42.

17. Cade, "Out of the Mouths of Ex-Slaves," 336.

18. "Scholars Will Study Ex-Slaves through FERA," *Pittsburgh Courier*, October 20, 1934.

19. "Proceedings of the Annual Meeting of the Association for the Study of Negro Life and History Held in Houston, Texas, November 10 to 14, 1934," *Journal of Negro History* 20 (January 1935): 1–12.

20. "Negro History Week Celebration Planned by Kentucky School," *Negro Star* (Wichita, KS), February 1, 1935.

21. "Dillard to Celebrate History Wk.," *Chicago Defender*, February 8, 1936; "Dillard to Stage Great History Week," *Plaindealer* (Kansas City, KS), February 7, 1936.

22. George P. Rawick, *The American Slave: A Composite Autobiography*, Vol. 1: *From Sundown to Sunup: The Making of the Black Community* (Westport, CT: Greenwood, 1972), xvi.

23. Library of Congress, "About this Collection," *Born in Slavery: Slave Narratives from the Federal Writers' Project, 1936 to 1938*, https://www.loc.gov/collections/slave-narratives-from-the-federal-writers-project-1936-to-1938/about-this-collection/ (accessed on April 14, 2020). See also Sterling A. Brown, "No Way to Disremember, Review of *Lay My Burden Down* by B. A. Botkin," *Journal of Negro Education* 15 (Spring 1946): 194–96; and Catherine A. Stewart, *Long Past Slavery: Representing Race in the Federal Writers' Project* (Chapel Hill: University of North Carolina Press, 2016).

24. Yetman, "The Background of the Slave Narrative Collection," 543.

25. Henry G. Alsberg quoted in Yetman, "The Background of the Slave Narrative Collection."

26. A. J. Negrotto to Reddick, April 30, 1936, box 10, LDRP-SC.

27. For a frank discussion of the issues involved in using the ex-slave interviews as historical sources, see John W. Blassingame "Using the Testimony of Ex-Slaves: Approaches and Problems," *Journal of Southern History* 41 (November 1975): 473–92.

28. Yetman, "The Background of the Slave Narrative Collection," 542.

29. L. D. Reddick, review of *American Minority Peoples*, by Donald Young, *Journal of Negro History* 19 (January 1934): 87–89; L. D. Reddick, review of *Social Attitudes*, edited by Kimball Young, *Journal of Negro History* 19 (April 1934): 208–10; "Proceedings of the Annual Meeting of the Association for the Study of Negro Life and History Held in Houston, Texas, November 10 to 14, 1934," *Journal of Negro History* 20 (January 1935): 11.

30. Kimball Young et al., eds., *Social Attitudes* (New York: Holt, 1931).

31. Reddick, review of *Social Attitudes*, 209, 210.

32. Rockefeller Foundation records, fellowships, fellowship recorder cards, RG 10.2 (FA426), folder "Reddick, Lawrence Dunbar—GEB-N," box 21.

33. Joe M. Richardson, "A White New Orleans Philanthropist Helps Build a Black University," *Journal of Negro History* 82 (Summer 1997): 328–42.

34. "Dillard Univ. Announces New Faculty Appointments," *Pittsburgh Courier*, May 11, 1935; Wayne J. Urban, *Black Scholar: Horace Mann Bond, 1904–1972* (Athens: University of Georgia Press, 1992), 61.

35. Allison Davis, Burleigh Gardner, and Mary Gardner, *Deep South: A Social Anthropological Study of Caste and Class* (Chicago: University of Chicago Press, 1941).

36. David A. Varel, "Bending the Academic Color Line: Allison Davis, the University of Chicago, and American Race Relations, 1941–1948," *Journal of Negro Education* 84 (November 2015): 534–46.

37. David A. Varel, *The Lost Black Scholar: Resurrecting Allison Davis in American Social Thought* (Chicago: University of Chicago Press, 2018), 91–98.

38. Reddick to Horace Mann Bond, June 24, 1937, HMBP-UMAL.

39. Pero Gaglo Dagbovie, *African American History Reconsidered* (Urbana: University of Illinois Press, 2010), 56–57.

40. L. D. Reddick, "Memorandum: Outline of Plan for Dept History at Dillard," February 8, 1937, box 10, LDRP-SC; "Lawrence Reddick Is Radio Speaker," *Chicago Defender*, February 26, 1938.

41. Varel, *Lost Black Scholar*, 110–11.

42. Akwasi B. Assensoh, "Obituaries: Lawrence Dunbar Reddick," *OAH Newsletter* 23 (November 1995): 19.

43. Reddick to President Trenholm, June 21, 1956, box 8, LDRP-SC. For more on the "politics of respectability," a term first coined by Evelyn Brooks Higginbotham, see Evelyn Brooks Higginbotham, *Righteous Discontent: The Women's Movement in the Black Baptist Church, 1880–1920* (Cambridge, MA: Harvard University Press, 1994); and Victoria W. Wolcott, *Remaking Respectability: African American Women in Interwar Detroit* (Chapel Hill: University of North Carolina Press, 2001).

44. "Missouri, Tennessee Club Women Hold Meet," *Pittsburgh Courier*, July 8, 1938.

45. Reddick to St. Clair Drake, April 21, 1959, box 41, LDRP-SC.

46. Ruth Reddick, "Toussaint and Haiti," *New History Bulletin* 4 (January 1941): 75; Ruth Reddick, "Glorious Palmares," *New History Bulletin* 4 (February 1941): 99; Ruth Reddick, "Cold Canaan," *New History Bulletin* 4 (April 1941): 168; Ruth Reddick, "J. W. Loguen," *New History Bulletin* 5 (November 1941): 40; Ruth Reddick, "T. Thomas Fortune," *New History Bulletin* 5 (November 1941): 42–43.

47. For an effective model to interrogate the sexism of the archives and piece together women's lives, see Jill Lepore's *Book of Ages: The Life and Opinions of Jane Franklin* (New York: Knopf, 2013). For two innovative books that center the romantic life of two black leftist activists, see Sara Rzeszutek Haviland, *James and Esther Cooper Jackson: Love and Courage in the Black Freedom Movement* (Lexington: University Press of Kentucky, 2015); and Stephen M. Ward, *In Love and Struggle: The Revolutionary Lives of James and Grace Lee Boggs* (Chapel Hill: University of North Carolina Press, 2016).

48. Andrew J. Rosa, "The Roots and Routes of 'Imperium in Imperio': St. Clair Drake, The Formative Years," *American Studies* 52 (November 2012): 62.

49. St. Clair Drake, "Studies of the African Diaspora: The Work and Reflections of St. Clair Drake," in *Against the Odds: Scholars Who Challenged Racism in the Twentieth Century*, ed. Benjamin P. Bowser and Louis Kushnick (Amherst: University of Massachusetts Press, 2002), 90–91.

50. Roger M. Williams, *The Bonds: An American Family* (New York: Atheneum 1971), 113.

51. L. D. Reddick, ed., "The Crescent," December 1935, box 27, LDRP-SC.

52. Savage and Reddick, *Our Cause Speeds On*, 95.

53. Reddick, ed., "The Crescent," December 1935.

54. Erik S. Gellman, *Death Blow to Jim Crow: The National Negro Congress and the Rise of Militant Civil Rights* (Chapel Hill: University of North Carolina Press, 2012), 2.

55. Savage and Reddick, *Our Cause Speeds On*, 97.

56. Gellman, *Death Blow to Jim Crow*, 25.

57. Savage and Reddick, *Our Cause Speeds On*, 99; "National Negro Congress Which Met in Chicago Acclaimed a Success," *New York Age*, February 22, 1936.

58. "Randolph Says Hope of Negro People Lies in Unity with Labor," *Daily Worker*, March 1, 1936.

59. Savage and Reddick, *Our Cause Speeds On*, 99.

60. Reddick, ed., "The Crescent," December 1935.

61. Gellman, *Death Blow to Jim Crow*, 26.

62. Savage and Reddick, *Our Cause Speeds On*, 99.

63. James H. Meriwether, *Proudly We Can Be Africans: Black Americans and Africa, 1935–1961* (Chapel Hill: University of North Carolina Press, 2002), 3.

64. "Protest New Orleans Italian Victory Parade: Fascists in Class against Teachers," *Pittsburgh Courier*, June 6, 1936; see also Kevin K. Gaines, *American Africans in Ghana: Black Expatriates and the Civil Rights Era* (Chapel Hill: University of North Carolina Press, 2006), 37–38.

65. L. D. Reddick, "Is the White College Better—for Blacks?," circa 1980, box 25, LDRP-SC.

66. See Davarian Baldwin, *Chicago's New Negroes* (Chapel Hill: University of North Carolina Press, 2007); Davarian L. Baldwin and Minkah Makalani, eds., *Escape from New York: The New Negro Renaissance beyond Harlem* (Minneapolis: University of Minnesota Press, 2013).

67. Margaret Walker, *How I Wrote Jubilee and Other Essays on Life and Literature*, ed. Maryemma Graham (New York: Feminist Press at the City University of New York, 1990), 50.

68. L. D. Reddick, "Arna Bontemps: Talent and Goodness," speech given in memoriam, Riverside Church, New York City, June 20, 1973, box 16, LDRP-SC.

69. Mary Ann Dzuback, *Robert M. Hutchins: Portrait of an Educator* (Chicago: University of Chicago Press, 1991), 142–44, quote on p. 143.

70. Michael Dennis, *Luther P. Jackson and a Life for Civil Rights* (Gainesville: University Press of Florida, 2004), 45.

71. L. D. Reddick University of Chicago Transcript, Julius Rosenwald Fund Papers, L. D. Reddick fellowship file, box 443, folder 3, FUSC.

72. Reddick to Horace Mann Bond, October 5, 1936, box 10, LDRP-SC; Reddick to Horace Mann Bond, March 26, 1937, box 10, LDRP-SC.

73. Reddick to Bond, March 26, 1937.

74. L. D. Reddick Fellowship Application, 1939, Julius Rosenwald Fund Papers, L. D. Reddick fellowship file, box 443, folder 3, FUSC.

75. Reddick Fellowship Application, 1939.

76. Marcus W. Jernegan, "Slavery and Conversion in the American Colonies," *American Historical Review* 21 (April 1916): 504–27.

77. Reddick to Horace Mann Bond, July 10, 1937, HMBP-UMAL.

78. Reddick, "Is the White College Better—for Blacks?"

79. Fred Arthur Bailey, *William Edward Dodd: The South's Yeoman Scholar* (Charlottesville: University Press of Virginia, 1997), ix.

80. L. D. Reddick, review of *The Old South: Struggles for Democracy*, by William E. Dodd, *Journal of Negro History* 23 (April 1938): 250–51.

81. "Dr. Johnson Receives Honor; Is Elected to Vice Presidency of Sociologists," *Capitol Plaindealer* (Topeka, KS), January 10, 1937.

82. Reddick to Horace Mann Bond, January 3, 1937, box 10, LDRP-SC.

83. Reddick to W. E. B. Du Bois, January 26, 1938, Du Bois Papers, SCUA UMAL.

84. Eric Foner, *Reconstruction: America's Unfinished Revolution, 1863–1877* (New York: Harper & Row, 1988), xx–xxii; Howard K. Beale, "On Rewriting Reconstruction History," *American Historical Review* 45 (July 1940): 807–27.

85. Reddick to W. E. B. Du Bois, January 15, 1938, Du Bois Papers, SCUA UMAL.

86. V. F. Calverton, "The Negro," in *America Now: An Inquiry into Civilization in the U.S.*, ed. Harold E. Stearns (New York: Scribner's, 1938), 488.

87. L. D. Reddick, review of *The First Negro Medical Society: A History of the Medico-Chirurgical Society of the District of Columbia, 1884–1939*, by W. Montague Cobb, *Journal of Southern History* 6 (February 1940): 130–31.

88. John B. Boles, "My Life with the Journal," *Journal of Southern History* 84 (February 2018): 10–11; John Hope Franklin, review of *Romanticism and Nationalism in the Old South*, by Rollin G. Osterweis, *Journal of Southern History* 15 (May 1949): 258–60; Elsie M. Lewis, "The Political Mind of the Negro, 1865–1900," *Journal of Southern History* 21 (May 1955): 189–202.

89. "60 Negro Professors Teach at White Colleges: Hired during War, They Retain Posts," *Chicago Defender*, February 8, 1947; James D. Anderson, "Race, Meritocracy, and the American Academy during the Immediate Post–World War II Era," *History of Education Quarterly* 33 (Summer 1993): 151–75.

90. L. D. Reddick, "Research Barriers in the South," *Social Frontier* 4 (December 1937): 85–86.

91. John Hope Franklin, "The Dilemma of the American Negro Scholar," in *Race and History: Selected Essays, 1938–1988* (1963; repr., Baton Rouge: Louisiana State University Press, 1989), 304.

92. Reddick, "Research Barriers in the South," 85.

93. Herbert Aptheker, "Vindication in Speaking Truth to Power: Herbert Aptheker," in *Against the Odds: Scholars Who Challenged Racism in the Twentieth Century*, ed. Benjamin P. Bowser and Louis Kushnick (Amherst: University of Massachusetts Press, 2002), 209.

94. Reddick, "Research Barriers in the South," 85.

95. Reddick to Carter Woodson, April 19, 1937, box 10, LDRP-SC.

96. Avery Craven, *The Coming of the Civil War* (New York: Scribner's, 1942), vii.

97. L. D. Reddick, "Is the White College Better—for Blacks?"

98. L. D. Reddick, "Memorandum: Dissertation Proposal," box 10, LDRP-SC; Reddick to Bessie L. Pierce, October 6, 1936, box 10, LDRP-SC.

99. Merle Curti, *The Social Ideas of American Educators* (New York: Scribner's, 1935).

100. Bruce Kuklick, *Black Philosopher, White Academy: The Career of William Fontaine* (Philadelphia: University of Pennsylvania Press, 2008), 53–59.

101. L. D. Reddick Fellowship Application, 1939, Julius Rosenwald Fund Papers, L. D. Reddick fellowship file, box 443, folder 3, FUSC.

102. Elsie M. Lewis Fellowship Application, 1944, Julius Rosenwald Fund Papers, Elsie M. Lewis fellowship file, box 430, folder 4, FUSC.

103. See Rosalind Rosenberg, *Beyond Separate Spheres: Intellectual Roots of Modern Feminism* (New Haven, CT: Yale University Press, 1982).

104. When black intellectuals like Reddick constructed their masculinity along traditional lines, they did so in concert with powerful institutions promoting those identities. For a study of this within black newspapers, see D'Weston Haywood, *Let Us Make Men: The Twentieth-Century Black Press and a Manly Vision for Racial Advancement* (Chapel Hill: University of North Carolina, 2018).

105. Deborah Gray White, ed., *Telling Histories: Black Women Historians in the Ivory Tower* (Chapel Hill: University of North Carolina Press, 2008), 4–8. See also Julie Des Jardins, *Women and the Historical Enterprise in America: Gender, Race, and the Politics of Memory, 1880–1945* (Chapel Hill: University of North Carolina Press, 2003); and *The Gender of History: Men, Women, and Historical Practice* (Cambridge, MA: Harvard University Press, 1998).

106. Horace Mann Bond to Reddick, June 30, 1937, HMBP-UMAL; Horace Mann Bond to Reddick, July 9, 1937, box 10, LDRP-SC; Horace Mann Bond to Reddick, July 24, 1937, box 10, LDRP-SC.

107. L. D. Reddick, "The Negro in the New Orleans Press, 1850–1860: A Study in Attitudes and Propaganda" (PhD diss., University of Chicago, 1939), 1, 2, 6.

108. Reddick, "The Negro in the New Orleans Press," 5.

109. Chicago Committee on Race Relations, *The Negro in Chicago* (Chicago: University of Chicago Press, 1922); Leonard W. Doob, *Propaganda: Its Psychology and Technique* (New York: Holt, 1935); Bruno Lasker, *Race Attitudes in Children* (New York: Holt, 1929); Harold D. Lasswell, *Propaganda Technique in the World War* (New York: Knopf, 1927); George Herbert Mead, *Mind, Self and Society* (Chicago: University of Chicago Press, 1934); Charles E. Merriam, ed., *The Making of Citizens*, 9 vols. (Chicago: University of Chicago Press, 1929–1933).

110. Charles H. Wesley, *The Collapse of the Confederacy* (Washington, DC: Associated Publishers, 1937).

111. Avery Craven, review of *The Collapse of the Confederacy*, by Charles H. Wesley, *American Journal of Sociology* 44 (March 1939): 775.

112. Reddick to Horace Mann Bond, April 7, 1939, HMBP-UMAL; Craven, review of *The Collapse of the Confederacy*, 775.

113. For a wide-ranging study of the American historical profession which takes up the politics of objectivity as its central theme, see Peter Novick, *That Noble Dream: The "Objectivity Question" and the American Historical Profession* (Cambridge: Cambridge University Press, 1998).

114. Horace Mann Bond to Reddick, March 27, 1939, HMBP-UMAL; Reddick to Horace Mann Bond, March 30, 1939, HMBP-UMAL; Horace Mann Bond to Reddick, April 3, 1939, HMBP-UMAL; Reddick to Horace Mann Bond, April 7, 1939, HMBP-UMAL.

115. Avery Craven, *The Repressible Conflict, 1830–1861* (Baton Rouge: Louisiana State University Press: 1939).

116. E. R. Thomas, review of *The Repressible Conflict, 1830-1861*, by Avery Craven, *Journal of Negro History* 24 (July 1939): 345-48. A letter from Bond to Reddick, which he addresses as "Alas Dr. E R Reddick Thomas / Alas Dr. L D Reddick Thomas," confirms that Reddick is the author of the review. See Horace Mann Bond to Reddick, July 21, 1939, HMBP-UMAL.

117. James Hugo Johnston and Luther Porter Jackson quoted in August Meier and Elliot Rudwick, *Black History and the Historical Profession, 1915-1980* (Urbana: University of Illinois Press, 1986), 103-4.

118. Avery Craven quoted in Meier and Rudwick, *Black History and the Historical Profession*, 103.

119. E. Merton Coulter, review of *The Repressible Conflict, 1830-1861*, by Avery Craven, *Mississippi Valley Historical Review* 26 (September 1939): 265-66; Charles W. Ramsdell, review of *The Repressible Conflict, 1830-1861*, by Avery Craven, *Journal of Southern History* 5 (November 1939): 553-54.

120. L. D. Reddick, "As I Remember Woodson," *Negro History Bulletin* 17 (November 1953): 38.

121. L. D. Reddick, "A New Interpretation for Negro History," *Journal of Negro History* 22 (January 1937): 19, 21-22, 25, 21.

122. For a book that treats nineteenth-century black historians with the seriousness they deserve, see Stephen G. Hall, *A Faithful Account of the Race: African American Historical Writing in Nineteenth-Century America* (Chapel Hill: University of North Carolina Press, 2009).

123. Reddick, "A New Interpretation for Negro History," 27, 27, 20, 20, 25, 28; W. E. B. Du Bois, *Black Reconstruction in America* (New York: Harcourt Brace, 1935); Pero Gaglo Dagbovie, a leading scholar of Carter Woodson and the black history movement, spent two whole pages discussing the content and significance of Reddick's essay. He wrote, for instance, that Reddick anticipated the pioneering work of Robin D. G. Kelley in his calls for studies of ordinary black folk. See Pero Gaglo Dagbovie, *African American History Reconsidered* (Urbana: University of Illinois Press, 2010), 24-25. For other discussions of Reddick's essay, see Lawrence Crouchett, "Early Black Studies Movement," *Journal of Black Studies* 2 (December 1971): 195; W. T. Fontaine, "An Interpretation of Contemporary Negro Thought from the Standpoint of the Sociology of Knowledge," *Journal of Negro History* 25 (January 1940): 7; Ella Forbes, "African Resistance to Enslavement: The Nature and the Evidentiary Record," *Journal of Black Studies* 23 (September 1992): 50; Earl E. Thorpe, *Black Historians: A Critique* (New York: William Morrow, 1971), 20-21; William D. Wight, *Black History and Black Identity: A Call for a New Historiography* (Westport, CT: Praeger, 2002), 60; Jeffrey Lynn Woodward, "Evolution of a Discipline: Intellectual Antecedents of African American Studies," *Journal of Black Studies* 22 (December 1991): 244-45.

124. L. D. Reddick, "Carter G. Woodson (1875-1950): An Appreciation," *Phylon* 11 (1950): 179.

125. Jacqueline Goggin, "Countering White Racist Scholarship: Carter G. Woodson and the *Journal of Negro History*," *Journal of Negro History* 68 (Autumn 1983): 361.

126. L. D. Reddick, review of *Adam's Ancestors*, by L. S. B. Leakey and F. Gowland Hopkins; *Stone Age Africa*, by L. S. B. Leakey, *Journal of Negro History* 22 (April 1937): 257–59; L. D. Reddick, review of *We Europeans*, by Julian S. Huxley, A. C. Haddo, and A. M. Carr-Saunders, *Journal of Negro History* 22 (April 1937): 255–57; L. D. Reddick, review of *Pro-Slavery Thought in the Old South*, by William Sumner Jenkins, and *Gone with the Wind*, by Margaret Mitchell, *Journal of Negro History* 22 (July 1937): 363–66; L. D. Reddick, review of *The Old South: The Geographical, Economic, Political and Cultural Expansion, Institutions, and Nationalism of the Ante-Bellum South*, by R. S. Cotterill, *Journal of Negro History* 23 (January 1938): 97–98; L. D. Reddick, review of *The Old South: Struggles for Democracy*, by William E. Dodd, *Journal of Negro History* 23 (April 1938): 249–51; L. D. Reddick, review of *Origins of Class Struggle in Louisiana: A Social History of White Farmers and Laborers during Slavery and After, 1840–1875*, by Roger Wallace Shugg, *Journal of Negro History* 25 (January 1940): 116–18; L. D. Reddick, review of *Let My People Go: The Story of the Underground Railroad and the Growth of the Abolition Movement*, by Henrietta Buckmaster, *Journal of Negro History* 26 (April 1941): 255–57.

127. Janette Hoston Harris, "Charles Harris Wesley, Educator and Historian, 1891–1947" (PhD diss., Howard University, 1975), 136–38.

128. Carter Woodson to Reddick, December 22, 1936, box 10, LDRP-SC; Rayford W. Logan to Members of the ASNLH Executive Council, December 14, 1936, box 10, LDRP-SC.

129. Reddick to Carter Woodson, January 7, 1937, box 10, LDRP-SC.

130. Reddick to Rayford Logan, January 11, 1937, box 10, LDRP-SC.

131. Rayford W. Logan to Reddick, January 23, 1937, box 10, LDRP-SC.

132. Carter Woodson, "Woodson Cites Brawley's Misrepresentations," June 10, 1936, box 10, LDRP-SC.

133. Benjamin Brawley to Reddick, January 23 and February 9, 1937; Reddick to Benjamin Brawley, February 6, 1937, box 10, LDRP-SC.

134. Carter G. Woodson quoted in Thorpe, *Black Historians*, 111.

135. Reddick to Horace Mann Bond, n.d., HMBP-UMAL; Horace Mann Bond to Reddick, December 11, 1938, HMBP-UMAL.

136. Edwin R. Embree to Charles S. Johnson, June 28, 1939, Fellowship Application, 1939, Julius Rosenwald Fund Papers, L. D. Reddick fellowship file, box 443, folder 3, FUSC.

137. Edwin R. Embree to Edgar B. Stern, July 27, 1939, Fellowship Application, 1939, Julius Rosenwald Fund Papers, L. D. Reddick fellowship file, box 443, folder 3, FUSC.

138. Reddick to Horace Mann Bond, n.d., HMBP-UMAL. For more on Claude Barnett and his pioneering work with the Associated Negro Press, see Gerald Horne, *The Rise and Fall of the Associated Negro Press: Claude Barnett's Pan-African News and the Jim Crow Paradox* (Urbana: University of Illinois, 2017).

139. Jerry Gershenhorn, "St. Clair Drake, Pan-Africanism, African Studies, and the Politics of Knowledge, 1945–1965," in "St. Clair Drake: The Making of a Scholar-Activist" symposium, *Journal of African American History* 98 (Summer 2013): 423.

140. "Forum Chiefs," *Chicago Defender*, February 11, 1939.

Chapter Three

1. Edwin R. Embree to Edgar B. Stern, July 27, 1939, Fellowship Application, 1939, Julius Rosenwald Fund Papers, L. D. Reddick fellowship file, box 443, folder 3, FUSC.

2. Elinor Des Verney Sinnette, *Arthur Alfonso Schomburg: Black Bibliophile and Collector* (Detroit: Wayne State University Press, 1989), 193.

3. Reddick to Horace Mann Bond, August 3, 1939, HMBP-UMAL.

4. L. D. Reddick, "Anti-Semitism among Negroes," *Negro Quarterly* 1 (Summer 1942): 122.

5. Rufus E. Clement to W. E. B. Du Bois, December 19, 1939, DBP-UMAL.

6. "Library of Congress Emancipation Festival Started Wednesday," *Negro Star* (Wichita, KS), December 20, 1940.

7. "Negro Leaders Meet Princess at White House Reception," *Negro Star* (Wichita, KS), December 27, 1940.

8. "N. Y. Fair Group Is Formed," *Pittsburgh Courier*, June 15, 1940.

9. "Radio Today," *New York Times*, August 26, 1941.

10. "Hear Reddick on Air Lanes," *New York Amsterdam Star-News*, September 6, 1941.

11. Lester A. Walton, "Library Is Barometer of Race's Growth in N.Y.," *Pittsburgh Courier*, August 15, 1925.

12. Rhonda Evans, "Catherine Allen Latimer: The New York Public Library's First Black Librarian," *New York Public Library* (blog), March 20, 2020, https://www.nypl.org/blog/2020/03/19/new-york-public-library-first-black-librarian-catherine-latimer.

13. Mission statement quoted in Sinnette, *Arthur Alfonso Schomburg*, 134.

14. Mission statement quoted in Sinnette, 131–36. See also Phyllis Dain, *The New York Public Library: A History of Its Founding and Early Years* (New York: New York Public Library, 1972).

15. "Evenings with Negro Authors," January 1943, HMPB-UMAL.

16. Reddick to William C. Haygood, November 13, 1945, L. D. Reddick Fellowship Application, 1945, Julius Rosenwald Fund Papers, L. D. Reddick fellowship file, box 443, folder 3, FUSC.

17. "Stage Stormy Session over 'Strange Fruit,'" *Pittsburgh Courier*, December 29, 1945.

18. L. D. Reddick, "A Record of Achievement," circa 1947, HMBP-UMAL.

19. Margaret Walker, *How I Wrote Jubilee and Other Essays on Life and Literature*, ed. Maryemma Graham (New York: Feminist Press, 1990), 50.

20. Lorenzo Greene to Reddick, February 17, 1943, box 33, folder 5, LJGP-LC; Lorenzo Johnston Greene, *The Negro in Colonial New England, 1620–1776* (New York: Columbia University Press, 1942).

21. L. D. Reddick, foreword to *Freedom's Soldier and Other Poems*, by Ricardo Weeks (New York: Wendell Malliet, 1947).

22. "Announce Outstanding Race Achievers for '39," *Chicago Defender*, February 13, 1940.

23. Reddick to Dr. Bousfield, January 7, 1941, L. D. Reddick Fellowship Application, 1939, Julius Rosenwald Fund Papers, L. D. Reddick fellowship file, box 443, folder 3, FUSC.

24. L. D. Reddick, "The Honor Roll in Race Relations," January 6, 1944, HMBP-UMAL.

25. Editorial Board, "Rating Negro Achievements," *New York Age*, February 10, 1940.

26. Benjamin Brawley to Reddick, January 23, 1937, box 10, LDRP-SC.

27. "Dr. L. Reddick At City College, Curator Assigned to Lecture on Negro History at School," *New York Amsterdam Star-News*, October 18, 1941.

28. "Negro History and Culture," College of the City of New York, the School of Education, L. D. Reddick Biographical Files, ARC-AU.

29. "Committee for Defense of Public Education Joint Committee," press release, May 3, 1941, box 33, LDRP-SC.

30. "Yergan Dismissal Arouses Speculations," *Chicago Defender*, May 10, 1941.

31. Carol Polsgrove, *Divided Minds: Intellectuals and the Civil Rights Movement* (New York: Norton, 2001), 107.

32. "1943 Negro Congress Program Set," *Chicago Defender*, March 6, 1943.

33. "'America Needs Negro Scholars,' Says Reddick," *Pittsburgh Courier*, April 4, 1942.

34. "60 Negro Professors Teach at White Colleges: Hired during War, They Retain Posts," *Chicago Defender*, February 8, 1947. See also James D. Anderson, "Race, Meritocracy, and the American Academy during the Immediate Post–World War II Era," *History of Education Quarterly* 33 (Summer 1993): 151–75; David A. Varel, "Bending the Academic Color Line: Allison Davis, the University of Chicago, and American Race Relations, 1941–1948," *Journal of Negro Education* 84 (Fall 2015): 534–46; and Fred G. Wale, "Chosen for Ability," *Atlantic Monthly* 180 (July 1947): 81–85.

35. "Eight Gotham Colleges Employ Negroes on Teaching Staffs," *Chicago Defender*, May 10, 1947.

36. "'New School' Adds Expert Staff for Race History," *Chicago Defender*, January 18, 1947.

37. See Keisha N. Blain, *Set the World on Fire: Black Nationalist Women and the Global Struggle for Freedom* (Philadelphia: University of Pennsylvania Press, 2018).

38. Kevin Gaines, "A World to Win: The International Dimension of the Black Freedom Movement," *OAH Magazine of History* 20 (October 2006): 16.

39. "Dr. Reddick to Visit Haiti for Library," *Negro Star* (Wichita, KS), May 2, 1941.

40. Reddick to Melville Herskovits, June 17, 1941, box 2, folder 3, MJHP-NU.

41. "Port-Au-Prince, Haiti," *Negro Star* (Wichita, KS), June 13, 1941.

42. "Friendship of Negroes Asked, Wants Them to Know They Have Two Countries—Haiti and U.S.," *New York Amsterdam Star-News*, June 28, 1941.

43. "1,000 Books Given to Haiti: Library Here Presents Duplicate Works on United States," *New York Times*, October 23, 1941.

44. Mercer Cook, "Trends in Recent Haitian Literature," *Journal of Negro History* 32 (April 1947): 230.

45. "Interview with Dr. John Karefa-Smart," in A. B. Assensoh, *Kwame Nkrumah of Africa: His Formative Years and the Beginning of His Political Career, 1935–1948* (Ilfracombe, UK: Stockwell, 1989), 240–41.

46. Kwame Nkrumah, *Ghana: The Autobiography of Kwame Nkrumah* (Edinburgh: Thomas Nelson, 1957), 44.

47. L. D. Reddick, "My Memory and Appreciation of K. Nkrumah," in *Kwame Nkrumah of Africa*, 247, 248.

48. L. D. Reddick, "What the 'Brothers' Need to Know," *African Interpreter* 1 (Summer 1943): 11.

49. Office of the Historian, United States Department of State, "The Atlantic Conference & Charter, 1941," https://history.state.gov/milestones/1937-1945/atlantic-conf (accessed April 14, 2020).

50. North Atlantic Treaty Organization, "The Atlantic Charter," August 14, 1941, https://www.nato.int/cps/en/natohq/official_texts_16912.htm.

51. P. Olisanwuche Esedebe, *Pan-Africanism: The Idea and Movement, 1776–1963*, 2nd ed. (Washington, DC: Howard University Press, 1994), 120.

52. Penny M. Von Eschen, *Race against Empire: Black Americans and Anticolonialism, 1937–1957* (Ithaca, NY: Cornell University Press, 1997), 26; James H. Meriwether, *Proudly We Can Be Africans: Black Americans and Africa, 1935–1961* (Chapel Hill: University of North Carolina Press, 2002), 2.

53. Nnamdi Azikiwe quoted in Kenneth Robert Janken, *Rayford W. Logan and the Dilemma of the African-American Intellectual* (Amherst: University of Massachusetts Press, 1993), 168.

54. "African Leaders Plead for Arms to Meet Axis Foe," *Pittsburgh Courier*, May 23, 1942.

55. L. D. Reddick, "Africa Speaks," *Opportunity* 20 (July 1942): 205–6. Quote from L. D. Reddick, "Africa: Test of the Atlantic Charter," *Crisis* 50 (July 1943): 217.

56. Reddick, "Africa Speaks," 205–6.

57. Adom Getachew, *Worldmaking after Empire: The Rise and Fall of Self-Determination* (Princeton, NJ: Princeton University Press, 2019), 1–3.

58. "Roosevelt Speech Is Given to Library," *New York Times*, September 25, 1942.

59. Horace Mann Bond to Reddick, October 7, 1942, HMBP-UMAL.

60. "African Students Hold Meet in New York: Urge Arms for Fellow Countrymen Ready to Fight," *Chicago Defender*, September 19, 1942.

61. L. D. Reddick, "What About Africa?," review of *The Atlantic Charter and Africa from an American Standpoint*, by Committee on Africa, the War, and Peace Aims," *Opportunity* 20 (September 1942): 283–84; Committee on Africa, the War, and Peace Aims, *The Atlantic Charter and Africa from an American Standpoint* (New York: Committee on Africa, 1942); Kingsley Ozuomba Mbadiwe, *British and Axis Aims in Africa* (New York: Wendell Malliet, 1942).

62. L. D. Reddick, "The Battle of Africa and the African People," *Opportunity* 20 (December 1942): 357.

63. L. D. Reddick, "Africa Is People," *New Masses*, box 27, folder 6, MJHP-NU.

64. Reddick to Herskovits, May 26, 1943, box 30, folder 12, MJHP-NU.

65. Reddick to Herskovits, June 16, 1943, box 30, folder 12, MJHP-NU.

66. L. D. Reddick, "Africa: Test of the Atlantic Charter," *Crisis* 50 (July 1943): 202–4, 217–18.

67. Horace R. Cayton, "Charter for Africa: Real Opportunities for Allies to Demonstrate Four Freedoms, Not Empty Words," *Pittsburgh Courier*, July 31, 1943.

68. "Scholars Plan Peace Strategy," *Pittsburgh Courier*, August 7, 1943.

69. L. D. Reddick, "South Africa: A Case for the United Nations," *Crisis* 50 (May 1943): 137, 137, 139; Von Eschen, *Race against Empire*, 61–62. See also Nicholas Grant, *Winning Our Freedoms Together: African Americans and Apartheid, 1945–1960* (Chapel Hill: University of North Carolina Press, 2018).

70. W. E. B. Du Bois to Reddick, January 8, 1945, DBP-UMAL; Janken, *Rayford W. Logan*, 175.

71. Reddick to W. E. B. Du Bois, March 6, 1945, DBP-UMAL; W. E. B. Du Bois to Reddick, March 6, 1945, DBP-UMAL.

72. Reddick to W. E. B. Du Bois, April 5, 1945, DBP-UMAL.

73. Meriwether, *Proudly We Can Be Africans*, 63.

74. George S. Schuyler, "Logan Gives Plan for Colonial Trusteeship," *Pittsburgh Courier*, April 14, 1945.

75. "Resolution of the Colonial Conference in New York," April 6, 1945, DBP-UMAL.

76. Gerald Horne, *Black and Red: W. E. B. Du Bois and the Afro-American Response to the Cold War, 1944–1963* (Albany: State University of New York Press, 1986), 29.

77. For more on the Manchester conference and subsequent anticolonial activism, see John Munro, *The Anticolonial Front: The African American Freedom Struggle and Global Decolonisation, 1945–1960* (Cambridge: Cambridge University Press, 2017).

78. Reddick to W. E. B. Du Bois, December 10, 1946, DBP-UMAL.

79. L. D. Reddick, "Random Notes of Preliminary Conferences of R. W., C. L. R. J., St.C. D. & L. D. R," box 33, LDRP-SC; Polsgrove, *Divided Minds*, 107.

80. Reddick to W. E. B. Du Bois, June 14, 1945, DBP-UMAL.

81. "World Negro Course to Begin at Library," *People's Voice*, September 23, 1944; "New York in Review," *Chicago Defender*, November 25, 1944; "The World View of the Negro Question," A Fifteen Week Course at the New School for Social Research in New York City, chaired by L. D. Reddick, Reddick, L. D., Biographical Files, ARC-AU.

82. L. D. Reddick, "Japanese as Citizens," 1944, box 33, LDRP-SC.

83. "Society Issues Two Pamphlets," *Pittsburgh Courier*, August 7, 1943.

84. L. D. Reddick, "Anti-Semitism among Negroes," *Negro Quarterly* 1 (Summer 1942): 120.

85. L. D. Reddick, "Prefatory Note" to *Should Negroes and Jews Unite?*, by Louis Harap and L. D. Reddick (New York: Negro Publication Society of America, 1943).

86. *The New York Amsterdam Star News*, August 22, 1942, in L. D. Reddick and Louis Harap, "Should Negroes and Jews Unite?," 3.3.0.320, MLKP-AU.

87. George Schuyler in L. D. Reddick and Louis Harap, "Should Negroes and Jews Unite?," 3.3.0.320, MLKP-AU.

88. Clayborne Carson Jr., "Blacks and Jews in the Civil Rights Movement," in *Strangers and Neighbors: Relations between Blacks and Jews in the United States*, ed. Maurianne Adams and John H. Bracey (Amherst: University of Massachusetts Press, 1999), 574.

89. L. D. Reddick, "The Negro in the United States Navy During World War II," *Journal of Negro History* 32 (April 1947): 205, 206, 204, 204; "Negro Hero Identified: Messman Who Manned Gun at Pearl Harbor Is Honored," *New York Times*, March 13, 1942.

90. Christopher Paul Moore, *Fighting for America: Black Soldiers—The Unsung Heroes of World War II* (New York: Ballantine, 2006), 33-34.

91. For a recent book on Dorie Miller, see Thomas W. Cutrer and T. Michael Parrish, *Doris Miller, Pearl Harbor, and the Birth of the Civil Rights Movement* (College Station: Texas A&M University Press, 2018). For a textbook that opens a chapter with a vignette of the Miller story, see Darlene Clark Hine, William C. Hine, and Stanley Harrold, *The African American Odyssey, Combined Volume, Second Edition* (Upper Saddle River, NJ: Prentice Hall, 2005), 485-86. For a distinguished research scientist's account of the inspiration she derived from the story, see Naomi W. Ledé, "Remembering a Hero of World War II," *Huntsville Item*, December 15, 2012.

92. Reddick, "Negro in the United States Navy," 206.

93. Christine Knauer, *Let Us Fight as Free Men: Black Soldiers and Civil Rights* (Philadelphia: University of Pennsylvania Press, 2014), 21.

94. John Stevens, *From the Back of the Foxhole: Black Correspondents in World War II* (Lexington, KY: Association for Education in Journalism, 1973), 13.

95. A. Russell Buchanan, *Black Americans in World War II* (Santa Barbara, CA: Clio Books, 1977), 71.

96. In 2006, historian Maggi Moorhouse still argued that "scant attention has been paid to the contributions of individual black soldiers of World War II." Maggi M. Morehouse, *Fighting in the Jim Crow Army: Black Men and Women Remember World War II* (Lanham, MD: Rowman & Littlefield, 2006), xiii. This marginalization is even more egregious for black women GIs. See Sandra M. Bolzenius, *Glory in Their Spirit: How Four Black Women Took On the Army during World War II* (Urbana: University of Illinois Press, 2018). See also Maria Hohn and Martin Klimke, *A Breath of Freedom: The Civil Rights Struggle, African American GIs, and Germany* (New York: Palgrave Macmillan, 2010).

97. "WANTED: Make Appeal for Letters from Servicemen and Women for the Schomburg Collection," *Pittsburgh Courier*, December 9, 1944.

98. "Minutes of Meeting of 7 February 1946," Committee on Negro Studies, box 32, folder 5, MJHP-NU.

99. Richard Wright quoted in Constance Webb, *Richard Wright: A Biography* (New York: Putnam, 1968), 227-28.

100. Two studies include Neil A. Wynn, *The Afro-American and the Second World War* (New York: Holmes & Meier, 1976); and Moore, *Fighting for America*. Moore

served as a curator at the Schomburg, and he relied extensively on Reddick's war-letters archive for his book. Wynn acknowledged Reddick as someone who "gave advice and encouragement, and suggested areas of study" (vii).

101. Charles H. Dubra quoted in Moore, *Fighting for America*, 70.

102. Marjorie McKenzie, "Pursuit of Democracy: Significance of Many Letters from Soldiers Analyzed by Writer," *Pittsburgh Courier*, February 10, 1945.

103. Reddick to Dorothy A. Elvidge, May 15, 1945, and Edwin Embree to Reddick, June 1, 1945, Fellowship Application, 1945, Julius Rosenwald Fund Papers, L. D. Reddick fellowship file, box 443, folder 3, FUSC.

104. "To Collect and Edit the Writings of Frederick Douglass," Grant Application Statement in Fellowship Application, 1945, Julius Rosenwald Fund Papers, L. D. Reddick fellowship file, box 443, folder 3, FUSC; "Annual Report of the Director," *Journal of Negro History* 30 (July 1945): 253.

105. Reddick to Charles Dollard, June 5, 1945, Fellowship Application, 1945, Julius Rosenwald Fund Papers, L. D. Reddick fellowship file, box 443, folder 3, FUSC.

106. L. D. Reddick, "The Negro Policy of the United States Army, 1775–1945," *Journal of Negro History* 34 (January 1949): 10.

107. Reddick, "Negro in the United States Navy," 214.

108. See, for instance, Thomas A. Guglielmo, "A Martial Freedom Movement: Black G.I.s' Political Struggles during World War II," *Journal of American History* 104 (March 2018): 883; and Chris Dixon, *African Americans and the Pacific War, 1941–1945: Race, Nationality, and the Fight for Freedom* (Cambridge: Cambridge University Press, 2018).

109. "Dr. Reddick Hits Ex-92nd Officer's Anti-Negro Story," *Chicago Defender*, April 20, 1946.

110. "'Unbiased Record' Asked: Negro Veterans at Conference Propose Own War History," *New York Times*, February 14, 1947.

111. W. E. B. Du Bois to Reddick, May 15, 1944, DBP-UMAL.

112. L. D. Reddick, "Library Resources for Negro Studies in the United States and Abroad," in *Encyclopedia of the Negro: Preparatory Volume* (Phelps-Stokes Fund Publishers, 1944), 164.

113. "Move to Get Slave's Name Immortalized," *Chicago Defender*, February 3, 1940.

114. David W. Blight, "'For Something Beyond the Battlefield': Frederick Douglass and the Struggle for the Memory of the Civil War," *Journal of American History* 75 (March 1989): 1156–78. See also David W. Blight, *Frederick Douglass: Prophet of Freedom* (New York: Simon & Schuster, 2018).

115. "Present 1st Copy of New Book on Life of Douglass," *Chicago Defender*, March 29, 1941.

116. L. D. Reddick, "To Collect and Edit the Writings of Frederick Douglass," Fellowship Application, 1945, Julius Rosenwald Fund Papers, L. D. Reddick fellowship file, box 443, folder 3, FUSC.

117. "A Project to Microfilm Negro Newspapers Published in U.S. Prior to 1900," n.d., box 32, folder 5, MJHP-NU.

118. Jerry Gershenhorn, *Melville J. Herskovits and the Racial Politics of Knowledge* (Lincoln: University of Nebraska Press, 2004), 158–66; Robert L. Harris Jr., "Segregation and Scholarship: The American Council of Learned Societies Committee on Negro Studies, 1941–1950," *Journal of Black Studies* 12 (March 1982): 325–30. See also Zachery R. Williams, *In Search of the Talented Tenth: Howard University Public Intellectuals and the Dilemmas of Race, 1926–1970* (Columbia: University of Missouri Press, 2009), 166–67.

119. Jerry Gershenhorn, "'Not an Academic Affair': African American Scholars and the Development of African Studies Programs in the United States, 1942–1960," *Journal of African American History* 94 (Winter 2009): 51.

120. Committee on Negro Studies, "Minutes of Meeting of November 10 and 11, 1944," box 32, folder 5, MJHP-NU.

121. Eric Williams, *Capitalism and Slavery* (Chapel Hill: University of North Carolina Press, 1944). Williams's insight continues to bear fruit. See, for example, Edward E. Baptist, *The Half Has Never Been Told: Slavery and the Making of American Capitalism* (New York: Basic Books, 2016). For a discussion of Reddick's mentorship of Williams, see Brinsley Samaroo, "Eric Williams, the Bibliophile and Scholar," *Journal of Caribbean History* 37, no. 2 (2003): 279–80.

122. Kenneth Porter, "Tentative Suggestions for Studies in American Negro History," October 28, 1946, box 37, folder 4, MJHP-NU; Gershenhorn, *Melville J. Herskovits*, 159–60.

123. "Early Negro Newspapers Now Being Microfilmed," *Chicago Defender*, August 9, 1947.

124. August Meier and Elliot Rudwick, *Black History and the Historical Profession, 1915–1980* (Urbana: University of Illinois Press, 1986), 233.

125. See, for instance, James Q. Whitman, *Hitler's American Model: The United States and the Making of Nazi Race Law* (Princeton, NJ: Princeton University Press, 2017); and Bradley W. Hart, *Hitler's American Friends: The Third Reich's Supporters in the United States* (New York: St. Martin's, 2018).

126. "4 Killed in Harlem Rioting; 195 Hurt, 300 Held in Looting," *New York Post*, August 2, 1943; Dominic J. Capeci, *The Harlem Riot of 1943* (Philadelphia: Temple University Press, 1977), 100–103. See also *Nathan Brandt, Harlem at War: The Black Experience in WWII* (Syracuse, NY: Syracuse University Press, 1996).

127. "Report of the Citizens Emergency Conference for Interracial Unity," September 25, 1943, New York City, folder 001527-028-0730, Papers of the NAACP, Part 07: The Anti-Lynching Campaign, 1912–1955, Series A: Anti-Lynching Investigative Files, 1912–1953.

128. L. D. Reddick, "Adult Education and the Improvement of Race Relations," *Journal of Negro Education* 14 (Summer 1945): 488.

129. "To Discuss Negro Culture," *Trenton Evening Times* (Trenton, New Jersey), February 8, 1946; "Dr. Reddick Assails Lax Rights By Colleges," *Chicago Defender*, April 13, 1946; Reddick, "Adult Education and the Improvement of Race Relations"; L. D. Reddick, "What Should the American Negro Reasonably Expect as the Outcome of a Real Peace?," *Journal of Negro Education* 12 (Summer 1943): 568–78.

130. L. D. Reddick, review of *Pro-Slavery Thought in the Old South*, by William Sumner Jenkins, and *Gone with the Wind*, by Margaret Mitchell, *Journal of Negro History* 22 (July 1937): 363–66; "Southern Writer 'Roasts' Leaders," *Pittsburgh Courier*, September 16, 1939; "Prize Book Is Called 'Worst,'" *Atlanta Daily World*, November 7, 1941; "'U. S. Can't Win without Negro,' Says Dr. Reddick," *Pittsburgh Courier*, January 3, 1942; "Events Today," *New York Times*, February 7, 1942; "White Color No Criterion of Superiority—Mrs. FDR," *Chicago Defender*, November 13, 1943.

131. L. D. Reddick, "Educational Programs for the Improvement of Race Relations: Motion Pictures, Radio, the Press and Libraries," *Journal of Negro Education* 13 (Summer 1944): 367.

132. Reddick, "Educational Programs for the Improvement of Race Relations," 369, 376.

133. Reddick, "Educational Programs for the Improvement of Race Relations," 368.

134. L. D. Reddick, "Some Stereotypes of American Minority Peoples," Supper-Conference for Anthropologists, April 16, 1948, L. D. Reddick Biographical Files, ARC-AU. Reddick's article continued to be cited by scholars and commentators for decades. See, for example, Edward Mapp, *Blacks in American Films: Today and Yesterday* (Metuchen, NJ: Scarecrow, 1972), 30–31, 54–55, 80; and Ishmael Reed, "A Palooka He Ain't," review of *The Greatest*, by Muhammad Ali, *New York Times*, November 30, 1975.

135. L. D. Reddick, "Foreword," *Journal of Educational Sociology* 17 (January 1944): 258.

136. "Dr. L. D. Reddick Analyzes Fight of Negroes in North," *Pittsburgh Courier*, February 5, 1944.

137. Reddick, "Foreword," 260; L. D. Reddick, "What the Northern Negro Thinks about Democracy," *Journal of Educational Sociology* 17 (January 1944): 296–306. Key works in the Chicago School of Sociology include Frederick Thrasher, *The Gang* (Chicago: University of Chicago Press, 1927); Louis Wirth, *The Ghetto* (Chicago: University of Chicago Press, 1928); Robert Park, Ernest Burgess, and Roderick McKenzie, *The City* (Chicago: University of Chicago Press, 1922); and William I. Thomas and Florian Znaniecki, *The Polish Peasant in Europe and America: Monograph of an Immigrant Group* (Boston: Badger, 1918). Key works in the black Chicago School tradition include E. Franklin Frazier, *The Negro Family in Chicago* (Chicago: University of Chicago Press, 1932); and St. Clair Drake and Horace Cayton, *Black Metropolis: A Study of Negro Life in a Northern City* (New York: Harcourt, Brace, 1945).

138. New York Public Library, "Press Release," September 20, 1945, box 33, LDRP-SC.

139. See, for instance, Anna-Lisa Cox, *The Bone and Sinew of the Land: America's Forgotten Black Pioneers and the Struggle for Equality* (New York: PublicAffairs, 2018).

140. L. D. Reddick, "The New Race-Relations Frontier," *Journal of Educational Sociology* 19 (November 1945): 137–41; "Survey Shows: West Coast New Racial Frontier," *Pittsburgh Courier*, November 24, 1945.

141. L. D. Reddick, "The College Graduate Faces a City World," 1947, box 33, LDRP-SC.

142. "Reddick Tells Why He Quit Schomburg Post," *Chicago Defender*, January 31, 1948.

143. W. E. B. Du Bois to Ralph Beals, January 28, 1948, DBP-UMAL.

144. Horace Mann Bond, "The Library's Schomburg Collection," *New York Times*, January 29, 1948.

145. "The Schomburg Collection," *New York Times*, February 13, 1948; George S. Schuyler, "Views and Reviews," *Pittsburgh Courier*, January 31, 1948.

146. "Bias on Collection Denied by Library," *New York Times*, March 16, 1948.

147. "Library Is Picketed after False Report," *New York Herald Tribune*, March 16, 1948.

Chapter Four

1. St. Clair Drake to Reddick, November 19, 1948, box 8, folder 30, SCDP-SC.

2. Reddick to St. Clair Drake, July 2, 1948, box 8, folder 30, SCDP-SC.

3. L. D. Reddick, "Africa, the Confederate Myth and the New Frontier," 1961, box 26, folder 2, MLKP-BU.

4. L. D. Reddick, "Persons and Places: Dizzy Gillespie in Atlanta," *Phylon* 10 (1949): 44.

5. Reddick to Alex Haley, Leonard Jeffries, and Courtney Brown, May 17, 1974, box 9, LDRP-SC.

6. "A Neglected Area of Scholarship," *Chicago Defender*, May 4, 1946. For Reddick's take on Atlanta, see L. D. Reddick, *Crusader without Violence: A Biography of Martin Luther King, Jr.* (New York, Harper, 1959), 24–41.

7. Reddick to St. Clair Drake, July 12, 1948, box 8, folder 30, SCDP-SC.

8. "The Trevor Arnett Library," n.d., box 13, LDRP-SC.

9. James H. Meriwether, *Proudly We Can Be Africans: Black Americans and Africa, 1935–1961* (Chapel Hill: University of North Carolina Press, 2002), 58.

10. Sarah Azaransky, *This Worldwide Struggle: Religion and the International Roots of the Civil Rights Movement* (New York: Oxford University Press, 2017), 3–5.

11. St. Clair Drake to Reddick, November 19, 1948, box 8, folder 30, SCDP-SC.

12. "Photo Standalone 3—No Title," *Chicago Defender*, January 13, 1951.

13. Benjamin E. Mays to William McKelvey, September 16, 1949, box 8, LDRP-SC. For a full-length study of Mays, see Randal Maurice Jelks, *Benjamin Elijah Mays, Schoolmaster of the Movement: A Biography* (Chapel Hill: University of North Carolina Press, 2012).

14. For more on the intellectual roots of anticolonial activism, see Minkah Makalani, *In the Cause of Freedom: Radical Black Internationalism from Harlem to London, 1917–1939* (Chapel Hill: University of North Carolina Press, 2014); and John Munro, *The Anticolonial Front: The African American Freedom Struggle and Global Decolonisation, 1945–1960* (Cambridge: Cambridge University Press, 2017).

15. L. D. Reddick, "The Relative Status of the Negro in the American Armed Forces," *Journal of Negro Education* 22 (Summer 1953): 380.

16. "'We Are on the Road to War,' Says L. D. Reddick," *Norfolk Journal and Guide*, August 14, 1948.

17. L. D. Reddick, "How Much Higher and Professional Education Does the Negro Need?," *Journal of Negro Education* 17 (Summer 1948): 238–39.

18. Reddick, "How Much Higher and Professional Education," 239.

19. Two key texts of the World Federalist Movement include Wendell Willkie, *One World* (New York: Simon & Schuster, 1943); and Emery Reves, *The Anatomy of Peace* (New York: Harper, 1945).

20. "'We Are on the Road to War,' Says L. D. Reddick," *Norfolk Journal and Guide*, August 14, 1948.

21. Reddick to R. E. Clement, March 16, 1949, box 400, folder 6, Atlanta University Presidential Records, Rufus E. Clement Records, ARC-AU.

22. Eddie Billingsley, "African Students Honor Dr. Reddick," *Atlanta Daily World*, June 8, 1955.

23. "Historical News," *Journal of Negro History* 38 (April 1953): 254–55.

24. Jerry Gershenhorn, "'Not an Academic Affair': African American Scholars and the Development of African Studies Programs in the United States, 1942–1960," *Journal of African American History* 94 (Winter 2009): 44–68.

25. Reddick to Horace Mann Bond, December 14, 1949, HMBP-UMAL.

26. Horace Mann Bond to Reddick, December 16, 1949, HMBP-UMAL.

27. W. Sherman Savage and L. D. Reddick, *Our Cause Speeds On: An Informal History of the Phi Beta Sigma Fraternity* (Atlanta: Fuller, 1957), 170, 169.

28. "Africans Will Fight for Freedom—Azikiwe," *Atlanta Daily World*, January 1, 1950.

29. Reddick to Horace Mann Bond, April 27, 1950, HMBP-UMAL; "Political Stew Boiling in Nigeria, Reports Hold," *Afro-American*, May 13, 1950; "Azikiwe Call Off U. S. Tour," *Chicago Defender*, May 6, 1950.

30. Savage and Reddick, *Our Cause Speeds On*, 170.

31. Reddick to William E. Doar Jr., February 7, 1955, box 41, LDRP-SC.

32. Savage and Reddick, *Our Cause Speeds On*, 183, 203–4.

33. Mary L. Dudziak, *Cold War Civil Rights: Race and the Image of American Democracy* (Princeton, NJ: Princeton University Press, 2011). See also Thomas Borstelmann, *The Cold War and the Color Line: American Race Relations in the Global Arena* (Cambridge, MA: Harvard University Press, 2003).

34. Glenda Gilmore, *Defying Dixie: The Radical Roots of Civil Rights, 1919–1950* (New York: Norton, 2009), 7.

35. Ellen Schrecker, *Many Are the Crimes: McCarthyism in America* (Boston: Little, Brown, 1998), xiii.

36. Ellen W. Schrecker, *No Ivory Tower: McCarthyism and the Universities* (New York: Oxford University Press, 1986), 4–5.

37. Horace Mann Bond to Reddick, May 14, 1947, HMBP-UMAL.

38. Reddick to Horace Mann Bond, May 16, 1947, HMBP-UMAL.

39. Civil Rights Congress, *We Charge Genocide: The Historic Petition to the United Nations for Relief from a Crime of the United States Government Against the Negro People* (New York: Civil Rights Congress, 1951), xi.

40. David Levering Lewis, *W. E. B. Du Bois: The Fight for Equality and the American Century 1919-1963* (New York: Holt, 2001), 688-91; Gerald Horne, *Black and Red: W. E. B. Du Bois and the Afro-American Response to the Cold War, 1944-1963* (New York: State University of New York Press, 1985).

41. "Many to Fete Dr. DuBois at Public Meet," *New York Amsterdam News*, September 29, 1951.

42. W. E. B. Du Bois, *In Battle for Peace: The Story of My 83rd Birthday* (1952; repr., New York: Oxford University Press, 2007), 58.

43. "Text of the address of L. D. Reddick at the 'DuBois meeting' Town Hall, New York City, September 28, 1951," box 8, LDRP-SC.

44. Marion Howe to Reddick, October 23, 1951, box 8, LDRP-SC.

45. Federal Bureau of Investigation, "Re: Communist Influence in Racial Matters Internal Security—C," September 9, 1966, folder 001606-012-0544, Martin Luther King Jr. FBI File, including FBI Report on King, August–October 1967, Federal Bureau of Investigation.

46. David J. Garrow, *The FBI and Martin Luther King, Jr.: From "Solo" to Memphis* (New York: Norton, 1981), 116, 265.

47. "Leaders Hit Jim Crow in Atlanta City Plan: Oppose Move to Shift Auburn Business Area," *Chicago Defender*, June 7, 1952.

48. "The remarks of Dr. L. D. Reddick at the Luncheon-Forum on the City Plan for Atlanta, at the Hungry Club, April 23, 1952," L. D. Reddick Biographical Files, ARC-AU; Robert E. Johnson, "University Historian Charges Plan Blueprints Future Jim Crow," *Atlanta Daily World*, April 29, 1952.

49. "Remarks of L. D. Reddick at the public hearings, Metropolitan Planning Commission, Municipal Auditorium, Atlanta, Georgia, May 26, 1952," L. D. Reddick Biographical Files, ARC-AU; Robert E. Johnson, "Business League Speaker Makes 4-Point Criticism," *Atlanta Daily World*, May 27, 1952.

50. "Leaders Hit Jim Crow in Atlanta City Plan: Oppose Move to Shift Auburn Business Area," *Chicago Defender*, June 7, 1952.

51. "Atlanta Planning Program Hungry Club Topic Wed.," *Atlanta Daily World*, April 10, 1955.

52. William Gordon, "Panel Group Sees Improvement in Atlanta's Planning Program," *Atlanta Daily World*, April 14, 1955.

53. "The Defender News Reel," *Chicago Defender*, May 15, 1948. See Nancy Joan Weiss, *Farewell to the Party of Lincoln: Black Politics in the Age of F.D.R.* (Princeton, NJ: Princeton University Press, 1983).

54. "Southern Teachers OK Rights Plank," *Chicago Defender*, August 2, 1952.

55. "Democrats Endorsed: Three Teachers Urge Southern Negroes to Back Stevenson," *New York Times*, August 13, 1952.

56. "Photo Standalone 19—No Title," *Chicago Defender*, August 9, 1952.

57. J. T. Carlton, "Don't Tell Us How to Vote," *Pittsburgh Courier*, September 6, 1952.

58. "Dobbs, Reddick Open Debate on Politics Here," *Atlanta Daily World*, September 30, 1952.

59. L. D. Reddick, "Around the U.S.A.: Victory in Atlanta," *The Nation*, May 30, 1953.

60. "The Defender Newsreel," *Chicago Defender*, December 21, 1946.

61. See Jeff Woods, *Black Struggle, Red Scare: Segregation and Anti-Communism in the South, 1948–1968* (Baton Rouge: Louisiana University Press, 2004).

62. "Is Guilt to Be by Association?," *Atlanta Daily World*, December 3, 1953. The *Atlanta Daily World*'s general cautiousness did not mean it was not a crucial part of the local civil rights movement. See Thomas Aiello, *The Grapevine of the Black South: The Scott Newspaper Syndicate in the Generation before the Civil Rights Movement* (Athens: University of Georgia Press, 2018).

63. L. D. Reddick, "The Negro Policy of the United States Army, 1775–1945," *Journal of Negro History* 34 (January 1949): 11–12.

64. L. D. Reddick, "The Relative Status of the Negro in the American Armed Forces," *Journal of Negro Education* 22 (Summer 1953): 387.

65. L. D. Reddick, "The Negro Policy of the American Army Since World War II," *Journal of Negro History* 38 (April 1953): 194–215. The research was supported by the Carnegie Research Fund. For more information, see Atlanta University Presidential Records, Rufus E. Clement Records, box 400, folder 6, ARC-AU.

66. Reddick, "The Relative Status of the Negro in the American Armed Forces," 386.

67. L. D. Reddick, "The Great Decision," *Phylon* 15 (1954): 196, 199, 194–95.

68. Reddick, "The Great Decision," 199.

69. Gertrude Martin, "Book Reviews," *Chicago Defender*, September 18, 1954.

70. Reddick, "The Great Decision," 196.

71. Reddick Press Release, circa 1954, box 8, LDRP-SC; "Article 1—No Title," *Chicago Defender*, August 28, 1954.

72. L. D. Reddick, "The Education of Negroes in States Where Separate Schools Are Not Legal," *Journal of Negro Education* 16 (Summer 1947): 297–98, 300.

73. Reddick to Horace Mann Bond, March 22, 1954, HMBP-UMAL.

74. "Pioneering Negro Aided Nation's Economy: College Prexy Lauds Carver Achievements," *Chicago Defender*, January 23, 1960.

75. H. K. Riggs, S. M. Nabrit, J. P. Brawley, B. R. Brazeal, and J. H. Robinson, *Our Colleges and the Industrialization of the South*, ed. L. D. Reddick (Atlanta: Fuller, 1953), 3–7, Countee Cullen-Harold Jackman Memorial Collection, box 29, folder 3, ARC-AU.

76. Riggs et al., *Our Colleges and the Industrialization of the South*, 5.

77. L. D. Reddick, "What the People Say: WAKE UP COLLEGES!," *Chicago Defender*, June 27, 1953.

78. William Gordon, "Reviewing the News: A Challenge to the Colleges," *Atlanta Daily World*, June 9, 1953; "Let's Move with the Times," *Chicago Defender*, June 6, 1953.

79. Reddick to St. Clair Drake, circa 1955, box 8, folder 30, SCDP-SC.

80. Reddick to William E. Doar Jr., February 7, 1955, box 41, LDRP-SC.

81. "Dr. Luther P. Jackson Dies at Virginia State," *Atlanta Daily World*, April 14, 1950; L. F. Palmer, "He Left a Lonesome Place," *Negro History Bulletin*, June 1, 1950, 198, 214.

82. Pero Gaglo Dagbovie, *The Early Black History Movement, Carter G. Woodson, and Lorenzo Johnston Greene* (Urbana: University of Illinois Press, 2007), 204–5.

83. Reddick to Lorenzo Greene, August 17, 1950, box 73, folder 12, LJGP-LC; "Set 1st History Meet Since Woodson's Death," *Chicago Defender*, September 30, 1950.

84. Dagbovie, *The Early Black History Movement*, 207.

85. Lorenzo Greene to Reddick, September 13, 1950, box 73, folder 12, LJGP-LC.

86. Lorenzo Greene to Reddick, October 6, 1950, box 73, folder 12, LJGP-LC; "Proceedings of the Annual Meeting of the Association," *Journal of Negro History* 36 (January 1951): 7–8.

87. "Logan Elected to Former Woodson Post, Director of History Study," *Chicago Defender*, November 11, 1950.

88. Reddick to Fellows, October 2, 1950, box 73, folder 12, LJGP-LC; Lorenzo Greene to Reddick, May 31, 1940, box 33, folder 5, LJGP-LC.

89. L. D. Reddick to Members of the ASNLH Executive Council, November 1, 1950, box 22, LDRP-SC.

90. Rayford Logan to Charles Wesley, December 18, 1951, box 22, LDRP-SC.

91. Lorenzo Greene to Reddick, November 8, 1950, box 73, folder 12, LJGP-LC.

92. William M. Brewer to Reddick, September 13, 1952, box 22, LDRP-SC.

93. Reddick to Lorenzo Greene, October 30, 1951, box 73, folder 12, LJGP-LC.

94. Charles Wesley to L. D. Reddick, September 9, 1952, box 22, LDRP-SC; Reddick to Lorenzo Greene, September 24, 1952, box 73, folder 12, LJGP-LC; William M. Brewer, "Proceedings of the Annual Meeting of the Association for the Study of Negro Life and History Held in Detroit, Michigan, October 24–26, 1952," *Journal of Negro History* 38 (January 1953): 6.

95. Rufus E. Clement to Reddick, April 21, 1954, DBP-UMAL.

96. Reddick to Rufus E. Clement, April 22, 1954, DBP-UMAL.

97. Rufus E. Clement to Reddick, February 17, 1955, DBP-UMAL.

98. Glovina Virginia Perry Banks to W. E. B. Du Bois, June 4, 1955, DBP-UMAL.

99. L. D. Reddick to C. A. Bacote, April 1, 1955, Clarence A. Bacote papers, box 12, folder 20, ARC-AU.

100. Reddick to Rufus E. Clement, March 1, 1955, DBP-UMAL; Rufus E. Clement to Reddick, March 2, 1955, DBP-UMAL.

101. Rufus E. Clement to Reddick, March 2, 1955, DBP-UMAL; Rufus E. Clement to Reddick, March 4, 1955, DBP-UMAL.

102. Reddick to Horace Mann Bond, March 9, 1955, HMBP-UMAL.

103. Reddick to St. Clair Drake, March 9, 1955, box 8, folder 30, SCDP-SC.

104. W. E. B. Du Bois to Reddick, March 28, 1955, DBP-UMAL.

105. W. E. B. Du Bois to Reddick.

106. W. E. B. Du Bois to Reddick, April 18, 1955, DBP-UMAL.

107. Reddick to Chairman and Members of the Atlanta University Senate, March 19, 1955, DBP-UMAL.

108. "Reddick Dismissed from Atlanta Univ.," *Cleveland Call and Post*, June 18, 1955.

Chapter Five

1. Robert D. Nesbitt to whom it may concern, January 31, 1959, box 90, folder 3, MLKP-BU.
2. Ralph David Abernathy, *And the Walls Came Tumbling Down* (New York: Harper & Row, 1989), 63.
3. "Reddick Says College to Aid Student Thinking," *Atlanta Daily World*, November 17, 1955.
4. L. D. Reddick, "Education or Propaganda: Report on the Encyclopedias," *Negro History Bulletin*, October 1, 1956, 11.
5. Reddick to Lorenzo Greene, September 23, 1955, box 8, LDRP-SC.
6. Department of History and Political Science, Alabama State University, https://www.alasu.edu/clas/history-political-science/department-history-and-political-science (accessed April 14, 2020).
7. L. D. Reddick, "Africa, the Confederate Myth and the New Frontier," 1961, box 26, folder 2, MLKP-BU.
8. Reddick to St. Clair Drake, April 11, 1956, box 8, folder 30, SCDP-SC.
9. Montgomery Improvement Association Newsletter, Vol. 1, No. 1, June 7, 1956, box 99, folder 2, MLKP-BU.
10. Danielle L. McGuire, *At the Dark End of the Street: Black Women, Rape, and Resistance—A New History of the Civil Rights Movement from Rosa Parks to the Rise of Black Power* (New York: Vintage, 2011), xvii.
11. Barbara Ransby, *Ella Baker and the Black Freedom Movement: A Radical Democratic Vision* (Chapel Hill: University of North Carolina Press, 2003), 171.
12. Mary Fair Burks, "Women in the Montgomery Bus Boycott," in *Women in the Civil Rights Movement: Trailblazers and Torchbearers 1941–1965*, ed. Vicki L. Crawford, Jacqueline Anne Rouse, and Barbara Woods (Bloomington: Indiana University Press, 1993), 71–83; Jo Ann Gibson Robinson, *The Montgomery Bus Boycott and the Women Who Started It: The Memoir of Jo Ann Gibson Robinson* (Knoxville: University of Tennessee Press, 1987).
13. Reddick to W. E. B. Du Bois, April 11, 1956, DBP-UMAL.
14. Reddick to C. V. Troup, June 13, 1956, box 8, LDRP-SC.
15. Troy Jackson, *Becoming King: Martin Luther King, Jr. and the Making of a National Leader* (Lexington: University Press of Kentucky, 2008), 96–97.
16. Reddick to C. V. Troup, June 13, 1956, box 8, LDRP-SC.
17. Martin Luther King Jr., "Recommendations Made to Executive Board of Montgomery Improvement Association," May 24, 1956, box 96, folder 4, MLKP-BU.
18. Norman W. Walton, "The Walking City, A History of the Montgomery Boycott, Part I," *Negro History Bulletin*, October 1, 1956, 17–20.
19. Evelyn Brooks Higginbotham, *Righteous Discontent: The Women's Movement in the Black Baptist Church, 1880–1920* (Cambridge, MA: Harvard University Press, 1994).
20. L. D. Reddick, "The Bus Boycott in Montgomery," *Dissent* 3 (Spring 1956): 108.
21. Reddick, "Bus Boycott in Montgomery," 111, 111, 115, 117. See also L. D. Reddick, "Whose Ordeal?," *New Republic* (September 24, 1956): 9–10.

22. Jacquelyn Dowd Hall, "The Long Civil Rights Movement and the Political Uses of the Past," *Journal of American History* 91 (March 2005): 1235.

23. U.S. District Court for the Middle District of Alabama, *Browder v. Gayle*, 142 F. Supp. 707 (M.D. Ala. 1956), June 5, 1956, https://law.justia.com/cases/federal/district-courts/FSupp/142/707/2263463/.

24. Martin Luther King Jr., Statement by the President of the MIA, December 20, 1956, box 98, folder 5, MLKP-BU.

25. Alabama Council on Human Relations Newsletter, June 1957, box 99, folder 2, MLKP-BU.

26. Maude L. Ballou to King, January 30, 1959, box 90, folder 2, MLKP-BU.

27. Montgomery Improvement Association Newsletter, September 27, 1958, box 99, folder 2, MLKP-BU.

28. P. L. Prattis, "Plain Murder," *Pittsburgh Courier*, January 18, 1958.

29. United States Congress, "Declaration of Constitutional Principles," March 12, 1956, http://alvaradohistory.com/yahoo_site_admin/assets/docs/4SouthernManifesto.1134251.pdf.

30. Tom P. Brady, foreword to *Black Monday* (Jackson, MS: Citizens' Councils of America, 1955).

31. "A Preview of the Declaration of Segregation," circa March 1956, box 23, LDRP-SC. On the wider history of the Citizens' Councils, see Stephanie R. Rolph, *Resisting Equality: The Citizens' Council, 1954–1989* (Baton Rouge: Louisiana University Press, 2018).

32. L. D. Reddick, "How SCLC Began," circa 1965, box 20, folders 6, MLKP-KC.

33. Aldon D. Morris, *The Origins of the Civil Rights Movement: Black Communities Organizing for Change* (New York: Free Press, 1984), 83.

34. Reddick, "How SCLC Began."

35. Morris, *The Origins of the Civil Rights Movement*, 88.

36. Reddick to King, January 26, 1965, MLKP-KC, box 20, folders 5.

37. "Constitution and By-Laws of the Southern Christian Leadership Conference" [final printed booklet], box 111, folder 1, MLKP-BU.

38. Memo by L. D. Reddick, "Bylaws and Preamble," November 5, 1958, box 109, folder 2, MLKP-BU; "Suggested Preamble [for instituting SCLC]," October 22, 1958, box 111, folder 1, MLKP-BU.

39. Ransby, *Ella Baker*, 184, 183–92.

40. L. D. Reddick, "A Few of My Impressions of India," May 3, 1959, box 22, LDRP-SC.

41. Reddick to King and Wyatt Tee Walker, September 15, 1961, box 109, folder 2, MLKP-BU.

42. "Reddick Notes on SCLC Administrative Committee Meetings on 2 April and 3 April 1959," in *Threshold of a New Decade: January 1959–December 1960*, Vol. 5, ed. Clayborne Carson, Tenisha Armstrong, Susan Carson, Adrienne Clay, and Kieran Taylor (Berkeley: University of California Press, 2005), 177.

43. Charles M. Payne, *I've Got the Light of Freedom: The Organizing Tradition and the Mississippi Struggle* (Berkeley: University of California Press, 1995), 3.

44. Ransby, *Ella Baker*, 172, 190–92.

45. "Anderson Criticized for 'Boycott' Article," *Pittsburgh Courier*, December 7, 1957.

46. Trezzvant W. Anderson, "How Has Dramatic Bus Boycott Affected Montgomery Negroes? Second Article in a Series," *Pittsburgh Courier*, November 16, 1957.

47. "Anderson Criticized for 'Boycott' Article."

48. "MIA Did Help Rosa Parks," *Pittsburgh Courier*, December 14, 1957.

49. "Anderson Criticized for 'Boycott' Article."

50. Jackson, *Becoming King*, 163.

51. Anderson, "How Has Dramatic Bus Boycott Affected Montgomery Negroes?"; Jackson, *Becoming King*, 161–67.

52. Akwasi B. Assensoh, "Obituaries: Lawrence Dunbar Reddick," *OAH Newsletter* 23 (November 1995): 19.

53. Archival Introduction, American Committee on Africa, box 83, folder 3, MLKP-BU.

54. Ransby, *Ella Baker*, 177.

55. *The Crusader*, Vol. 1, No. 1, February 1959, box 114, folder 4, MLKP-BU.

56. Thomas R. Peake, *Keeping the Dream Alive: A History of the Southern Christian Leadership Conference from King to the Nineteen-Eighties* (New York: Peter Lang, 1987), 52–60.

57. Martin Luther King Jr., *Stride toward Freedom: The Montgomery Story* (New York: Ballantine, 1958); L. D. Reddick, *Crusader without Violence: A Biography of Martin Luther King, Jr.* (New York: Harper, 1959).

58. Carol Polsgrove, *Divided Minds: Intellectuals and the Civil Rights Movement* (New York: Norton, 2001), 109.

59. Clayborne Carson, introduction to *The Papers of Martin Luther King, Jr.*, Vol. 4, *Symbol of the Movement: January 1957–December 1958*, ed. Clayborne Carson, Susan Carson, Adrienne Clay, Virginia Shadron, and Kieran Taylor (Berkeley: University of California Press, 2000), 29.

60. Memo on Martin Luther King Jr., Manuscript, May 1958, box 14, folder 3, MLKP-BU; "Notes from Dr. Reddick to Dr. King on the book, 1958," 2.1.2.30, MLKP-AU.

61. Reddick to St. Clair Drake, March 21, 1957, box 8, folder 31, SCDP-SC.

62. Reddick to St. Clair Drake, May 6, 1957, box 8, folder 31, SCDP-SC.

63. Reddick to St. Clair Drake, July 25, 1958, box 8, folder 31, SCDP-SC.

64. Taylor Branch, *Parting the Waters: America in the King Years, 1954–63* (New York: Simon & Schuster, 1998), 250.

65. Reddick, *Crusader without Violence*, 1, 131, 131.

66. Reddick, 17, 14–18.

67. Reddick, 81, 81, 19.

68. Wilma Dykeman and James Stokely, "McCarthyism under the Magnolias," *The Progressive* (July 1959): 6–10; Jeff Woods, *Black Struggle, Red Scare: Segregation and Anti-Communism in the South, 1948-1968* (Baton Rouge: Louisiana University Press, 2004), 4–5.

69. Reddick, *Crusader without Violence*, 233, 22, 233, 233.

70. "Carolina Leader Lashes Critics," *Chicago Defender*, May 16, 1959.

71. For Williams's full story, see Timothy B. Tyson, *Radio Free Dixie: Robert F. Williams & the Roots of Black Power* (Chapel Hill: University of North Carolina Press, 1999).

72. Reddick to W. E. B. Du Bois, April 11, 1956, DBP-UMAL.

73. "So What Does Non-Violent Resistance Profit a Dead Man?," *Los Angeles Tribune*, July 17, 1959.

74. Reddick, *Crusader without Violence*, 21.

75. Tyson, *Radio Free Dixie*, 210.

76. Reddick to Melvin Arnold, July 18, 1959, box 41, LDRP-SC.

77. Reddick to St. Clair Drake, November 24, 1959, box 8, folder 31, SCDP-SC. Reddick would later republish some parts of the book. See L. D. Reddick, "Martin Luther King and the Republican White House," in *Martin Luther King, Jr.: A Profile*, ed. C. Eric Lincoln (New York: Hill and Wang, 1970), 72–89.

78. Ernestine Cofield, "Book Review," *Chicago Defender*, November 10, 1959.

79. Anna Arnold Hedgeman, "A Great Book About the Negro People," *Negro History Bulletin*, February 1, 1960, 115.

80. "King Once Tried Suicide, Says New Book," *Los Angeles Tribune*, June 26, 1959.

81. "Auburn Ave. History Told in New Book," *Atlanta Daily World*, June 2, 1959; "New Book on King Tells Story of Famous Street," *Chicago Defender*, June 27, 1959.

82. "Book Tells Little Known Facts about M. L. King," *Chicago Defender*, July 18, 1959.

83. The notable exception here was Hugh H. Smythe, an anthropologist who had studied under Melville Herskovits at Northwestern and seemed to have a grudge against Reddick. In *Phylon*, Smythe savaged the book, writing that it "is poorly written, has no real continuity, lacks a smooth flowing narrative pattern, and reads like something put together from clippings and inserts." Smythe also took issue with Reddick calling King a "charismatic leader," insisting that "he isn't and never could be in the United States." See Hugh H. Smythe, "Man from Montgomery," review of *Crusader without Violence*, by L. D. Reddick, *Phylon* 20 (1959): 409–10.

84. James Baldwin to Martin Luther King Jr., May 26, 1960, in *The Papers of Martin Luther King, Jr.*, Vol. 5, *Threshold of a New Decade*, 461.

85. Saunders Redding, "Book Review: A Live Biography," *Afro-American*, June 20, 1959.

86. Benjamin E. Mays, "My View: Crusader without Violence," *Pittsburgh Courier*, July 25, 1959.

87. W. E. B. Du Bois, quoted in Gerald Horne, *Black and Red: W. E. B. Du Bois and the Afro-American Response to the Cold War, 1944–1963* (Albany: State University of New York Press, 1986), 239.

88. "Quakers Sponsor Trip of Dr. and Mrs. King to India," *Arkansas State Press*, January 30, 1959; Martin Luther King Jr. to the Christopher Reynolds Foundation, March 7, 1958, box 90, folder 2, MLKP-BU.

89. W. Sherman Savage and L. D. Reddick, *Our Cause Speeds On: An Informal History of the Phi Beta Sigma Fraternity* (Atlanta: Fuller, 1957), 204; Phi Beta Sigma Press Release, 1949, box 8, LDRP-SC.

90. L. D. Reddick, "An Afterword by Dr. L. D. Reddick," in *Rev. Dr. Martin Luther King, Jr. and America's Quest for Racial Integration* by A. B. Assensoh (Ilfracombe, UK: Stockwell, 1987), 79.

91. James E. Bristol to Corinne B. Johnson, March 11, 1959, in *The Papers of Martin Luther King, Jr.*, Vol. 5, *Threshold of a New Decade*, 139.

92. James E. Bristol to Corinne B. Johnson, March 10, 1959, in *Papers of Martin Luther King, Jr.*, Vol. 5, 141.

93. L. D. Reddick, "A Few of My Impressions of India," May 3, 1959, box 22, LDRP-SC.

94. "Reddick Notes on SCLC Administrative Committee Meetings on 2 April and 3 April 1959," in *The Papers of Martin Luther King, Jr.*, Vol. 5, *Threshold of a New Decade*, 179.

95. Pranshankar Someshwar Joshi to Martin Luther King Jr., 1959, box 90, folder 2, MLKP-BU.

96. James E. Bristol to King, January 3, 1958, box 90, folder 2, MLKP-BU.

97. Reddick, "An Afterword by Dr. L. D. Reddick," 79.

98. King, "My Trip to the Land of Gandhi," box 90, folder 1, MLKP-BU.

99. Reddick to Richard Wright, April 29, 1959, box 3, folder 105, Richard Wright Papers, Yale Collection of American Literature, Beinecke Rare Book and Manuscript Library.

100. Coretta Scott King, *My Life with Martin Luther King, Jr.* (New York: Holt, Rinehart and Winston, 1969), 174–75.

101. "Notes for Conversation between King and Nehru," February 10, 1959, box 90, folder 1, MLKP-BU.

102. "Account by Lawrence Dunbar Reddick of Press Conference in New Delhi on 10 February 1959," in *The Papers of Martin Luther King, Jr.*, Vol. 5, *Threshold of a New Decade*, 127–29.

103. Reddick to King, April 9, 1959, box 28, LDRP-SC; Martin Luther King Jr., "My Trip to the Land of Gandhi," *Ebony*, July 1959, 84–92. For more on *Ebony*'s central role within African American intellectual life, see E. James West, *Ebony Magazine and Lerone Bennett Jr.: Popular Black History in Postwar America* (Urbana: University of Illinois Press, 2020).

104. Martin Luther King Jr., "Statement of Dr. Martin Luther King upon Landing at New York City," March 18, box 90, folder 1, MLKP-BU.

105. Reddick, "A Few of My Impressions of India."

106. L. D. Reddick, "India's Progress Against Untouchability," July 22–24, 1959, box 22, LDRP-SC.

107. August Meier, "The Successful Sit-ins in a Border City: A Study in Social Causation," *Journal of Intergroup Relations* 2 (Summer 1961): 230–37.

108. For a good discussion of Lawson and his methods, see Wesley C. Hogan, *Many Minds, One Heart: SNCC's Dream for a New America* (Chapel Hill: University of North Carolina Press, 2007), 13–44.

109. For a broader look at student activism on black colleges in this era, see Joy Ann Williamson, *Radicalizing the Ebony Tower: Black Colleges and the Black Freedom Struggle in Mississippi* (New York: Teacher's College Press, 2008).

110. Wayne A. Wiegand and Shirley A. Wiegand, *The Desegregation of Public Libraries in the Jim Crow South: Civil Rights and Local Activism* (Baton Rouge: Louisiana State University Press, 2018), 118.

111. Nikole Hannah-Jones, "The Resegregation of Jefferson County," *New York Times*, September 6, 2017.

112. Robinson, *The Montgomery Bus Boycott and the Women Who Started It*, 169.

113. Levi Watkins, *Fighting Hard: The Alabama State Experience* (Detroit: Harlo, 1987), 28.

114. Montgomery Students Sit-In Story, circa April 15, 1960, box 99, folder 3, MLKP-BU.

115. "Sitdown Staged in Alabama Shop; Courthouse at Montgomery Is Scene of First Protest in the Deep South," *New York Times*, February 26, 1960.

116. Montgomery Students Sit-In Story, circa April 15, 1960, box 99, folder 3, MLKP-BU; "ASC Negroes Roar Approval of Campus Walkout Threat," *Montgomery Advertiser*, March 1, 1960; "Police Thwart Negro Services at Capitol: Whites Held at Distance by Officials," *Montgomery Advertiser*, March 7, 1960; Dick Hines and Arthur Osgoode, "City Police Arrest 37 Negro Agitators for Demonstration," *Montgomery Advertiser*, March 9, 1960; Herschel Cribb, "32 Students Given Fines; File Appeals," *Montgomery Advertiser*, March 12, 1960.

117. Reddick, "The State vs. the Student," *Dissent* 7 (Summer 1960): 224, 219–20, 228.

118. Watkins, *Fighting Hard*, 33.

119. "Trenholm Plans Purge of 'Disloyal' Faculty," *Montgomery Advertiser*, March 27, 1960.

120. For a good discussion of the false narratives surrounding the student sit-ins, which the *Montgomery Advertiser* was important in spreading, see L. D. Reddick, "Sit-In Mythology," box 23, LDRP-SC.

121. Watkins, *Fighting Hard*, 30–31.

122. Reddick quoted in Watkins, *Fighting Hard*, 36.

123. Reddick to King, April 13, 1960, box 37, folder 1, MLKP-BU.

124. Reddick to King, April 25, 1960, box 63, folder 2, MLKP-BU.

125. SCLC to John Malcolm Patterson, April 14, 1960, in *The Papers of Martin Luther King, Jr.*, Vol. 5, *Threshold of a New Decade*, 426.

126. Robinson, *The Montgomery Bus Boycott and the Women Who Started It*, 168–70; Abernathy, *And the Walls Came Tumbling Down*, 164–65.

127. Carol Polsgrove has documented how this report, upon which Reddick's firing was purportedly based, has vanished from the archives. See Polsgrove, *Divided Minds*, 118.

128. Bob Ingram, "Negro Teacher Linked to Reds, Ordered Fired," *Montgomery Advertiser*, June 15, 1960.

129. Reddick to W. E. B. Du Bois, June 25, 1960, Du Bois Papers, SCUA UMAL.

130. "Reddick Denies Ties with Reds; Lashes Governor," *Atlanta Daily World*, June 18, 1960.

131. "Reddick Fired Because of Book, Sit-Ins," *Chicago Daily Defender*, June 20, 1960.

132. "Reddick to Ghana, Wants Ala. Hearing," *Atlanta Daily World*, July 1, 1960.

133. Patrick Malin, "News Release," June 17, 1960, box 61, folder 3, MLKP-BU; "Civil Liberties Union Hits Firing of Dr. Reddick, *Atlanta Daily World*, June 22, 1960.

134. Martin Luther King Jr., SCLC Press Release, June 16, 1960, box 112, folder 1, MLKP-BU; Roy Wilkins to John Patterson, June 17, 1960, MLKP-KC, box 20, folders 4.

135. "Reddick to Ghana, Wants Ala. Hearing," *Atlanta Daily World*, July 1, 1960.

136. C. Vann Woodward, "The Unreported Crisis in the Southern Colleges," *Harper's Magazine*, October 1962, 86. While trying to win back accreditation in 1979, the Alabama state government and the board of trustees at Alabama State College offered Reddick an apology and $1,000 to get him to revoke his condemnation of the school. He rejected the offer as too little, too late. See Jordan E. Kurland to Reddick, May 25, 1979, box 5, LDRP-SC.

137. King to A. Philip Randolph, August 9, 1960, box 109, folder 2, MLKP-BU.

138. Bob Ingram, "Negro Teacher Linked to Reds, Ordered Fired," *Montgomery Advertiser*, June 15, 1960.

139. "Alabama Dismisses a Negro Educator," *New York Times*, June 16, 1960.

140. Clayton Knowles, "Truman Believes Reds Lead Sit-Ins," *New York Times*, April 19, 1960.

141. "Academic Freedom Dies in Colleges as Desegregation Fight Rages," *Chicago Defender*, October 6, 1962.

142. Mercer Cook, "Historical News," *Journal of Negro History* 45 (July 1960): 212–13.

143. "Dr. Reddick in Coppin State Post," *Atlanta Daily World*, September 28, 1960.

144. L. D. Reddick, "The Negro as Southerner and American," in *The Southerner as American*, ed. Charles Grier Sellers Jr. (Chapel Hill: University of North Carolina Press, 1960), 147.

Chapter Six

1. Reddick to St. Clair Drake, December 15, 1958, box 8, folder 31, SCDP-SC.

2. George M. Houser, "A Report on the All Africa People's Conference Held in Accra, Ghana, December 8–13, 1958," box 83, folder 3, MLKP-BU. See also Adom Getachew, *Worldmaking after Empire: The Rise and Fall of Self-Determination* (Princeton, NJ: Princeton University Press, 2018).

3. Reddick to MLK, April 27, 1959, box 109, folder 2, MLKP-BU.

4. Tom Mboya, "Key Questions for Awakening Africa," *New York Times Magazine*, June 28, 1959, box 83, folder 3, MLKP-BU.

5. Martin Luther King Jr., Introductory Remarks at Africa Freedom Dinner, in *The Papers of Martin Luther King, Jr.*, Vol. 5, *Threshold of a New Decade*, 203–4.

6. St. Clair Drake to Reddick, April 10, 1959, box 8, folder 31, SCDP-SC.

7. Reddick to St. Clair Drake, November 24, 1959, box 8, folder 31, SCDP-SC.

8. St. Clair Drake to Reddick, June 12, 1959, box 8, folder 30, SCDP-SC.

9. Reddick to St. Clair Drake, May 2, 1961, box 8, folder 30, SCDP-SC; St. Clair Drake to Nana, June 13, 1962, box 8, folder 31, SCDP-SC.

10. "Reddick to Ghana, Wants Ala. Hearing," *Atlanta Daily World*, July 1, 1960; "Dr. Reddick to Greet Azikiwe," *Chicago Defender*, November 19, 1960.

11. "Dr. Reddick Tells of Trip to Nigeria," *Afro-American*, December 17, 1960.

12. Reddick to St. Clair Drake, May 2, 1961, box 8, folder 30, SCDP-SC.

13. See Kevin K. Gaines, *American Africans in Ghana: Black Expatriates and the Civil Rights Era* (Chapel Hill: University of North Carolina Press, 2006).

14. "Nkrumah Confers with 2 American Professors," *Afro-American*, July 30, 1960.

15. St. Clair Drake to Reddick, September 14, 1960, box 8, folder 31, SCDP-SC.

16. L. D. Reddick, "Contrast: 1965 versus 1975," *Black Scholar* 19 (January/February 1988): 8.

17. Reddick to MLK, May 9, 1961, box 109, folder 2, MLKP-BU.

18. Reddick to MLK and Wyatt Tee Walker, September 15, 1961, box 109, folder 2, MLKP-BU.

19. Reddick to MLK and Wyatt Tee Walker, December 8, 1961, box 20, folder 4, MLKP-KC.

20. King to Reddick, March 8, 1962, box 20, folder 4, MLKP-KC.

21. Reddick to MLK and Wyatt Tee Walker, February 17, 1962, box 20, folder 4, MLKP-KC.

22. Reddick to MLK and Wyatt Tee Walker, October 6, 1961, box 109, folder 2, MLKP-BU.

23. Reddick to MLK, May 9, 1961, box 109, folder 2, MLKP-BU.

24. "Civil War Fetes Decried by Negro," *New York Times*, April 23, 1961.

25. L. D. Reddick, "Africa, the Confederate Myth and the New Frontier," 1961, box 26, folder 2, MLKP-BU.

26. "Civil War Fetes Decried by Negro," *New York Times*, April 23, 1961; "Dr. Reddick Blasts Glorifying Civil War," *Chicago Defender*, May 2, 1961; "N.Y.C. Teachers' President Lashes Slow Integration . . . North, South," *New Pittsburgh Courier*, May 6, 1961.

27. Reddick to MLK and Wyatt Tee Walker, September 15, 1961, box 109, folder 2, MLKP-BU.

28. Reddick to King, October 16, 1962, box 20, folder 4, MLKP-KC.

29. Reddick to King, August 2, 1963, box 20, folder 4, MLKP-KC.

30. Clarence B. Jones and Stuart Connelly, *Behind the Dream: The Making of the Speech that Transformed a Nation* (New York: Palgrave MacMillan, 2011), 106–7.

31. Jones and Connelly, *Behind the Dream*, 60, 62, 112, 54–61; L. D. Reddick, "An Afterword by Dr. L. D. Reddick," in *Rev. Dr. Martin Luther King, Jr. and America's Quest for Racial Integration* by A. B. Assensoh (Ilfracombe, UK: Stockwell, 1987), 80–82.

32. Thomas R. Peake, *Keeping the Dream Alive: A History of the Southern Christian Leadership Conference from King to the Nineteen-Eighties* (New York: Peter Lang, 1987), 124–28.

33. Reddick to Bayard Rustin, September 27, 1963, box 20, folder 4, MLKP-KC.

34. Reddick to Roy Wilkins and King, June 29, 1963, box 20, folder 4, MLKP-KC.

35. Taylor Branch, *Pillar of Fire: America in the King Years, 1963–65* (New York: Simon & Schuster, 1998), 212.

36. "Reddick Notes on SCLC Administrative Committee Meetings on 2 April and 3 April 1959," in *The Papers of Martin Luther King, Jr.*, Vol. 5, *Threshold of a New Decade: January 1959–December 1960*, ed. Clayborne Carson, Tenisha Armstrong, Susan Carson, Adrienne Clay, and Kieran Taylor (Berkeley: University of California Press, 2005), 177.

37. H. Blake to Reddick, October 22, 1963, Folder 001581-020-0658, Bayard Rustin, General Correspondence, January–December 1963, Bayard Rustin Papers, A. Philip Randolph Institute, New York.

38. Reddick to King, October 11, 1963, box 20, folder 4, MLKP-KC. For more on Rustin, see John D'Emilio, *Lost Prophet: The Life and Times of Bayard Rustin* (Chicago: University of Chicago Press, 2003). For more on the politics of sexuality during the Cold War, see David K. Johnson, *The Lavender Scare: The Cold War Persecution of Gays and Lesbians in the Federal Government* (Chicago: University of Chicago Press, 2004).

39. Reddick to King, November 27, 1963, box 20, folder 4, MLKP-KC.

40. "Assignments of the Black Mountain Retreat," MLKP-AU, 6.1.0.1490; "Tentative Agenda for SCLC Retreat," MLKP-AU, 6.1.0.1500.

41. Martin Luther King Jr., *Why We Can't Wait* (New York: New American Library, 1964).

42. David J. Garrow, *Bearing the Cross: Martin Luther King, Jr., and the Southern Christian Leadership Conference* (New York: Morrow, 1986), 311–12.

43. Carol Polsgrove, *Divided Minds: Intellectuals and the Civil Rights Movement* (New York: Norton, 2001), 201–2.

44. Reddick to King, November 27, 1963, box 20, folder 4, MLKP-KC. See also Reddick to King, January 29, 1964, box 20, folder 5, MLKP-KC.

45. Reddick to King, January 6, 1964, MLKP-AU, 6.1.0.1480.

46. Garrow, *Bearing the Cross*, 312.

47. "Martin Luther King, Jr.—A Current Analysis," March 12, 1968, Folder 001606-014-0326, Martin Luther King Jr. FBI File, including SCLC, Student Nonviolent Coordinating Committee, and Racial Situation in Florida, June–August 1968, Federal Bureau of Investigation.

48. Garrow, *Bearing the Cross*, 332.

49. L. D. Reddick, "Lessons from the Wallace 'Victory,'" to MLK and Advisory Group, June 19, 1964, box 20, folder 5, MLKP-KC; Dan T. Carter, *From George Wallace to Newt Gingrich: Race in the Conservative Counterrevolution, 1963–1994* (Baton Rouge: Louisiana State University, 1996), 1–23.

50. Reddick, "Lessons from the Wallace 'Victory.'"

51. Reddick, "An Afterword by Dr. L. D. Reddick," in *Rev. Dr. Martin Luther King, Jr.*, 82.

52. Reddick to King, November 25, 1964, box 20, folder 5, MLKP-KC.

53. Martin Luther King Jr., Acceptance Speech for the Nobel Peace Prize in Oslo, Norway, December 10, 1964, the Nobel Prize Organization, https://www.nobelprize.org/prizes/peace/1964/king/26142-martin-luther-king-jr-acceptance-speech-1964/.

54. Reddick to King, November 25, 1964, box 20, folder 5, MLKP-KC; Reddick to King, January 26, 1965, box 20, folder 5, MLKP-KC.

55. L. D. Reddick, "How SCLC Began," 1965, box 20, folder 6, MLKP-KC; Betty Washington and Edward T. Clayton, "The Men Behind Martin Luther King," *Chicago Defender*, May 22, 1965.

56. Jacquelyn Dowd Hall, "The Long Civil Rights Movement and the Political Uses of the Past," *Journal of American History* 91 (March 2005): 1234.

57. Reddick to King, Ralph Abernathy, and Andrew J. Young, January 16, 1967, 6.2.0.3720, MLKP-AU.

58. For a basic introduction to the historiographical shifts, see Hall, "The Long Civil Rights Movement," 1233–63; and Peniel E. Joseph, "The Black Power Movement: A State of the Field," *Journal of American History* 96 (December 2009): 751–76.

59. L. D. Reddick, *Crusader without Violence: A Biography of Martin Luther King, Jr.* (New York: Harper, 1959), 230–31.

60. For a useful framing of the spectrum of African American political thought, see Manning Marable and Leith Mullings, eds., *Let Nobody Turn Us Around: Voices of Resistance, Reform, and Renewal*, 2nd ed. (New York: Rowman & Littlefield, 2009), xxi–xxix.

61. Reddick, *Crusader without Violence*, 231.

62. For good studies of how this played out in particular cities, see Robert O. Self, *American Babylon: Race and the Struggle for Postwar Oakland* (Princeton, NJ: Princeton University Press, 2003); and Matthew J. Countryman, *Up South: Civil Rights and Black Power in Philadelphia* (Philadelphia: University of Pennsylvania Press, 2006).

63. L. D. Reddick, "Critical Review: The Politics of Desegregation," *Journal of Negro Education* 31 (Summer 1962): 414–20, 418.

64. Ibram H. Rogers, *The Black Campus Movement: Black Students and the Racial Reconstitution of Higher Education, 1965–1972* (New York: Palgrave Macmillan, 2012), 163.

65. Reddick, "Critical Review: The Politics of Desegregation," 419–20.

66. Peake, *Keeping the Dream Alive*, 105. See also Katherine Mellen Charron, *Freedom's Teacher: The Life of Septima Clark* (Chapel Hill: University of North Carolina Press, 2009).

67. "Add History Books on Negro to School List," *Chicago Defender*, March 16, 1965.

68. Harry Gilroy, "Minorities' Story Traced in Series," *New York Times*, January 23, 1965; Fred M. Hechinger, "News of the Week in Education: For Minorities a Place in History," *New York Times*, October 25, 1964.

69. L. D. Reddick, "T.U. Story: Pilgrimage to the White University," box 21, LDRP-SC.

70. "Add History Books on Negro to School List," *Chicago Defender*, March 16, 1965.

71. "A Glorious Age in Africa," *New York Times*, February 21, 1965. See also William S. Murphy, "The Reader: Leisure Literature for Teens," *Los Angeles Times*, January 31, 1965; and "Courier Book Shelf: History for Our Youth," *Pittsburgh Courier*, March 6, 1965.

72. Agnes McCarthy and L. D. Reddick, *Worth Fighting For: The History of the Negro in the United States During the Civil War and Reconstruction* (Garden City, NY: Doubleday, 1965), 111.

73. L. D. Reddick, "Speech at Jacksonville, Fla Delta Affair," box 33, LDRP-SC.

74. "Negro's Role in History Depicted in New Books," *New York Times*, March 15, 1965.

75. See Rose Casement, *Black History in the Pages of Children's Literature* (New York: Scarecrow, 2008).

76. Reddick to John Sargent, November 22, 1966, box 5, LDRP-SC.

77. Reddick to Loretta Barnett, January 11, 1967, box 5, LDRP-SC.

78. John Hope Franklin, "The Dilemma of the American Negro Scholar," in *Race and History: Selected Essays, 1938–1988* (Baton Rouge: Louisiana State University Press, 1989), 295–308.

79. Reddick to John Sargent, November 22, 1966, box 5, LDRP-SC.

80. Reddick to W. E. B. Du Bois, November 10, 1959, Du Bois Papers, SCUA UMAL.

81. Still the best study of SNCC and its changing politics is Clayborne Carson's *In Struggle: SNCC and the Black Awakening of the 1960s* (Cambridge, MA: Harvard University Press, 1981).

82. Stokely Carmichael and Charles V. Hamilton, *Black Power: The Politics of Liberation in America* (New York: Random House, 1967), 53.

83. L. D. Reddick, "The New Racism in American Higher Education," conference paper presented at the National Black Think Tank conference at the University of Maryland, September 25, 1976, box 25, LDRP-SC.

84. Peake, *Keeping the Dream Alive*, 108.

85. L. D. Reddick, "A Summary View," n.d., box 16, LDRP-SC.

86. Taylor Branch, *At Canaan's Edge: America in the King Years, 1965–68* (New York: Simon & Schuster, 2006), 196.

87. Andrew J. Young to L. D. Reddick, November 3, 1965, box 20, folder 6, MLKP-KC; Robert L. Green to L. D. Reddick, November 15, 1965, box 20, folder 6, MLKP-KC. See also James T. Patterson, *Freedom Is Not Enough: The Moynihan Report and America's Struggle over Black Family Life—from LBJ to Obama* (New York: Basic Books, 2010).

88. Federal Bureau of Investigation, "Martin Luther King, Jr. Security Matter—C," September 1966, Folder 001606-010-0438, Martin Luther King Jr. FBI File, Part 1, Federal Bureau of Investigation.

89. Peake, *Keeping the Dream Alive*, 200–203.

90. Reddick to King, Ralph Abernathy, and Andrew J. Young, January 16, 1967, 6.2.0.3720, MLKP-AU.

91. Branch, *At Canaan's Edge*, 584.

92. Peake, *Keeping the Dream Alive*, 214–16.

93. Reddick to King, August 17, 1967, box 5, LDRP-SC.

94. L. D. Reddick, "Two Fatal Blunders: LBJ & MLK," n.d., box 25, LDRP-SC.

95. Branch, *At Canaan's Edge*, 640–41; Garrow, *Bearing the Cross*, 575.

96. "Dr. L. D. Reddick Named OIC Director," *Atlanta Daily World*, September 28, 1966.

97. The amicable relations seemed to stem from the wide latitude the history department gave to Reddick to pursue his various activist endeavors. In his resigna-

tion letter, Reddick oozed gratitude to the department chair: "You know, without my saying it, that my years at Coppin have been among the most fruitful of my entire life." Reddick to Parlett L. Moore, June 28, 1968, box 5, LDRP-SC.

98. "Photo Standalone 8—No Title," *Chicago Defender*, July 3, 1967.

99. OIC, "Draft of Contract," box 16, LDRP-SC; "OIC Institute in Philly Gets New Director," *Chicago Defender*, November 9, 1968.

100. "Dr. Sullivan to Address Mass Meet," *Atlanta Daily World*, October 28, 1962; Peake, *Keeping the Dream Alive*, 109.

101. Countryman, *Up South*, 102–3.

102. L. D. Reddick, *The Essence of OIC: Manpower Training for Disadvantaged Adults* (Philadelphia: Opportunities Industrialization Center, 1971), 81–88; Guian A. McKee, *The Problem of Jobs: Liberalism, Race, and Deindustrialization in Philadelphia* (Chicago: University of Chicago Press, 2008), 117–30.

103. Reddick, *Essence of OIC*, 80, 124; V. P. Franklin, "Pan-African Connections, Transnational Education, Collective Cultural Capital, and Opportunities Industrialization Centers International," *Journal of African American History* 96 (Winter 2011): 55–58.

104. For Sullivan's widely read treatments of this topic, see Leon Howard Sullivan, *Build, Brother, Build: From Poverty to Economic Power* (Philadelphia: McCrae Smith, 1969); and Leon H. Sullivan, *Moving Mountains: The Principles and Purposes of Leon Sullivan* (Valley Forge, PA: Judson, 1998).

105. Reddick to St. Clair Drake, November 1, 1966, box 8, folder 30, SCDP-SC.

106. Reddick, *Essence of OIC*, 69.

107. L. D. Reddick, "The Urban Rebellion and OIC," n.d., box 13, LDRP-SC; L. D. Reddick, "What to Do About the Urban Rebellion," n.d., box 16, LDRP-SC.

108. Franklin, "Pan-African Connections," 54.

109. Richard Nixon to Leon Sullivan, August 26, 1970, box 16, LDRP-SC; "Vice President Humphrey on O.I.C.," n.d., box 16, LDRP-SC.

110. "Antipoverty Goal Hit by Educator," *Washington Post*, May 21, 1966.

111. Reddick, *Essence of OIC*, 40, 122.

112. "Isom of OIC in Training," *Greater Milwaukee Star*, January 18, 1969.

113. Reddick, *Essence of OIC*, 65; L. D. Reddick, "Awareness of Minority History," n.d., box 16, LDRP-SC.

114. L. D. Reddick, "Afro-American History" Take-Home Exam, circa 1969, box 28, LDRP-SC.

115. Reddick, *Essence of OIC*, 65; L. D. Reddick, "Progress Report, OIC Managerial Training Program to National Industrial Advisory Council," January 30, 1969, box 16, LDRP-SC.

116. Reddick to St. Clair Drake, October 19, 1966, box 8, folder 30, SCDP-SC.

117. L. D. Reddick, "Exploratory Memorandum," n.d., box 8, folder 30, SCDP-SC.

118. Reddick, *Essence of OIC*, 21, 119, 44, 43.

119. Reddick, *Essence of OIC*, 32, 22.

120. Countryman, *Up South*, 110–19; McKee, *The Problem of Jobs*, 180.

121. "Reddick Quits OIC," *Chicago Defender*, April 7, 1970; "Reddick Leaves OIC for Temple," *New Courier*, April 11, 1970.

122. L. D. Reddick, "T.U. Story: Pilgrimage to the White University," box 21, LDRP-SC.

123. L. D. Reddick, "OIC National Board—Farewell," March 16, 1970, box 13, LDRP-SC.

Chapter Seven

1. Fabio Rojas, *From Black Power to Black Studies: How a Radical Social Movement Became an Academic Discipline* (Baltimore: Johns Hopkins University Press, 2007), 21.

2. Martha Biondi, *The Black Revolution on Campus* (Berkeley: University of California Press, 2012); Ibram H. Rogers, *The Black Campus Movement: Black Students and the Racial Reconstitution of Higher Education, 1965–1972* (New York: Palgrave Macmillan, 2012). The scholarship on the black campus movement has proliferated in recent years. See also Stefan Bradley, *Harlem vs. Columbia University: Black Student Power in the Late 1960s* (Champaign: University of Illinois Press, 2009); Stefan M. Bradley, *Upending the Ivory Tower: Civil Rights, Black Power, and the Ivy League* (New York: New York University Press, 2018); Donald Downs, *Cornell '69: Liberalism and the Crisis of the American University* (Ithaca, NY: Cornell University Press, 1999); Willium Exum, *Paradoxes of Protest: Black Student Activism at a White University* (Philadelphia: Temple University Press, 1985); Wayne Glasker, *Black Students in the Ivory Tower: African American Student Activism at the University of Pennsylvania, 1967–1990* (Amherst: University of Massachusetts Press, 2002); Richard McCormick, *The Black Student Protest Movement at Rutgers* (New Brunswick, NJ: Rutgers University Press, 1990); Joe Turner, *Sitting In and Speaking Out: Student Movements in the American South, 1960–1970* (Athens: University of Georgia Press, 2010); Ann Williamson, *Black Power on Campus: The University of Illinois, 1965–1975* (Champaign: University of Illinois Press, 2003).

3. Stephen Ward, "'Scholarship in the Context of Struggle': Activist Intellectuals, the Institute of the Black World (IBW), and the Contours of Black Power Radicalism," *Black Scholar* 31 (Fall/Winter 2001): 43.

4. See, for instance, Ashley Farmer, *Remaking Black Power: How Black Women Transformed an Era* (Chapel Hill: University of North Carolina Press, 2017); Peniel E. Joseph, "The Black Power Movement: A State of the Field," *Journal of American History* 96 (December 2009): 751–76; Peniel E. Joseph, *Waiting 'Til the Midnight Hour: A Narrative History of Black Power in America* (New York: Holt, 2007); Robyn C. Spencer, *The Revolution Has Come: Black Power, Gender, and the Black Panther Party in Oakland* (Durham, NC: Duke University Press, 2016); Rhonda Y. Williams, *Concrete Demands: The Search for Black Power in the 20th Century* (New York: Routledge, 2015).

5. For a recent scholarly assessment of the Poor People's Campaign, see Sylvie Laurent, *King and the Other America: The Poor People's Campaign and the Quest for Economic Equality* (Berkeley: University of California Press, 2019).

6. "Poverty: End of the Dream," *Newsweek*, July 8, 1968, 19.

7. Reddick to Ralph Abernathy, July 3, 1968, box 5, LDRP-SC.

8. Reddick to St. Clair Drake, July 24, 1969, box 8, folder 30, SCDP-SC.

9. Thomas R. Peake, *Keeping the Dream Alive: A History of the Southern Christian Leadership Conference from King to the Nineteen-Eighties* (New York: Peter Lang, 1987), 237–42, 264–65.

10. "Our 53rd Anniversary Convention at the New York Hilton," *Negro History Bulletin* 31 (December 1968): 4; L. D. Reddick, "Martin Luther King and the Republican White House," in *Martin Luther King, Jr.: A Profile*, ed. C. Eric Lincoln (New York: Hill and Wang, 1970), 72–89; "SCLU [sic] Blasts 'King' for Distorted Facts," *New Journal and Guide* (Norfolk, VA), March 3, 1978; "Program Keeps King's Memory Alive," *Twin Cities Courier*, March 30, 1978.

11. "Letter from L. D. Reddick to Colleagues [of OIC, copied to Coretta King, Stanley Levison, Benjamin Mays, and Rayford Logan]," November 21, 1966, MLKP-DC, http://www.thekingcenter.org/archive/document/letter-l-d-reddick-colleagues#.

12. Derrick E. White, *The Challenge of Blackness: The Institute of the Black World and Political Activism in the 1970s* (Gainesville: University Press of Florida, 2011), 204, 75.

13. Ward, "'Scholarship in the Context of Struggle,'" 51, 50.

14. White, *Challenge of Blackness*, 77.

15. Biondi, *Black Revolution on Campus*, 187; St. Clair Drake to Reddick, May 21, 1985, box 17, LDRP-SC.

16. "Trustees Air Policies Of Md. State Colleges," *Washington Post*, March 9, 1965; L. D. Reddick, "Remarks: Conference on Urban Education at Michigan State University," May 16, 1967, box 16, LDRP-SC; L. D. Reddick, "Y-003: Final Report," May 1967, box 13, LDRP-SC.

17. Reddick to St. Clair Drake, July 24, 1969, box 8, folder 30, SCDP-SC.

18. "'Generation Gap' A Part of the Black Revolution," *Los Angeles Sentinel*, May 22, 1969.

19. L. D. Reddick, "Glimpse of a Possible Future," April 19, 1969, speech before at the Centennial Inauguration of Vivian Henderson as President of Clark College, Atlanta, Georgia, Vivian Wilson Henderson papers, box 69, folder 6, ARC-AU.

20. Black Studies Seminar, vols. 1–3, July 19–25, 1970, box 21, LDRP-SC.

21. "Anguish over Relevance Strains Three Social Sciences, Psychologists: One Session Taken Over, Five Dissident Groups Seek Changes," *Chronicle of Higher Education*, September 15, 1969; "Disciplines Experiencing Rifts Between Old Guard and Proponents of Change," *Chronicle of Higher Education*, September 15, 1969; "Educators Find Black Studies Are Changing Higher Education," *New York Times*, June 4, 1972.

22. "Black Academy of Arts and Letters Created," *Chicago Defender*, April 3, 1969.

23. "Black Academy of Arts, Letters, Established for Pride in Race," *New York Amsterdam News*, March 29, 1969.

24. "Black Academy of Arts, Letters, Established."

25. Simon Anekwe, "3 Blacks Enter Own Hall of Fame," *New York Amsterdam News*, September 26, 1970.

26. Benjamin Mays, "Black Academy Made Great First-Year Strides," *Chicago Defender*, October 10, 1970.

27. Ethel L. Payne, "Senegal President Seeks Closer Ties with America," *Chicago Defender*, July 1, 1971.

28. "Black Academy Admits President of Senegal," *Afro-American*, June 26, 1971.

29. Reddick to St. Clair Drake, February 6, 1975, box 8, folder 31, SCDP-SC.

30. Temple University News Release, February 21, 1975, box 21, LDRP-SC.

31. Valfoulaye Diallo to Mbiu Koinange, February 20, 1975, box 23, LDRP-SC.

32. For an overview, see Martin Meredith, *The Fate of Africa: A History of Fifty Years of Independence* (New York: PublicAffairs, 2005).

33. L. D. Reddick, "T.U. Story: Pilgrimage to the White University," box 21, LDRP-SC.

34. L. D. Reddick, "Chairman Don and Chairman Ernst," n.d., box 25, LDRP-SC.

35. "Historian L. D. Reddick Joins Full-Time Staff at Temple U.," *Philadelphia Tribune*, March 24, 1970.

36. Reddick, "T.U. Story."

37. "Temple Offering Black Studies," *New Journal and Guide*, September 27, 1969.

38. "Historian L. D. Reddick Joins Full-Time Staff at Temple U.," *Philadelphia Tribune*, March 24, 1970.

39. L. D. Reddick, "The Condition of Temple University Library for Afro-American Studies," box 25, LDRP-SC.

40. L. D. Reddick, "Silence in the Temple Library," *Philly Talk*, September 1971, box 28, LDRP-SC.

41. "Historian L. D. Reddick Joins Full-Time Staff at Temple U.," *Philadelphia Tribune*, March 24, 1970.

42. "American Civil War," syllabus, n.d., box 13, LDRP-SC.

43. "20th Century: Economic History," syllabus, n.d., box 13, LDRP-SC.

44. "Oppression Is Key to Black History, Says Temple Scholar," *Philadelphia Tribune*, December 30, 1969.

45. Vincent Harding published one of the more influential treatises on the revolutionary nature of black history, and he circulated it widely among black intellectuals, including Reddick. See Vincent Harding, *Beyond Chaos: Black History and the Search for the New Land* (Atlanta: Institute of the Black World, 1970).

46. "Oppression Is Key to Black History, Says Temple Scholar," *Philadelphia Tribune*, December 30, 1969.

47. John F. Morrison, "F. Elaine DeLancey, 68, Drexel Professor," *Philadelphia Daily News*, August 4, 2001.

48. For a concise overview, see Jeanne Theoharis, "Gary Convention," in *Encyclopedia of African-American Culture and History* 3 (Detroit: Macmillan, 2006): 907. For the broader context of the Modern Black Convention Movement and Black Power, see Komozi Woodard, *A Nation within a Nation: Amiri Baraka (LeRoi Jones) and Black Power Politics* (Chapel Hill: University of North Carolina Press, 1999).

49. "Black Political Convention," March 16, 1972, box 13, LDRP-SC.

50. L. D. Reddick, "The Great Debate," n.d., box 25, LDRP-SC.

51. L. D. Reddick, "What the Negro Thinks About Democracy," box 33, LDRP-SC.

52. L. D. Reddick, "Introduction of Vine Deloria," Temple University, n.d., box 16, LDRP-SC.

53. Reddick to Members of the College Committee on African Studies, December 15, 1971, box 32, LDRP-SC.

54. L. D. Reddick, "Toward Community Self-Determination," remarks at Utopia and Urban Development forum, Franklin Institute, May 19, 1975, box 17, LDRP-SC. See Robert L. Allen, *Black Awakening in Capitalist America: An Analytic History* (New York: Anchor, 1970).

55. L. D. Reddick, "The New Racism in Higher Education," spring 1978, box 13, LDRP-SC.

56. For two excellent studies of the contributions and obstacles faced by earlier generations of black scholars, see Jonathan Scott Holloway, *Confronting the Veil: Abram Harris, Jr., E. Franklin Frazier, and Ralph Bunche, 1919–1941* (Chapel Hill: University of North Carolina Press, 2002); and Francille Rusan Wilson, *The Segregated Scholars: Black Social Scientists and the Creation of Black Labor Studies, 1890–1950* (Charlottesville: University of Virginia Press, 2006).

57. Ira Berlin, *Slaves without Masters: The Free Negro in the Antebellum South* (New York: Pantheon, 1974); Eugene D. Genovese, *Roll, Jordan, Roll: The World the Slaves Made* (New York: Pantheon, 1974); Peter H. Wood, *Black Majority: Negroes in Colonial South Carolina from 1670 to the Stono Rebellion* (New York: Knopf, 1974).

58. Stanley M. Elkins's *Slavery: A Problem in American Institutional and Intellectual Life* (Chicago: University of Chicago Press, 1959); Kenneth Stampp, *The Peculiar Institution: Slavery in the Ante-bellum South* (New York: Knopf, 1956).

59. Another white scholar published a similar and similarly influential book three years later: Lawrence W. Levine, *Black Culture and Black Consciousness: Afro-American Folk Thought from Slavery to Freedom* (New York: Oxford University Press, 1977).

60. Peter Novick, *That Noble Dream: The 'Objectivity Question' and the American Historical Profession* (Cambridge: Cambridge University Press, 1998), 487–90.

61. Fogel and Engerman, *Time on the Cross*, 11, 5, 5–6.

62. Fogel and Engerman, 9. The authors also published an entire volume on their methods. See Robert William Fogel and Stanley L. Engerman, *Time on the Cross: Evidence and Methods—A Supplement* (Boston: Little, Brown, 1974).

63. Fogel and Engerman, *Time on the Cross*, 6.

64. C. Vann Woodward in *Interpreting American History: Conversations with Historians*, ed. John A. Garraty (New York: Macmillan, 1970), 65.

65. Quotes from L. D. Reddick, "Complaint," *New York Review of Books*, August 8, 1974. See also C. Vann Woodward, "The Jolly Institution," *New York Review of Books*, May 2, 1974.

66. "Slavery Is Topic of Meeting Here," *New York Times*, April 13, 1975. For more on Aptheker, see Gary Murrell, *"The Most Dangerous Communist in the United States": A Biography of Herbert Aptheker* (Amherst: University of Massachusetts Press, 2015).

67. Reddick to St. Clair Drake, April 24, 1975, box 8, folder 31, SCDP-SC.

68. L. D. Reddick, "Corporate Scholarship Takes Over Black History and Squeezes Out the Black Scholar," April 11, 1975, box 21, LDRP-SC.

69. C. Gerald Fraser, "Black Historians Report Inattention," *New York Times*, February 12, 1975.

70. "William Still," National Underground Railroad Freedom Center, https://freedomcenter.org/content/william-still (accessed April 14, 2020).

71. Fraser, "Black Historians Report Inattention."

72. John Hope Franklin, "The History of African-American History," in *The State of Afro-American History: Past, Present, and Future*, ed. Darlene Clark Hine (Baton Rouge: Louisiana University Press, 1986), 22, 17; John Hope Franklin, *Mirror to America: The Autobiography of John Hope Franklin* (New York: Farrar, Straus and Giroux, 2005), 44–45, 59–60. To be sure, Reddick's politics did not preclude him from recognizing the positive interactions and relationships he had had with white scholars throughout his career, such as Howard Beale, Melville Herskovits, and Theodore Currier. Elsewhere, for instance, Reddick acknowledged, "I learned much [from Currier] about the trends of social thinking that I have found useful throughout my academic life." See L. D. Reddick, "Is the White College Better—for Blacks?," circa 1980, box 25, LDRP-SC.

73. David Brion Davis, *The Problem of Slavery in Western Culture* (Ithaca, NY: Cornell University Press, 1966).

74. David Brion Davis, "Slavery and the Post–World War II Historians," in *Slavery, Colonialism, and Racism*, ed. Sidney W. Mintz (New York: Norton, 1974), 2.

75. Elsa Dixler, "David Brion Davis, Prizewinning Historian of Slavery, Dies at 92," *New York Times*, April 15, 2019.

76. Lorenzo Johnston Greene, *The Negro in Colonial New England, 1620–1776* (New York: Columbia University Press, 1942); Eric Williams, *Capitalism and Slavery* (Chapel Hill: University of North Carolina Press, 1944).

77. To be fair, Davis himself acknowledged and condemned black marginalization. However, belated acknowledgment by white scholars did nothing to change the racist past. See, for instance, David Brion Davis, "Of Human Bondage," review of *Slavery and Social Death: A Comparative Study*, by Orlando Patterson, *New York Review of Books*, February 17, 1983.

78. Dixler, "David Brion Davis."

79. L. D. Reddick, "Are Blacks Losing Control of Black History," speech before Central State College, February 14, 1974, box 16, LDRP-SC; Reddick to ASALH, n.d., box 32, LDRP-SC; L. D. Reddick, "The New Racism in American Higher Education," conference paper presented at the National Black Think Tank conference at the University of Maryland, September 25, 1976, box 25, LDRP-SC.

80. L. D. Reddick, "Black History as a Corporate Colony," *Social Policy* (May/June 1976): 2, 5, 2.

81. Moss H. Kendrix, "Editorial Comment," *Negro History Bulletin* 38.5 (June/July 1975): 407.

82. Betty P. Smith to August Meier, October 11 and 20, 1983, box 133, folder 7, August Meier Papers, Sc MG 340, Schomburg Center for Research in Black Culture, the New York Public Library.

83. Alton Hornsby Jr., "The Sixty-Second Annual Meeting," *Journal of Negro History* 63 (April 1978): 152.

84. L. D. Reddick, "Black Participation in the Bicentennial," October 24, 1974, box 16, LDRP-SC.

85. Reddick, "Black Participation in the Bicentennial."

86. L. D. Reddick, "Semi-Final Report of Black Bicentennial Citizens Committee," May 1974, box 16, LDRP-SC.

87. Reddick, "Semi-Final Report of Black Bicentennial Citizens Committee."

88. Andrea A. Burns, *From Storefront to Monument: Tracing the Public History of the Black Museum Movement* (Amherst: University of Massachusetts Press, 2013), 55.

89. Charles L. Blockson to Fellow Board Members of Afro American Historical and Cultural '76 Bicentennial Corporation, April 17, 1975, box 16, LDRP-SC.

90. Charles L. Blockson, *"Damn Rare": The Memoirs of an African-American Bibliophile* (Tracy, CA: Quantum Leap, 1998), 297.

91. Biondi, *Black Revolution on Campus*, 243–46.

92. "National Urban League to Issue Black Essays," *Milwaukee Star Times*, January 22, 1976.

93. L. D. Reddick, *Blacks and U.S. Wars* (New York: National Urban League, 1976), 3.

94. L. D. Reddick, "The Real Issues in the Reddick Case," January 1976, box 25, LDRP-SC.

95. L. D. Reddick, "The New Racism in Higher Education," Spring 1978, box 13, LDRP-SC.

96. Reddick to Marvin Wachman, December 8, 1975, box 13, LDRP-SC.

97. "Chronology Lists Events Leading to Reddick Attack," *Temple Times*, May 6, 1976, box 25, LDRP-SC.

98. L. D. Reddick, "The Issues Before Us," January 1976, box 25, LDRP-SC.

99. Department of History, Temple University, "Resolutions," January 28, 1976, box 25, LDRP-SC.

100. L. D. Reddick, "Farewell: Open Letter to the Members of the Department of History," March 12, 1976, box 25, LDRP-SC.

101. L. D. Reddick, "Progress Report to the People on the Fight Against Racism at Temple U.," delivered at rally, Wednesday, June 16, 1976, Student Activities Center, Temple U., box 25, LDRP-SC.

102. L. D. Reddick, "Submitted to the Committee of the Pennsylvania State Legislature, Investigating Racism and Related Matters at Temple University, Wed. Sept. 29, 1976," box 13, LDRP-SC.

103. T. Harris, "TU Black Faculty Caucus Critical of Dr. Reddick," *Philadelphia Tribune*, June 4, 1977.

104. "Legislators Okay $66 Million for U," *Temple Times*, July 1, 1976, box 25, LDRP-SC; "Reddick Not Discouraged by Vote," *Temple Times*, July 1, 1976, box 25, LDRP-SC; Len Lear, "State Lawmakers Charged with Taking Payoffs: Allegation Issued by Rep. Richardson," *Philadelphia Tribune*, July 13, 1976.

105. "Review Panel Finds Reddick Charges Baseless, Hits 'Provocation,'" *Temple Outlook*, June 21, 1976. For Reddick's rejoinder, see Reddick to James M. Shea, August 6, 1976, box 13, LDRP-SC.

106. T. Harris, "TU Black Faculty Caucus Critical of Dr. Reddick," *Philadelphia Tribune*, June 4, 1977.

107. Harry Amana, "Black Historian Hits Racism at Temple: Dr. L. D. Reddick Lists Charges in a 17-Page Report," *Philadelphia Tribune*, April 24, 1976.

108. Reddick to A. Philip Randolph, December 20, 1966, box 5, LDRP-SC; Reddick to Charles Harris, May 5, 1968, box 5, LDRP-SC; "Interview Granted by Mother Divine," *New Day*, July 31, 1971, box 16, LDRP-SC.

109. Malcolm X with the assistance of Alex Haley, *The Autobiography of Malcolm X* (New York: Grove, 1965).

110. L. D. Reddick, "Kinte Project," 1972, box 33, LDRP-SC.

111. Alex Haley, "General Staff Memorandum," December 10, 1973, LDRP-SC; L. D. Reddick, "The Alex Haley Project," June 29, 1972, box 33, LDRP-SC; J. Herman Blake, "Kinte Library Project: Oral History—USA," March 1976, box 30, LDRP-SC.

112. L. D. Reddick, "Kinte Project."

113. L. D. Reddick, "Prolog," in L. D. Reddick and others, "Draft: Search for the Black Family in America: An Intellectual Adventure," June 1976, box 30, LDRP-SC.

114. Reddick, "Prolog."

115. L. D. Reddick, "Kinte Project."

116. St. Clair Drake, "New Research Perspectives on the Black Family," October 21, 1975, box 30, LDRP-SC.

117. David A. Varel, *The Lost Black Scholar: Resurrecting Allison Davis in American Social Thought* (Chicago: University of Chicago Press, 2018), 154–60.

118. Andrew Billingsley, *Black Families in White America* (Englewood Cliffs, NJ: Prentice Hall, 1968).

119. Andrew Billingsley, "Black Families and White Social Science," in *The Death of White Sociology*, ed. Joyce A. Ladner (New York: Random House, 1973), 437.

120. John W. Blassingame, *The Slave Community: Plantation Life in the Antebellum South* (New York: Oxford University Press, 1972); Herbert G. Gutman, *The Black Family in Slavery and Freedom, 1750–1925* (New York: Pantheon, 1976); George P. Rawick, *From Sundown to Sunup: The Making of the Black Community* (Westport, CT: Greenwood, 1972).

121. See, for instance, Sterling Stuckey, "Through the Prism of Folklore: The Black Ethos in Slavery," *Massachusetts Review* 9 (Summer 1968): 417–37.

122. L. D. Reddick, "Social Scientists and Public Policy," June 7, 1974, box 30, LDRP-SC; Reddick, "Black History as a Corporate Colony," 3–4.

123. L. D. Reddick, "Myth Versus Fact and the Black Family," 1975, box 30, LDRP-SC; Drake, "New Research Perspectives on the Black Family."

124. Alex Haley, *Roots* (Garden City, NY: Doubleday, 1976).

125. Henry Louis Gates Jr., foreword to *Reconsidering Roots: Race, Politics, and Memory*, ed. Erica L. Ball and Kellie Carter Jackson (Athens: University of Georgia Press, 2017), xi, xiv.

126. Reddick, "Beyond Roots."

127. See Dan T. Carter, *From George Wallace to Newt Gingrich: Race in the Conservative Counterrevolution, 1963–1994* (Baton Rouge: Louisiana State University, 1996).

128. Rogers, *Black Campus Movement*, 164–65.

129. Anne E. Bartlett, "Student Forum Protests Policy toward Afro," April 1976, box 32, LDRP-SC.

130. Afro-American Studies Concentrators, "Do You Know that Dr. Ephraim Isaac Will Not Be Teaching Next Year!!!," n.d., box 32, LDRP-SC.

131. L. D. Reddick, "Blacks at Harvard, 1850–1978, NEH Project Proposal," circa 1978, box 32, LDRP-SC.

132. Reddick to the Fellowship Committee of the National Endowment for the Humanities, May 16, 1978, box 32, LDRP-SC.

133. Reddick, "Is the White College Better—for Blacks?"

134. L. D. Reddick, "Blacks at Harvard, 1850–1978, NEH Project Proposal," 1978, box 32, LDRP-SC; L. D. Reddick, "The Black College Experience," 1978, box 32, LDRP-SC. For Reddick's notes and manuscripts on this research, see box 17 of his papers. For subsequent publications on the black experience at Harvard, see Werner Sollors, Thomas A. Underwood, and Caldwell Titcomb, eds., *Varieties of the Black Experience at Harvard: An Anthology* (Cambridge, MA: Harvard University Press, 1986); Marcia Graham Synnott, *The Half-Opened Door: Discrimination and Admissions at Harvard, Yale, and Princeton, 1900–1970* (Westport, CT: Greenwood, 1979). For an earlier study study, see Nell Painter, "Jim Crow at Harvard: 1923," *New England Quarterly* 44 (December 1971): 627–34.

135. Easy Klein, "The Ebony Tower," June 1975, box 13, LDRP-SC.

136. Moton Center for Independent Studies, "1977–78 Research Scholars," box 13, LDRP-SC.

137. "A History of the Association of Black Women Historians," Association of Black Women Historians, http://abwh.org/history/history/ (accessed April 14, 2020).

138. L. D. Reddick, "The New Racism in Higher Education," Spring 1978, box 13, LDRP-SC.

139. Reddick, "The New Racism in American Higher Education," conference paper presented at the National Black Think Tank conference at the University of Maryland, September 25, 1976, box 25, LDRP-SC.

140. Reddick, "The New Racism in Higher Education."

Conclusion

1. Reddick to St. Clair Drake, May 16, 1978, box 8, folder 30, SCDP-SC.

2. "Prof Quits White College for Fisk," *Afro-American*, February 24, 1973.

3. Reddick to Valfoulaye Diallo, circa 1978, box 13, LDRP-SC; Reddick to J. Rupert Picott, June 11, 1980, box 17, LDRP-SC.

4. Martha Biondi, *The Black Revolution on Campus* (Berkeley: University of California Press, 2012), 8–9.

5. Tony Brown, "Tony Brown's Journal," *Columbus Times* (Columbus, GA), September 23, 1980.

6. "Black College Petition Drive," *New Pittsburgh Courier*, January 24, 1981.

7. Brown, "Tony Brown's Journal."

8. Tony Brown, "A Slow Fade to White: The Destruction of Public Black Colleges," *Black Collegian*, March/April 1979, box 25, LDRP-SC.

9. L. D. Reddick, "The Education of Negroes in States Where Separate Schools Are Not Legal," *Journal of Negro Education* 16 (Summer 1947): 300.

10. Dena Kleiman, "Can Black Colleges Survive?," *New York Times*, December 20, 1981.

11. L. D. Reddick, "The Need for Black Colleges," *New York Times*, January 31, 1982.

12. L. D. Reddick, "Toward a History of the Black College in America," box 25, LDRP-SC; St. Clair Drake to Reddick, June 16, 1981, box 8, folder 30, SCDP-SC.

13. L. D. Reddick, "Upper South: Paradise to Lose," box 25, LDRP-SC.

14. See, for example, Jelani M. Favors, *Shelter in a Time of Storm: How Black Colleges Fostered Generations of Leadership and Activism* (Chapel Hill: University of North Carolina Press, 2019).

15. St. Clair Drake, Benjamin Quarles, and L. D. Reddick, "A Brief Proposal for a Comprehensive History of the Black College in America," box 8, folder 30, SCDP-SC.

16. Delece Smith-Barrow, "H.B.C.U.s' Sink-or-Swim Moment," *New York Times*, October 21, 2019.

17. "Future Gains Dim," *New Pittsburgh Courier*, March 15, 1980.

18. "Summary Remarks of L. D. Reddick at Amistad Conference," January 8, 1981, box 5, LDRP-SC; Neil Postman, *Amusing Ourselves to Death: Public Discourse in the Age of Show Business* (New York: Viking, 1985).

19. L. D. Reddick et al., *Thoughts Round About Midnight* (New Orleans: L. D. Reddick, 1988).

20. L. D. Reddick, "An Afterword by Dr. L. D. Reddick," in *Rev. Dr. Martin Luther King, Jr. and America's Quest for Racial Integration*, by A. B. Assensoh (Ilfracombe, UK: Stockwell, 1987), 81–82.

21. L. D. Reddick, "Another Side of the Story," *Louisiana Weekly*, April 10, 1982, box 25, LDRP-SC.

22. Reddick to St. Clair Drake, September 28, 1984, box 8, folder 31, SCDP-SC.

23. Drake to Reddick, June 16, 1981; St. Clair Drake to Reddick, May 21, 1985, box 17, LDRP-SC.

24. Reddick to St. Clair Drake, September 28, 1984, box 8, folder 31, SCDP-SC.

25. Darlene Clark Hine, ed., *The State of Afro-American History: Past, Present, and Future* (Baton Rouge: Louisiana State University Press, 1985).

26. John Hope Franklin, "On the Evolution of Scholarship in Afro-American History," in *State of Afro-American History*, 18–19.

27. Mary Frances Berry, "Blacks in Predominantly White Institutions of Higher Learning," in *The State of Black America 1983* (New York: National Urban League, 1983), 304; Fox Butterfield, "Blacks Decrease but Women Increase on University Faculties," *New York Times*, January 28, 1984.

28. Reddick to Catherine F. Barton, August 26, 1985, box 17, LDRP-SC; Reddick to "H," September 30, 1985, box 25, LDRP-SC; Reddick to Darlene Clark Hine, October 7, 1985, box 17, LDRP-SC.

29. Darlene Clark Hine to Reddick, September 10, 1985, box 17, LDRP-SC; Darlene Clark Hine to Reddick, September 16, 1985, box 25, LDRP-SC.

30. Reddick to Robert L. Harris Jr., October 3, 1977, box 13, LDRP-SC; Robert L. Harris Jr., "Segregation and Scholarship: The American Council of Learned Societies Committee on Negro Studies, 1941–1950," *Journal of Black Studies* 12 (March 1982): 325–30.

31. James D. Anderson, "Secondary School History Textbooks and the Treatment of Black History," in *State of Afro-American History*, 253–74.

32. L. D. Reddick, "Can We Call It Truth?," box 5, LDRP-SC.

33. Eric Pace, "Lawrence Reddick, 85, Historian and Writer," *New York Times*, August 16, 1995.

34. "Award-Winning Author to Discuss Apartheid," *Montgomery Advertiser*; March 16, 2009; "The Thirty-Second Annual ATWS Meeting in Denver, Colorado," *Journal of Third World Studies* 32 (Spring 2015): 377.

35. There is currently no other book, or even significant article, on Reddick, even though a veritable cottage industry has grown up around select black intellectuals such as W. E. B. Du Bois and James Baldwin. Reddick has been cited or discussed in countless books and articles, but only a few sources provide more than passing treatment. See Pero Gaglo Dagbovie, *The Early Black History Movement, Carter G. Woodson, and Lorenzo Johnston Greene* (Urbana: University of Illinois Press, 2007), 18–19, 24–25, 204–7; August Meier and Elliot Rudwick, *Black History and the Historical Profession, 1915–1980* (Urbana: University of Illinois Press, 1986), 19, 93, 103–4, 127–28, 132–33, 153, 233–34, 240; and Carol Polsgrove, *Divided Minds: Intellectuals and the Civil Rights Movement* (New York: Norton, 2001), 67, 107–11, 116–21.

36. "Our Shame: The Sins of Our Past for All to See," *Montgomery Advertiser*, April 26, 2018.

37. Brent Staples, "When Southern Newspapers Justified Lynching," *New York Times*, May 5, 2018.

38. James Baldwin, "The White Man's Guilt," *Ebony* 20 (August 1965): 47.

39. Martin Luther King Jr., Letter from Birmingham Jail, April 16, 1963, King Papers, Stanford University, http://okra.stanford.edu/transcription/document_images/undecided/630416-019.pdf.

40. W. E. B. Du Bois quoted in W. Sherman Savage and L. D. Reddick, *Our Cause Speeds On: An Informal History of the Phi Beta Sigma Fraternity* (Atlanta: Fuller, 1957), 195.

41. L. D. Reddick, *Crusader without Violence: A Biography of Martin Luther King, Jr.* (New York: Harper, 1959), 234.

Index

Abernathy, Ralph: at Alabama State College, 123, 148; as influential activist, 5, 162, 188, 212; SCLC and, 122, 126–27, 130–32, 158, 176, 187

Africa: American culture and education and, 25, 52–53, 61, 71, 92, 182, 196, 198–200, 216, 219; anticolonialism and decolonization generally, 3, 5–6, 8, 11, 66, 73–81, 135, 142, 160, 163; as covered by the *Crisis*, 19; post-colonization and independence of, 80, 116, 154–58, 192–93, 225; Reddick's early life in, 14, 19, 25; Reddick's possible job in, 120; Soviet Union and, 152. *See also* African diaspora; Ethiopia; Ghana; Nigeria; Pan-Africanism; slavery; South Africa

African American Intellectual History Society, 230

African diaspora, 13, 46, 48, 89, 188, 191; Arturo Schomburg's collections on, 23–24, 68; in New York City, 64–65; Reddick's tenure at the Schomburg and, 69, 73–78, 87

African Interpreter, 75

African Studies. *See* Black Studies

Afro-American, The, 34, 141, 157–58

Alabama: Birmingham, 131, 139, 161, 163–64, 231; organizing and uprisings in, 47–48, 90, 167–68; racism and segregation in, 129, 147–49, 151, 164, 167–68. *See also* Montgomery (AL)

Alabama State College (ASC): cultural and intellectual life of, 121–23; history department at, 2, 5, 121, 125, 127; Reddick's legacy at, 227; Reddick's firing from, 6, 124, 150–52, 154–55, 158, 160, 211, 268n136; student protests at, 148–50

Alexander, Raymond Pace, 88

Allen, Celia Jane, 73

Allen, Robert, 198

Alsberg, Henry G., 42

American Civil Liberties Union (ACLU), 150–51

American Council of Learned Societies (ACLS), 66, 88–89

American Historical Association (AHA), 54

American Negro Academy, 190

American Sociological Association, 21

American Sociological Society, 53

Amistad Society, 172–73, 225

Amos, Miles G., 111

Anderson, James D., 227

Anderson, Trezzvant, 133–34

anti-Semitism, 1, 51, 82–83

Aptheker, Herbert, 55, 201

Arkansas, 47, 135, 146

Armstrong, Louis, 50

Asante, Molefi, 212

Assensoh, Akwasi B., 225

Associated Negro Press, 64, 70

Association for the Study of African American Life and History (ASALH), 204–5, 216

Association for the Study of Negro Life and History (ASNLH): *Negro History Bulletin* and, 45, 117, 140; Negro History Week and, 24–25, 41–42, 69, 181; Reddick and, 6, 10, 91, 100, 117–19, 133; slave testimonies sponsored by, 39, 41–42; Woodson and, 3–4, 19, 25, 26, 39, 62–63, 117–18

Association of Black Psychologists, 190
Association of Black Sociologists, 190
Association of Black Women Historians, 220
Atlanta (GA): King's ties to, 137, 188; organizing and public gatherings in, 108–9, 112, 114, 132, 146, 189, 204, 216; racism and segregation in, 96, 107–9; thriving black community in, 96, 111, 122–23, 130, 156, 196; Urban Crisis Center in, 1. *See also* Atlanta University Center
Atlanta Daily World, 102, 109–11, 116, 260n62
Atlanta University Center (AUC), 11, 43, 99, 118, 188; alumni, 16; consortium, 96; faculty, 98, 109–10, 115; Pan-Africanism and, 100; Reddick's departure from, 5, 95, 116, 119–21, 150, 156; students, 31, 110; Trevor Arnett Library within, 2, 94, 97, 100, 115. See also *Phylon* (periodical)
Atlantic Charter, 76–79
Augustine, Byron, 49
Australia, 80
Azaransky, Sarah, 98
Azikiwe, Nnamdi: at Lincoln University, 100, 156–57; as Pan-Africanist leader, 5, 75–76, 101–3, 142, 154; Phi Beta Sigma and, 37, 101, 103

Bacote, Clarence, 50, 97, 109–10, 114, 118, 204
Baez, Joan, 177
Baker, Ella, 5, 8, 130, 132–33, 136, 156
Baldwin, James, 141, 165, 230, 283n35
Baltimore (MD): 6, 152, 159, 168, 176. *See also* Maryland; Coppin State College
Banks, Glovina Virginia Perry, 120
Barnett, Claude, 64, 155
Bass, Herbert, 208–9, 220
Beale, Howard K., 54, 140, 278n72
Beals, Ralph, 94–95
Beard, Charles, 62

Bearden, Romare, 190
Belafonte, Harry, 188
Bennett, Lerone, 140, 190
Berlin, Ira, 199, 201, 216
Bethune, Mary McLeod, 17, 117
Bevel, James, 163, 177
Bhave, Vinoba, 144
bicentennial celebrations, 205–8, 217
Billingsley, Andrew, 215–16
Biondi, Martha, 207
Black Academy of Arts and Letters (BAAL), 6, 187, 190–92
black family life, 6, 176, 212–17, 219
Black Lives Matter, 230
Black Panthers, 169, 178, 196
Black Power, 2, 6, 180, 183, 191–92, 214; appeal of, 7, 168–72, 175–76, 184, 188; civil rights movement generally and, 7, 9–10, 172; electoral politics and, 196; militarism and nationalism of, 11, 139, 189; Reddick's route to, 154–68; universities and, 186, 198, 211, 220. *See also* Carmichael, Stokely; Pan-Africanism
Black Studies: as African Studies, 89, 100; institutionalization of, 186–90, 207, 213, 220, 227; at Temple University, 6, 10, 194–97, 218
Blake, J. Herman, 216
Blassingame, John, 215
Blockson, Charles, 207
Blyden, Edward, 169
Boas, Franz, 89
Bolin, Jane, 69
Bond, Horace Mann: anti-Communism and, 105; at Dillard University, 43–44, 46, 58, 64; at Fisk University, 21, 23–24, 27–29; King Center and, 188; *Negro Education in Alabama* by, 27; Pan-Africanism and African Studies programs and, 89, 100–101, 155–56; Reddick's correspondence with, 52–53, 59, 64–65, 78, 114, 120; Schomburg Library and, 78, 94–95; University of Chicago and, 27, 50

Bond, Julian, 188, 189
Bontemps, Arna, 50, 190
Boston University, 44, 85, 122, 188
Brady, Tom P., 129
Branch, Taylor, 137, 163, 177–78
Brawley, Benjamin, 61, 63, 70
Brewer, William, 62, 117–18
Bristol, James, 142–43
Brooks, Gwendolyn, 50
Brown, Sterling, 62, 66, 89
Brown, Tony, 222–23
Brown, Troy, 134
Browning, James B., 62
Brown v. Board of Education (1954): fate of HBCUs after, 6, 13, 171–72, 222; SCLC, 135; white resistance to, 111–15, 129–30, 138, 147
Budenz, Louis F., 107
Bunche, Ralph, 12, 30, 140
Burgess, John W., 40
Burks, Mary Fair, 125, 151
Burns, Andrea, 207

Cade, John B., 39–41
Caribbean, 6, 16, 24, 44, 69, 79; islands and countries in, 46, 74, 81, 82
Carmichael, Stokely, 169, 175–76, 189, 198
Carnegie Corporation, 88, 213–14
Carpenter, Marie, 34
Carson, Clayborne, 82, 136
Carter, Ambrose, 101
Cayton, Horace: on Atlantic Charter and Pan-Africanism, 76, 79, 81; as sociologist, 50, 53, 68, 93, 195
Cheek, Cordie, 22
Chicago (IL): black community and culture in, 50, 68, 69, 96, 145; as black gathering place, 38, 47–48, 79; Chicago Campaign in, 176–77; public education in, 172–73. *See also* Roosevelt University; University of Chicago
Chicago Defender, 73, 109, 113, 116, 140–41, 152
China, 14, 66, 82, 100

Churchill, Winston, 76–77
City College of New York (CCNY), 71–73, 76
Civil Rights Act of 1957, 135
Civil Rights Act of 1964, 158, 163, 166
Civil War: black education following, 16, 20; black experience of, 173, 207–8, 216; general historical interpretations of, 4, 58, 195, 229; racist historical interpretations of, 32–34, 40, 55–56, 59, 88, 92, 96, 160. *See also* slavery; *Worth Fighting For* (Lawrence Reddick)
Clark, Kenneth, 73, 214–15, 223–24
Clark, Septima, 172
Clark College, 96, 189
Clarke, John Henrik, 190
Clement, Rufus, 111, 119–21
Cobb, Montague, 54
Cofield, Ernestine, 140
Cold War: and anti-Communism generally, 6, 99–100, 104–5; and Communist Party USA (CPUSA), 31, 107; intellectuals during the, 46, 55, 72, 163, 191, 201; internationalism and, 98–100, 102; Jim Crow and civil rights during the, 125, 127, 130, 138–39, 152; Red Scare and repression during the, 6, 8–9, 11, 94–97, 104–8, 111, 120, 151–52, 163–64, 229. *See also* McCarthyism
Cole, Nat King, 139
Colin, Frank, 1–2
Colson, Edna, 34
Columbia University, 40, 69, 75, 203
Colvin, Claudette, 125, 127
Committee on Negro Studies (CONS), 66, 88–89, 100, 227
Communism. *See* Cold War, McCarthyism
Confederacy: celebration of, 96, 106–7, 123–24, 160, 229; scholarship on, 59, 160–61, 195
Congress of Racial Equality (CORE), 155, 163, 188

Index   287

Cook, Mercer, 74, 155
Cook, Samuel DuBois, 222
Coppin, Fannie Jackson, 152
Coppin State College, 152, 159, 172, 176, 178–79, 189, 272–73n97
Countryman, Matthew, 184
Cowper, William, 14
Cox, Oliver Cromwell, 190
Craven, Avery O.: and his relationship with black students, 55–57, 59–60, 63, 200; as part of Lost Cause school of historiography, 55–56, 58–60
Crescent, The (periodical), 38, 46–48, 103
Crisis (magazine), 18–19, 27, 29, 79, 106
Crozer Theological Seminary, 138, 140
Crusader without Violence (Lawrence Reddick), 5, 136–41, 151, 169, 228, 265n83
Cruse, Harold, 198
Cuba, 74
Currier, Theodore, 21, 23, 202, 278n72
Curti, Merle, 56

Dagbovie, Pero, 117, 247n123
Dartmouth College, 202–3
Davis, Allison, 43–44, 46, 50, 215
Davis, Barbara, 193
Davis, David Brion, 202–4, 278n77
Davis, Elizabeth Stubbs, 44
Davis, Jefferson, 124
Davis, John Aubrey, 89, 100, 155
Davis, John P., 48, 66
Davis, Ossie, 190
DeLancey, F. Elaine, 196
Deloria, Vine, Jr., 197
Democratic Party, 109–10, 166, 210, 217, 226
De Priest, Oscar, 50
Dillard University: history department at, 2, 36, 43, 222, 225; Reddick's activism at, 49, 225–26; Reddick's colleagues at, 43–44, 46, 58; Reddick's departure from, 64, 119, 221
Dissent, 127, 149
Dodd, William E., 52, 55
Dominican Republic, 74
Dorsey, Thomas, 50
Doubleday, 172–74
Douglas, Aaron, 24
Douglass, Frederick, 88, 191
Doyle, Bertram, 21
Drake, St. Clair: career generally of, 11–12, 68, 93; and collaborations with Reddick, 5, 179, 182, 190, 224; at Dillard University, 44, 46, 49, 50; and friendship and correspondence with Reddick, 50, 96, 120, 124, 137, 189, 201, 226; on generational divisions among African Americans, 214–15; internationalism of, 81, 98, 116, 155–58, 192; at University of Chicago, 50
Du Bois, W. E. B., 232, 283n35; accomplishments and scholarship of, 97, 191, 195, 214; and correspondence with Reddick, 126, 139, 151, 175; and the *Crisis* magazine, 19, 29; and his *Encyclopedia of the Negro* project, 62, 87; at Fisk University, 24; and influence on Reddick generally, 32, 164; on Martin Luther King, Jr., 141; and Pan-Africanism and colonialism 5, 73, 79–81, 101–3, 155, 157; persecution and marginalization of, 106–7, 120, 138, 219; slave testimony efforts by, 39; at Schomburg Library, 68, 94
Duckett, Al, 165
Dudziak, Mary, 104
Duke, David, 1–2
Dunbar, Paul Laurence, 13
Dunning, William Archibald, 40, 56
Dunning School, 40, 56, 199
Dzuback, Mary Ann, 51

economy: and economic justice, 8, 102, 104, 138–39; and fair employment, 7, 9, 39, 69, 130, 160; and labor movement, 11, 17, 30, 47–49, 72, 115, 176, 195; and poverty, 7, 80, 90, 93, 143, 165–69, 175–77, 180, 183, 187, 218.

See also Great Depression; National Negro Congress; New Deal; Opportunities Industrialization Center; Poor People's Campaign
Edmonds, Helen G., 220
education: and academic culture, 201–4; and Reddick's early life, 14–17; segregation within, 22, 54–55, 73, 97, 111–15, 135, 147, 171–72, 220–24; struggle for public education, 16–17, 27–28, 146–47; student sit-ins and, 124, 133, 147–48, 151–52, 154; textbooks and encyclopedias relating to, 3, 25, 33–35, 87, 91, 123, 172–74, 227; as tool of oppression, 25–26. *See also* Black Studies; *Brown v. Board of Education* (1954); Fisk University; historically black colleges and universities; University of Chicago
Eisenhower, Dwight D., 109–11, 135
Elkins, Stanley, 199
Ellington, Duke, 190
Ellison, Julian, 201
Ellison, Ralph, 68, 81
Embree, Edwin, 64–65, 86
Encyclopedia of the Negro. See Du Bois, W. E. B.
Engerman, Stanley, 200–202
Ethiopia, 48–49, 73, 103, 192
Europe: colonialism and imperialism and, 5, 58, 71, 80, 87, 90, 155, 194, 197–98, 214–16; Fisk's Jubilee singers in, 26; Reddick's education and, 14; Schomburg collection on, 24; World War II generally, 76, 80, 102
Evers, Medgar, 164
Exman, Eugene, 136

Faris, Ellsworth, 43
Faubus, Orval, 135
Fauntroy, Walter, 158, 162
Federal Bureau of Investigation (FBI), 106–7, 151, 165, 178, 191–92
Federal Emergency Relief Administration (FERA), 40–42

Fisk, General Clinton B., 20
Fisk Herald, 28
Fisk University: alumni, 54, 57, 179, 202, 222; as HBCU, 41, 43, 51, 54, 216, 222, 224; Reddick's experience with, 13, 16, 19–33, 36–37, 39, 75, 224; Wranglers at, 23, 28, 32, 53
Florida: political mobilization in, 17, 69, 166, 179; Reddick's childhood in, 13–19
Fogel, William, 200–202
Foner, Eric, 203
Ford, Gerald, 191
Forman, James, 188
France, 100, 124, 144–45, 191
Frankfort (KY), 37–38, 41. *See also* Kentucky State Industrial College
Franklin, John Hope: ASNLH, 117; Fisk University and, 22–23, 202; general prominence of, 11–12, 21, 140, 172–73, 190; SCLC, 188; scholarly writings of, 54, 173, 195, 202, 226
Frazier, E. Franklin, 140; and the New School, 82; as sociologist, 21, 30, 53, 93, 214–16; University of Chicago and, 50
Freedom Summer, 166

Gaines, Kevin, 38, 73, 157
Gandhi, Mohandas: and internationalism, 100; and land reform, 144; principles of nonviolent resistance generally, 98, 128, 137–38, 141–42, 146, 155
Gandi, Julio Pinto, 81
Garrow, David, 107
Garvey, Amy Ashwood, 73
Garvey, Marcus, 73, 98, 169
Gates, Henry Louis, Jr., 217
Gellman, Erik, 47
General Education Board, 43, 50
Genovese, Eugene, 199, 201
Gershenhorn, Jerry, 89, 100
Ghana: Akwasi B. Assensoh, 225; Drake, 116, 157, 179; Nkrumah, 5, 75, 103, 135, 146, 155, 157

Index 289

Gibson, Kenneth, 196
Gillespie, Dizzy, 96
Gilmore, Glenda, 104
Glazer, Nathan, 165, 219
Gold Coast (Africa), 75, 77, 101
Goodman, Benny, 69
Gordon, Mittie Maude Lena, 73
Gordon, William, 156
Grant, Edmonia W., 21
Grant, Ulysses S., 107
Great Depression, 27; cultural impact, 7, 13; shaping Reddick's life and career, 10, 29–31, 35–43, 65, 115, 165, 231; Southern Agrarians and the, 32
Great Migration, 50, 67
Greene, Lorenzo Johnston: Carter Woodson and, 62–63, 117–18; Lincoln University in Missouri and, 152, 224; *The Negro in Colonial New England*, 69, 203; Reddick's correspondence with, 123
Greener, Richard T., 219
Gutman, Herbert, 215

Haley, Alex, 6, 213, 217
Hall, Jacqueline Dowd, 9, 128
Hansberry, Lorraine, 50
Harap, Louis, 82
Harding, Vincent, 164, 188–90, 201, 215, 276n45
Harlem, 170; Adam Clayton Powell in, 48; black culture and, 50, 65, 80–81, 98, 113; Schomburg Library and, 4, 67–68; uprising (1943), 90
Harmon Foundation, 70, 72
Harper & Brothers, 136, 140
Harris, Abram, 30, 195
Harris, Charles, 172–74
Harris, Jessica, 38
Harris, Robert L., Jr., 89, 227
Harvard University, 55; David Brion Davis and, 203; Du Bois and, 106; other universities, 20, 50, 97, 116; Reddick at, 1–2, 208, 212–14, 218–20; Theodore Currier and, 21, 24, 202

Helstein, Ralph, 165
Herndon, Angelo, 48, 88
Herskovits, Melville, 74, 79, 89, 100, 265n83, 278n72
Higginbotham, Evelyn Brooks, 127
Hill, Herbert, 11
Hill, Robert, 216
Hine, Darlene Clark, 227
Hines, Earl, 50
historically black colleges and universities (HBCU), 5, 20, 212; Bond's defenses of, 28; desegregation of, 6, 10, 115–16, 171–72, 218–25; protest movements at, 127, 186; Reddick's critiques of, 31, 37, 115–16; Reddick's experience with, 2, 5, 13, 22, 75, 203, 225, 230; Woodson's critiques of, 25–26, 28. *See also* Alabama State College; Atlanta University Center; Dillard University; education; Fisk University; Howard University; Kentucky State Industrial College; Lincoln University
Holt, Thomas C., 227
Hook, Sidney, 165
Horne, Gerald, 81
Houser, George, 155–56
Howard University: desegregation workshop at, 223; faculty and administration at, 21, 30, 57, 138; as an HBCU, 13, 20, 43, 75, 97; *Journal of Negro Education* and, 33; students, 31
Hughes, Langston, 39
Hunton, W. A., 81
Hutchinson, William T., 57

India: decolonization and internationalism of, 66, 77, 81–82, 138, 163; and Jawaharlal Nehru, 101; Martin Luther King Jr.'s trip to, 5, 98, 124, 132, 141–47; religious conflict within, 102
Indiana, 41, 166, 196
Institute of the Black World (IBW), 188–90

intelligence tests, 27, 43
Isaac, Ephraim, 218–19
Italy, 44, 48–49, 73

Jackson, Jesse, 177, 226
Jackson, Luther Porter, 50–51, 60, 62, 117
Jackson, Mahalia, 162
Jackson, Maynard, 196
Jackson, Sara Dunlap, 4
James, C. L. R., 81, 98, 191
Japan, 73, 76, 83–84, 124
Japanese internment, 82, 93
Jeffries, Leonard, 213, 216
Jencks, Christopher, 219
Jernegan, Marcus, 52, 55
Jim Crow: and Cold War, 104; defenses of, 130, 147–49; Dixiecrats and, 109; end and limitations of, 167–70, 224; Reddick's childhood and, 14, 17–18; scholarship during, 26, 33–34, 55, 228; struggle against generally, 3, 6–7, 48, 75, 86, 98, 108, 124, 129, 136, 231; unions and, 47. *See also* education; lynching; police
Johns Hopkins University, 178
Johnson, Charles S.: gradualist approach of, 26–27, 53; mentor to Reddick, 26–27, 29, 64, 86; prominence and influence of, 21, 23, 53; scholarly work of, 26–27, 39, 93; University of Chicago and, 50
Johnson, James Weldon, 16, 21, 37–39, 46, 82
Johnson, Lyndon, 164–69, 176–77, 180
Johnson, Mordecai, 138, 142
Johnston, James Hugo, 50, 60, 62
Jones, Clarence, 158, 161–62, 164–65, 167
Jones, Lewis Wade, 21, 179
Jordan, Vernon E., 207
Joshi, Pranshankar Someshwar, 144
Journal of Educational Sociology, 92–93
Journal of Negro Education, 172; Reddick's writings in, 33, 91, 112, 114, 171, 223

Journal of Negro History: Reddick's writing and editorial work for, 42, 59–60, 62, 66, 86, 112; Woodson and, 4, 25, 33, 39–40, 117

Kalibala, Ernest, 82
Karefa-Smart, John, 74–75
Keats, John, 14
Kelley, Robin D. G., 247n123
Kelly, Colin, 84
Kennedy, John F., 160–61, 163–64
Kennedy, Robert, 160, 181
Kentucky State Industrial College, 36–37, 41. *See also* Phi Beta Sigma
Kenya, 155–56, 192
Kenyatta, Jomo, 192
Keyes, Ulysses S., 51
Kilson, Martin, 190
King, Charles, 1, 101
King, Coretta Scott, 5, 124, 142–43, 188
King, Martin Luther, Jr., 122; assassination of, 9, 154, 178; books by, 124, 136–41, 51, 164–65, 179; charismatic male leader and celebrity of, 12, 127–28, 132, 134–35, 137; criticisms of, 141, 169–70, 175–77, 191; decolonization and, 135, 144–46, 156; economic justice and, 138–39, 176–78; India and, 5, 98, 124, 141–47; legacy of, 179, 188, 212, 226; as mentee of Reddick, 2, 8, 142, 158, 185, 189, 231; Montgomery Improvement Association (MIA) and, 126, 129; Morehouse College and, 96, 222; nonviolence and, 98, 127–28, 137–42, 145–47, 167, 175, 177, 225; SCLC and, 129–31, 150, 158–69. See also *Crusader without Violence* (Lawrence Reddick)
King Center, 188–89
Kinte Library Project, 213–14, 216–17, 219
Knauer, Christine, 84
Korean War, 99, 112
Korstad, Robert, 9
Ku Klux Klan, 1, 40, 69, 116, 123, 129–30

Lamar, Nat, 165
Langston University, 171
Latimer, Catherine Allen, 68
Latin America: Reddick's archival collections on, 69, 74, 87, 89; Reddick's general engagement with, 16, 44, 61, 64; University of Chicago scholars and, 52
Lawson, James M., 147, 164
Lawson, James R., 98
League of Nations, 27
Lee, Bernard, 162
Lee, Robert E., 106
Lescot, Elie, 74
Levison, Stanley, 130; King and, 136, 158, 162, 165, 177
Lewinson, Paul, 89
Lewis, Elsie Mae, 21, 50, 54, 57, 205–6
Lewis, Hylan, 97
Liberia, 27, 49, 101, 103
librarianship: activism and remedying insufficient attention to black resources, 4, 10, 39, 42, 84–90, 97, 126–27, 194–95, 197, 213–14, 217, 219; criticisms of Reddick and his, 119–20; Library Documentation Project and, 188–89; racism and, 18, 55; Reddick's career generally and, 2, 4, 10, 228, 230; Reddick's early life and, 18, 24. *See also* Alabama State College; Atlanta University Center; Kinte Library Project; Schomburg Library
Library of Congress, 66, 88, 90, 213–14
Lincoln, Abraham, 16, 227
Lincoln, C. Eric, 188–90, 222
Lincoln University (Missouri), 103, 152, 171, 224
Lincoln University (Pennsylvania): HBCUs and, 20; Horace Mann Bond and, 28, 105;
international students and Pan-Africanism at, 75, 89–90, 100–101
Lindsay, Arnett, 62

Locke, Alain, 21, 37, 69, 73, 88, 103
Logan, Rayford, 5, 12, 62–63, 80–81, 117–18, 172
Lomax, John, 41
Los Angeles (CA), 90, 168, 179
Los Angeles Tribune, 139–40
Lost Cause. *See* Dunning School; Southern Agrarians
Louisiana, 39, 42, 130, 233. *See also* Dillard University; New Orleans
Louisiana State University, 59, 223, 227
Lowery, Joseph, 130
lynching: campaigns against and recognition of, 17, 106, 141, 229; justifications and instances of, 16, 22, 25, 34

Manly, Albert, 188
Mannheim, Karl, 56
Marable, Manning, 10
March on Washington Movement, 79, 162–64, 178
Maryland, 166, 171, 180. *See also* Baltimore (MD); Coppin State College
Marx, Karl, 62, 105, 139
May, Emmett, 38
Mays, Benjamin, 97–98, 108, 114, 141, 190–91
Mbadiwe, Kingsley, 77–78
Mboya, Tom, 155–156
McCarthy, Agnes, 173
McCarthyism, 105, 107, 138, 151–52, 160. *See also* Cold War
McGuire, Danielle, 125
McKee, Guian, 184
McWilliams, Carey, 82, 93, 160
Mehlinger, Louis, 62, 117–18
Meier, August, 90, 202
Meredith, James, 85, 176, 231
Meriwether, James H., 49, 98
Meyers, Michael, 223–34
military: colonialization and, 79; desegregation of, 109, 112; discrimi-

nation and segregation within, 83–86, 112; historians and the, 197, 208; mobilization and anti-Communism, 99, 105; Union Army, 20, 216
Miller, Doris "Dorie," 83–84
Milton, John, 14
Mis-education of the Negro, The, (Carter Woodson) 24–25
Mitchell, Vernon C., Jr., 38
Montgomery (AL): bus boycott in, 2, 5, 121, 124–30, 133–34, 136–38, 140, 144; churches in, 122; as cradle of civil rights movement, 124–25, 146–48; as cradle of Confederacy, 123–25, 130, 147, 229; and Montgomery Improvement Association (MIA), 126, 129, 134, 148, 151; Reddick in, 2, 5, 121–30, 147, 150–53, 156. *See also* Alabama; Alabama State College
Morehouse College, 96–97, 141, 222
Morgan v. Virginia (1946), 159
Morris, Aldon, 131
Moton, Robert Russa, 37
Moton Center for Independent Studies, 218–20
Moynihan, Daniel Patrick, 176, 214–15, 219
Mullings, Leith, 10
Mussolini, Benito, 44, 48
Myrdal, Gunnar, 89, 165

Nashville (TN), 22, 32, 112, 147, 159, 161. *See also* Fisk University; Vanderbilt University
Nation, 111, 160
National Archives, 4, 89, 213
National Association for the Advancement of Colored People (NAACP): and divisions within black community, 134, 161, 163; and education, 34, 196, 223; and electoral politics and protests, 17, 49, 64, 106, 112, 150–52, 177; and its second Amenia Conference, 30; leaders and organizers of, 11, 16, 47, 125, 132, 152; nonviolence and, 139; as outlawed in South, 130; Spingarn Awards of, 70, 72. *See also Crisis* (magazine)
National Endowment for the Humanities (NEH), 205, 219
National Labor Relations Act, 47
National Negro Congress (NNC), 47–48, 50, 60, 72, 133
National Urban League, 26, 29, 115, 165, 207
Negro History Bulletin. *See* Association for the Study of Negro Life and History
Negro History Week. *See* Association for the Study of Negro Life and History
Nehru, Jawaharlal, 101, 142, 145
Nelson, Stanley, 224
New Deal, 7, 27, 39–42, 47
New Negro Renaissance, 16, 26, 69
New Orleans (LA), 41, 43–44, 49–50, 58, 60, 222–23, 227. *See also* Dillard University; Louisiana
New School for Social Research, 73, 82
Newsweek, 163, 187
New York City, 91, 94, 107, 112, 160, 204; capital of African diaspora and vibrant community, 4–5, 64, 96; organizing and meeting place, 48, 66, 75, 130, 145–46, 163, 176–77, 201; public education within, 34, 72. *See also* City College of New York; Queens College
New York Review of Books, 200
New York Times: general coverage, 69, 77, 87, 109, 177, 203; Reddick and, 152, 161, 173, 201, 224, 227; Schomburg Library and, 77, 94
New York University, 23, 45, 213
Nigeria, 5, 74–77, 101–2, 111, 156–57, 179
Nixon, E. D., 126, 134
Nixon, Richard, 140, 169, 180, 191

Index   293

Nkrumah, Kwame: St. Clair Drake and, 137; Ghana and, 135, 146, 157, 193; Lincoln University and, 100; Pan-Africanism and Ghana and, 5, 75, 81, 103, 154–55, 157–58; Phi Beta Sigma and, 75, 101, 103; Schomburg Library and, 68–69
Nobel Peace Prize, 167, 177
North Carolina, 55, 59, 139, 147, 164, 220
Northwestern University, 23, 89, 265n83

One World Movement. *See* World Federalist Movement
Operation Breadbasket, 176–77
Opportunities Industrialization Center Institute (OIC): cultural empowerment at, 6, 180–82; employment opportunities generally at, 9, 189; *The Essence of OIC* (Lawrence Reddick), 179–80; Reddick's work with, 2, 7, 10, 169, 178–85, 192–93, 228
Opportunity, 26, 27, 29–30, 77–79
Organization of American Historians (OAH), 60
Orizu, Akweke Abyssinia Nwafor, 74–75
Ortiz, Paul, 16–17

Padmore, George, 98
Pan-Africanism, 4–7, 11, 73–81, 90, 106, 214; Phi Beta Sigma and, 97–103; Reddick's travel abroad for, 73–75, 135, 155–58, 185, 191–92. *See also* African diaspora
Park, Robert E., 21, 43
Parker, Eleanor, 220
Parks, Rosa, 125, 127
Patterson, John, 6, 124, 147–52, 164, 229
Payne, Charles, 133
Peirce, Bessie, 52
Phelps-Stokes Fund, 26, 62
Phi Beta Sigma, 10, 37–39, 75; campaigns and internationalism of, 47–49, 99–103; Reddick's involvement with generally, 10, 37–39, 46, 70, 91, 108, 133; Reddick's writings for, 60, 103, 115, 228
Philadelphia, 1, 6, 195, 201, 210–11, 218; bicentennial celebration and, 205–8; OIC in, 178–79, 181, 184, 193. *See also* Temple University
Philadelphia Tribune, 193, 195
Phillips, Ulrich Bonnell, 40, 56, 201
Phylon (periodical), 66, 96–97, 113, 265n83
Pittsburgh Courier: Jim Crow South and, 129, 133–34; Reddick and, 79, 85, 93, 134, 141, 225; Schomburg Library and, 68, 85; World War II and, 49, 76
Podhoretz, Norman, 165
Poor People's Campaign, 176–78, 187
Poitier, Sidney, 190
police: brutality and violence by, 7, 80, 90, 129, 138, 167–68; repression and harassment by, 49, 126, 128–29, 148–50, 187
Polsgrove, Carol, 267n127
Popper, Hermine, 136
Popular Front, 47, 104, 165
Porter, Dorothy, 66
Postman, Neil, 225–26
Powell, Adam Clayton, 48, 178
Pride, Armistead, 89–90
Progressive School, 52, 54, 62
Puerto Rico, 74, 81

Quakers, 142–43
Quarles, Benjamin, 12, 190, 195, 224
Queens College, 201–2, 204

Radin, Paul, 21
Randolph, A. Philip, 48, 72, 79, 141, 165, 178, 212
Ransby, Barbara, 132
Ransom, John Crowe, 32
Rawick, George P., 42, 215
Reagan, Ronald, 226, 231

Reconstruction, 51, 91, 111, 113, 217; *Black Reconstruction* (W. E. B. Du Bois), 54, 62; oppression and resistance during, 16–17, 229; racist historical portrayals of, 4, 32–34, 40, 55; Reddick on, 62, 173; Second Reconstruction, 168; struggle for education and other civil rights during, 14–16, 109

Reddick, Amos Richard, 13–15, 19

Reddick, Ella Ruth Thomas: education and teaching of, 44–45, 122; life with Lawrence Reddick, 46, 94, 119, 122, 157, 222, 227

Reddick, Fannie Ethridge, 13–15

Reddick, Fannie M., 14–15

Reddick, Harold N., 14–15, 227

Redding, J. Saunders, 68, 141

Red Power, 197

Republican Party, 109, 180, 217–18

Reuter, Edward B., 43

Richardson, Bill, 210

Rippy, Fred, 52, 57

Robeson, Paul, 105, 138, 191

Robinson, Cleveland, 158, 162–63, 165, 177

Robinson, Jo Ann, 125–27, 148, 151

Rodell, Marie, 136

Rojas, Fabio, 186

Roosevelt, Eleanor, 66, 70, 78, 111

Roosevelt, Franklin, 27, 38, 47, 76–79

Roosevelt University, 11, 157, 189

Roots, 6, 213, 217

Rosenwald Fund, 26, 27, 56, 64, 86

Rustin, Bayard: and controversy over homosexuality, 163–64; movement work of, 79, 98, 130–31; as part of Martin Luther King Jr.'s inner circle, 5, 8, 136, 158, 162–65, 177

Sargent, John, 174

Savage, William Sherman, 62, 103, 152

Schandorf, Joseph, 77

Schlesinger, Arthur, 140

Schomburg, Arturo, 4, 23–24, 32, 62, 65

Schomburg Library: and contributions to mass education and black history, 4, 11, 23, 188, 207, 228; Reddick's curatorship at, 2, 10, 36, 63–71, 73–81, 84–95; Reddick's departure from, 97, 119, 211

Schrecker, Ellen, 104–5

Schuyler, George, 76, 81–82, 95

Scott, C. A., 109

Scott, William Edouard, 50

Scottsboro Boys, 31

Selassie, Haile, 103

Senghor, Léopold, 191–92

Settle, Ophelia, 39

Shamsee, M. A., 77

Shaw, George Bernard, 30

Shelley, Percy Bysshe, 14

Shridharani, Krishnalal, 82

Shuttlesworth, Fred, 130–31, 188

Sierra Leone, 74

Sims, George, 213

Slaughter, Henry P., 66

slavery: Confederacy and Jim Crow South on, 123, 229, 231; Du Bois on, 141; excuses for, 32, 52, 56; freed enslaved peoples under, 20; genocide and, 106; historical records on, 24, 39 42, 58–61, 87–88, 90, 213–14; indentured servitude versus, 53, 131; Jubilee Singers, 26; landmark books on, 89, 173, 199–203, 215–17; mainstream white portrayals of, 4, 25, 33–34, 88, 194–95, 206; outside the United States, 27, 74, 80; preventing education under, 14–16; Reddick's writings and curriculum on, 174, 182; Republican party and, 109; resistance to, 122, 175; slave trade, 1

Smith, Eleanor, 220

Smith, Lillian, 68

Smythe, Hugh, 172, 265n83

Social Attitudes (book review), 42–43

Social Policy (periodical), 204

sociology: Chicago School of, 21, 28, 93, 97; limited integration of, 53, 92–93; racial biases and exclusion within, 43, 60, 215; Reddick's work within, 41, 56, 59, 83, 92–93, 97, 182; scholars in Reddick's circle generally, 21, 26–27, 50, 93, 106, 157, 189, 215
South Africa, 72, 144, 167; apartheid within, 80, 135, 226
South Carolina, 109, 130, 178, 200
Southern Agrarians, 32–34
Southern Association of Colleges and Secondary Schools, 20, 120
Southern Christian Leadership Conference (SCLC): anti-Communist hysteria and, 191;
The Crusader (periodical) by, 133; King and Reddick within 2, 5, 141, 163–65, 167–69, 176, 185, 189; leaders and campaigns of, 122, 130–36, 152, 158–69, 172, 175–78, 184, 187–88; Reddick's involvement with, 8, 10–11, 124, 131–32, 150–53, 159–70, 175–76, 187–88
Southern Negro Youth Congress, 48
Southern University, 39, 223
Soviet Union: Cold War politics of, 94, 99, 102, 105, 152, 156, 191; Reddick and, 111; United Nations and, 100; World War II and, 76. *See also* Cold War
Spelman College, 96, 147
Stampp, Kenneth, 199, 201–2
Stanford University, 11, 214, 219
Stanton, Edwin M., 16
Stanton School, 16–17, 19, 21
Stephens, Alex, 124
Stevenson, Adlai, 109–10
Still, William, 201
Stuckey, Sterling, 172, 215
Student Nonviolent Coordinating Committee (SNCC), 133, 163, 175, 188
Sullivan, Leon, 178–81, 184, 212

Talmadge, Herman, 111–14, 116
Taylor, Alrutheus Ambush, 21, 24, 62
Temple University: Black Studies program at, 6, 9, 193–96, 198; Reddick's confrontations and departure from, 197–98, 208–12; Reddick general involvement with, 2, 178, 182, 185, 193, 218–19
Tennessee, 22, 44. *See also* Nashville (TN)
Terborg-Penn, Rosa, 220
textbooks, racist representations, 3, 25, 33–35, 87, 91, 123, 172–73, 227
Third World: Communism, 99, 102; decolonization and liberation, 3, 106, 226; Studies, 218, 227
Thomas, Julius A., 115
Thompson, Charles H., 33
Thoreau, Henry David, 128, 138
Thorpe, Earl, 140
Thurman, Howard, 98
Thurmond, Strom, 109
Till, Emmett, 123
Trenholm, H. Councill, 150, 152
Truman, Harry S.: civil rights and, 87, 104–5, 109, 112–13, 152; foreign policy of, 98–99, 102, 104–5
Tun, Maung Saw, 81
Ture, Kwame. *See* Carmichael, Stokely
Turner, Lorenzo Dow, 21, 23, 50, 89
Tuskegee Institute, 21, 37

Uganda, 81–82
United Nations: decolonization and, 77, 79–80; genocide and, 106; internationalism and, 100, 108, 163
United States Constitution: constitutional rights generally and, 7, 131, 158, 173; First Amendment, 1; Fifteenth Amendment, 168; Fourteenth Amendment, 16, 129, 168, 218; segregation, 108, 112–14, 129, 159; shortcomings of, 206; Thirteenth Amendment, 66. *See also Brown*

v. Board of Education (1954); voting rights
United States Department of State, 191–92
University of California v. Bakke (1978), 218, 220
University of Chicago: alumni, 21, 26–27, 50; Chicago School, 21, 28, 93, 97; Franklin, John Hope and, 12; general racism at, 51–52, 54–58; Reddick as student at, 2, 13, 36, 43, 46, 50–53, 55–58, 151, 224
University of Pennsylvania, 75, 182

Vanderbilt University, 32–33
Vietnam War, 168–169, 177, 191, 217, 225
Virginia, 161, 177, 229
Virginia State College, 172
voting rights: campaigns, 72, 132, 135, 167–68, 177; political enfranchisement, 110–11; Voting Rights Act, 168–69
Vyshinski, Andrei, 111

Wachman, Marvin, 208, 210
Wachtel, Harry, 158, 165–67, 169
Walden, A. T., 108, 111
Walker, Margaret, 50, 69, 190
Walker, Wyatt Tee, 158, 161, 163–64, 174
Wallace, George, 164, 166
Walton, Norman, 127
Ward, Stephen, 186
Warren, Robert Penn, 32–33
Washington, Booker T., 37, 61, 178, 195
Washington, DC, 101, 106, 146, 177, 226; ASNLH headquarters in, 117, 205. See also March on Washington
Washington, George, 107
Washington Post, The, 177
Watkins, Levi, 148, 150
Watson, Bernard, 210
Weeks, Ricardo, 69
Wesley, Charles, 54, 59–60, 62, 117–19, 190, 195

West African Pilot (newspaper), 76, 101
White, Walter, 17, 39, 76
Wilberforce University, 20
Wilkins, Roy, 47, 141, 152, 163
Williams, Eric, 79, 82, 89, 203
Williams, George Washington, 61, 191
Williams, Hosea, 177
Williams, Marco, 224
Williams, Robert F., 139–40
Willkie, Wendell, 84
Wirth, Louis, 79
Wofford, Harris, 136
Wood, Peter, 199
Woodson, Carter: and ASNLH, 3–4, 19, 25–26, 39, 42, 62–63, 117–18, 247n123; exclusion of, 54; Fisk University and, 24–25; influence on Reddick, 4, 19, 25, 42–43, 53, 62, 86, 195; inner circle of, 4, 19, 21, 53, 69, 97, 103, 109; John Hope Franklin on, 202; legacy of, 61, 117–18, 191; Library of Congress and, 66; *The Mis-Education of the Negro* by, 24–26; OIC and, 181; support of Reddick at the University of Chicago, 50, 53, 55, 59–60
Woodward, C. Vann, 200
Work, Nathan Monroe, 54
Works Progress Administration (WPA), 41–42, 201
World Federalist Movement, 100, 108, 114, 223
World War I, 40, 68
World War II: anti-Communism after, 104; David Brion Davis serving in, 202; decolonization and civil rights during, 5, 11, 49, 64, 67, 70, 73–83; disregard of black contributions to, 4, 83–87; postwar Germany and, 161; Reddick as archivist and scholar of, 84–87, 112, 207–8; Reddick during, 2, 44, 64–66, 90. See also Ethiopia; Miller, Doris; military
Worth Fighting For (Lawrence Reddick), 173–74, 195, 228

Wright, Marian, 177, 188
Wright, Richard, 50–51, 68–69, 81, 85, 144–45
Wynn, Neil A., 253–54n100

Yale University, 33, 203
Yergan, Max, 48, 72, 81, 88, 105
Yetman, Norman, 42

YMCA, 72, 98
Young, Andrew, 158, 164, 176, 187–88
Young, Whitney, 114, 165

Zenith Books series, 172–74
Zeta Phi Beta, 37–38
Zikists, 101–2, 142
Znaniecki, Florian, 43

www.ingramcontent.com/pod-product-compliance
Lightning Source LLC
Chambersburg PA
CBHW030524230426
43665CB00010B/752